Homeward Bound

A HISTORY OF THE BAHAMA ISLANDS TO 1850
with a Definitive Study of Abaco in the American Loyalist Plantation Period

by

Sandra Riley

A RILEY HALL PUBLICATION

A RILEY HALL PUBLICATION

Homeward Bound-A History of the Bahama Islands to 1850

ALSO BY SANDRA RILEY

Sisters of the Sea: Anne Bonny and Mary Read—Pirates of the Caribbean

Sometimes Towards Eden: Anne Bonny in Jamaica

The Lucayan Taino: First People of the Bahamas

Bahamas Trilogy: Miss Ruby, Matt Lowe, Mariah Brown
A collection of Solo Dramas

Stone Poems/Wotai: Help on the Way

The Greenbear Chronicles

WITH PEGGY C. HALL

Gus Greenbear and the Beijing Fortune Cookie Caper

Bicentennial Edition 1983, Fourth Printing 2000
ISBN#0-9665310-2-7

For further information visit www.rileyhall.com or email Riley Hall at
rileyhall@gmail.com

Riley, Sandra.
    Homeward bound : a history of the Bahama Islands to 1850
with a definitive study of Abaco in the American loyalist plantation period / by Sandra Riley.—Bicentennial ed. — Miami, Fla.
: Island Research ; Green Turtle Cay, Abaco, The Bahamas :
Albert Lowe Museum, c1983.

    xi, 308 p. : ill. ; 23 cm.
    Bibliography: p. 278-284.
    Includes index
    ISBN 0-941072-06-1 (pbk.)

    1. Bahamas—History. 2. Abaco (Bahamas)—History. 1. Title.
F1656.R5   1983   972.96—dc19   83-214208
                                                  AACR 2   MARC
Library of Congress

Cover painting *Homeward Bound*—an original oil painting by Alton Lowe
Courtesy of the Albert Lowe Museum

To Lydia Austin Parrish and Thelma Peters who went before, and to my mother, Florence Riley, who made it possible for me to come after.

MINISTRY OF EDUCATION & CULTURE
PUBLIC RECORDS OFFICE, ARCHIVES SECTION,

P O Box N3913/14   Nassau Bahamas

BICENTENNIAL MESSAGE

The year 1983 marks the Bicentennial of the Loyalists advent into the Bahamas. Many American Loyalists with their slaves left their homes and bravely sought a new life in the Bahama Islands, of which they knew little. Among the Loyalists were planters, tradesmen and professionals. These people increased the population, founded new settlements and towns and infused new energy into Bahamian life. Their impact on Bahamian history has been profound.

To mark this important event in our history, Sandra Riley, an American keenly interested in Bahamian history, after much research, has produced a history of the Bahama Islands to 1850, with a definitive study of Abaco in the American Loyalist Plantation Period. She is to be congratulated for gathering together so much information, much of it little known, and for presenting it in such a readable style.

D. Gail Saunders
Chief Archivist
Department of Archives
Ministry of Education
Commonwealth of The Bahamas

iv

Foreword

The allure of gleaming seascapes and the tranquil murmur of casuarinas may have drawn Sandra Riley to The Bahamas, but it was the history of these islands that entrapped her. Perhaps this book, in which she has put the history of the Bahamas on wide screen, is an effort on her part to exercise a spell. This would explain her dedication.

But a work of such depth and perception can come only from years of disciplined effort, of searching records, correlating information, shaping all the pieces into a meaningful mosaic. Fortunately the British were good record-keepers. Dull records? You will not think so when you read, quote and unquote, the author's many excerpts from there. They are so interlarded with skullduggery, cruelty and tidbits of scandal as to make society hang its head in shame.

This is a people book—real people with names and descriptions—pirates, privateers, Puritans, slavers and slaves, wreckers and benighted Loyalists. It reads like fiction but it is fact, meticulously documented. If you find it hard to "take" violence, injustice and suffering unless it is fiction, you may have to read this book with clenched fists; for a persistent theme is "man's inhumanity to man." But there are counter forces of bravery, of coping under hardship, of sharing and caring and winning through to successful settlement.

Perhaps you are looking for roots? Thousands of people living today have ancestors mentioned here: ancestors who lived by the sea or struggled on the land, who raked salt, built boats, raised pineapples, turtles or salvaged wrecks; some, too, who knew the curse of slavery and the joy of becoming free. Using the resources of this book and its valuable appendices, you may be able to forge a link making you a part of it so that you, too, can identify with the past and feel, in spirit, homeward bound.

Thelma Peters

Preface

In August of 1972 I was given the opportunity to work as an historian for Columbus Landings, a land development company on San Salvador in The Bahamas. I began researching pirates and the American Loyalists at the Historical Society of Southern Florida where I met Thelma Peters for the first time. She was busily supervising the organization of the library but took time from her task and from her own personal research, which would portray pioneer South Florida in *Lemon City* and *Biscayne Country,* to assist me. When I mentioned to her that I was primarily a play director, not an historian, she responded emphatically, "Well, you're an historian now." So I got on with it. Almost a year later, due to the recession, I lost that job but not my interest in Bahamian history and went on to continue my research whenever and wherever I could.

Several years ago Dr. Peters turned over to me all her dissertation notes on the American Loyalists in the Bahamas; and in 1980, thanks to the kind hospitality of Cande Key, I stayed in the same conch house in New Plymouth, Green Turtle Cay, that Thelma had stayed in years before. Since it seemed that I was destined to dog her tracks just as she had followed upon the work of Lydia Austin Parrish, I decided to devote all my time and energy to this study. Irwin and Rosemary McSweeney made it possible for me to spend two months in Nassau, enabling me to finish my research. During the writing of the book Alton Lowe provided constant support with his incessant *You can do it!,* and wordsmith Bonnie Hance made sense out of my scribbling once I had finished it.

March, 1983
Nassau, The Bahamas   Sandra Riley

Author's Acknowledgements

I should like to express my thanks to the staff members of the following archives, museums and libraries who allowed me to use their special collections pertaining to the American Loyalists and who were so helpful to me in my research:

British Library, London, England

Caroliniana Library, Columbia, South Carolina

Charleston Historical Society Library, Fireproof Building, Charleston, South Carolina

Clements Library, University of Michigan, Ann Arbor, Michigan

Georgia Department of Archives and History, Atlanta, Georgia

Georgia Historical Society Library, Savannah, Georgia

Historical Society of Southern Florida, Miami, Florida: especially Becky Smith, Librarian, and Linda Williams, Curator of Collections

Institute of Commonwealth Studies, London University, London, England

Lands and Surveys, Nassau, The Bahamas: especially Clement Albury and Leonard Ferguson

Library of Congress, Washington, D.C.

Albert Lowe Museum, Green Turtle Cay, Abaco, The Bahamas

Wyannie Malone Museum, Hope Town, Abaco, The Bahamas

Miami Public Library, Genealogy Room, Miami, Florida: especially Pat Warren

Monroe County Public Library, Key West, Florida: especially Betty Bruce and Sylvia Knight

Nassau Library, Nassau, The Bahamas: especially former Head Librarian Edna Rolle, Chief Librarian Winifred Murphy and her staff: Joy Dean, Faith Maycock, Gretal Murphy, and Olive Rolle

New-York Historical Society Library, New York, New York

New York Public Library, Rare Books and Manuscripts Division, New York, New York: especially Anastacio Teodoro, III

Public Archives, Nassau, The Bahamas: especially Gail Saunders, Chief Archivist, and her staff: Lynette Ferguson, Alexis Pearce, Elaine Toote, Sherriley Voiley, Patrice Williams, and Eugene Wood

Public Records Office, London, England

South Carolina Department of Archives and History, Columbia, South Carolina: especially Wylma Wates, Chief Archivist; Alexia Helsley, Research Archivist; and Robert McIntosh

St. Augustine Historical Society, St. Augustine, Florida: especially Jacqueline Beardon

Turton House, Nassau, The Bahamas, Methodist Records

University of Miami Archives, Otto G. Richter Library, Coral Gables, Florida

Wilson Library, University of North Carolina, Chapel Hill, North Carolina

P. K. Yonge Library of Florida History, University of Florida, Gainesville, Florida

I would like to thank the following individuals for their research assistance:

Don and Kathy Gerace of the College Center of the Finger Lakes, Bahamian Field
   Study School, San Salvador, The Bahamas;
Dr. Paul and Joan Albury at the Bahamas Historical Society Nassau, The Bahamas;
William Holowesko and his staff members Cyd Gay and Merthlyn Hanna at the
   Bahamas Title Research Company;
Dorie Hall also at Nassau, The Bahamas;
Iris Lowe Powers and her father, Harold Lowe at Green Turtle Cay, Abaco, The
   Bahamas;
Ginny Curry and Terry and Barbara Herlihy for the many hours spent deciphering
   almost illegible documents;
Sylvia Heller and Alton Lowe for helping me research on jaunts to the Southern U.S.
   Archives;
Irwin McSweeney, Betty Bruce, and Antonina Canzoneri for providing a continual
   flow of information.

Many thanks to Marlene Adams for design, Elisabeth Zanger for artistic embellish-
ments, Liz Basile for promotional assistance and to Ellen Edelen, Dr. Thelma Peters,
Dr. Eileen Rice, O. P., Gail Saunders, and Dr. Dorothy Yehle, O. P., for advice during
stages of the manuscript production.

I wish to express my gratitude to the following for their financial contributions:
Frances Armbrister, Tony Armbrister, Sylvia Cole-Tierney, Barbara Evans, Myrtie
Saunders Hall, William Holowesko, Carl H. and Minnie C. Lowe: The New Plymouth
Club and Inn, William Saunders, Derek Taylor, *The Tribune*, Harold Williams, and
especially the CCFL Bahamian Field Station, Harold J. and Minnie C. Lowe, The
Nassau Shop, Garth Sweeting, Peter Sweeting, and Roscoe Thompson.

HOMEWARD BOUND

CONTENTS

List of Illustrations

This statue of Woodes Rogers before the British Colonial Hotel on Bay Street, Nassau, depicts him as the man of action who expelled the pirates from New Providence. (Photograph by Stanley Toogood.)

1

In the Beginning . . .
Enigma

In the Bahamas nature has created a playground of breathtaking beauty and presented a mystifying geological enigma which is wonderfully unique. There is, in truth, no other place on earth quite like these islands.

About two hundred million years ago, when dinosaurs began to appear on the earth but before there was an Atlantic Ocean, the shifting of huge earth plates initiated a rift running south to north through the middle of a vast land mass called Pangaea.[1] The rift opened an inland ocean in the area now known as the Bahamas. The wedge-shaped chasm quickly filled to sea-level with rocks and sediment dumped from the splitting continents onto a "basement of oceanic crust." Further continental drifting left behind a plateau about half the size of Texas, called the Bahama Platform.[2] Once again algae and coral growth could develop and out of the deposit of these and other calcarious organisms, the Bahama Islands grew.

The action of the sea pounded, crushed and ground the remains of coral polyps and abandoned shells, spreading the carbons over coral reefs where they seeped into every crevice, forming masses which evolved into cays. On the western shore of what is now Abaco, sediment from the eroding coral reefs drifted in and chalky mud or white marl began to ooze in the flats. Dried by the winds, coralline sand brushed over the shore, creating beaches of blinding whiteness. In some places the wind swept the sand into high dunes which later became cemented into ridges of hard limestone.

Under the water the sea artist created colourful gardens of feather bars, grasses, luxuriant coral reefs and shoals, and milky flats reflecting the exquisite varying hues of the blue water. While the wind artist shaped the edges of the limestone cliffs, the crashing waves cut sea caves and carved giant arches where the sea could rush into a honeycomb of caverns and blow up through myriad holes in the rock.

The generally accepted geological theory is that the Bahama Islands grew from this sedimentary build-up of shallow-water carbonates which took the shape of coral reefs, shoals, flats, Aeolian dunes, limestone cliffs, and dazzling beaches. As the masses of sediment built up and solidified, they sank; and more sediment piled on top. The enigma is that "the Bahama Platform is composed of flat-lying shallow water carbonate caps thicker than the ocean is deep;" and because of this unique geological event it contains "the oldest sediments so far discovered in the entire

Atlantic Ocean."[3] The question puzzling geologists is this: since the giant caps do not rest on submersed volcanoes, how did the platform maintain itself above sea level?

Modern geologists such as Dietz, Holden and Sproll suggest that the "Atlantic Ocean was initially created by the rifting of Pangaea in the vicinity of the Bahamas" and the newly created ocean basin provided "an excellent sediment trap." New rivers fingering into the land surrounding the hole dumped vast amounts of rock and sediment into the tiny ocean on top of a hidden lower section of ancient rock which Dietz named the "Bahama Cryptobasin." When this fill approached sea level, the process of carbonate sedimentation could, in principle, begin.[4]

Further rifting took place and as Pangaea broke up, huge ocean slabs shifted and split apart, leaving gaps which filled with crust and became part of the moving plates. As the sea floor spread, the new continents of North America, South America and Africa drifted apart. The Bahama Platform clung to the southern tip of North America, nearly isolated in an ever-widening Atlantic Ocean. Throughout this activity the plateau maintained sea level but was severely cut by deep passes which seemed to reach toward the deep ocean masses moving farther and farther away. The Great Bahama Canyon separates the Bahama Banks, one part following the Northwest Providence Channel to join the Tongue of the Ocean north of New Providence and stretches seaward along the Northeast Providence Channel. This deep trough, which passes between the southern tip of Abaco and Eleuthera, has submarine canyon walls almost three miles high and is perhaps the largest underwater canyon in the world.[5]

During the Pleistocene Era vast amounts of water were drawn from the ocean to form huge glaciers. The process exposed coral atolls on the Bahama Plateau and the sedimentary deposits soon hardened and Aeolian dunes built up to form large land masses. As time passed, ocean levels rose again to sculpt the land into the shapes of the islands, cays, and rocks known today as the Bahamas.[6]

The Tropic of Cancer traverses the Bahama Archipelago, and warming currents drifting up from the Caribbean Sea bless the isles with a temperate climate while prevailing northeast trade winds waft fresh breezes across the land. The island group begins at the northward Matanilla Reef and stretches southward, picturesquely dotting the shallow sea until it ends at Mayaguana.

In 1864 Governour Rawson W. Rawson reported the exact number of land formations "never hitherto counted" as 29 islands, 661 cays, and 2,387 rocks.[7] Surprisingly, no one else has ever attempted an exact count. All the islands, including the Turks and the Caicos, demonstrate basically the same physical character. Calcareous rock, hardened into compact masses of somewhat stratified limestone, is generally perforated with caves and punched with holes that plunge in some spots to unfathomable depths. The fossil remains of ancient coral atolls which fringe parts of the land are indications of the time the land spent under the water. The highest cliff rises to 220 feet at the Hermitage, Cat Island.[8]

Numerous inland salt-water lakes and salinas rise and fall with the tides. Andros, the largest island in the Bahamas, enjoys the only fresh water river. On most of the other islands, wells reach to pockets of rain water caught in the coral rock. Although these wells are quite deep, at the bottom salt water intrudes the coralline network from the sea and beyond a certain depth only brackish water may be drawn.

Three kinds of soil afford suitable planting: the rich black soil of the valley land in which forests and fruit trees flourish, the red pineapple soil, and the white sandy soil on the margin of the beaches, which nurtures Indian corn and other vegetables.

The even climate of these northern tropics has now and then been visited by unusual climatic and natural disturbances: it once snowed in Nassau and earthquake shocks have tremored in Inagua; but more frequently, hurricanes have left a wake of, destruction, usually between the months of August and October.[9]

In the northernmost reach of the Bahamas, Great and Little Abaco lie on the Little Bahama Bank in a cluster of 82 cays and 208 rocks. Separated from Grand Bahama by a "convulsion of nature," the Abacos form a crescent southward from the Matanilla Reef to the tip of Great Abaco, called Hole in the Wall.[10]

A Bishop Churton, struck by the island's beauty, the colouring of the sea—especially the white water within the reef, the lovely bays, and the "rock promontories, clothed with luxuriant vegetation," described Abaco this way:

> It is a splendid island to look at, full of the most gorgeous colouring. Nowhere have the rocks been worn into more picturesque shapes. The rich green of the cays, the white sand in the little bays, seem somehow to shine out more brilliantly than on any other shore of ours; and I can never think of Abaco without its billows flashing as they break mile after mile upon the barrier reefs which protect its eastern shore.[11]*

This luxuriant vegetation sown by nature from seeds carried from distant shores by birds, by the wind, and by the water is not only prolific but virtually self-sustaining.

In 1905 a leading botanist, William Coker, reported 795 flowering plants and ferns, and a variety of tasty fruits indigenous to the Bahamas.[12] Vast pine forests cover Abaco where other hardwoods were, at one time, more abundant. In 1725, artist-naturalist Mark Catesby visited New Providence, Eleuthera, Andros, and Abaco and observed very large trees growing in solid rock. The largest, the mahogany, used domestically and in shipbuilding, measured three to four feet across. He marvelled at its tenacity, for the roots sometimes ran at length along the smooth rocky surface until they found "hollows or chinks" to insinuate and thereby feed on the "rotten wood, Leaves and other Vegetables digested into Mould" deposited there. The growth of the trees eventually split the rock, creating fissures to collect fresh nutrients carried by the wind and rain.[13]

A fertile verdure covered the land and the isles began to fill with noises. From the pine barrens of Abaco to the prairies of Inagua the islands buzz, twitter, sing, grunt, hum, and shriek with life. (See plate 1.) A medley of noises issues from the innumerable birds, beasts, and fishes, some ringed, tipped, or spotted in brilliant

---

* Punctuation in direct quotations has been emended: spelling and capitalization have not been altered.

PLATE 1
In his painting, *Other Bahamians*,
Alton Lowe makes a subtle
statement that parrots and
flamingos, the original
inhabitants of the Caribbean,
are the true natives. (From the
collection of Dr. Ulrich Baench.)

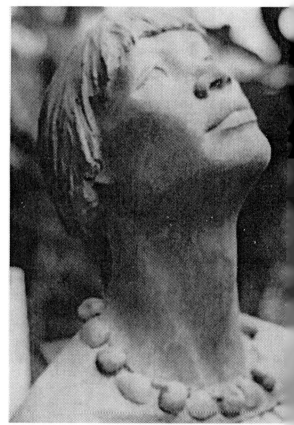

PLATE 2
Lucayans believed that tying
a board to an infant's head
hardened the bone, rendering
the warrior's forehead
invincible to enemy blows.
(Sculpture by James Mastin;
courtesy of the Albert Lowe
Museum.)

yellows, reds, and blues. Some reptiles and many lizards rustle through the vegetation. The iguana and a rabbit-like rodent called the agouti would provide food sources for the Indians.

Storrs Olson, a biological archaeologist at the Smithsonian Institution, studied the fossilized remains of the ancient hutia, a rodent similar to the agouti, which he found in Abaco along with its predators, the giant hawk and the large barn owl. Olson maintains that extinct organisms give the most information regarding the forms of life and vegetation present on the island before man arrived and altered the environment.[14]

And so, before there was an ear to hear and a mind to interfere, the islands burst with a thousand wonders. The haunting cry of the whale, the shriek of the parrot, the whisper of the pines and the music of the songbirds mingled with fragrant odours of the flowering trees and spicy hints of herbs, filling the isles with what in *The Tempest*, Shakespeare called, "Sounds and sweet airs, that give delight, and hurt not."

The first people to enjoy the sights and sounds of the Bahamas were the Lucayan Arawak Indians. (See plate 2.) Surely something stirred inside Columbus's breast when he first set eyes on the variant blue of the water on the west side of San Salvador on 13 October 1492.[15] In 1982, a group of Canadian high school students screamed out when they first saw those leeward Bahamian seas. Certainly such a spontaneously exuberant response never passed the admiral's lips. After all, he had important matters on his mind, such as the discovery of new worlds, not to mention the riches he thought they possessed. Still, one wonders what feeling he left unrecorded on that historic day, and we will never know what the Arawaks thought of the bearded men in strange clothes who arrived in vessels shaped like fire-breathing monsters.

The few days Columbus spent in the Bahamas in October of 1492 afford the only first-hand information about the Lucayan Arawaks. Since not even one of the estimated forty thousand Lucayans remains in the Bahamas,[16] anthropologists who study the people in other parts of the Caribbean culture area and archaeologists who study their sites and pottery in the Bahamas have supplied further knowledge. The first published archaeological account appeared in 1888 and resulted from a survey of the Bahamas conducted by W. K. Brooks.[17] Over these last one hundred years there have been several surveys and a few excavations, and now extensive research in every area of Bahamian archaeology is progressing in an effort to find out more about the "lifeways" of the peace-loving Lucayans, the first people to discover and enjoy the Bahama Islands.[18]

Since the Lucayans spoke the language known as Arawak, they may have migrated from the northern provinces of South America to the Antilles, then pushed their way up in to the Bahamas. Columbus may well have been the first European to encounter them there. At 2 A.M. on October 12, 1492, Columbus recorded landfall, and on the 13th, truly an inauspicious day for the Lucayans, the natives of Guanahani paddled out to greet him. (See plates 3 and 4.)[19] Columbus later changed the island's name, which in the Arawak language meant "iguana," to San Salvador. The natives' name for themselves—*lukku* (man) and *kairi* (island), "men of the

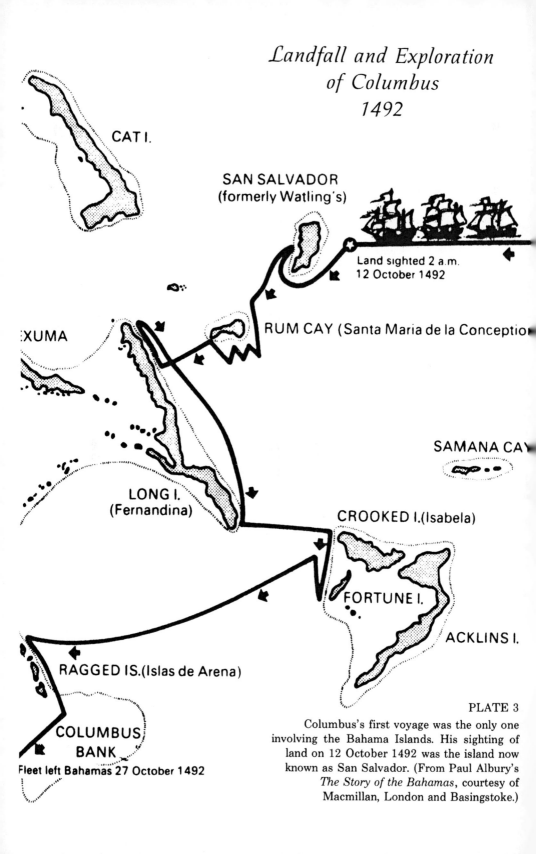

Landfall and Exploration
of Columbus
1492

CAT I.

SAN SALVADOR
(formerly Watling's)

Land sighted 2 a.m.
12 October 1492

XUMA

RUM CAY (Santa Maria de la Conceptio

SAMANA CAY

LONG I.
(Fernandina)

CROOKED I.(Isabela)

FORTUNE I.

ACKLINS I.

RAGGED IS.(Islas de Arena)

PLATE 3
Columbus's first voyage was the only one
involving the Bahama Islands. His sighting of
land on 12 October 1492 was the island now
known as San Salvador. (From Paul Albury's
The Story of the Bahamas, courtesy of
Macmillan, London and Basingstoke.)

COLUMBUS
BANK
Fleet left Bahamas 27 October 1492

islands"—underwent some corruption but remains as "Lucayan" to this day.[20] "Bahamas" is probably a corruption of the Spanish word *Bajamar*, which connotes shallow waters.

Naked except for paint, the young men possessed small but handsomely shaped bodies, firm and straight limbed. Even to Spanish eyes, the women were beautiful with their hair, coarse as horse hair, hanging long and straight about their guileless faces. Under their artificially flattened foreheads the natives' dark eyes reflected their honest, friendly, and hospitable nature.[21] Ironically, the natives thought the Spaniards had come from Heaven.

The Arawak language, described as the softest of all the Indian tongues, was depicted by the linguist Peter Martyr as rich in vowels, sweet, sonorous, and "most pleasing to the ear."[22] The people's manner was as delicate as their speech. They knew no iron, for when Columbus showed them his sword, the young men naively grasped the blade and cut themselves. Several of the men had some scars on their bodies which they said they had received while defending themselves when people came "from the other islands in the neighborhood . . . to take them prisoner." What

PLATE 4: An engraving by Theodore de Bry shows Columbus exchanging gifts with the Lucayans who were vastly impressed by the admiral, his men, and the three ships, the like of which they had never seen.

impressed Columbus more than the excellent qualities of their character was the bits of gold hanging from their noses.

Refusing their gifts of cotton, parrots, spears, and healing leaves, Columbus presented them with glass beads, hawk's bells and other trinkets.[23] The Spaniards who came after Columbus, driven by insatiable avarice for gold and pearls, would rob the gentle Lucayans of that which no one will ever willingly relinquish—their freedom.

The Lucayans were simple agricultural people and had neither the will nor the means to wage war against the massive invasion staged by the Spaniards. Their javelins, merely sticks pointed with fish teeth and bones and "other things," were used more in hunting and fishing rather than in fighting.[24]

That they came is a certainty, but the questions of how, when, and especially why, the Arawaks came to the Bahamas are debatable. There is evidence in many areas, however. During an archaeological reconnaissance of the Bahamas in 1937, Herbert Krieger uncovered data from artifacts "pointing to a close cultural contact between the Lucayans and the Arawak of Hispaniola."[25] In the 1950s Irving Rouse demonstrated that Bahamian pottery shared stylistic similarities with that of Haiti.[26] Recently John Winter conducted a chemical computer analysis in a significant number of imported pottery pieces to trace elements which indicate that the trade ware in the Bahamas came by way of Cuba rather than Hispaniola.[27] In 1871 Dr. Brinton stated that when the Arawaks of Guiana were asked about their origin, they pointed north to Trinidad; but in 1953 Irving Rouse presented his Circum Caribbean Theory that suggested that the migratory pattern of the Arawaks was, perhaps, a circuitous one.[28] It is enough to say that the Lucayan Arawaks shared the same language, culture, and pottery types as the Antillian Arawaks. And for reasons purely speculative, these sturdy seafarers migrated over 1,500 miles to the Bahamas some time between 500 and 1300 A.D.

The most exciting and popular reason for the peopling of the Bahamas is that the peaceful Arawaks were chased to the islands by the man-eating Caribs. Brinton thought this theory doubtful, for in 1871 there was no actual "evidence that the Caribs had gained a permanent foothold on any of the Great Antilles at the period of discovery, some careless assertions of the old authors to the contrary notwithstanding." He offers instead that "man in his migration" from his ancestral home in the far south to the doorstep of the North American continent "followed the lead of organic nature around him."[29] One hundred years later scientists like Winter, Sullivan, Mitchell, Keegan, Olson, and others relentlessly examine the environment to learn more about the lifeways of the first Bahamians.

Aruac means meal-eaters. A bread made from the root of the bitter manioc or cassava was a "staple food of the historic Indians of the Greater Antilles."[30] In 1978 Sears and Sullivan maintained that temperature and rainfall requirements of the bitter manioc limited cultural expansion. Of the fifty-three prehistoric open air midden sites Sears and Sullivan discovered in the Bahamas, only one small site on New Providence was located in the northern climatic zone. Andros, Grand Bahama, and Abaco had none. Although moist, Abaco may have been too cold to support bitter manioc cultivation, which needs a minimum of one year's growth. However, other root products such as sweet manioc and sweet potato adapt well to cooler climates.[31] Sears and Sullivan may not subscribe to that view today and did in fact state in their report that Andros and Great Abaco have the marine resources important to Lucayan settlers of the more densely populated central area.[32] It is therefore hoped that future investigation will uncover permanent habitational sites on Abaco and supply more detail of the Indians' early migrations.

Sears and Sullivan suspect that Antillian Arawaks first came to the Caicos (southern Bahamas) to gather salt and shellfish and for unknown reasons spread into the middle Bahamas, establishing agricultural settlements as far north as Eleuthera.[33] Salt was easily gathered and used for trade. Shellfish may have been exported from the Caicos to Hispaniola but were also used for food.

The bivalve *Codakia*, a clam found in estuaries or in shallow near shore environments, constituted a major food source for the inhabitants of the central Bahamas.[34] By studying the growth patterns of hundreds of living shells extracted from Pigeon Creek in San Salvador and comparing them with those of hundreds more excavated from a prehistoric site near there, Mitchell discovered a varying use of *Codakia* by the Arawaks in the village. He concluded that ceremonial feasts might have accounted for the consumption of large quantities at some times, while other seasonal foods might have been utilized at others. Seasonal migration to other parts of the island or to other islands for trade, salt-gathering, ceremonies, or other events might have reduced the demand for shellfish. Since the varying demand for *Codakia* occurred on the site at approximately the same time each year, Mitchell believes that some type of ceremonial calendar system might have been in use. The largest consumption seemed to coincide with major solar and astral events.[35]

Like clams, conch is high in protein. William Keegan believes that there was perhaps a stronger dependence on conch as a food source among Lucayans than has been stressed by archaeologists because of the absence of shell data. Because of their size, conch shells are awkward to transport and for this reason only shells that would be reworked into tools would have been brought to the village; the rest would have been left behind.[36] Throughout the historic period conch has been, and still is, a major food source for Bahamians. Further study may determine the amount of conch used as well as what other kinds of fish Lucayan Arawaks included in their diet.

At a site on Pine Cay in the Caicos, when Keegan tested prehistoric subsistence fishing techniques to determine what kinds of fish were eaten by the Indians, grunts comprised almost one-half the fish population on the reef. Snapper and porgy were next in number and parrot fish third. He used the native bow and arrow, poison spears, and hooks made of fish bone to catch the fish and in the tidal environment, nets and weirs constituted the primary method of channeling fish into pens. Keegan believes his data to be non-conclusive because his reef traps "suffered a variety of indignities:" wave action, sharks and theft.[37] Lucayans probably hunted the hutia to supplement their diet of fish as well as to add variety to their menu.

Pottery vessels used in food preparation and consumption provide the essential data for archaeologists to study in order to define cultural influences. In 1965 Charles Hoffman excavated the Palmetto Grove Site on the northwest side of San Salvador. He found no whole vessels but many shards with thick soft walls made of a reddish, shell-tempered paste. Except for some basketry impressions or mat marking, the surfaces were for the most part undecorated. He called this pottery, formed out of material purely indigenous to the Bahamas, palmetto ware.[38] Pottery in this series "drew upon other regional traditions while evolving decorative and formal modes of its own" and can be "dated no earlier than 900 A.D. nor later than 1100 A.D."[39]

Because pottery made from the Bahama red loam is generally brittle, the shape of the vessels can only be inferred from the shards. Some appear rounded, some boat-shaped. Griddles for making cassava bread are thick and flat; some rims are incised, but generally flat or rounded. Lugs are wedge-shaped or made from strips of paste draped across the rim.[40] Some surfaces are incised or punctated with cross hatched lines and small dotted decorations.[41]

Richard Rose, currently excavating the Pigeon Creek Site on San Salvador, discovered that two types of imprints appear on larger vessels—leaf and mat. Rose thinks palm leaves may have been used to shape the object and perhaps less durable clay had to be molded and supported by a basket, after which clay and mat were probably fired together.[42]

No habitational sites have been found on Abaco to date, but there is sufficient evidence to prove that Arawaks visited and perhaps even named the island. The Lucayans told Columbus that there were so many islands in the neighbourhood that "they could not be numbered," but they did name for him over one hundred.[43] To this day Abaco retains its Arawak name, and while the old maps are confusing, a linguistic explanation might serve.[44] *Abba* means the number one. The suffix *coa* might mean a place since the definition of *barbacoa* is a loft for drying maize or a place for storing provisions. Hence, Abaco may mean first place or first island, which, if one is travelling from north to south, it is. Another word in the Arawak language bears study in this regard. It is *arcabuco*, a wood or the swaying to and fro of trees. Brinton states that to the aboriginal man every object presented itself as doing something. "Therefore his adjectives are all verbal participles."[45] Perhaps *arc* is the motion part of the word which means a wood, and Abaco is "the island of the swaying pines."

Some pottery shards have been found on Abaco but not in quantities sufficient to determine sites or provide other data as yet. However, artifacts of the non-ceramic variety have been discovered in the island group. During a survey of the Bahamas in 1912, Theodoor De Booy found a wooden canoe paddle in a cave on Mores Island, Abaco. In view of the fact that very few wooden artifacts have survived the rigours of the climatic conditions in the Bahamas, this paddle oar was a rare archaeological find. Two factors played important roles in the remarkable preservation of this Lucayan object: the paddle was fashioned from a single piece of cedar and the cave where it lay on a shelf for centuries was dry. (See plate 5.)

The paddle displays excellent handcraft. The crosspiece has a knob at the un-

PLATE 5: This cedar paddle, in a remarkable state of preservation, was found on Mores Island, Abaco. (Courtesy of Museum of the American Indian, Heye Foundation.)

derside of each end, obviously designed to provide a better hold. The slender shaft widens as it nears the blade, which tapers to a rounded end. De Booy mentioned that one of the petroglyphs on the wall of a cave in Rum Cay is "an exact representation of the type of paddle found on Mores Island." The Spanish historian Oviedo described canoes "propelled by wooden oars (*nahos*) that were provided with a crosspiece at one end and a blade at the other."[46]

De Booy's published account does not mention that he found any celts or axeheads, commonly called "thunderbolts," which have been found on the island. Celts were made from serpentine marble, usually polished and cut into flower petal shapes of varying size, and range in colour from vivid green to olive.[47] They may have been used on ceremonial occasions.

In his study of boat building in the Bahamas, William Glover found that thunderbolts were considered good luck pieces and were prized by boat builders who placed a celt "under the mast before it was stepped." At one time Abaco was a major boat building centre, and for this reason Sears and Sullivan believed that celts of diverse origins would have been brought in by boat purchasers, hence making Abaco unreliable in celt distributional evidence.[48]

Goggin, in his 1937 field notes, mentioned that at one time Mr. Elgin Forsyth, former commissioner at Andros, had a collection of eight celts from Mores Island, and in his 1952 notes he cited an even larger collection belonging to Mrs. Hugh Johnson of Nassau, containing one celt from Mores Island and one from Cherokee Sound, Abaco.[49] Granberry does not say whether the celts in these collections were found or purchased.

Several handsome celts have been found on sites away from the boat building areas of Abaco. Cecil G. Ford, superintendent of schools for Abaco in the 1950s, found a few celts and some barbed arrowheads on the island. Michael Gerassimos happened on two large axeheads and Donald Lowe of Marsh Harbour found one.[50] These artifacts are in the collection of the Albert Lowe Museum on Green Turtle Cay, Abaco.

In 1958, a young Alton Lowe scooped up a splendid artifact in a bucket of dirt from under his father's house at Green Turtle Cay. It was the figure of a bird standing on two small gourds. (See plate 6.)The bird pecks the earth and its upright tail acts as a spout for the hollow vessel. This ceremonial piece was probably brought to Green Turtle from a cave on the main of Abaco in a load of guano or bat dirt used by

PLATE 6: This ceremonial vessel, found at Green Turtle Cay and now in
the Albert Lowe Museum, is unlike any other artifact found to date in The
Bahamas and may link Lucayan and Floridian Indian cultures. (Photograph
by Robert Carr.)

farmers to fertilize the soil. The Arawaks used caves for burial and perhaps other
ceremonial purposes.

The origin of the bottle presents puzzling yet fascinating considerations. The
vessel is more typical of ceramic bottles found in the Gulf area of southeastern
North America than of Lucayan or Antillian pottery. The clay, "superficially similar
to the paste of the St. Johns series of Florida," indicates that the vessel could have
originated in North or Central Florida, perhaps in the vicinity of Tampa.

Archaeologists believe that contact between Florida and the Bahamas did
occur; however, "until this discovery there have been no prehistoric artifacts or material reported from the Bahamas that can be shown to have had their origins from

the North American mainland." Further research might yield more evidence and possibly determine what this interaction meant in terms of its effect on Lucayan and Florida Indian cultures.[51]

Columbus did not go to Abaco; instead he headed south in search of the Great Khan and the riches of Cathay (China), which he thought were nearby. En route to Cuba Columbus named and took possession of Rum Cay, Long, Crooked, and Ragged Islands, saying "once taken it would answer for all time."[52] Again he was wrong. Except for brief periods of Spanish occupation, Great Britain held the Bahamas from the sixteenth century until Independence in 1973.

During the early part of the nineteenth century the islands enjoyed a flourish of European trade but some trade had always been carried on in the Bahamas, even in prehistoric times. On October 15, 1492, Columbus recorded in his journal that he had met a man in a canoe. The native "canoes," constructed from a "single trunk of a tree," usually mahogany, could contain as many as forty to forty-five men and were rowed with an oar "like a baker's peel," and "wonderfully swift."[53] He was told that Arawak canoes could travel seven leagues a day or about twenty-one nautical miles. This man was going from Rum Cay to Long Island, a distance of twenty-two miles.[54] Columbus's entry clarifies some aspects of Lucayan life and trade. This particular Lucayan trader had with him

> a piece of the bread which the natives made, as big as one's fist, a calabash of water, a quantity of reddish earth, pulverized and afterwards kneaded up, and some dried leaves which are in high value among them, for a quantity of it was brought to me at *San Salvador*; he had besides a little basket made after their fashion, containing some glass beads, and two *blancas* (copper Spanish coins) by all which I knew he had come from *San Salvador*, and had passed from thence to *Santa Maria* [Rum Cay].[55]

It would seem from this passage that Lucayan traders travelled light, carrying with them only what was essential for trade and sustenance.

The only meal this man allowed himself on the day's journey was a fist-sized piece of cassava bread and a gourd of water. The natives' sleek figures were obviously due to the small meals they consumed. Las Casas remarked that a Spaniard consumed enough food in one day to feed thirty Indians for one month.[56] Perhaps this is why Columbus gave the detail about the size of the bread and took the man on board to give him something to eat.

The trade items he carried in his handcrafted basket possibly indicate that he had completed trading and would end his journey at Long Island. What had he traded for the Bahama red loam, the healing herbs, and the few prestige items he had gotten in San Salvador? If, in fact, Long Island was his home, he probably traded salt, for there are numerous salt deposits on Long Island and Inagua.

Sears and Sullivan determined from the mode of trade ware in the Caicos and other factors that the Lucayans there carried salt and dried conch to the Greater Antillian Islands of Hispaniola or Cuba or both.[57] Salt is light weight and easily gathered. To demonstrate the relative ease of salt-gathering, Shaun Sullivan conducted an experiment at Armstrong Pond, Middle Caicos, in July, 1977. In fifteen minutes, using conch shells as scoopers, sixteen people collected enough salt to fill 120 gallon containers and projected that in a six-hour day this crew could have gathered 139 bushels of salt.[58]

The little clothing Lucayans wore was made of cotton. Cotton fabric also may have been suitable for trade because Columbus's journal relates that upon arrival the natives rowed out to greet him bringing, among other things, rolls of spun cotton.[59] Sears and Sullivan offer the interpretation that probably "historic trade relationships mirror the prehistoric."[60] Today salt and shellfish are still exported from the Caicos to the neighbouring island of Hispaniola. The theory provides speculation, in this regard, relative to the middle and northern Bahamas. John Winter determined that trace elements in trade ware found in the middle Bahamas came from Cuba. Perhaps the historic practices of Bahamians to fish for turtle in Cuban waters and later carry lumber from Abaco to Cuba prove this connection. Except during times of war when Spanish vessels were forbidden entry into the Port of Nassau, the traffic between the Bahamas and Cuba was as heavy as it was consistent.

In the historic mirror theory Abaco may reflect a larger role in the lifeways of the Lucayans. Indians may have come to Abaco to hunt hutia, iguana and turtle, to fish, to get the red loam needed to make pottery, and perhaps even to build their canoes.

Archaeologists are also investigating long distance travel by Lucayans. The existence of prized religious objects such as zemis (idols), monolithic ceremonial axes, and celts formed of minerals from distant and perhaps volcanic lands warrants consideration. The discovery of more items like the Guatamalan jade piece found by Richard Rose on the Pigeon Creek Site, San Salvador, and the large celts acquired by Alton Lowe from Abaco might substantiate the theory that Lucayans were open ocean and long distance navigators.

Shaun Sullivan recently examined, and is still studying, the ball court on one of the prehistoric sites on Middle Caicos. The ball court was outlined by flat limestone rocks in the shape of a compressed parallelogram. In the middle of the court sat a stone slightly depressed in the centre. A series of smaller stones arranged in relation to the centre stone recorded astrological events. Using this calendar, Sullivan hopes to date the terminal occupation of the site since the stones had been adjusted up to the point when there was nobody left to do it.

At another site on Middle Caicos Sullivan found a pile of rocks that he believed to be a navigational aid. Small stones laid in lines with hooks at the end formed a kind of map; the hooks represented the destination of the voyage. Following in the direction of these stone lines on MC8 would take these Lucayan travellers directly to Tortuga.[61]

It is not a far-fetched notion to go further into these relatively sophisticated areas of astrological events and ocean maps recorded on Lucayan sites. An analysis of the symbols contained in the Arawak myth relating the origin of the sea bears a distinct similarity to the geological event which formed the Bahama Islands. The theory is even more accurate when the Lesser and Greater Antilles are included.

The fable was recorded in the early 1500s by Peter Martyr, who thought it childish, utterly absurd, and indicative of the primitive and heathenish people who told it to him. In the Arawak fable Iaia represents the presence of an absolute power who buried his only son within a great round gourd, the world. Within the calabash his bones transformed into sea monsters. Then four brothers born of one woman, symbolizing the continents of North and South America, Eurasia, and Africa within Pangaea, come to break the gourd. The sea pours forth out of the "rifts" and overflows the plains, leaving only the mountain peaks that formed the islands.

Here is Peter Martyr's version of the fable of the origin of the sea as told to him by the Arawaks, complete with Martyr's sarcastic final remark:

> For they say that there was once in the Island, a man of great power, whose name was *Iaia*; whose only son being dead, he buried him within a great gourd. This *Iaia*, grievously taking the death of his son, after a few months, came again to the gourd: The which when he had opened, there issued forth many great whales and other monsters of the sea: whereupon he declared to such as dwelt about him, that the sea was enclosed in that gourd. By which report, four brethren (borne of one woman who died in her travail) being moved, came to the gourd in hope to have many fishes. The which when they had taken in their hands, and espied *Iaia* coming, (who oftentimes resorted to the gourd to visit the bones of his son) fearing lest he should suspect them of theft and sacrilege, suddenly let the gourd fall out of their hands: which being broken in the fall the sea forthwith broke out at the rifts thereof, and so filled the vales, and overflowed the plains, that only the mountains were uncovered, which now contain the islands which are seen in those coasts. And this is the opinion of these wise men as concerning the origin of the sea.[62]

2

"The Flag That Bears No History But Blood and Tears"

Once at the dinner table, Columbus stood an egg upright simply by cracking the end of it. After his demonstration, all those who had tried and failed protested they could have done the same. "But none of you thought of doing it," he said, "and so it was *I* discovered the Indies." He went on to say that many things thought impossible appear easy after someone has achieved them. "I found the Indies and now every ignorant pilot can find his way there."[2]

Columbus was a skilled navigator but not a prophet. He could not have known the heinous deeds that were to be the aftermath of his "discovery." Pandoralike, Columbus opened the way to the New World and through that door Spain would send some of its most despicable criminals into a paradise. Time spent in the islands gave him a glimpse of the beginning of the destruction of the Indies, but he did not live to see the final extermination of the peaceful Lucayans, who were the first to welcome him with food and gifts to their island home.

In 1542, the Dominican friar Bartolomé de Las Casas looked back over his forty years spent in the American colonies, set pen to paper, and wrote his brief account of the *Devastation of the Indies*. He outlined in the most vivid terms the details of a holocaust in which Spanish Christians unjustly exterminated by strange and cruel murders "more than twelve million men, women, and children. In truth, I believe without trying to deceive myself that the number of the slain [in the New World] is more like fifteen million."[3]

Down through the centuries the reception of the *Brief Account* has not been kind. Critics have labeled the author fraud, hypocrite, madman, and traitor. Las Casas's opponents have tried to convince scholars not to trust the monk's figures, and it has been the practice of historians writing on the West Indies and Bahamas to use figures offered by other Spanish historians instead.

In the *Brief Account*, Las Casas states that 500,000 Lucayans were exterminated. William Robertson uses Peter Martyr's estimate of forty thousand and cites a twenty-page bibliography of Spanish books and manuscripts as the proof of his research for his work. At the same time his contemporary, Bryan Edwards, foremost nineteenth century historian of the West Indies, followed suit as did Southey and other scholars of the twentieth century. Even Las Casas in his *History of the Indies* quotes the figures of Peter Martyr, the only Spanish historian he trusted.[4]

The question of numbers may not be important here, but the issue of Las

Casas's credibility is vital in light of the astounding accounts he uncovered during his long fight for the civil rights of the Indians. Recent historians tend to respect his scholarship, which seems to have passed the rigourous test of time. Ramón Pidal, the most respected Spanish historian of the twentieth century, published a book "which sought to exorcise the spirit of Las Casas once and for all."[5] Hans Enzensberger in his introduction to the *Brief Account* cites the demographic research of two American scholars working in Old Mexico who "reached the conclusion that in the 30 years between Cortez's landing and the writing of the *Brief Account* the population of Central Mexico dwindled from 25 to roughly 6 million. That means that the conquista must have had *19 million victims in Mexico alone;* Las Casas names only 4." (Emphasis added.)[6]

Did Las Casas exaggerate his figures in some places in his *Brief Account* and not in others? If he did exaggerate, did he do it to shock people? Did he use the more conservative figures in his documented history because he was intimidated by his critics or because he was afraid no one would believe him?

Bryan Edwards admits he wrote, "with trembling hand," Las Casas's account of Indians being roasted over a slow fire, all the time "wishing it could be proved false."[7] Las Casas spent forty years in the Indies and watched with his own eyes the extermination of millions, about which he feared to tell because he thought he might have dreamed it.[8]

The devastation of the Indies came on the heels of the terrifying Spanish Inquisition. Who could not believe it? A people capable of devising the cruel torments used to punish their own heretics could certainly exterminate what they thought to be a heathen race. It is understandable, however, how one can witness horrors and doubt the proof of one's own eyes. In the Army Museum in Honolulu a sixteenth century Spanish crucifix is displayed in a manner which allows the viewer to see the front, on which hangs the body of Christ. On the back of the cross are affixed little replicas, in silver, of the implements of torture used in the Inquisition.[9]

Reality or dream, the bitter fact remains that the tyrannical Conquistadors were no less guilty for murdering 40,000 or 500,000 as the following accounts may prove.

Las Casas was particularly grieved over the extermination of the Lucayans, for he thought them the most "blessed among all Indians in gentleness, simplicity, humility, and other natural virtues."[10] Of their islands he said:

> They have the healthiest lands in the world, where lived more than five hundred thousand souls; they are now deserted, inhabited by not a single living creature. All the people were slain or died after being taken into captivity and brought to the Island of Hispaniola to be sold as slaves.[11]

It was not until after the death of Queen Isabella in 1504 that the worst atrocities were perpetrated on the people of Hispaniola. Once the natives were deprived of her "zealous care," Las Casas watched the entire island destroyed[12]

... in 1508, there were 60,000 people living on this island, [Hispaniola] including the Indians; so that from 1494 to 1508, over three million people had perished from war, slavery and the mines. Who in future generations will believe this? I myself writing it as a knowledgeable eyewitness can hardly believe it, but it is a fact born of our sins, and it will be well that in time to come we lament it.[13]

With his work force thus diminished, Governour Ovando of Hispaniola became desperate and petitioned the King with a proposal "to transport the inhabitants of the Lucayo islands to Hispaniola, under pretence that they might be civilized with more facility, and instructed to greater advantage in the Christian religion,..."[14] This blatant lie deceived King Ferdinand and he gave his sanction to the enterprise. Robertson tells the story of how the "civilized" Spanish tricked the guileless Lucayans into captivity.

> Several vessels were fitted out for the Lucayos, the commanders of which informed the natives, with whose language they were now well acquainted, that they came from a delicious country, in which their departed ancestors resided, by whom they were sent to invite them to come thither, to partake of the bliss which they enjoyed. That simple people listened with wonder and credulity, and fond of visiting their relations and friends in that happy region, followed the Spaniards with eagerness. By this artifice 40,000 were decoyed into Hispaniola, to share in the sufferings which were the lot of the inhabitants of that island, and to mingle their groans and tears with those of that wretched race of men.[15]

During the passage from the Bahamas to Hispaniola it is reported that each Spanish vessel lost almost one-third of its human cargo. Left without food or drink, many Indians perished in the suffocating holds of the Spanish vessels and never reached Hispaniola. One Spaniard told Las Casas that "their ships in these regions could voyage without compass or chart, merely by following for the distance between the Lucayos Islands and Hispaniola, which is sixty or seventy leagues, [about two hundred miles] the trace of those Indian corpses that had been cast over board by earlier ships."[16]

It was not uncommon for the Indians to commit suicide rather than submit to a life of slavery. Many of the Lucayans displayed quiet acts of desperation wrought from homesickness. This story by Peter Martyr supports Las Casas's claim that the "Indians when uprooted from their native land very soon perished."[17]

> Many of them in the anguish of despair, obstinately refuse all manner of sustenance, and retiring to desert caves and unfrequented woods, silently give up the ghost. Others, repairing to the sea-coast on the northern side of Hispaniola, cast many a longing look towards that part of the ocean where they suppose their own islands to be situated; and as the sea-breezes rise, they eagerly inhale it; fondly believing that it has lately visited their own happy vallies, and comes fraught with the breath of those they love, their wives and children. With this idea they continue for hours on the coast, until nature becomes utterly ex-

hausted; when stretching out their arms towards the ocean, as if to take a last embrace of their distant country and relations, they sink down, and expire without a groan.[18]

Not all Lucayans so calmly "gave up the ghost;" some tried to escape. One courageous man made a dugout canoe from the trunk of a wild cotton tree and lashed calabashes of water to it. With another man and one woman he paddled to the Bahamas and was almost within sight of his homeland when the three were seized by a Spanish ship and brought back to Hispaniola.[19]

In relating this story, Las Casas also mentioned that perhaps more Lucayans tried to escape and return to their islands but their efforts would have been in vain. During the years 1508-1513 the Spanish continuously raided the Bahamas. Sometimes they would choose "the rockiest and most inaccessible island to corral all the Indians taken from the neighboring islands" and keep them under guard until a ship could return to carry another load. Once seven thousand Indians and their seven guards died of starvation when Spanish vessels were destroyed in a sudden gale just as they neared the shore.[20]

Not all Lucayans died on the plantations or in the mines of Hispaniola. About this time Don Diego Columbus, son of the admiral, was appointed one of the governours of the Indies and was instructed by his king to settle Cubagua, one of the pearl islands near Marguerita.[21] The Lucayos had no gold or silver but the Lucayans were excellent swimmers; and when the Spaniards discovered pearls at Cubagua and decided to exploit them, Lucayans were sold for 150 gold pesos whereas the going price for slaves had been four pesos.[22]

Greed for pearls finally put an end to all the Lucayans. They died in a most excruciating manner diving for pearls. Las Casas relates:

The pearl fishers dive into the sea at a depth of five fathoms, and do this from sunrise to sunset, and remain for many minutes without breathing, tearing the oysters out of their rocky beds where the pearls are formed. They come to the surface with a netted bag of these oysters where a Spanish torturer is waiting in a canoe or skiff, and if the pearl diver shows signs of wanting to rest, he is showered with blows. . . .

The food given the pearl divers is codfish, not very nourishing, and the bread made of maize, the bread of the Indies. At night the pearl divers are chained so they cannot escape.

Often a pearl diver does not return to the surface, for these waters are infested with man-eating sharks . . . that can kill, eat, and swallow a whole man.

. . . And in this extraordinary labor, or, better put, in this infernal labor, the Lucayan Indians are finally consumed. . . .[23]

Exactly how many Lucayans were exterminated Las Casas could not say. His *History* says a "multitude of people were extinguished, the *Brief Account* numbers "More than five hundred thousand souls."[24] Yet, regarding one idea he was certain:

"I have no doubt we the tormentors are less fortunate than they who suffered our torments. . . ."[25]

Unfathomable greed turned some Spaniards into ravaging beasts. Loosed upon a sheepfold they terrorized, tortured, and killed "with the strangest and most varied new methods of cruelty."[26] Gold fever consumed them; their thirst for the metal was insatiable. Inestimable treasures poured into Spain from the New World; enough, as one Spanish historian put it, to 'pave the streets of Seville with blocks of gold and silver.' "[27]

Before he took a hard look at himself and the other settlers, Las Casas confessed that he had cared more about his plantations and mines than about Christian teaching.[28] With this realization, he gave up all his possessions and became the solitary spokesman for human rights in the Indies. The revered admiral lost his fortune in quite another way. In 1785 the *Bahama Gazette* reprinted, for the benefit of the newly settled inhabitants of the Lucayos, a letter recently found in an old book in Jamaica. In the letter dated 1503 and addressed to the King of Spain, Columbus sorrowfully imparts that his enemy, one Bevadilla, robbed him of all his gold.[29]

The lust for gold, silver, pearls, and emeralds proved the cause of the wholesale slaughter that ensued. The conversion of the Indians to Christianity, absurdly purported to be the chief aim of the Spanish conquerors, shows the extent to which these colonial masters would go in order to enslave, rob, and murder their victims.

Las Casas records the words of one "wretch of a Governor [Pedro Arias d' Avila]"[30] who prefaced a raid on a settlement which was reported to have gold with these words: "Caciques [chiefs] and Indians! We notify you that there is but one God and one Pope and one King of Castile. Show obedience!" or "we will slay you or take you into captivity." The message is clear enough. By colonial rule the victim, not the murderer, is the guilty party.[31] Once, under the pretence of religion, Spaniards baptized hundreds and immediately cut their throats. Religious fervour did not fool one old cacique named Hatuey. As he was roasting at the stake, a Franciscan friar, "an artless rascal," preached at him something about God, the articles of faith, and the blessings of heaven in an effort to save the chief's soul from the fires of hell. Hatuey asked if all Christians went to Heaven. "When told that they did, he said he would prefer to go to Hell."[32]

The *Brief Account* is an unparalleled book of horrors in which Las Casas insists he has described "only the ten-thousandth part of what was actually done." Countless cruelties bloody the pages. Human beings were cut to pieces, roasted over slow fires, wrapped in straw and burned, hanged in lots of thirteen (in memory of the Saviour and the twelve apostles), devoured by dogs, buried alive, and tortured in numerous bizarre ways. Many were killed for sport. The Spanish would take bets on who could split a man in two or cut off his head in a single stroke.

These murderers treated their animals better than the Indians. One account reveals that eighty Indians were traded for a single mare. The Spaniards had butcher shops where corpses of Indians were hung up for display. A customer might ask for "a quarter of that rascal hanging there, to feed my dogs until I can kill another one for them."[33]

It seemed to Las Casas that one criminal was trying to outdo the other, each killing and torturing as many as he liked. Las Casas did not name even one of the leaders of the Conquista in his *Brief Account*. In this way he intended to eradicate their memory from human recollection. He was not successful however, for history "cannot be written without naming its criminals."[34] All the bloody governours can be named including the "latest tyrant-Governor" appointed "with a great to-do" in 1538.

In Florida this governour terrorized and massacred the natives. He also forced his captives to carry "intolerable loads" like beasts of burden. When "one of the burden-bearers sank under the load, they cut off his head at the neck-chain, so as not to interrupt the march of the others, since they were all chained together." His name—Hernando de Soto.[35] Over two hundred years later the Florida Indians could not forget what the Spanish had done to their grandfathers. In 1783, when East Florida was ceded by England to Spain, the Indians were most irate and demanded that Britain provide asylum for them along with the other American Loyalists. They also threatened to kill any Spaniard who set foot on Florida soil.[36]

Consistently throughout the *Brief Account*, Las Casas asks: "how many tears were shed, how many groans were uttered, how many people were left alone, how many were condemned to eternal servitude...." How many? In Cuba seventy thousand children, "whose fathers and mothers had been sent to the mines, died of hunger." On the Darien Coast between present-day Panama and Colombia one captain, acting upon his governour's orders, slew forty thousand Indians in a single attack. Countless others died of hunger and exhaustion on plantations, in the mines, at pearl fishing and boat building. Others were driven to desperate acts. One woman killed and ate her own child. In Hispaniola, two hundred natives fled to the mountains, and there husbands and wives hanged themselves together with their children because the cruelties perpetrated by Roderige Albuquerque were so horrifying.[37]

Soon all the acts of terror and murder required to maintain colonial rule depleted the workforce; and the Spanish soon learned that even their particularly economical brand of slavery, in the long view, was not profitable. In 1515 Las Casas petitioned the king to enact laws to eliminate the system of slavery. Spain, entirely dependent on the profits of West Indian colonialism, could not support such a bold and naive notion. Some laws were instituted but were later revoked, and once again Las Casas stood alone in his fight for human rights.

In one audience with his king in 1520, Las Casas was maneuvered into pointing out the delicate constitution of the Indians and suggesting that Africans were better suited to work in mines and on plantations. Ironically, this slip of the tongue initiated one of the biggest business deals in the history of the world—fifteen to twenty million Africans were dragged off and sold as slaves in America.[38] As early as 1503, ships from Africa brought slaves to Hispaniola.[39]

In that same year there had been orders to stop the importation of Africans into Hispaniola because many had run away to the Indians and taught them to resist the Spanish.[40] However, in 1570, when Las Casas suggested African labour Spain responded eagerly. This might explain how Las Casas came to be blamed for initiating the African slave trade. In his *History of the Indies*, Las Casas does not try to whitewash his mistake but admits it.

> The priest Las Casas was the first to suggest that one should introduce Africans to the West Indies. He did not know what he was doing. When he heard that the Portuguese were catching people in Africa against all laws and made them into slaves he bitterly regretted his words . . . [and maintained that] the right of the blacks is the same as that of the Indians.[41]

It was too late. The Africans seemed to flourish in Hispaniola. At first the Spanish thought them immortal, for it was a long time before anyone saw a black man die.[42]

It is strangely ironic that the same colonial system which depopulated the Bahamas in the early 1500s would repopulate the islands in the late 1700s. The British colonial system of granting land to the heads of families, with so many acres allotted for family members and slaves, differs somewhat from the *ecomedia*, in that the land complete with inhabitants was granted to the Spanish colonists. Driven by greed, the Spanish could not follow Las Casas's vehement urging and abolish the evil system of slavery. England would be the first nation to do that. The British treatment of their slaves, especially in the Bahamas, was for the most part humane, and certainly cannot be compared with the treatment of the Lucayans by the Spanish. Yet it has been shown that degree cannot ameliorate the crime. Slavery of any kind in any shape or guise is an appalling evil and not to be tolerated for any reason.

Today's Bahamians bear striking similarities to the Lucayans. It is almost as if the spirit of those unfortunate Lucayans reached out to give a sympathetic touch to victims like themselves, a touch that might draw out all bitterness and imbue the sufferer with the positive qualities of their nature. For like the Lucayans, many Bahamians are "humble, patient and peaceable . . . devoid of rancors, hatreds or desire for vengeance."[43]

Visiting the Out Islands, now called the Family Islands, and meeting some of their people would almost cause one to wonder if, indeed, the Lucayan holocaust had survivors. Ponce de Leon in his search for the fountain of youth in 1513 found people on some of the northern Bahamas, but the southern islands were depopulated by that time.[44] Las Casas tells of a kind merchant, Pedro de Isla, who, moved by the horrors inflicted on the Lucayans, had obtained permission to outfit a ship at his own expense and send a crew to the Lucayos in search of survivors whom he intended to keep out of the reach of raiders. "After three years they found only eleven persons whom I saw with my own eyes because they disembarked at Puerto de Plata where I lived at the time." Las Casas relates that he could not keep from staring at one old man

> . . . who was tall and venerable and had a long face, dignified and authoritative. To me he looked like our father Adam before the Fall, and thinking how many like him there were all over these islands, and how in so short a time and almost under my eyes they had been destroyed without offending us in the

least, nothing was left for us to do but lift our eyes to Heaven and tremble at divine judgment.[45]

It is human to hope. Perhaps there were other survivors besides the lost eleven.

Thelma Peters found a clipping from the Washington *Daily News*, dated 13 October 1937, in which Dr. Krieger of the National Museum suggested that some Lucayans' descendants might inhabit the unexplored regions of Andros Island. "There is no proof that the Lucayans still exist," the article stated. "But Dr. Krieger pointed to legends told by Negroes who now inhabit the coast of Andros Island and to his own discovery of a Lucayan canoe and various implements in caves on the island."[46]

Lucayan artifacts have been found on Andros, but the Indians Dr. Krieger spoke about were Seminoles, not Arawaks. Weary of English and Spanish political intrigues various groups of Indians from the Carolinas and Georgia migrated to Florida. They were called the Seminoles, which in the Creek dialect means runaway.[47] Eventually these exiles settled in Cape Florida, which at the time was a kind of station for Bahamian wreckers "who plundered wrecks in the Florida Keys."[48]

At some time in the first half of the nineteenth century, these Seminoles paddled their dugout canoes to Andros to escape slave catchers. Red Bays settlement, now located on the northwest coast of Andros, was in Dr. Krieger's time more remote. Living deep in the pine forest of northern Andros, Seminoles shunned even the free Blacks; hence legends grew about the small band of aloof people.[49]

Elmore Nairn of San Salvador relates that his great grandmother was a descendant of an Arawak. Perhaps she possessed a happy mingling of eighteenth century slave descent and Lucayan Arawak and passed on qualities of kindness, generosity, fine looks, honesty, wisdom, friendliness, and hospitality to her great grandson. Long ago, when a Scottish whaler anchored at Long Island, the sailor Nairn met Elmore's great grandmother. He was obviously smitten by the woman's loveliness, for he abandoned his vessel to stay with her. When his captain was ready to return to Scotland, he came back to Long Island and caught the sailor. Nairn told his captain, that "Before I'll go back to Scotland, you can cut off my head." Unlike Columbus, who abandoned paradise to die unhappy and alone, material goods meant nothing to the sailor. He had found paradise in the arms of this woman, who meant more to him than his own life. The captain understood and sailed away, leaving the sailor to live out the rest of his days in the islands.[50]

3

The Re-Peopling of the Bahamas and
Other Disastrous Accounts

Even a child knows it is always easier to destroy than to build. In less than five years the Spanish had denuded the Lucayos of at least forty thousand people; it would take nearly 350 years for the islands to reach that population again.[1] "Re-peopling" the Bahamas evolved slowly from settlement fraught with anxiety, bordering, at times, on sheer desperation, and sustained by raw courage and oceans of hope.

From the time of the Lucayan Arawaks to this very day, the history of the Bahamas can truly be said to have been "writ on water."[2] As a provider, the sea has always been bountiful, not only for subsistence, but also for profit, first from whales and turtle, later from sponge and crawfish. Bahamians, inveterate opportunists, turned even the destructive forces of the sea into livelihood: for over four hundred years wrecking answered as the most consistent Bahamian occupation. Before the sea swallowed them up, goods foraged from wrecks were either recycled or sold for profit. Sometimes a castaway vessel would yield salt, beef, candles, clothing, and other necessities of life for these early European settlers. Throughout the centuries, the perpetually dangerous waters of the Bahamas served as access to the open ocean for new world travellers, a haven for pirates, a theatre for wars, the hunting ground of the wreckers, and the chief highway for trade, licit and illicit.

In 1513, Ponce de Leon wandered through the islands in search of the legendary fountain of youth. On the first leg of his journey he spotted Great Abaco but did not stop. After Spaniards left San Salvador, Abaco was the first large land mass in their northerly course and a logical place to begin their search. Lawson believes that the lookout could have seen all of Man-O-War Cay, but from the crow's-nest of the *San Cristoval*, the hills of Great Abaco probably looked like other small islands and not worthy of further investigation. Juan Ponce decided to go on, and after making what appeared to be a roundabout in the open ocean, he beat across the Gulf and made landfall in the neighbourhood of St. Augustine. On the last leg of his journey, the discoverer of Florida found himself once again in the Little Bahama Bank, this time on the north-western side in the vicinity of Memory rock. The explorer named this "island of rocks alone at the edge of the deep," La Viega, after the old woman who directed him south to the land of Bimini and the magic spring. Afraid to be caught in the mighty ocean current of the Gulf Stream and swept northward, the expedition turned from south to east, missed Bimini, and crossed the Northeast

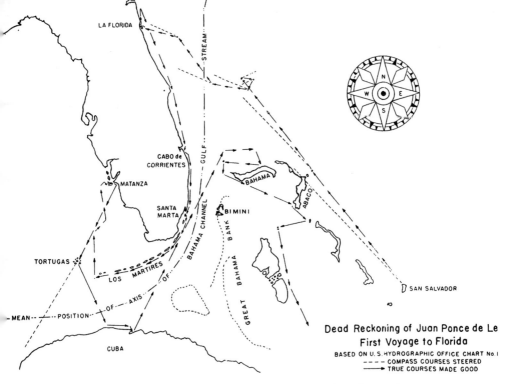

Dead Reckoning of Juan Ponce de Le
First Voyage to Florida
BASED ON U.S. HYDROGRAPHIC OFFICE CHART No. 1
---- COMPASS COURSES STEERED
——→ TRUE COURSES MADE GOOD

PLATE 7: In his search for the Fountain of Youth in 1513, Juan Ponce de Leon traversed most of the Bahamas as well as Florida. (From Edward Lawson's *The Discovery of Florida.*)

Providence Channel past the southern tip of Abaco, zigzagging through the Bahamas homewards. (See plate 7.)[3]

Although he made a great discovery in Florida, the eternal fountain eluded Ponce de Leon. Perhaps the Lucayans spoke only figuratively when they told stories about a well of perpetual youth in the northern reaches of their homeland. In some of the unspoiled islands today where the tendency is to follow the easy rhythm of the place and climate, several people have lived to be upwards of one hundred years old.

Although known to seafarers and traders, the Bahamas remained relatively unexplored and virtually uninhabited during the sixteenth century. The French, English and some Dutch appeared in the West Indies to trade, to explore and to trouble Spanish fleets in the Old Bahama Channel between Cuba and the Bahamas. As did the Spanish, men like Cabot, John Hawkins, the first English slave trader in America, and Francis Drake used the Gulf of Bahama or the Straits of Florida as it is called today.

Spanish galleons and fleets of vessels called *flotas* coming from Mexico and South America would rendezvous at Havana and, together, thus protected from plunder, would speed home through the favoured channel.[4] More often the Gulf passage proved more treacherous than enemy ships and the best road to Spain very often became the swiftest way to heaven. By the end of the century all knew the hazards of the Gulf Stream. Erratic currents coupled with fierce winds and the angry Gulf dragged many treasure-laden vessels to a watery grave, spewing undigested bits of bones and gold onto the Florida coast.

If the voyager was willing to beat against the wind there were other ways out of the Indies. Vessels from Hispaniola could pass out through the Caicos Islands or from South America through the Windward Passage and out to the ocean deep.

Vessels coming from Spain could enter the Bahamas by way of the Northeast Providence Channel. Some speculate that the wild boars and horses on the main of Abaco may have swum ashore from wrecks of Spanish vessels cast upon the dangerous windward side of the island. Although there is no documented evidence to prove it, it is reasonable to suspect that some islands might have had a few scattered inhabitants, survivors of shipwrecks, escaped Lucayans, or even a few runaway African slaves. In 1728, Spaniards were forbidden to carry any Negroes from Hispaniola to Cuba "because they escaped from thence."[5] Perhaps they fled to the Bahamas, knowing that those islands were seldom visited by the Spanish any more. It is even more difficult to prove that there were any organized attempts at settlement during the sixteenth century.

In his report to the Colonial Office, in 1721, Woodes Rogers states that the Spaniards had a settlement on Cat Island for a time and mentions "foundations of brick in two places where they had towns."[6] The island could have been used as a temporary base during the period of the raids. However, Cat Island is long and high in some places, a description which does not seem to fit the image of the rocky island corral mentioned by Las Casas. It is central, and was perhaps strategic to the Spanish for that reason.

There may have been one English claim to the islands in the sixteenth century. Some historians maintain that Queen Elizabeth included the Bahamas in a grant to Sir Humphrey Gilbert in 1578, but there is no record of Gilbert's making any attempt to settle the islands.[7] Perhaps he never had the chance to do so. One bleak afternoon in 1583 off Newfoundland, as Sir Humphrey's frigate recovered from being nearly swamped by waves, he called out to his comrades on the *Golden Hind* saying, "'We are as near to Heaven by sea as by land.'" That same night the sea devoured Sir Humphrey's frigate. The *Hind* searched all that night to no avail; ship, general and crew were lost to the deep.[8]

The French were perhaps the first Europeans to attempt a permanent settlement in the Bahama Islands. Jacques-Nicholas Bellin recorded in his *Déscription Géographique* that a company had been formed in France to establish the *Lucayes*. Based upon a reliable source he called the *Memoires*, Bellin went on to say that in 1565 French colonists embarked on a munitions ship bound for *Lucayoneque* (Abaco). Having delayed too long, the second envoy found no one there when they arrived at the island. According to the *Memoires* Abaco had good ports, safe harbours, a quantity of pigs and salt, and many sources of good water.[9]

During the seventeenth century England laid formal claim to the Bahamas amid almost insurmountable difficulties occasioned by hostilities with France and Spain and the depredations of the bloody buccaneers. In 1629 England granted to its Attorney General, Sir Robert Heath, certain territories in America

betwixt 31 and 36 degrees of North Latitude [Carolinas], not inhabited by the subjects of any Christian King, but partly inhabited by barbarous men who have not any knowledge of the Divine Deity . . . together with the Islands of Veajus [probably Ponce de Leon's rocks on the Little Bahama Bank including Abaco] and Bahamas [Grand Bahama], and all other islands lying southerly or near upon said continent. . . .

The grant clearly indicated that "Sir Robert should plant the same according to certain instructions signed by his Majesty. . . ."[10] Once again there is no record of English colonization.

Although the Heath grant established England's first official recognition of the Bahama Islands and marked the beginning of their political history as well as a more than thirty year relationship with the British Empire, the document is vague compared to the grant issued by Cardinal Richelieu in 1633. The prime minister of France specified the islands of "Abaco, Inaugua, Mariguana, and Gilatur (?)," as not occupied by Europeans and to be included in the Barony of the Bahamas granted to Guillaume De Caen. This grant, however, left the Protestant Baron with nothing more than an empty title; while he could build forts, he could not bring Protestants to colonize the islands."[11]

At the same time Frenchmen of quite a different sort gained a foothold in the West Indies. Along with the planters who colonized Hispaniola came the buccaneers or hunters, and in 1632, the *filibustiers* or freebooters took possession of the island of Tortuga. The bloody combination of these two groups would later become the terror of the Spanish Main.[12]

Near mid-century the first group of English planters to settle the Bahamas came from Bermuda, or Somers' Island, as it was sometimes called because Sir George Somers had been shipwrecked there in 1609. News of the incident reached London soon after and pricked the imagination of the Bard, who immortalized both wreck and enchanted island in his last comedy, *The Tempest*. Shakespeare probably read this account of the Bermuda wreck in Howe's *Annals*. A company of adventurers were bound for Virginia when a sudden and violent storm scattered their fleet of eight sail. Seven ships managed to continue on course for Virginia, but Somers' vessel sprang a leak. Spent from their efforts to bail out the shattered hull, the company had only one request of their admiral and that was to die on "any shore whatsoever."

> Sir George Somers, sitting at the stern, seeing the ship desperate of relief, looking every minute when the ship would sink, he espied land, which according to his and Captain Newport's opinion they judged it should be that dreadful coast of the Bermodes, which islands were of all nations said and supposed to be enchanted and inhabited with witches and devils, which grew by reason of accustomed monstrous thunder, storm, and tempest, near unto those islands. Also for that the whole coast is so wondrous dangerous of rocks that few can approach them but with unspeakable hazard of shipwreck. Sir George Somers, Sir Thomas Gates, Captain Newport, and the rest suddenly agreed of two evils to choose the least, and so in a kind of desperate resolution directed the ship

mainly for these islands, which by God's divine providence at a high water ran right between two strong rocks, where it stuck fast without breaking. Which gave leisure and good opportunity for them to hoist out their boat, and to land all their people [about 160] as well sailors, as soldiers, and others in good safety, and being come ashore, they were soon refreshed and cheered, the soil and air being most sweet and delicate.[13]

Forty years later a company of adventurers left Somers' Island for the "sweet and delicate" air of the Bahamas, which they renamed "Eleutheria" (now Eleuthera) because in Greek the word connotes freedom.[14]

The religious disputes in Bermuda echoed the turmoil in England. Puritans, incensed at London decadence, fought to separate from the Established Church, a break resulting in their subsequent exodus to the Massachusetts Bay Colony. Puritanism, unleashed in America, was regarded by Charles I as a "'wolf held by the ears.'" The strength of the Puritan ethic was indeed powerful enough to become the heritage of America to this day.

Civil wars erupted in England, Cromwell's Army defeated Charles I, who was imprisoned for a time but later would lose both his crown and his head. Basically, the economic structure of England remained unchanged despite the religious turmoil. Trevelyan suggests that settlers in Virginia, the West Indian islands, and, even to a large extent, New England did not emigrate for religious reasons.

The ordinary colonist had been drawn oversea by the Englishmen's characteristic desire to "better himself," which in those days meant to obtain land. Free land, not free religion, was the promise held out in the pamphlets issued by the companies promoting the emigration.[16]

One of these pamphleteering promoters was William Sayle. On 9 July 1647, his company of Eleutheran adventurers agreed on their "Articles and Orders of Incorporation," which insisted on freedom of religion and opinion and held out the promise of land, but actually offered much more. The document is remarkable in that politically it proposes the establishment of a republic.[17] If it had succeeded, the Bahamas would have been the first democratic state in the New World.

According to the "Articles and Orders," each member of the company (limited to one hundred persons) paying £100 was to be granted three hundred acres, to be cultivated for joint benefit at first, then divided into individual lots to which would be added two thousand acres more.[18]

All ordinance "recovered of any wraks" shall "serve for the fortification of the Plantation." But other wrecked goods, together with "all mynes of Gold, Silver, Copper, Brass or lead, Ambergreise, Salt and Woods" found on unoccupied land or islands, were to be divided in three equal shares: the first to the finder or owner in the case of occupied land, the second to the first adventurers, and the third to the public treasury. Nothing could be fished, mined, raked, or cut without a warrant from the governour and council, a body which was to be elected from the senate made up of the first one hundred adventurers.[19] However, Captain Sayle was commissioned by Parliament to be governour for the first three years.[20]

A particularly commendable part of the document relates to the adventurers' humanitarian treatment of any natives they might find on the islands. It was ordered that "no Inhabitant of these Plantations, shall in their converse with any of the Natives of any of those parts, offer them any wrong, violence, or incivility whatsoever: but shall deal with them with all justice and sweetness. . . ." Furthermore, since the company had been informed that some Indians had "been taken and sold at some of the Caribe Islands," it was agreed and ordered that they should be "sought out" and after they had been given religious instruction should "be then returned to the places from which they were taken. . . ."[21]

The idealistic intentions of the settlers expressed in their "articles" soon faltered under the harsh realities of pioneer life. The expedition seemed ill-fated even before it got under way. In March, 1646, William Rener of Bermuda wrote to John Winthrop in Massachusetts relaying the regrettable news that of the two ships which had been sent to the Bahamas to find a suitable island to settle upon, the first had never returned and the second had returned, "but without discoverye of that islande we aimed at." Rener also informed the Puritan governour that he and Captain Sayle had purchased half interest in a vessel (*William*) and a shallop of six tons designed expressly for sailing in the Bahamas and that they proposed to leave "about [the] firste of 3ᵈ monthe [March 1646 old calendar]."[22]

Nothing is certain about the voyage, not the date of departure, the place of arrival in the Bahamas, or what became of the adventurers themselves. Some time between the spring of 1646 and the fall of 1648, William Sayle set out with seventy prospective settlers, a group composed of religious Independents from Bermuda and some people from England.[23]

Reverend Patrick Copeland had renounced the Church of England some years ago, and now this godly Independent of nearly eighty years had the courage to leave his Bermuda home and embark on an expedition to a primitive island. Like old Gonzalo in *The Tempest*, he probably had his own image of Utopia. What follows in the only contemporary account of the arrival of the Eleutheran adventurers in the Bahamas reads like the scenario of Shakespeare's comedy. Just as Sebastian plots to kill his brother to gain the throne of Naples, Captain Butler rebels against the government set forth in the "Articles" agreed on by the adventurers. It is curious that both men, stranded on primitive islands, with no hope of ever returning to civilization, should behave as they would back in Italy or England.

> . . . in the way to Eleutheria, one captain Butler, a young man who came in the ship from England, made use of his liberty to disturb all the company. He could not endure any ordinances or worship &c. and when they arrived at one of the Eleutheria Islands, and were intended there to settle, he made such a faction, as enforced captain Sayle to remove to another island, and being near the harbour, the ship struck and was cast away. The persons were all saved, save one, but all their provisions and goods were lost, so as they were forced (for divers months) to lie in the open air, and to feed upon such fruits and wild creatures as the island afforded.[24]

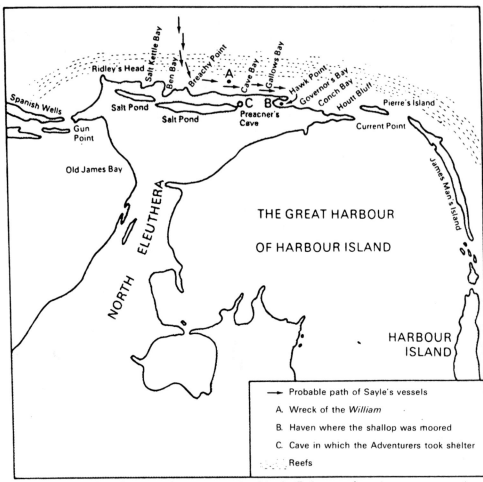

PLATE 8: The Eleutherian Adventurers arrived in the Bahamas aboard
the *William*, but their claim to the islands would not survive the political
turmoil of the Restoration in England. (From Paul Albury's *The Story
of the Bahamas*, courtesy of Macmillan, London and Basingstoke.)

Although Abaco and Eleuthera lie nearest to Bermuda, it is conjectured that the
adventurers first landed at the northern bulge of Eleuthera. Sayle later removed to
St. George's Cay (Spanish Wells), a small island to the leeward. (See plate 8.) Unable
to stand by and watch his people perish, Sayle provisioned the shallop as best he
could and, taking eight men, set out to find help. After nine days their supplies were
exhausted, but Sayle reached Virginia where religious sympathizers furnished him
"with a barque and provisions for the relief of the settlers in the Bahamas."[25]

The legality of Eleutheran Proprietorship has always been questionable due to
the shifts in government in England at the time. Charles I was executed 30 January
1649 and *The Journal of the House of Commons* of Cromwell's Parliament recorded

that on 31 August 1649 "An Act for Settling the Islands in the West Indies betwixt the Degrees of Twenty-four and Twenty-nine North Latitude was passed." But no further official record has been found. However an original letter of attorney from one John Bolles to Joseph Bolles, his brother, dated August 15, 1654, cites an act passed in 1650 "for encouragement of adventurers to some newly discovered Islands" by which it was enacted that:

> William Saile, Cornelius Holland, John Hutchinson, George Hutchinson, Gregory Clement, Nathaniell Rich, Thomas Westrowe, Thomas Jopson, John Bolles, John Humphry, Nicholas Bond, Peter Chamberlaine, Owen Rowe, John Rushworth, Robert Haughton, John Sparrowe, Gualter Frost, Nicholas West, Thomas Smith, Robert Norwood, William Rowe, John Blackwell, junior, Arthur Squib, Samuel Spurstow, John Elliston, Azariah Husbands theire Heires Successors and Assignes should be from thenceforth deemed and adjudged the true and lawful Proprietors of all those Islands lying betwene the degrees of twenty fower and twenty nyne Northlatitude from the Equinoctiall and in longitude from Florida to the Sumers Islands whereof discovery hath bin made at the Charge of the aforesaid Persons And that the said Persons theire Heires and Assignes should have hold possesse and enjoye the Islands forever. . . .[26]

"Forever" turned out to be twenty years. Sayle had to abandon his claim to the Bahamas, for in 1670 the islands officially fell to the six Lords Proprietors in their Carolina grant.

There is little doubt that the adventurers mentioned in the House Journal of 1649 were the twenty-six Proprietors named in Bolles' letter of attorney.[27] Of the twenty-six, only William Sayle actually emigrated to Eleuthera. Joseph Bolles, John Blackwell Jr., John Humphry, and Nicholas West went to New England. Cornelius Holland had an estate in Bermuda and the rest remained in England.

Many were Cromwell's men, and five were regicides: Gregory Clement, Cornelius Holland, John Humphry, John Hutchinson, and Owen Rowe signed the death warrant for the execution of King Charles I. Upon the restoration of King Charles II, Gregory Clement was executed and Owen Rowe died in the London Tower. It was a chaotic time in England's history as the last lines of George Wither's poem eulogizing Thomas Westrowe indicate: "They will not much mistake therein, who shall/This Isle, Great Bedlam, now Great Britain call."[28]

In 1649 the Bermudian Royalists acknowledged Charles II as king, took up arms, and exiled Reverend Nathaniel White and his Independent congregation to the "little Island" in the Bahamas where the Eleutheran adventurers struggled to cultivate "barren Rock" and "shallow Earth." News of their plight reached Boston where £800 was collected from several churches to purchase provisions which arrived in the Bahamas 17 June 1650. The grateful colony sent back ten tons of brasilwood for the use of Harvard College.[29] Besides ambergris, brasiletto was the most valued export of the Bahamas at this time. The wood produced fine furniture, and the small seeds sheathed in white flower pods contained a useful dye.[30]

Despite Puritan generosity the infant colony collapsed. Seventy settlers returned to Bermuda in 1650. Mr. Forster reported that "the ruder sort of people" threatened to send them all away from Bermuda again and only "by the blessing of the Lord" was he able to pacify them.[31] In all likelihood these seventy people represented most, but not all, of the original colonists.

More settlers probably joined the remnant of the first adventurers because by 1656 ships commuted between Bermuda and Eleuthera on a regular basis.[32] In that same year Reverend White and some others went home, but the Bermuda Council banished "some troublesome slaves" as well as native Bermudians, and "all the free Negroes to the Eleutherian Settlement."[33] Respected Bahamian historian Paul Albury believes that both New England and Virginia used the Bahamian colony as a dumping ground for undesirables and trouble-makers.[34]

In December, 1656, Cromwell's Council of State wrote to the commander of the British Fleet in America advising him to send a vessel to rescue about sixty English Protestants from Somers' Island, who "through the violent persecution of some ill-affected persons there" had gone to Eleuthera and suffered much hardship. The Council suggested that the commander "invite them to Jamaica" and if they were "not free to go to Jamaica to send them to England." There is no record that anyone from Eleuthera accepted Cromwell's invitation.[35]

Robert Ridley departed the island at some point, but he left his name behind on the treacherous channel that cuts through menacing patches of coral just off the northwest point of North Eleuthera. Ridley Head Channel is the quickest way for shallow draft vessels leaving Spanish Wells to pass to Abaco.[36] Along with three others, "Robert Ridlye" had signed the letter which accompanied the gift of wood to Harvard College.[37]

In March, 1657, William Sayle, his wife and three children and thirteen other persons arrived in Bermuda in the ship *John*.[38] A few months later Richard Richardson and his two associates, John Williams and Aser Eley, arrived in Eleuthera. A man named Curtise who lived in William Sayle's house invited the company to stay there. In a few weeks Richardson had a falling out with his companions and "went to live in the cave where they [the first adventurers] did formerly goe to service."

Around the 22nd of August Curtise came to the cave and told Richardson that he had heard about the wreck of a Spanish treasure ship on "Jeames man's Iland." One historian, Bates, argues that the Spanish vessel did not wreck on Man Island but on Abaco, and another authority, Craton, also mentions that a Spanish ship was "cast ashore at Abaco in July, 1657." Their information was obtained from Lefroy's introduction to Richardson's sworn statement in the *Bermuda Memorials* which is misleading. However, Richardson's statement is clear enough.[39]

Richardson quickly patched up his differences with his companions. They borrowed the governour's shallop and retrieved a substantial amount from their first voyage, some £2600, which they divided at Governour's Bay. The group had originally agreed to share and share alike. However, after "a great deal of wrangling" Richardson managed to get an additional half share. They "went downe" again to the wreck for more treasure and this time sailed "up to Spanish Wells" to divide the money.[40]

Evidence presented in Richardson's account proves helpful in establishing the landfall of the first adventurers. He indicates that Sayle's house and the first Eleutheran settlement lay in the vicinity of Governour's Bay and what is now called Preacher's Cave. Also, the reference to Spanish Wells may possibly confirm that island as the one to which the settlers removed after the quarrel with Butler.

William Sayle had not permanently abandoned the colony as it might seem. In London he received some backing to promote a trading voyage that would benefit the Eleutheran pioneers. Thomas Sayle, the governour's son, captained the *William*, which would first carry passengers and goods from London to Bermuda, then proceed to the Bahamas to cut brasilwood, collect seal oil and ambergris, and engage in wrecking. This merchandise would then be taken and sold at the "Cariba Islands," probably Barbados and some of the other English-held islands in the Windward Antilles. Thomas Sayle received his orders in 1658 and departed for Eleuthera 23 June 1660 with much needed supplies and at least one passenger; for on 21 June Governour William Sayle and the Bermuda Council had found Neptula, wife of Benjamin Downeham, guilty of adultery and exiled her to Eleuthera.[41]

Another son, Nathaniel, was appointed governour of Eleuthera after his father's departure. The document, dated 19 December 1661, was laid before the Bermuda Commission examining Nathaniel Sayle's claim to the Bahamas. At the investigation Peter Sands swore that he and "Mr. Nathaniell Sayle were at Elutheria together" and recalled seeing a "paper that had a Seale at it" which was published "in the Cave" but he did not know the contents of the paper. Another witness, William Barnet, said the paper "had a brave seal unto it" but whether or not it was the King's grand seal, he could not say. However, he did swear that he was present "in the cave" where Nathaniel Sayle read his commission:[42]

> By virtue of a Commission granted unto Captain William Sayle, and divers others, by the Kinge and Parliament of England, to enjoy the Bohamo Islands, and from him to mee, I doe appoint Mr. Thomas Houtt and Mr. Thomas Haies to be Deputy Governours under mee. And in my absence to govern the people uppon Elutheria, and to Administer Oath to any of the Inhabitants for the clearing of matter brought before them. Likewise I doe require all the Inhabitants uppon that Island to yeald all lawfull obedience unto the sayd Thomas Houtt and Thomas Haies, as they will answer the contrary at their peril. . . .[43]

On one of his voyages to Carolina, William Sayle had luckily been driven by a storm into an island harbour rather than onto a deadly reef or into the ocean deep. He named that island Providence. A group of Bermudians who had been cruising Bahamian waters whale fishing and looking for Spanish wrecks and ambergris settled the island in 1666 and initiated a second wave of Bermudian colonization in the Bahamas.[44] At first they called it Sayle's Island in honour of its discoverer; but later as more and more settlers poured in, inhabitants changed the name back to

Providence. In fact, they had taken to calling the island New Providence in order to distinguish it from Old Providence off the coast of present-day Nicaragua.[45]

Bermuda had become overpopulated and a land shortage resulted; hence there was no longer a way for a man to "better himself." Too poor to transport themselves, their fellow Bermudians John Dorrell and Hugh Wentworth providently assisted the emigrants with ships and money, extending credit until the pioneers could raise funds from their plantations. For these settlers there could be no turning back; they had to make the new settlement work.[46]

PLATE 9: This 17th Century engraving of a buccaneer shows the origin of the name, (bottom left) and indicates the life style with a duel (middle) and a wild boar hunt (right). (From Maurice Besson's *The Scourge of the Indies*, courtesy of Routledge and Kegan Paul, London.)

PLATE 10
No fictional buccaneer could ever match the true history of L'Ollonais the Cruel, whose atrocities inflicted on his Spanish prisoners became legend. (From John Esquemeling's *The Buccaneers of America*.)

Trevelyan maintains that "the makers of early American settlements must have been men and women of most admirable versatility, endurance and courage.[47] One must include here Bahamian settlers, who also had virgin soil to tame and households to furnish from whatever the primitive island could provide. Unlike their American counterparts they had no old inhabitants to battle, but they were forced to defend themselves against French and Spanish raiders because the settlement of New Providence coincided with the heyday of the buccaneers.

The term buccaneer came in part from *boucan*, a wooden gridiron on which the French hunters on Hispaniola used to cook and cure their meat. These butchers looked as if they had virtually crawled inside the animals they slaughtered. They dressed in bloodied pantaloons and wore shoes made from the skin of a boar's foreleg. (See plate 9.)[48] Soon tired of supplying passing ships with meat, these hunters formed a kind of fraternity called the Brethren of the Coast and rode out to plunder the sea. In a later period the term buccaneer became synonymous with privateer, a man who raided only enemy vessels during times of war and under letters of marque, official pirating licenses issued by his king. Those who plied their trade in peacetime were called pirates. Woodes Rogers, who in 1718 crushed the pirates in the Bahamas, had been a privateer.

Nonetheless, pirates, "by any other name," were men and women with strong personalities, uncommon energy, and a thirst for independence. Pirates "lived for the moment," were "swaggerers, lovers of glory, sometimes cruel, often generous, but cowards never."[49]

PLATE 11: Despite this romantic picture, Henry Morgan was better known for his destruction of the Spanish than for the capture of lovely women. (From Maurice Besson's *The Scourge of the Indies*, courtesy of Routledge and Kegan Paul, London.)

During the peak of activity, Henry Morgan led the British buccaneers at Jamaica and Francis L'Ollonais led the French at Tortuga against Spain, their common enemy. During the decade of the 1660s, these two and their bands, along with some Portuguese and Dutch buccaneers, were the scourge of the Indies. They sacked towns in New Spain (now Mexico) and mercilessly inflicted the tortures of the damned on their prisoners, taking Spain's wealth and repaying Spaniards for their treatment of the Indians.

As unimaginable as it may seem, the Spanish had met their match in L'Ollonais the Cruel. This formidable enemy murdered all his prisoners, cutting them to pieces, pulling out their tongues and committing other atrocities upon the Spaniards. His rage even displayed a certain macabre flair. Once he took his cutlass, cut open a captive's breast, jerked out his heart, and "began to bite and gnaw it with his teeth, like a ravenous wolf." (See plate 10.)[50]

In 1668, Henry Morgan, the future Governour of Jamaica, sacked the city of Porto Bello on the Darien coast of the Province of Costa Rica. In order to strike fear in the inhabitants, he shut up all the soldiers and officers in one room and set fire to the powder magazine below them and "blew up the whole castle into the air, with all the Spaniards that were within." (See plate 11.)[51]

Although the Spaniards were held at bay for a time, the infant settlements at New Providence, North Eleuthera, Spanish Wells, and Harbour Island were always under the threat of Spanish invasion as they struggled to plant roots in Bahamian soil. They dragged their livelihood from the sea and carried their wares to market in the Windwards across Caribbean waters infested with the deadliest marauders the New World had ever known, the buccaneers.

4

Lords, Knaves, and "They That Go Down to the Sea in Ships"

In the face of colonization and buccaneer invasion, the ownership of the Bahama Islands remained unsettled until 1663. William Sayle and the first adventurers of Eleuthera soon learned that a grant is an empty document without the corresponding patent. The next, finally official, claim would be made by a group of men called the Lords Proprietors.

On 24 March 1663 King Charles II granted the Province of Carolina to his "right trusty, and right well beloved Cousins and Councellors:"

> Edward, Earl of Clarendon, our high Chancellor of England; and George, Duke of Albemarle, Master of our horse and Captain General of our Forces; our right trusty and well beloved William, Lord Craven; John, Lord Berkeley, our right trusty and well beloved Counsellor; Anthony, Lord Ashley, Chancellor of our Exchequer; Sir George Carteret, Knt. and Baronet, Vice Chamberlain of our household; and our trusty and well beloved Sir William Berkeley, Knt.; and Sir John Colleton, Knight and Baronet. . . .[1]

On 11 July 1668 six of the eight Carolina Proprietors (Albemarle, Craven, Ashley, Carteret, Colleton, and John Berkeley) were granted the "islands of Bahama, Elutheria, Ventris [probably Abaco], Providence, Inagua, and all other islands lying within 22 degrees to 27 degrees north latitude commonly called the Bahama Islands or the Lucayos." The patent included the rights to whales, sturgeons, and all other "royal fishes" in the sea, bays, inlets, and rivers. Powers were extended to the Proprietors to make grants of land, levy customs' fees and appoint governours.[2]

William Berkeley, John's brother, was governour of Virginia at this time, and the reason he was excluded from the Bahama grant is not known. Although Clarenden was acquitted of charges of high treason, the king dismissed him as chancellor in 1667 and in 1668 the earl was banished from England.[3]

The Bahama grant stipulated, according to medieval custom, that a "rent of one pound of fine silver" be paid "as often as the King, his heirs and successors, shall visit said islands."[4] The king never visited the islands, nor did any of the Lords Proprietors, for that matter. They took little interest in colonial affairs; redresses received little notice.

A Captain John Russell, late master of the *Port Royal*, had occasion to appeal to Sir Peter Colleton "concerning his condition." The Lords Proprietors had fitted out an expedition of three ships, the *Carolina*, the *Port Royal*, and the *Albemarle*, which set sail from Kinsale, Ireland, bound for Barbados. Since plantations there had been severely damaged by hurricanes, the fleet was to recruit colonists from Barbados for the Carolinas. In the Bahamas, the *Port Royal* experienced foul weather, and on 12 January 1669 the vessel was "cast away upon the island of Munjake near Abaco." Everyone reached shore safely in the ship's boat, but many survived the storm and the wreck only to die of neglect waiting for a new boat to be completed. "Our inhuman carpenter," Russell reported, had created so much trouble and by his refusing to work caused so much delay "that many of our people lost their lives." However, Russell was not a man to sit idly by and watch his passengers perish. He took the loathsome carpenter to another island, marooned him there, then returned to Munjake to build the boat himself. Captain Russell successfully piloted the survivors to Eleuthera, where he commissioned another vessel to take them to New Providence where some remained while others secured transport to Bermuda.[5]

John Dorrell chanced to meet Captain O'Sullivan, Surveyor General, who had acquainted him with Lord Ashley's desire to promote new plantations. In a letter dated 17 February 1670 Dorrell told the Proprietor about the Bermudian settlement of about three hundred inhabitants on New Providence, an island with "gallant harbours." In an effort to rank the Bahamas with the Provinces of Carolina and Virginia, he also informed Ashley that the land produced "as good cotton as is ever grown in America, and gallant tobacco." However, the settlers were in need of "small arms and ammunition, a godly minister and a good smith." Dorrell reminded his lordship that he and his friend Hugh Wentworth had encouraged the settlement from the start and urged Ashley to patronize the colony "by gaining a patent for all the Bahama Islands, so they may be governed according to his majesty's laws."[6]

Dorrell sent another letter to Ashley dated "Somers Island March ye 13th 1670/71" His detailed account of the Bahama Islands included their accurate latitudes reckoned by one "Solomn [sic] Robinsone Master of the ship *Barmudians Adventure* who hath been a Coaster among ye said Islands." Before he offered the advantages of each island, he assured Lord Ashley that plentiful amounts of brasilwood covered the whole of the group.

Travellers from Bermuda and America generally approached "Elutheriah" before going to any other islands. It was about 140 miles long and very narrow in some places, "Well watered," and had a "good harbour for shipping." Harbour Island "Lyeth in a bite of Elutheriah" and at its eastern end is a "Small Island [St. George's Cay (Spanish Wells)] and amongst these 3 Islands and about them is the most and Best Ambergreece found." The inhabitants there numbered "about 20 families of Barmudians."

New Providence had "near 500 inhabitants," many of them children. The land produced "good cotton and tobacco, Suggar Cains," and "Indico Weed." Abaco and "Andrews [Andros]" had plenty of good cedar and pine trees. Exuma had "a Salt pond on a Small Island belonging to it . . . and two years ago a Sperma Cetta Whale" had been found there. Dorrell assured his lordship that "there is not more Abler men in the English Nation for Killings of Whales than our Natives here [Bermuda]." He also reminded Ashley that the management of the whaling industry in the Bahamas rested in good hands, for Hugh Wentworth was "chief husband."

Evidently Lord Ashley had expressed some desire to visit the islands because Dorrell ends his letter by advising his lordship to bring his vessel to Bermuda first. He would need to take on a pilot experienced in sailing Bahamian waters because several vessels had been cast away on Eleuthera.[7]

Ashley's influence prevailed; on 1 November 1670 the Proprietors' grant became officially recorded in the "Patent Roll."[8] The Proprietors had appointed old William Sayle to be the first governour of South Carolina. He died at Albemarle Point on 4 March 1691.[9] Since Sayle is generally thought to have been the first governour of the Bahamas, Hugh Wentworth is considered the first proprietory governour.

Hugh Wentworth died around 1670 and Bahamians elected as governour Hugh's brother, John Wentworth, who in 1671 received his commission from the governour of Jamaica and the Lords Proprietors.[10] John Wentworth sent a particularily colourless report to Thomas Lynch, the governour of Jamaica, in which he pointed out that the entrance from the northward ocean lies between the islands of Abaco and Eleuthera, which are about thirty leagues in length "but with little habitable land." Eastward and southward of New Providence for "40 or 50 leagues are islands of no value, with shallow water and banks navigable only for barques and shallops."[11]

Highly displeased with Captain Wentworth's government, John Dorrell wrote to Ashley declaring that the governour "'debauches himself and has corrupted the people.'" He encourages young men to "'run a-coasting in shallops which is a lazy course of life and leaveth none but old men, women and children to plant.'" Dorrell suggested that the Proprietors restrict the number of boats allowed to go turtling in order to preserve the species, and to prohibit the cutting of brasiletto except by license and to encourage planting by awarding grants of land.[12]

In 1672, Lord Ashley was created First Earl of Shaftesbury and soon became the most important statesman in the reign of Charles II. He alone of all the Proprietors took an interest in colonial affairs and as his interest was wholly commercial, he was not about to allow Wentworth to ruin his prospects in the Bahamas.[13]

Ashley wrote to John Wentworth in 1675 and warned him not to deal with adventurers but to look out for the best interests of the Proprietors. Regarding the cutting of brasiletto, he reminded him that the Lords Proprietors had good right to the land and the wood that grew upon it. It is obvious from his concluding remark that Shaftesbury was a man to be reckoned with. He told Wentworth to decide whether he held his place as governour because he was chosen by the people or by appointment of the Proprietors. "For if by the former the latter will quickly try how safe the island will be under another."[14]

This proved no idle threat. John Wentworth was recalled and on 1 July 1676 the Proprietors commissioned Charles Chillingworth governour of the Bahama Islands. Their instructions to him seemed to reflect John Dorrell's suggestions to Ashley a few years before. As governour, Chillingworth was to prohibit the cutting of brasiletto, cedar, or other wood, coasting for ambergris, whalefishing, or wrecking without a license. The governour was to persuade the people to plant provisions, tobacco, indigo, and cotton, as well as to propose a bill for the preservation of the turtle if that were necessary.[15]

Prior to the arrival of Woodes Rogers in 1717, the proprietory governours proved by and large an unsavory lot of tyrants, despots, drunkards, thieves, and cowards. The few who tried to maintain a modicum of order were met with resistance and either abandoned their posts or were driven off the island by the inhabitants. The colony grew more and more unruly and rebellious. Trevelyan believed the independent attitude of English settlements stemmed from the fact that "they had not been founded by an act of State but by private initiative."[16] Often the success of government, or the decision to have any government at all in the Bahamas, rested on the whims of the inhabitants. Such was the fate of Mr. Chillingworth. At New Providence some of the people "living a lewd, licentious Sort of Life" grew "impatient" with the governour, seized him and shipped him off to Jamaica.[17] In 1682 Governour Lynch of Jamaica reminded the Board of Trade the "Bahama Islands were once under this government and must return to the King's or they will remain nests of robbers. . . ."[18]

The Proprietors were quick to safeguard their own interests but slow to protect the lives of the islanders. Bahamians carried on secret trade with Hispaniola and Cuba in spite of the danger of being captured and imprisoned by the Spanish.[19] France and Spain realized the strategic nature of the island of New Providence, but no matter how often they were importuned, the Proprietors took no steps to fortify the island. The result of their neglect was inevitable.

In 1682 the Spanish attacked New Providence, destroyed the settlement, killed all the cattle "they could not or would not carry off, and took the Governor away with them in Chains." Mr. Trott told Oldmixon that the "Spaniards roasted Mr. Clark [Robert Clarke] on a spit after they had killed him," but another account states that the Spanish roasted him alive. The Spanish attacked New Providence again in 1684. Colonel "Lilborn [Robert Lilburne]" escaped to Jamaica and the inhabitants "dispersed in the Holes and Woods amongst the Islands."[20]

On the 5th of August, 1686, the people of Boston were busily taking up collections at all their meeting houses to aid French Protestant refugees lately driven from "France for Religion's sake." They also generously included "fifty persons, Men, Women and Children, which were by the cruelty of the Spaniards beaten off from Eleatheria" and had managed to sail to Boston, where they arrived "naked and in great distress."[21]

The Eleutheran refugees finally settled the township of North Yarmouth on Casco Bay near Portland, Maine, which in colonial days lay within the Province of Massachusetts. On 6 January 1686, Jeremiah Dunmer, Simeon Stoddard, and Walter Gendall petitioned the governour of Massachusetts, Sir Edmund Andros, in behalf of the destitute Bahamians. This petition, submitted to the council and president, was filed 15 September 1686 and states:

... in July last past, arrived at this Town of Boston from Eleuthera, one of the Bahama Islands, many families having been spoiled by the Spaniards of all they possessed and driven off naked and destitute, who on their arrival here were like to be a continued charge unto this place. Your Petitioners, considering the same, made application unto the President and Council offering that if the interjacent land ... might be granted unto us, who have each of us some land upon the place, that we would advance money for their support and supply and settlement on said land. [We] were pleased thereupon to have an order for removing the said distressed people unto that place, declaring they would recommend our request unto His Majesty for his Royal favor therein. Whereupon we were at the charge of removing about *nine families* of the distressed people and have been at considerable charge in furnishing them with necessaries for their supply and support this winter. (Emphasis added.)[22]

Somehow the settlers survived the winter but by the summer of 1787 they were in such dire straits that again they had to petition Governour Andros for relief. According to the Eleutherans, their benefactors had not kept their part of the bargain.

Nicholas Davis, Nath. Sanders, John Alberry, and Daniell Sanders, in behalfe of selves, families and the rest of our Company, Humbly sheweth your Excellency that whereas we agreed with some gentlemen here, namely, Mr. Jeremiah Dunmer, and Major Gidney of Salem, for the settlement of a plantation about Casco Bay, according to articles drawne upp betweene us, we have performed our part, but inasmuch as these gentlemen have not performed their obligation to us, in which they were bound to supply us that wee might carry on the plantation, we were forced to desert the plantation, because we had not food to subsist there, to our great damage and undoing—for we are now in a farr worse condition than we were before we went thither, not knowing what course to take to subsist, having worne out our clothes and wasted the little we had. Our humble petition to your Excellency is that we might have relief in the matter; for if we had forfeited our bonds to these gentlemen, as they have forfeited their bonds to us, the law would have been open to them.[23]

The unfortunate circumstances of the Eleutherans were fortuitous in the respect that without the petition of Davis, Sanders, and Alberry, the Bahamian refugees to New England in 1686 would have remained anonymous. With at least three of their names the historian can snatch a thread and begin to examine at least a remnant of the cloth.

In 1670 Dorrell estimated the population of Eleuthera, Harbour Island, and Spanish Wells at ten families, all Bermudians. In July, 1686, about fifty persons arrived in Boston after the Spanish raid on the islands. The Dunmer petition, filed 15 September 1686, stated that nine families had removed to Casco Bay. Even if Dorrell underestimated the population, at least one family stayed behind in Eleuthera. Peter Sands, one of the men who testified in Bermuda at the 1665 investigation of the proprietory rights dispute, probably stayed in the Bahamas. His name or that of his son appeared on the 1731 census with his place of residence—Eleuthera.[24] From that time to this, there have been, and still are, many Sands living on Eleuthera and New Providence.

Davis, Sanders (Saunders), and Alberry (Albury) are names well known in the Bahamas today, especially in Eleuthera and Abaco. And nowhere is the New England flavour more pronounced than at Harbour Island and Green Turtle Cay, Abaco. The houses in Dunmore Town, Harbour Island, Governor's Harbour, Eleuthera, and Spanish Wells reflect not just American colonial but New England colonial architecture. New Plymouth, Green Turtle Cay's settlement, has the look of a New England fishing village. (See plate 12.)

PLATE 12
Alton Lowe's original oil painting captures
the New England-like charm of this
colonial cottage on Harbour Island.
(From the collection of Alfred Meister.)

Various interpretations of this similarity are conceivable. It is reasonable to infer that at the Peace of 1783 American loyalist refugees came from New England colonies to settle Eleuthera and Abaco. It is true that there may have been some New Englanders in the large contingency of New York evacuees, but New York could hardly be considered a New England town. Among the New York and East Florida refugees were soldiers, politicians, merchants, and planters, not many seafarers. Very few Loyalists settled in Harbour Island or Spanish Wells and, after only a few years, the Abaco Loyalists moved on to other islands. A decade or so of habitation is hardly enough time to initiate, let alone implant, an architectural style, especially on the town of New Plymouth, which in all probability had not even been settled. This is not to say that Harbour Islanders did not invite their American relatives to come to the Bahamas after the Revolutionary War. It is reasonable that New Englanders as well as Loyalists from other American colonies would naturally migrate to the areas where they had kin.

Since many of the early Bahamians were seafarers, it is possible that they maintained a constant connection with the American colonies from the early days of settlement. It is curious to speculate as to why the Eleutheran refugees of 1686 went to Boston when Virginia was much closer not only in distance but by virtue of many Bermudians having settled there. Perhaps it was because many of the Eleutherans were whalers, an occupation they had in common with New Englanders at the time.

Of the first Bermudian adventurers who came to Eleuthera in about the year 1647, the ones who stayed were probably those who were bred to the sea. These wreckers, whalers, and turtlers survived Spanish and French attacks and pirate invasions.[25] Their hunting grounds were the Abacos and the only planting they did was strictly for subsistence. In 1783 Lieutenant Wilson, the engineer from East Florida, commented that the inhabitants of Harbour Island never bothered about cultivation. Without clearing the land, they went into the bush, dug holes with a stick between the trees, dropped in a few seeds and took no more care until they came back to harvest the crop.

Until about 1806, Harbour Islanders did not give a thought to settling Abaco. For the most part they lived aboard their vessels when cruising Abaco waters. Eric Whittleton states that prior to the Loyalist influx in 1783 Abaco was no more than "a home for a few squatters."[26] Perhaps a Bermudian or a Nantucket whaler or an Eleutheran wrecker tented there; and it is certain that pirates careened their vessels in the sheltered harbours of Green Turtle Cay.

During the Loyalist or plantation period, trading activity became heavy and wrecks increased. All vessels coming from northern American ports sailed along the treacherous eastern coast of Abaco, then rounded Hole in the Wall in order to reach New Orleans, New Providence or Cuba. About 1806 Harbour Islanders decided to join the few remaining Loyalists on Abaco and settled there, predominantly on the windward cays in order to be near the wrecking action. During the nineteenth century the town of New Plymouth grew to prominence. Many wealthy wreckers resided there and toward the end of the century the island became a centre for the disposal of wrecked goods. Possibly this trade brought many old Eleutheran family names such as Bethel, Albury, Lowe, Pinder, Russell, Roberts, Sawyer, Sweeting, and Curry to Abaco.

Many inhabitants deserted the islands after the Spanish raids, but more settlers came in from Jamaica. Try as they might, the Spanish were never able to depopulate the Bahamas a second time.

In the late 1600s pirates began to look on New Providence as a kind of resort. Lieutenant Governour Malesworth of Jamaica was more than a little concerned that the lack of good government as well as the dubious character of the new inhabitants of the Bahamian island would render the island incapable of withstanding any kind of outside invasion. Malesworth wrote from Jamaica in 1686 that the new governour elected in New Providence was

> . . . a broken down merchant, who with six or eight more indebted persons were gone to shelter themselves in the windwardmost part of the island in order to slip away by some boat. I hope, however, that my orders will have been in time to stop them. The modeller of their Government is one Patterson, a Whig lawyer, who, meeting with no encouragement here [Jamaica], fell upon this project, declaring that he knew of many discontented, good people in England, who would gladly leave it to settle in some island where they might be quiet and easy. One of the rules excludes all Jews, Quakers, and Roman Catholics. This Patterson, together with one Bridges, a conventicle preacher, and a whole sloopload of passengers, left the Island [Jamaica] a few days since with tickets, as if bound for Providence, where others will join them, under colour of cutting braziletto. This Bridges lived here in very good esteem with his congregation, but having married has lost his interest with the sisterhood who were his main supporters. His consequent discouragement seems to be the occasion of his joining with his father-in-law Patterson in the new design. Its result could have been only to make the people a prey to the Spaniards or a nursery of pirates.[27]

Perhaps Thomas Bridges would not have been Malesworth's choice for governour of the Bahama Islands. Recorded in the minutes of the Council of Jamaica 21 February 1687 was a proclamation for the recall of Thomas Bridges and others from New Providence.[28] Nonetheless, the Lords Proprietors commissioned the former preacher as governour in 1688 and sent along instructions that above all else "piracy is to be strictly put down."[29]

In 1690 the Proprietors appointed Cadwallader Jones and sent him to New Providence with only four barrels of powder "to support his government." The despicable Governour Jones set himself up as an absolute power. He pardoned violent criminals, neglected the defense of the island, seized and converted to his own use not only the public treasury, but the Lords Proprietors' royalties. While banishing the most virtuous and useful inhabitants without a trial, Jones invited pirates to the port and openly consorted with them. He was twice arrested and imprisoned by the inhabitants, who petitioned for a new governour. Nicholas Trott arrived in 1694 with a commission from their lordships whereupon he permitted Jones to leave the island without a trial.[30]

At the same time as Jamaica endeavoured to recover from the horrifying earth-quake which had swallowed up the city of Port Royal along with about three thou-sand inhabitants, Governour Trott proceeded to rebuild the settlement of New Providence, which had been equally devastated by the Spanish.[31] Before his commission expired, the town, which he named Nassau, had 160 houses in it. The governour maintained the peace by literally wearing out the few inhabitants by hav-ing them keep the watch around the clock.

Henry Avery's pirate vessel of forty-six guns appeared in the harbour at a time when the island had little defence, however, and the governour's integrity was put to the test. Since Avery had twice as many men aboard his vessel as Trott had on his entire island, the governour chose diplomacy over bravado. Trott told the chronicler Oldmixon that he received Avery to prevent the "Pirate's beating down the Town, and taking that by Force. . . ." The governour was later in a better position to de-fend Nassau against the French, who made several unsuccessful attempts on the island.[32] However, the incident with the notorious pirate Avery might have eventual-ly cost him the governourship of the Bahamas. Whether or not Trott actually consorted with pirates was never proved.

In March, 1697, Nicholas Webb arrived in the Bahamas to succeed Mr. Trott and that year the Peace of Ryswick put an end to privateering. The age of the buc-caneer had ended and the great age of piracy had begun. Oldmixon recounts that "Wrecks and Pirates were the only hope of Providence, there being no Product to trade with except Brasiletto Wood and Salt." At this time Exuma panned great quantities of salt for export.[33] Edward Randolph made a tour of English plantations in America and reported that there was sufficient salt in the Bahamas "'to supply England.'"[34]

In his *History of the Isle of Providence* Oldmixon described the seventeenth cen-tury Bahamian's attitude toward wrecking:

> As for Wrecks, the People of Providence, Harbour-Island and Eleuthera, dealt in them as it is said the good men of Sussex do: All that came ashore was Prize, and if a Sailor had, by better Luck than the rest, got ashore as well as his Wreck, he was not sure of getting off again as well. This perhaps is Scandal, but it is most notorious, that the Inhabitants looked upon every Thing they could get out of a Cast-away Ship as their own, and were not at any Trouble to enquire after the Owners.[35]

Besides land, which soon disappointed the first adventurers, their articles speci-fied as an inducement to colonizers the division of wrecked goods, salt, woods, and ambergris—the gold of the whale.

"Call me Ishmael." This line, perhaps the best known in all American litera-ture, rings up fantasies of sea adventure unparalleled. *Moby Dick*, the allegory of good and evil couched in the greatest whaling story of all time, immortalized the Nantucket whaler. The Bahamas never had a Herman Melville, but his description of Nantucket as "a mere hillock, and elbow of sand; all beach, without a back-ground" serves well for the cays of Abaco. And it was "no wonder" that the

Eleutheran like the Nantucketer "born on the beach, should take to the sea...
ploughing it as his own special plantation."[36]

The history of Bahamian whaling begins in Bermuda. Even before the Pilgrims
saw whales sporting about the *Mayflower* on their arrival in America in 1620, Bermudians had already attempted sperm whaling "in the deep." The following account of the whalers' first disappointing experiment is recorded in the *Historye of the
Bermudaes*, a work attributed to Captain John Smith, who established the first successful English colony in American at Jamestown in 1607. Smith is perhaps better
remembered for his story of how he was rescued from certain death by the Indian
chief's daughter Pocahontas.

In 1616, great numbers of whales could be seen off the Bermuda coast during
the months of January, February, and March. A company fitted out a tall ship, the
Neptune, and furnished it with skillful men and other necessaries. The governour
sent three new shallops, each manned with seven or eight men, to join the expedition:

> ... but the effect of this attempt answered not his hopes, for whether it were by
> reason of the extraordinary swift swimming and stoute mettall of this kind of
> whale (for it is the trunck whale, and is knowen by experience to have store of
> sparme), or the condition of the place, the sea being ther in some places very
> deepe, or that by reason of the rocks the hawsers could not be kept cleare, or
> what other mischiefe or mischance so ever it was, certaine it is that after many
> trialls, hazards, adventures, and continuall rayleinges upon poore mistris For-
> tune, not so much as one peece of a whale could ever be recovered, though di-
> vers of them were often strook and wounded; upon which ill luck the Governour
> for that time layd aside this sea-service and fell again to the land.[37]

About the same time William Sayle and his adventurers arrived at Eleuthera,
American colonists at Plymouth Bay, Cape Cod, Salem, and Long Island were killing
the slow-moving "right" whale along their shores as the Indians had done. Martha's
Vineyard was settled by whalers in 1652, and they also engaged in fishing there.[38]
The colony of Nantucket was established by Thomas Macy in 1659 and about 1672
James Loper, a successful Salem whaler, was invited by Macy to join the
Nantucket colony and start a whaling business there, which he did.[39]

The Lucayan was probably the first to see a sperm whale in Bahamian waters.
From the shore or in his canoe he watched its breath shoot out in a single stream and
hover over the whale like a cloud of steam, but whether any Indian ever tried to kill a
sperm whale is uncertain. What did the islander think of the whale's mammoth head,
a third the size of its huge body, and its jaw running the length of that head, with con-
ical teeth and a throat large enough to swallow a squid—or a man? Did a Bahamian
ever get close enough to look into its small cold eye?

Did an Eleutheran mate shout to his harpooner, "Stand and let him have it!"?
Did the Bahamian crew then feel the thrill of a "Nantucket sleigh-ride" before the
Nantucket whalers ever had a chance to name the experience of being towed at a
speed of fifteen knots by a sperm whale? Was ever a Bahamian shallop tossed into

the air by the head of a whale or struck by its tail to shatter like glass? Or seeing the huge jaw open about to bite his whaleboat in half, did a mate shout to his crew "Stern all for our lives!"?

Did any Bahamian ever watch a harpooned whale die in a "flurry," spouting scarlet, or did he sense like the poet Blake that the king of the deep was "drinking his soul away?"[40] Did an Eleutheran ever have the opportunity to confront the monster looming above him, and with harpoon in hand have the raw courage to bellow, "I spit my last breath at thee!"?[41]

Almost twenty years before Nantucketers solicited help to learn the art of whale fishing, it was a rapidly expanding industry in the Bahamas. In 1663, Hugh Wentworth received the title of " 'Husband in the Islands on the Behalfe of the Adventurers about the Whale Fishery.' " During the next five years, he hunted whales in Bermudian and Bahamian waters with his friends John Dorrell and old William Sayle. In 1669 they bought a ship called the *Blessing*, which they renamed the *Recovery*. Bates comments that whale fishing was "No easy livelihood."[42]

Offshore whaling in Bahamian waters must have been particularly hazardous due to the numerous rocks, coral heads, and in many places a dangerous sea of white water. Whale Cay, Abaco, is a sheer mass of solid, jagged rock on the windward side. In rough weather gigantic waves break over the entire island. The surf there is more treacherous than any sperm whale. If a harpooned whale should drag a boat through the narrow Whale Cay Channel, the likelihood of its being smashed against the rocks is almost a certain one.

The Bermudian surveyor and schoolmaster Richard Norwood, a relative of Robert Norwood, one of the original promoters of the Eleutheran adventurers, gives the only written account of seventeenth century whaling in the Bahamas. He probably received his information from Mr. Wentworth and company, and his letter to the Royal Society in London in 1667 describing the killing of whales is a testimonial to their skills.

> If [says Norwood] they [the whales] be struck in deep water, they presently make into the deep with such violence, that the Boat is in danger to be haled down after them, if they cut not the rope in time. Therefore they usually strike them in shoal-water. They have very good Boats for that purpose, mann'd with six oars, such as they can row forwards or backwards, as occasion requireth. They row gently up to the Whale, and so he will scarcely shun them; and when the Harpineer, standing ready fitted, sees his opportunity, he strikes his Harping-Iron into the Whale, about or before the Fins rather than towards the Tayl. Now the Harping-Irons are like those, which are usual in England in striking Porpoises, but singular good mettal, that will not break, but wind, as they say, about a mans hand. To the Harping-Iron is made fast a strong lythe rope, and into the Socket of that iron is put a Staffe, which, when the Whale is struck, comes out of the Socket; and so when the Whale is something quiet they hale up to him by the rope, and, it may be strike into him another Harping-Iron, or lance him with Lances in staves, till they have kill'd him. This I write by relation, for I have

PLATE 13: In his dry brush painting,
Robert Sticker gives a dramatic depiction
of "Whaling in Abaco." (Courtesy of the
Albert Lowe Museum.)

not seen any kill'd, my self. I hear not, that they have found any Sperma Ceti in
any of these Whales; but I have heard from credible persons that there is a kind
of such as have the Sperma at Eleutheria, and others of the Bahama-Islands
(Where also they find often quantities of Ambergreese) and that those have
great teeth (which ours have not) and are very sinewy. [43] (See plate 13.)

Although Norwood was not certain whether sperm whales had been killed in the
Bahamas, he did describe the whalers' use of harpoon with line attached which was
an especially dangerous practice in Bahamian waters because of the shoals and
rocks. Nantucketers did not employ that technique until about the mid-1700s.

The first American recorded to have captured a sperm whale was a Captain
Hussey of Nantucket. In 1712 a sudden storm drove his boat far out to sea where he
saw a great whale and was successful in killing it.[44] Mr. Atkins of Boston was the first
New Englander to go sperm whale fishing "in the deep" about 1720. His whalers
struck with harpoons to which were fastened drags (thick boards about fourteen
inches square) "after the Indian fashion." It was some time later that New Englanders had the courage to fix a line to the harpoon. The very idea of having their
boat attached to the fierce whale by a strong rope struck terror in the hearts of whaling crews, who in their imaginations saw themselves dragged to the bottom of the sea

or towed at great speeds to the other side of the world. Eventually overcoming their trepidation, New Englanders in the mid-1770s engaged in sperm whale fishing expeditions to the North and South Atlantic on a grand scale.[45] Stories of that kind of adventure live in the pages of *Moby Dick* where Melville's characters casually talk of whaling disasters and philosophize that "All men live enveloped in whale-lines."[46]

Profits were high for whale oil and well worth the risk, but ambergris, which often simply floated onto Bahamian shores, rendered more than its weight in gold. Ambergris is found in the intestines of sperm whales of both sexes, but more often in the male, and is the result of indigestion. If the whale cannot rid himself of the obstruction, he will die. Lumps of ambergris look like solidified sea foam or sponge and have been known to weigh as much as two hundred pounds. It is opaque in lustre and ashy in colour, which varies from black to whitish gray; gray ambergris is the most prized because it has been a long time in the whale. Ambergris has the pleasant smell of "newly ploughed earth" or a scent like musk and has the "curious property of retaining, or absorbing other odors to a wonderful degree." Perfumers have always valued the substance because it enables perfume to hold its fragrance for a long time.[47]

Not only ambergris but sometimes the whole sperm whale would wash ashore in the Bahamas. In 1668 one was found at Exuma.[48] Mr. Norwood said a Bermudian named John Perinchief found a dead sperm whale on one of the Bahama Islands, and although he was "ignorant in the business, yet he got a great quantity of spermaceti out of "its head.""[49]

That same year another Bermudian, Mr. Richard Stafford, a man proficient in the killing of black whales, had also seen dead sperm whales in Bermuda. "These have divers teeth, about the bigness of a man's wrist." He had also been at the Bahama Islands, "and there have seen this same sort of whale dead on the shore, with sperma all over their bodies." His next statement indicates that he intended to start a sperm whale fishery in the Bahamas. "Myself, and about 20 more have agreed to try whether we can master and kill them, for I could never hear of any of that sort that were kill'd by any man; such is their fierceness and swiftness." Stafford estimated that one "such Whale would be worth many hundred pounds." There is no documented proof that he was successful or even attempted the enterprise.[50] If he had been successful, Stafford would have preceded Captain Hussey in the killing of a sperm whale by almost fifty years.

In April, 1688, the governour of Jamaica sent a letter to the governour of Barbados, in which he states that a gentleman from Jamaica had sent a sloop whale-fishing in the Bahamas

> which he hopes may be profitable, many whales having been found in those parts; but it seems that it is difficult to take them there, as the seas are full of rocks and sands, so he succeeded in taking one small whale, while a larger one, which he struck got away. . . .[51]

Coincidentally, that same year the first mention of a sperm whaling voyage to Florida and the Bahamas is found in the New England records. George Dow wrote that in August, 1688, "the commander of the brigantine *Happy Return* petitioned Governour Andros for 'License and Permission, with one Equipage Consisting in twelve marines, twelve whalemen and six Divers—from this Port, upon a fishing design about the Bohamas Islands, and Cap Florida, for sperma Coety whales and Racks [wrecks] and so to return to this Port.' Whether this voyage was ever undertaken we do not know."[52]

Even at the end of the century Bermudians took an active role in the whaling industry. On 21 September 1699, the Lords Proprietors recommended to the care of the governour of the Bahamas, a Mr. Dudgeon, secretary of Bermuda, "to whom we have granted some land on Abucco [Abaco] and Andrews Island [Andros], with a liberty to fish for whales. . . ."[53] Edward Randolph seemed critical of the Lords who, according to him, had "granted away the royalty of the whale fishing and a great part of the island of Abbico" for thirty years to Mr. Dudgeon, a "sort of stock jobber."[54]

The lieutenant governour to whose care Mr. Dudgeon was recommended was Read Elding, a mulatto, who was commissioned by Governour Webb in 1698.[55] An earlier, somewhat suspicious incident involving Colonel Elding may have prompted Webb to desert his post in order to avoid reprisals. The governour had sent Elding out to find a pirate named Kelly. The pirate eluded him but Elding did not return empty-handed. He had seized a vessel, the *Bahama Merchant*, which he maintained had been abandoned. Webb claimed the prize until the owner complained and the crew mysteriously arrived in Nassau to force the Admiralty Court to reverse its decision. Edward Randolph later told the Council of Trade that Elding had piratically seized the *Bahama Merchant*, a brigantine from Boston, and forced its master Mr. Edwards to leave his vessel and "shift for his life." Randolph believed Elding to be a "known and late pirate" who was, in his opinion, illegally in possession of the government.[56]

Pirate or no, once given a free hand, Elding's ardour and courage in the pursuit of pirates knew no stops. Elding wrote England on 4 October 1699 that "about a fortnight now past" he had tried, condemned, and hanged a notorious pirate and intended to do his utmost to suppress others which might fall into his hands.[57]

Shortly thereafter, Elding captured a mongrel band of five infamous pirates: "Ounca Guicas, Frederic Phillips, John Floyd, John Vantein and Hendrick Van Hoven, alias Hynde, "the grand pirate of the West Indies.'" Vantein was released for lack of evidence, but the rest were convicted late in October for sailing "'under a bloody flag . . . as common pirates and robbers on the sea.' "[58] Read Elding summarily hanged them.

As the century closed, the tattered remnants of the first English settlements held on in spite of French and Spanish invaders. And now with Read Elding, forerunner of Woodes Rogers, at the helm, Nassau took a deep breath, secure from pirates—for the moment.

5

The Great Age of Piracy

Although Read Elding had hung out Mr. Hynde to sun dry, he had not heard the last of the pirate's gang, who threatened to come to New Providence and avenge their captain.[1] Besides trying to avert the designs of the rabble pirates, Elding had internal governmental troubles as well. Thomas Walker, Judge of the Vice Admiralty, claimed that Elding had refused to accept his commission and that he and the other proprietory representatives had been "molested, disturbed, and in danger of our lives of Read Elding, the assumed Deputy Governor of the Bahamas."[2] Whether Read Elding "assumed" the duties of the Vice Admiralty to get his fair share of wrecks and prizes, or whether Mr. Walker was displaying early signs of a later, but justified, paranoia is not certain.

Elding's successor, Elias Hasket, did not hold the welfare of the people worth a jot; his appointment proved once again the uncanny ability of their lordships to commission only greedy and profane wretches to the governourship of the Bahamas.

In 1702, two sail of Portuguese had been lost in the Gulf; and because the slavers were "in great want of provisions," the captain put in at Abaco, where he disembarked his slaves, and sailed on to New Providence. The arrival of the Portuguese vessels in Nassau Harbour greatly alarmed the townspeople, who ran to the fort to arm against attack. When he discovered that the Portuguese were no military threat, the governour became anxious to turn a profit on the misfortune that had befallen the slave captain. Hasket offered to buy from a Mr. Cole goods he had recently brought from Europe and the Carolinas. When Mr. Cole refused to sell at half price, the governour said that "he would be revenged on him." Mr. Cole goes on to relate that the Portuguese captain also "tried to hire a sloop to get his negroes." The governour would not allow anyone to come to terms with the captain. When Read Elding promised Hasket one-third his fee, "200 pistolls," then equivalent to that many English pounds, he was finally allowed to go to Abaco and bring the Blacks to New Providence.

Meanwhile, Cole goes on to say that "some poor people" brought provisions to sell to the Portuguese. The governour saw them come, took their provisions and paid "what he pleased." If they went away discontented, "he would swear and damn them" saying "he would cut their ears off."[3]

The inhabitants soon became "out of Humour" with Mr. Hasket. One day "they seized him, put him in Irons," and shipped him off the island. They then took it upon themselves to elect another governour, a Mr. Ellis Lightfoot. If the outraged citizens had waited two years before taking matters into their own hands, the Spanish might have cropped Mr. Hasket's ears for them. Oldmixon narrates the destruction wrought in New Providence by the combined French and Spanish forces who in July, 1703,

> ... landed, surprized the Fort, took the Governor Prisoner, plundered and stripped the English, burnt the Town of Nassau, all but Mr. Lightwood's [sic] House, together with the Church, spoilt the Fort and nailed up the Guns. They carried off the Governor and about half the Blacks. The rest saved themselves in the Woods: But in October they came again, and picked up most of the Remainder of the Negroes.[4]

Oldmixon goes on to relate how Mr. Lightfoot obtained his freedom from the Spanish prison at Havana through a ransom, went to Carolina, and "thence in a vessel on some Adventure" and was never heard of again. After this second invasion, the English inhabitants "thought it in vain to stay longer; so they removed, some to Carolina, some to Virginia, and some to New England." A few people remained scattered among the Out Islands.

Meanwhile the Proprietors had appointed another governour. When Mr. Birch arrived, he found the place practically deserted so he did not even "Trouble to open his Commission." Birch stayed on the island a few months but was forced to sleep in the woods all that time; he then went back to England.[5]

Although the Spanish had no permanent settlements in the islands at this time as England did, their claim to possession issued from the pope, to them an authority higher than any king.[6] The English claimed a kind of squatter's rights. The Spanish would continue to plunder the islands until the question was finally settled eighty years later. Displaced over these years by war, by pirates and then by war once again, many of the early Bermudian and English inhabitants who had taken refuge in several of the American colonies returned from time to time when things cooled off, so to speak. Many cautious but none the less loyal souls would not come home until after the Peace of 1783.

Even after the French and Spanish attack of 1703, Whitehall refused a request from the Bahamas for one hundred soldiers as "unseasonable at this time." The few inhabitants expressed willingness to repair the fort for "provisions and liquor."[7] A report on the state of the Carolinas dated Whitehall, 10 January 1705/6, placed the blame for the plight of the Bahamas squarely on the shoulders of the Lords Proprietors.[8] Their lordships seemed to have lost all interest in the islands and refused even to appoint a governour although in 1707 Robert Holden solicited them for the position. He had been given a patent for whaling and wrecking rights in the Bahama Islands and intended to go there.[9]

Mr. Holden informed the commission that he had purchased, out of his own funds, a "half a ton of shot and powder," which he intended to distribute among the people along with the "other things" he had bought for them. Holden felt that £300 to £400 would be enough to repair the damages to the island, but he advised against resettling or fortifying Providence during the war or inviting "the people scattered among the islands to return thither till a peace was concluded." Since New Providence had no natural fortifications, he proposed that Eleuthera might be a better place of defence because of its "good harbour."[10]

At that same meeting Mr. Stephen Dupont reported that the best place for English vessels to lie and wait for the enemy would be the east side of Abaco, "where they would not be perceived by the Spaniards."[11]

In January, 1708, the commission heard more testimony relative to the state of affairs in the Bahama Islands. British merchants hotly petitioned Her Majesty to take the government of the Bahama Islands "into her hands" in order to protect West Indian trade.

The bitter fact of the matter was that the Lord Proprietors had flatly refused to provide means for the security of British subjects in the Bahamas. Mr. Graves testified that, in the twenty-two years he had lived in New Providence, the Proprietors had sent over only four barrels of powder. As a result of all the testimony, the Lords of Trade and Plantations directed that a petition be drawn "requesting Her Majesty" to take the Bahama Islands "into her immediate protection and government."[12]

Queen Anne's War lasted until 1713 and during that time both French and Spanish pirates plundered the Bahamas. Letters to the Board of Trade told of the daily terror Bahamians suffered. In 1708 the French attacked the salt ponds at one island and five English vessels. In 1709 the French and Spanish possessed themselves of several of the Bahama Islands and committed great cruelties on Her Majesty's subjects.[13]

Captain Smith of the *H.M.S. Enterprise* wrote to the Board relating the hardships endured by the English settlers at Eleuthera. The inhabitants disclosed to the captain that as far as they knew there were no settlements of French in the Bahamas, but "they had been frequently visited by the enemy." Sometimes the French had taken whole families, forcing them "to confess where their money was hid." Their fear was so great that thirty-two families slept in the woods "so not to be surprized by the French" in the night. The Eleutherans had no "arms sufficient for their defense," but on Harbour Island Captain Thomas Walker had raised a "small battery" from the twelve families living there and had had four guns mounted.[14]

By 1710 Whitehall seemed ready to initiate a move to establish the Bahamas as a Royal Province. In September Mr. John Graves, long time resident and collector of customs at Nassau, received a letter asking him for the state of the islands so that government could go ahead with placing the Bahamas "under Her Majesty." His speedy but curt response informed the Lords only that the Spanish had "carried away most of the guns."[15] Mr. Graves either was tired of the bureaucracy or simply had no more to add to his eight page memorial delivered to the Lords Proprietors of the Bahamas Islands, to the honourable Commissions of Her Majesty's Customs, and to both Houses of Parliament, which was published in 1708.

In his *Short Account*, Graves once again stressed the convenience of the islands to trade. If the Bahamas fell into the hands of the enemy, no merchant vessel coming from Jamaica through the Gulf of Florida to the Carolinas or England would be safe. He himself had lived in Providence for twenty years and in that time it had been "three times plundered and layed in ashes."

In spite of everything Graves went on to write that the Bahamas "are the most healthy Islands of all our settlements and tho the ground be very Rocky, it will produce whatever is put into it, the best of Cotton in all the Indies, Dying woods, Sugarcanes, Indico, and great Quantities of Salt made by the sun out of the Sea, Tortoise shell, oyl of whale, seal and Nurse." At times spermaceti whales and, often, ambergris "washed up on the Bays." Salt was exported to the Carolinas. "Our Dying woods and what cotton we have are daily carried to the Dutch at Curazo and to the Danes at St. Thomas."

New Providence "needs a small man-o-war and a garrison" or else pirates would ruin the place. Already the settlers had to co-operate with the pirates in order to survive—an accommodation which Graves labeled "ill practices for filthy lucre." He flatly determined that "without good government and some strength," the Bahama Islands would always be a "shelter for Pyrates."[16]

The war of the Spanish Succession was ended in 1713 by a series of treaties known as the Peace of Utrecht. Great Britain confirmed Philip V's succession to the throne of Spain but insisted that he renounce the throne of France. The treaty with Spain ceded Gibraltar to Great Britain and afforded England with long sought-after commercial privileges. British merchants gained the monopoly of the slave trade with Spanish possessions in the West Indies and were allowed to carry one shipload of goods to trade at Porto Bello each year. Merchants cleverly got round the latter restriction by "simply unloading an entire fleet over the deck of the one ship after it docked at Porto Bello."[17]

Cessation of war meant the end of privateering and with so many British sailors unemployed, the West Indies was flooded with pirates. If Great Britain did not choose to recognize that New Providence lay directly in the course of trading vessels sailing from the New World to the Old, the pirates did. Pirates took Nassau and made it their headquarters.

The islands and cays of the Bahamas provided excellent shelter for their shallow draft vessels, especially the windward cays of Abaco where pirates often careened to await a chance to molest the Spanish. Pirates eventually held Harbour Island as an outpost where they manned Mr. Walker's battery with fighters from their own ranks.

In April, 1714, Lieutenant Governour Pulleine of Bermuda informed the Council of Trade that the Bahamas had become a retreat for three "sets of pyrates" and that the residents at Harbour Island, Eleuthera, and Providence lived "without any face of government," with "every man doing only what's right in his own eye." Furthermore, the governour reported that a pirate named Cochran had married the daughter of a Mr. Thomson, "one of the richest inhabitants of Harbour Island," and the pirate sailed Thomson's sloop to Curacao with brasiletto.[18]

The pirate mentioned here was probably Captain John Cochram, who later took the pardon. He and Benjamin Hornigold, another reformed pirate, successfully captured ten pirates at Green Cay, eight of whom were hanged in Nassau by Woodes Rogers in December of 1718.

In his March, 1715, correspondence to the Council, Thomas Walker assured their lordships that in "discharging his duty and loyalty to His Majesty" he had spent his "time in takeing upp pirats and routeing them from amongst these islands" and promised to "persevere" in these pursuits until a governour was sent out. When the governour arrives, he went on to say, he will be hard pressed "to curbe the exorbitante tempers of some people" and will find "inhabitants upon Ileatheria and the out Islands in arms to deffend themselves against justice."

Enclosed in Walker's correspondence were papers relating to his recent confrontation with Eleutheran pirates who had voyaged out against the Spanish. Included among those on a list of designated pirates were some inhabitants who may have decided that turnabout was indeed fair play:

> List of men that sailed from Ileatheria and committed piraceys upon the Spaniards, on the coast of Cuba, since the Proclamation of Peace: Danl. Stillwell, marryd to Jno. Darvill's daughter. John Kemp, Mathew Lowe, James Bourne, John Cary (all married). John Darvill sent his yong son of 17 yeares old a-piratting and was part owner of the vessell that committed the piraceys. Strangers that sailed from Ileatheria a-piratting:—Benja. Hornigold, Thomas Terrill, Ralph Blankershire, Benja. Linn.[19]

The pirate sloop *Happy Return* made two successful voyages. John Vicker's deposition of July, 1716, before Lieutenant Governour Spotswood of Virginia gives this account:

> About a year ago one Daniel Stillwell, formerly belonging to Jamaica and lately settled on Isle Aethera [Eleuthera], went in a small shallop with John Kemp, Matthew Low, two Dutchmen, and Darvill to the coast of Cuba and there took a Spanish lanch [launch] having on board 11,050 pieces of eight, and brought the same into Isle Aethera; and Capt. Thomas Walker of Providence having received advice thereof from the Governor of Jamaica, seized Stillwell and his vessell, but upon the coming of Hornigold to Providence, Stillwell was rescued and Capt. Walker threatened to have his house burned for offering to concern himself, Hornigold saying that all pirates were under his protection.[20]

Even if Hornigold had not interfered, Thomas Walker could not have tried the pirates in Nassau; for since the death of Queen Anne, his commission as judge of the Vice Admiralty Court had not been renewed. He had to send his prisoners to Jamaica, which was the nearest king's government, and on the way there the pirates escaped.

Now the inhabitants lived in deadly fear of Spanish retaliation for the outrages committed by the Eleutherans.[21] Another of Walker's enclosures shows that Bahamians knew the Spanish mind perhaps too well. A Captain Hearne had sent the following correspondence to Thomas Walker on 20 January 1715. It contained information he had gotten "after being 30 days on board a Spanish ship, upon the Bohamia Bank."

> Your takeing the piratts upp may save your life. . . . The Spaniards sent about two months agoe to cutt you off, and all men, women and children. But it may be said as of the Invincible Armado against England, God did turne them home either by bad weather or elce by bad pilotts. Sir, if you send the sloope you have seized to Havanna you will prevent their comeing and be rewarded well. . . .

Thomas Walker immediately set sail for Havana "where he accommodated all matters with the Governour there for ye peace and safety of the inhabitants of the Bohamia Islands."[22]

Perhaps nearly provoking another Spanish attack may have sobered the errant Eleutherans; and although they were protected by Benjamin Hornigold, Blackbeard's tutor in the art of piracy, it is doubtful that Lowe, Darvill, Kemp, or Cary ever went pirating again.

Despite the efforts of Thomas Walker, the pirate population on New Providence increased and began to threaten not only Bahamians but inhabitants of North America as well. The American colonies feared for the safety, not only of their merchant vessels, but of their very lives. A memorial from Richard Bereford on the current state of South Carolina in June, 1716, proposed that Great Britain encourage emigration to the Bahama Islands "(now inhabited only by a few scattered English settlements notorious for being without government)" by sending a small garrison to protect settlers. The defence of the Bahamas would be the "greatest security imaginable not only to Carolina but to other American colonies." Because of debts caused by the recent wars, Carolinians feared being "reduced to the miserable condition of their neighbours in the Bahama Islands, which we hope his most gracious Majesty the King under God will timely prevent."[23]

Governour Spotswood of Virginia wrote in July, 1716, that "a nest of pirates are endeavouring to establish themselves at Providence" and strongly urged that a government be established there and "the place made defencible." In spite of promises from the "gang at Providence that they will seize only French and Spanish ships," some trading vessels from the American colonies had already been plundered by the Nassau pirates.[24]

The deposition of John Vickers enclosed in Governour Spotswood's correspondence showed the height of disorder arising in New Providence in the wake of pirate occupation. Vickers testified that in November of 1715 Benjamin Hornigold arrived at Providence in a stolen sloop from Jamaica to dispose of Spanish booty. Captain Jennings came in April, 1716, and brought in a French prize mounted with thirty-two guns which he had taken at the Bay of Hounds. Pirates at Nassau robbed the inhabitants, burned their houses, and ravished the women; many settlers "had deserted their habitations for fear of being murdered." Some sailors at New Providence who called themselves the "flying gang" extorted money from the people. Mr. Stockdale, who had come to Virginia with Vickers, was whipped "for not giving them what they demanded." Thomas Barrow, pretending to be chief among the pirates at Providence,

> ... gives out that he only waits for a vessell to go out a pirating, that he is Governor of Providence and will make it a second Madagascar, and expects 500 or 600 men more from Jamaica sloops to join in the settling of Providence, and to make war on the French and Spaniards; but for the English, they don't intend to meddle with them, unless they are first attack'd by them; nevertheless Barrow and his crew robb'd a New England brigantine ... in the harbour of Providence and took a Bermuda sloop, beat the master and confined him for severall days, but not finding the said sloop fitt for their purpose, discharged her.[25]

When the pirates mounted guns in the fort in August, 1716, Thomas Walker fled to South Carolina. Not only had his life been threatened but Hornigold had promised to shoot his father as well.

Walker did not stay in Charleston long; he returned to the Bahamas sometime before July, 1717. Captain Musson reported to the Commissioners that on his way back to South Carolina, he stopped at Abaco where he found "Captain Thomas Walker with several other inhabitants" who had fled Providence "by reason of the rudeness of the pirates" and settled at Abaco.[26]

Walker's Cay, which bears his name, is situated just southeast of the Matanilla reef and is the northernmost island in all the Bahamas. Perhaps Captain Walker hid there to be as far away from the pirate headquarters as he could get without actually leaving the Bahamas. Captain Musson gives no indication where in Abaco he stopped. Exactly where Walker established residence may never be known, but his was the first recorded English settlement in Abaco.

Having discovered that dealing with pirates like Hornigold was not the same as bringing a few wayward Bahamians to justice, Walker had abandoned New Providence and none too soon. In 1717 Nassau was in the hands of professionals. The Golden Age of Piracy produced corsairs like Ned Teach (Blackbeard), Charles Vane, Henry Jennings, Stede Bonnet, Jack Rackam, Anne Bonny, and Mary Read, who ruled the coast of America, the Bahamas, and the Caribbean seas.

Daniel Defoe chronicled their lives in his *General History of the Robberies and Murders of the Most Notorious Pyrates* written under the pseudonym of Captain Charles Johnson and first published in 1724.[27] Besides the colonial records and the *London Gazette*, Defoe provides the only other contemporary account of the lives of these fascinating personalities. Defoe however displayed a tendency at times to extend his documented source material into the realm of fiction, protest as he did to the contrary.

According to Defoe, the Treaty of Utrecht accounted for the sudden increase in the numbers of pirates in 1713; his reasoning was that " 'Privateers in Time of War are a Nursery for Pyrates against a Peace.' " The sudden decline came with the death of Captain Bartholomew Roberts who " 'alone took 400 sail, before he was destroy'd.' "[28]

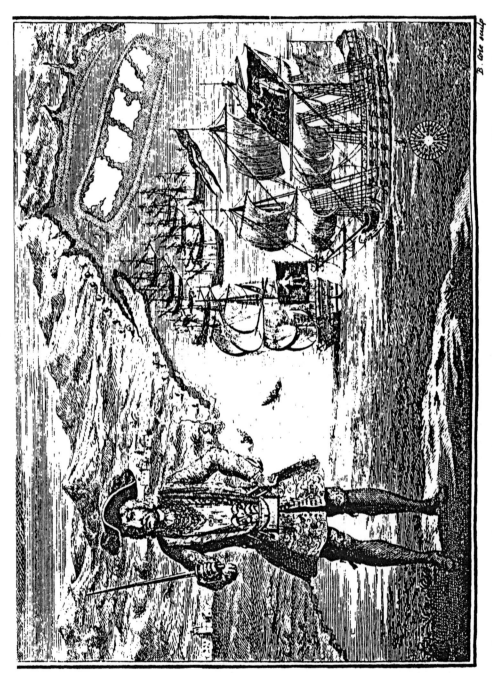

Captain Bartho. Roberts with two Ships, Viz. the Royal Fortune and Ranger, takes

Black Bart, perhaps the undisputed king of the pirates, generally displayed most unpiratelike behaviour. He drank tea instead of rum, followed his strict code to the eleventh article, and lived by his motto, "a merry Life and a short one." Although he did not drink strong liquor, Roberts was much addicted to music and dancing. However civilized this tall dark man appeared to be, he was deadly when provoked. Piqued at several flagrant attempts made by the governours of Barbados and Martinique to capture him, Roberts caused a new jack to be made which showed him standing upon two skulls, one signifying a Barbadian's head and the other a Martinican's head. With this dread ensign flapping in the mizzen peaks of the *Royal Fortune*, Black Bart roamed the Caribbean seas. (See plate 14.)[29]

Roberts cut a gallant figure standing on the quarterdeck "dressed in a rich crimson Damask Wastcoat and Breeches, a red Feather in his Hat, a Gold Chain round his Neck, with a Diamond Cross hanging to it, a Sword in his Hand, and two Pair of Pistols hanging at the End of a Silk Sling, slung over his Shoulders (according to the Fashion of the Pyrates)." He died boldly shouting orders to his crew until a charge of grapeshot struck him full in the throat. The man who found his captain dead is reported to have "gushed into Tears, and wished the next shot might be his Lot." The pirate crew then threw him overboard, with his Arms & Ornaments on," as their Captain had requested.[30]

Nineteenth and early twentieth century historians romanticized some of the already fictional elements in Defoe's account, but the popularity of Robert Louis Stevenson's classic *Treasure Island* created even more misconceptions about pirating. Colonial records contain no single case of anyone being forced to "walk the plank." Unlike the buccaneers, most pirates lusted solely after booty and had little desire to molest their prisoners so long as they offered no resistance. If opposed, pirates gave no quarter but fought until the red paint of the deck was washed with so much blood it literally ran out the scuppers.

Usually hoisting a black flag would be the only encouragement necessary to bring a vessel to the point of surrender; if not, once the pirates were aboard a splendid display of weaponry would be enough to terrify a hundred men into submission. Skill in the use of the cutlass gave the pirates of the Caribbean their dread reputation.

Captain John Smith maintained that boarding a vessel in a sea fight was more dangerous than charging the trench on the field of battle.[31] For this reason alone, cowardice in the face of death was rare among pirates. Mary Read never hesitated to board a fighting vessel, perhaps because she had had much practice as a soldier in Marlborough's Army, charging trenches in the Flanders Wars. Anne Bonny often-

PLATE 14 (opposite page):
Captain Bartholomew Roberts ("Black Bart") was a contradictory personality, even for a pirate. Here B. Cole, 18th C. engraver, depicts him against a background of ships, one of which flies an ensign showing Bart standing on the skulls of his enemies. (Originally published in Daniel Defoe's *General History of the Pyrates*, 1724.)

times fought beside her and together they quickly dispatched the most valiant opponents.

Usually pirates could judge when the vessel pursued was preparing to fight. Captain Smith illustrated the warning signs:

> ... if you see your chase strip himselfe into fighting sailes, that is to put out his colours in the poope, his flag in the maine top, his streamers or pendants at the end of his yards armes, furle his spret-sails, pike his mizen, and fling his maine yard, provide your self to fight.[32]

Probably the worst crime to the minds of the Puritan settlers in America was the pirates' love of life, for when ashore, they spent their days and nights in riotous living, drinking, dancing, and carousing. Pirates realized that their ill-gotten gains could just as easily be taken away and preferred to spend their wealth. What they did not spend on debaucheries ashore, they wore as decorations on their bodies, but they seldom buried their gold. Pirate crews threatened with capture, trial, and hanging made pacts to go into the hold, blow themselves up, and "go all merrily to hell together." Some pirates even displayed humanitarian feelings and gave chase to a slaver in order to set free the cargo, or to a hell ship to justly turn the captain over to his tortured prisoners.

The pirate ranks boasted several colourful characters like Stede Bonnet, the educated gentleman planter who left Barbados and took up a life of piracy to escape "a disagreeable marriage." Charles Bellamy was called the socialist pirate because in an impassioned speech he once damned " 'all those who will submit to be governed by Laws which rich Men have made for their own Security. . . .' " Bellamy railed against the rich scoundrels who " 'rob the Poor under the Cover of Law' " while pirates only " 'plunder the Rich under the Protection of our own courage. . . .' "[35]

Captain Jack Rackam distinguished himself by the striped calico breeches he always wore, but is perhaps better known for the fact that under his flag, showing a skull cradled in crossed cutlasses, sailed the pirates Anne Bonny and Mary Read. Rackam was quartermaster to the sadistic Captain Charles Vane before he put Vane and his mate Robert Deal in a longboat and bid them "go to the Devil." Anne and Mary may have been members of Vane's crew who voted him out and Rackam in as captain. It cannot be absolutely determined at what point the women joined Rackam's crew; however, they were captured with him that fateful November night at Negril, Jamaica, in 1720, when Captain Jonathan Barnet attacked their sloop. According to Defoe the men, including Captain Rackam, retired to the hold, leaving the two women to "keep the deck. Mary Read called to those under Deck, to come up and fight like Men, and finding they did not stir, fired her Arms down the Hold amongst them, killing one, and wounding other."[34] This information is from Defoe's account but it never appeared in the printed trial.

In his correspondence to the Colonial Office of 28 December 1720, Sir Nicholas Lawes, governour of Jamaica, wrote that "Rackam and 10 more have been tryed and executed."[35] Neither communication mentions the women, but he did send the official transcripts of their trial in his 12 June 1721 letter.

Rackam and ten of his crew were tried on the 16th and 17th and executed on the 18th of November, 1720. (See plate 15.)[36] The two women were tried separately on the 28th of November, 1720, and condemned for the same crimes. It was stated that in the perpetration of their "evil designs" on 3 September 1720 they did "piratically, feloniously, and in a hostile manner, attack, engage, and take Seven Fishing-Boats" about two leagues from Harbour Island, did "assault certain fishermen" names unknown, but "Subjects of His Majesty the King," whom they plundered of their fish and fishing tackle valued at £10 Jamaican currency. Three leagues off Haiti on 1 October, they did "set upon, Shoot at, and take two merchant Sloops" along with "Apparel and Tackle" valued at £1000. On 19 October five leagues from Port Maria Bay, Jamaica, they took a schooner belonging to Thomas Spenlow, and near Dry Harbour Bay, Jamaica, took a merchant sloop of which Thomas Dillon was master. Like Rackam and the others, the women pleaded not guilty to these charges.

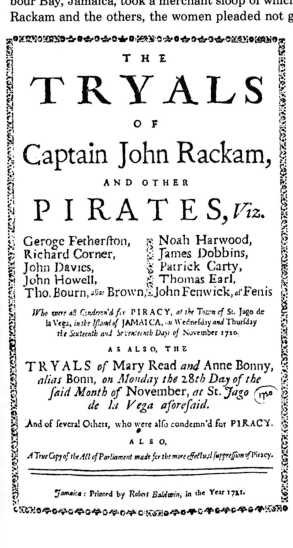

PLATE 15

The trials of Calico Jack Rackam and the two female pirates, Anne Bonny and Mary Read, were reported in a pamphlet printed in 1721, only months after their conviction. Details of their colourful lives were, unfortunately, not included. (CO 137/14f. 9, courtesy of Public Records Office, London.)

Several witnesses made statements to their active participation in these blatant acts of piracy. Thomas Spenlow swore that when he was taken, the women were aboard Rackam's sloop. John Besneck and Peter Cornelian, two Frenchmen who had been impressed into Rackam's service, said the women were "very active on Board, and willing to do any Thing." When Rackam "gave chase, or Attacked," Bonny and Read wore "men's Cloaths; and, at other Times, they wore Women's Cloaths." Thomas Dillon stated that, when Rackam's crew boarded his vessel, Anne Bonny "had a Gun in her Hand, That they were both very profligate, cursing and swearing much, and very ready and willing to do any Thing on Board."

Dorothy Thomas, whose canoe had been robbed of its "Stock and Provisions," testified that the two women "wore Mens Jackets, and long Trouzers, and Handkerchiefs tied about their Heads; and that each of them had a Machet and Pistol in their Hands and cursed and swore at the Men to murther the Deponent; and that they should Kill her, to prevent her coming against them; and the Deponent further said, That the Reason of her knowing and believing them to be women then was, by the largeness of their Breasts."

Dorothy Thomas' testimony was all that was necessary to put the women at the end of a rope. The trial ended this way:

> His Excellency the President, pronounced Sentence of Death upon them in the Words following, viz: You Mary Read, and Ann Bonny, alias Bonn, are to go from hence to the Place from whence you came, and from thence to the Place of Execution; where you, shall be severally hang'd by the Neck, 'till you are severally Dead. And God of His infinite Mercy be merciful to both of your Souls.
>
> After Judgment was pronounced, as aforesaid, both the Prisoners inform'd the Court, that they were both quick with Child, and prayed that Execution of the Sentence might be stayed.
>
> Whereupon the Court ordered, that Execution of the said Sentence should be respited, and that an Inspection should be made.[37]

In the four pages which comprised their complete trial there is no mention of the fascinating backgrounds of these women. Prior to the official trials there was probably an unrecorded but open hearing where the true sex of the women was discovered and where the women told the stories of their lives, which Defoe so colourfully recounts.

Defoe knew the market value of including the women in his history and of mentioning "the remarkable Actions and Adventurers of the two Female Pyrates, Mary Read and Anne Bonny" on his title page. He goes to great lengths in his preface to insure the credibility of his version which is the only contemporary account of their lives.

> As to the lives of our two female Pyrates, we must confess they may appear a little extravagant, yet they are never the less true for seeming so, but as they were publickly try'd for their Pyracies, there are living Witnesses enough to justify what we have laid down concerning them; it is certain, we have produced

some Particulars which were not so publickly known, the Reason is, we were more inquisitive into the Circumstances of their past Lives, than other People, who had no other Design, than that of gratifying their own private Curiosity: If there are some Incidents and Turns in their Stories, which may give them a little the Air of a Novel, they are not invented or contrived for that Purpose, it is a Kind of Reading this Author is but little acquainted with, but as he himself was exceeding diverted with them, when they were related to him, he thought they might have the same Effect upon the Reader.[38]

Indeed the reading public was "diverted" with their history, however fictionalized it may seem.

Both women were born illegitimate. Defoe begins Anne's story with the ridiculous circumstances surrounding her birth at a town near Cork, Ireland. If "Captain Johnson" had read the literature of his own time, he would have recognized the cast of characters from a Defoe novel or a Congreve play. They include Anne's father, gad-about and sometime attorney at law; Anne's mother, his maid servant and bed partner; and the attorney's wife, who accuses the serving maid of stealing three silver spoons when she knew all along the tanner had taken them. The wife commits the maid to jail, then installs herself in the maid's bed, where she enjoys a brief but fruitful communication with her own husband who thinks she is the maid. When his wife is delivered of twin boys, he rants and raves about her supposed infidelity. Finally the solicitor emigrates to North Carolina with Anne and the serving maid to become a successful planter.

Someone who knew Anne as a young woman in Carolina testified at the hearing that she had such a "fierce and couragious Temper . . . That she had kill'd an English Servant-Maid once in her Passion with a case-knife . . . but upon further Enquiry, I [Defoe] found this story to be groundless: It is certain she was so robust, that once, when a young Fellow would have lain with her, against her Will, she beat him so, that he lay ill of it a considerable Time."[39] Against her father's wishes Anne married the snivelling opportunist James Bonny. Disappointed when Anne's father disowned her, Bonny took her to New Providence where she first fell in love and then ran off to sea with the charming and dashing Jack Rackam.

Anne's reprieve was due to the fact that she was carrying Jack's child. Still angered by his cowardly behaviour on the night of their capture, she is reported to have said to him before his execution " 'that she was sorry to see him there, but if he had fought like a Man, he need not have been hang'd like a dog.' " Perhaps she regretted her harsh statement and sent him off to his death with a kinder word which no one overheard.[40]

Mary Read was born in England and disguised by her mother as her dead half-brother in order to gain an inheritance from the boy's grandmother. The disguise proved still profitable to the mother when she sent her daughter, at the age of thirteen, "to wait on a French Lady, as a Footboy." Unhappy in the brothel, Mary, still in the guise of a lad, ran off to sea aboard a man-o-war which carried English troops to Flanders. A taste of the brutality of naval and military discipline of the time encouraged her to desert her ship and enlist as a cadet in a regiment of foot in France. Her brave actions got her a transfer to a regiment of horse where "she behaved so well in Several Engagements, that she earned the esteem of all her officers," especially one, a Fleming with whom she had fallen in love. Mary did not know how to speak her love, but Defoe tells us that "love is ingenious," and since they were constantly together, and often shared the same tent, Mary found a "Way of letting him discover her Sex, without appearing that it was done with Design." Her comrade was overjoyed at the prospect of having a mistress: Mary, however, was determined not to grant any sexual favours until they were wed.

Miraculously, they both survived the bloodiest battle of the 1709 campaign at Malplaquet and returned to winter quarters at Breda. The wedding of the "two troopers" drew an army of curiosity seekers and Mary probably would have preferred storming some bastion to walking down the aisle. She and her husband kept a tavern at the "Sign of the Three Horse-shoes, near the Castle of Breda, North Brabant, Netherlands." Her husband died after only a few years, and once again Mary Read put on men's clothing and shipped herself aboard a Dutch vessel, bound for the West Indies and high adventure. Her ship was taken by "English Pyrates" and since Mary Read was the only English person on board, "they kept her amongst them. . . ." Whether this was Vane's or Rackam's vessel is not known.

While in Rackam's service, she fell in love with a carpenter whom Rackam had forced to serve aboard his pirate vessel. Once again, "she suffered the Discovery to be made, by carelessly shewing her Breasts, which were very white." Keeping her sex a secret, they made private vows of marriage and she remained constant, loyal and courageous in her love.

Her husband, who was no fighter, had foolishly argued with one of the pirates and when their vessel came to anchor at one of the Bahama Islands they proposed "to go ashore and fight according to the custom of the Pyrates." Since Mary "fear'd more for his Life than she did for her own," she devised a way to save his life and his pride. Mary quarreled with the same pirate but challenged him to a duel two hours before he was to meet her lover. Ashore "she fought him at Sword and Pistol, and killed him on the Spot." (See plate 16.)

At the hearing in Jamaica Mary refused to reveal the name of her lover lest he be tried for piracy with the rest. In answer to the court's questioning, Mary was required to declare that "she had never committed Adultery or Fornication with any Man. . . ."[41] It is history's loss that her interrogators were so bemused by her gender that they never thought to ask any questions of real value. No one asked Mary Read before she died of a fever in the Spanish Town jail how she had endured the march of over one hundred miles to Breda in 1708 during the bitterest winter in European history to date, or how she stayed alive climbing ramparts and jumping into enemy trenches onto bayonets poised to receive her, or what it felt like to charge her horse at full speed into the thick of clashing swords.

Both Anne and Mary suffered from the greatest of all piratical misconceptions. Since the time of Defoe, male historians of piracy have felt the need to belittle these strong women by dwelling on the active nature of their sexuality. So instead of

courageous or even despicable pirates, they have been labeled "great whores," despite clear evidence to the contrary. Each of the women was monogamous by nature and during most of their adventures, each of the women chose not to disclose her sex to anyone but her chosen lover.

One of the greatest whoremongers of the period was the notorious Captain Edward Teach, alias Blackbeard, who was born in Bristol, sailed in privateers out of Jamaica and often "distinguished himself for his uncommon Boldness and personal Courage." Late in 1716, Hornigold gave Teach the command of a sloop he had seized as a prize, launching the career of one of the most colourful pirates of the age—that is, if we can believe Defoe's report of him.

Blackbeard had fourteen "wives" and shared them with his crew from time to time. His appearance was designed to frighten the most courageous pioneers along the Carolina coast. The most singular feature of his visage was a full black beard, an adornment unusual for this period when men seldom wore facial hair of any kind, let alone a growth such as the one described by Defoe.

> ... Captain Teach, assumed the Cognomen of Black-beard, from that large Quantity of Hair, which, like a frightful Meteor, covered his whole Face, and frightened America more than any Comet that has appeared there a long Time.
>
> This Beard was black, which he suffered to grow of an extravagant Length; as to Breadth, it came up to his Eyes; he was accustomed to twist it with Rib-

bons, in small Tails, after the Manner of our Ramilies [sic] Wiggs, and turn them about his Ears: In Time of Action, he wore a Sling over his Shoulders, with three Brace of Pistols, hanging in Holsters like Bandaliers; and stuck lighted Gunner's Matches under his Hat, which appearing on each Side of his Face, his Eyes naturally looking fierce and wild, made him altogether such a Figure, that Imagination cannot form an Idea of a Fury, from Hell, to look more frightful.

If he had the Look of a Fury, his Humours and Passions were suitable to it. . . . (See plate 17.)[42]

Blackbeard guzzled barrel after barrel of rum mixed with gunpowder and would shoot one of his crew every now and then just so "they would not forget who he was."

He also devised little tests of their courage and his own. " 'Come,' says he, 'let us make a Hell of our own, and try how long we can bear it;' accordingly he, with two or three others, went down into the Hold, and closing up all the Hatches, filled several Pots full of Brimstone, and other combustible Matter, and set it on Fire, and so continued till they were almost suffocated. When some of the Men cry'd out for Air; he opened the Hatches, not a little pleased that he held out the longest."

His aim was to make his men believe "he was the Devil incarnate," and he succeeded. The night before he died "one of his Men asked him, in Case any Thing should happen to him in the Engagement with the Sloops, whether his Wife knew where he had buried his Money? He answered, that no Body but himself, and the Devil, knew where it was, and the longest Liver should take all."[43]

Blackbeard was killed by Lieutenant Maynard at Ocrocoke Inlet, North Carolina, 22 November 1718. After a bloody battle during which Maynard had inflicted no less than twenty-five wounds on the pirate's body, Maynard sailed into Bath Town with Blackbeard's head dangling from his bowsprit.[44]

Looking back on these events from the space of over 250 years, one might tend to view these criminals in the light of fantasy but must realize however, that " 'Romance is Crime in the Past Tense.' "[45] Unlike Defoe, the modern novelist and historian might characterize these figures in a more realistic light by following Shakespeare's directive to "hold a mirror up to nature."

Woodes Rogers came to the Bahamas in July, 1718, as its first Royal Governour. The prime directive of his commission was to clean up both Nassau, a crowded, lawless town, and the island of New Providence, a full blown pirate colony, by flushing the evil criminals out of their lurking holes in the tiny cays and inlets of the Bahama Islands. Some of the inhabitants with whom he had to deal had committed acts of sadistic torture, were guilty of every kind of perverse debauchery and foul murder, and used language which would bring colour to the cheeks of the Marquis de Sade.

PLATE 17 (opposite page): Daniel Defoe, in his *General History of the Pyrates*, relates the adventures of the fearsome Edward Teach, better known as Blackbeard. (Engraving by B. Cole, courtesy of the Bahamas Historical Society, photograph by Stanley Toogood.)

6

Old Rusty Guts

Between 1708 and 1711 Woodes Rogers commanded the frigates *Duke* and *Duchess* on a privateering expedition to the South Seas under letters of marque commissioned by Queen Anne's husband, Prince George of Denmark, the Lord High Admiral of England. A Bristol man bred to the sea, Rogers was fearless, bold, possessed of both great physical toughness and a keen sense of humour. Piloted by William Dampier, voyager and noted author, Rogers captured twenty vessels, sacked the city of Guayaquil, and seized the ultimate of Spanish prizes—the Manila Galleon.

Once a year the Manila Galleon, laden with gold and silver valued in the millions by today's standards, crossed the Pacific to Acapulco by a secret route. Built of Philippine teak and ironwood, the hull of the galleon was so strong and resilient that it swallowed up small cannon balls and bounced back the larger ones. Rogers had accomplished the impossible, but at great cost. In the raging sea battles of this expedition Rogers had gained fame and some wealth but had had parts of his upper jaw and left foot shot away. He lost many men, and to his "unspeakable sorrow" had seen his younger brother killed before his eyes.

On the return voyage he rescued Alexander Selkirk from Juan Fernandez Island off the coast of Chile. It was Selkirk's account of his being shipwrecked that fired the imagination of Daniel Defoe and resulted in the book *Robinson Crusoe.* Although Rogers could have retired in comfort, this ambitious man submitted a proposal to the Commissioners of Trade for "colonizing the Bahamas and stamping out piracy."[1]

After much badgering from Mr. Graves and the governours of Carolina and Virginia, the Proprietors had chosen another governour for the Bahamas; however, Roger Mostyn apparently lacked the intestinal fortitude to venture into pirate territory, for there is no record of his arrival. In order to protect larger interests in the Carolinas by ridding the Bahamas of pirates, their lordships reluctantly surrendered the civil and military rule of the islands to the Crown.

The intrepid Woodes Rogers was indeed the man for the job. The Board of Trade accepted his proposal, and the king appointed him the first royal governour of the Bahamas, bestowing on him the dubious privilege of exterminating the vermin and fumigating their haunt, the pirate stronghold at Nassau. Rogers and his partners managed to raise enough funds to provide an independent company of infantry of one hundred men and finance a group of industrious German Protestant settlers from the Palatinate.[2] It was these settlers who introduced the pineapple to the Bahamas.

The king's proclamation for the suppression of pirates, dated 5 September 1717, had been sent ahead to New Providence and many pirates would take advantage of the amnesty offered by surrendering before 5 September 1718 although Charles Vane would not be one of them.[3] A few days before Rogers officially appeared at New Providence, Charles Vane had arrived with a French prize, a brigantine of twenty-two guns filled with brandy, claret, sugar and indigo. He was determined to dispose of his plunder with or without the permission of the new royal governour. Vane had sent a letter out to Rogers' vessel stating that if the governour would allow him to keep his present goods, he and his company would accept the king's pardon. Rogers sent no reply. Vane unloaded the French brig and, putting the empty barrels back on the vessel, prepared to give Old Rusty Guts a warm welcome.

One of Rogers' consorts, the man-o-war *Rose*, put in a little too eagerly on the afternoon of July 25th. The governour prudently kept the *Delicia* at sea with the *Milford* and the other vessels in the fleet. Vane fired on the *Rose*, slicing some of its rigging, then setting fire to his French prize, forced the British vessel to cut its cables and run out in the night for fear of being burned. When Rogers neared the island the next morning, he saw the French vessel burning in the harbour and later reported that Vane "with about 90 men [and possibly two women] fled away in a sloop wearing the black flag, and fir'd guns of defiance when they perceiv'd their sloop out sayl'd the two that I sent to chase them." Other than the incident with Vane, Rogers met no opposition. The salute from the slightly disabled *Rose* was probably answered by ragged musketry from the shore when Rogers landed on the 27th of July, 1718. His company took possession of the fort; he read his commission before his officers, soldiers, and about three hundred inhabitants who, under the prudent leadership of Commodore Jennings, surrendered on the spot.[4]

Rogers submitted a lengthy report to the council in October, 1718, and although conditions in New Providence were not perfect, at least the town of Nassau had settled down somewhat. In October Charleston was in a state of turmoil with nightly riots and daily threats to burn the town. Recent Indian wars had exhausted the fighting strength of the military and the harbour was vulnerable. Pirates actively intercepted trade between Charleston and England.[5]

Governour Lawes, who had vowed to hang all pirates in the West Indies, was having troubles of his own in Jamaica. In spite of the king's pardon, the pirates were growing more "numerous and insolent," criminals from England were inciting Blacks to rebellion, and Spanish inhabitants were seeking restitution for losses to English pirates.[6]

In the face of continual raids by pirates and the threat of both French attack and Spanish invasion, Governour Rogers was determined to reintroduce a semblance of government to the islands. He asked the Board of Trade to confirm his Bahamian Council of twelve, along with the following appointments. He had chosen six men from the people he had brought with him: Robert Beauchamp, William Slater, replaced at his death by Christopher Gale (Chief Justice), William Fairfax (Assistant Justice and Judge of the Admiralty with no annual salary), William Walker, Wingate Gale, and George Hooper (Naval Officer). After investigating the characters of the inhabitants who had not been pirates, he chose six men from among them: Nathaniel Taylor, Richard Thompson, Edward Holmes, Thomas Barnard, Thomas Spencer and Samuel Watkins, replaced at his death by Thomas Walker (Assistant Justice).

Rogers admits some difficulty installing William Fairfax as Deputy Customs Collector:

> I did indeed receive an order from the Lords of the Treasury to appoint him [William Fairfax] Deputy to Mr. Graves, Collector, in case of that old man's inability to act, which he has not been able to do otherwise than in his chamber or bed, but is of so petulant a temper that I have been unwilling to interfere, and Mr. Fairfax not pressing to serve under such a peevish gentleman without the manner of his acting and pay, or fees, was settled, for which I have no direction how to divide it, and Mr. Graves having no other support but this employ which he has been several years possess'd of. I am very unwilling to meddle in this affair without its first being settled in England. But beg leave to propose for His Majesty's approbation that Mr. Graves may enjoy his annual sallary of £70, and the fees of Collector will content Mr. Fairfax during Mr. Graves's life. . . .[7]

It seems his many years' residence in Nassau battling Spanish invaders and suffering pirates' abuse had taken a toll on Mr. Graves's disposition; but his many good works in behalf of government warranted some consideration and it is to Governour Rogers' credit that he did not just dismiss the incompetent old man.

Graves had emigrated from Jamaica with Patterson and Bridges in 1686. In 1692 their lordships had appointed him Secretary of the islands and on Edward Randolph's recommendation he had been made Collector of Customs in 1697. He died some time before 1721. In his will, written 28 November 1718, he bequeathed to the church "when settled, my large Bible in Quarto, one large new Damask table cloath and two Damask Napkins." Woodes Rogers was one of the executors, and probate was signed by Thomas Walker—chief justice, and copied by William Fairfax.[8]

William Fairfax took on positions of importance in the colony and when Rogers returned to England in 1721 to recover his health, he appointed Fairfax deputy governour. In 1723 Sir William, a widower, married Sarah Walker. Their son, George William Fairfax, was baptized 20 January 1724.[9] The family later moved to Virginia where George William's sister Anne married Lawrence Washington, the half brother of George Washington. A frequent visitor in the Fairfax home, young George Washington became lifelong friends with George Fairfax.

Lord Thomas Fairfax had inherited some land in Virginia and came to stay with his cousin Sir William at Belvoir for a time. He became George Washington's friend and benefactor and was responsible for launching George's surveying career when he sent him along with his companion George William Fairfax on a surveying party to the remote south branch of the Potomac. Lord Fairfax, a "frank and open Loyalist," died in 1782 before Great Britain acknowledged the independence of the American colonies, but not before he had seen the boy who had surveyed his land in Virginia become the "great instrument to dismember the British Empire."[10]

Rogers reported in October, 1718, that upon their arrival in July last many of the soldiers, passengers, and sailors fell ill and it was a fortnight before Governour Rogers discovered the cause. A number of rawhides stacked on the shore near the town had "putrified the air." It seemed as though "only fresh European blood" drew the infection; his people were "seized so violently," wrote Rogers "that I have had above 100 sick at one time and not a healthfull officer, till now." The old inhabitants did not contract the strange illness and told Rogers that usually people "when they become sickley in most of the other American Plantations find relief when they come here."

The mortality rate among the soldiers was so high Rogers found it necessary in September to write to Governours Hunter of New York and Lawes of Jamaica to beg replacements from their garrisons. While Rogers worked to rebuild an old fort, he experienced the customary island labour problems. "One bastion fronting the sea last week fell down having only a crazy crack'd wall in its foundation. The wages of hired workmen are extravagantly dear, and I have buried most of those I brought with me." He feared he would not be able to hold New Providence in case of enemy attack. The "sickly season" was not the only reason why he could not "put the place" in a "better posture of defence;" another primary cause was the "excessive laziness of the people." Although poor, most of the people were "so addicted to idleness" that they would rather "starve than work." He doubted that among these indolent people he could find enough men he could depend on to fill the seats of the assembly. Although he had not taken a complete census as yet, he had determined that New Providence should have fifteen seats, Eleuthera two, and Harbour Island and Abaco one seat each.[11]

The energetic Woodes Rogers had big plans for promoting industry in the Bahamas. New Providence was overgrown with wood. "We may soon rake salt enough, for the several ponds amongst the Windward Islands, to supply Newfoundland and all North America." He also expected "experienc'd men from Bermudas" to begin a whale fishery.

Rogers probably never filled all the seats in his assembly and was in desperate need of inhabitants to execute his designs. On his way to Nassau, Rogers had stopped at Anguilla, one of the northernmost of the windward group of the West Indies. These "poor but industrious" people, barely surviving on the barren, defenceless island, threatened to become food for the Carib Indians. Rogers sent a vessel to inform them that he was securely installed on New Providence and hoped the vessel would return with some settlers. Rogers felt these people in particular would be an asset to the Bahamas because he had observed "that they live in perfect friendship with each other, and are of modest behaviour," and he hoped their assimilation into Bahamian society would "reform the contrary manners of the men and women now with us, which cannot be suddenly changed." The governour also expected some settlers from the overcrowded Bermudas and Carolina," where I hear they dread a worse Indian warr than the last and don't believe themselves secure under the Proprietors."

The governour had built a small fort of eight guns at the easternmost entrance of the harbour "where we keep watch" and had formed the inhabitants into three companies of militia. Spain threatened "to attempt these Islands;" this intelligence Rogers had on good authority, for Richard Taylor of Philadelphia had been a prisoner on a Spanish vessel when it landed on the southwest part of Cat Island on the 26th of July, the day Rogers dropped anchor in Nassau Harbour. The Spanish violently seized six women and several children, "but not one of the men, of the said Island, they all flying to the bushes for shelter." The raiders carried off all the goods belonging to those inhabitants "even to the meanest of their household utensils." From Taylor's report Rogers also learned that a new governour had arrived at Havana with orders to destroy all the English settlements on the Bahama Islands.[12]

Rogers informed the Council that "the French also cast their eyes on these Islands and I believe whenever they have an opportunity they'l not scruple it for want of title." Rogers had sent a messenger to inform the French general of Hispaniola about the brigantine Vane had left burning in Nassau Harbour. the emissary reported that the general "stamped with his foot and said in a passion that the French king his Master had [a] right to these Islands and that they would settle here very soon. . . ."[13]

Even with the threat of foreign invasion, Rogers could not "prevaile with Captain Whitney to stay longer than the 14th of September." They had expected Vane at Abaco any day. In fact "the very day after Captain Whitney sailed, I had an express sent me that three vessels supposed to be Vaine and his prizes were at Green Turtle Key near Abacoa and since I had no strength to do better, I got a sloop fitted under the command of Captain Hornygold to send and view them and bring me an account. . . ."

Hornigold was a long time returning and Rogers feared he had either been taken by Vane or had taken up with him to go about fresh piracies. At Nassau Rogers kept a "very strick't watch for fear of any surprize." Failing in an attempt to capture Vane, Hornigold returned to Nassau with a seized Bahamian sloop Woolfe and its master, Nicholas Woodall, who had gotten permission from the governour to go out turtling but had been trading with Vane instead. After getting news of Vane's activities from the merchant captain, Rogers slapped Woodall in irons to remain in jail until the next vessel going to England could take him to trial.

Vane now commanded a brigantine and had carried into Green Turtle Bay two ships, both out of Carolina: one of four hundred tons, the Neptune under Captain King, and the Emperour of two hundred tons with a load of "rice, pitch, tarr and skins bound for London." The pirate threatened Governour Rogers by stating he expected to be joined by Major Bonnet "or some other pirates. This Vaine had the impudence to send me word that he designs to burn my guardship and visit me very soon to return the affront I gave him on my arrival in sending two sloops after him instead of answering the letter he sent me."[14] Rogers later enclosed a statement made by Mr. Gale in November, 1718, confirming his fears that Vane could execute his threat. "The pirates yet accounted to be out are near two thousand men and of those Vaine, alias Vaughn, Thaitch [Blackbeard] and others promise themselves to be repossessed of Providence in a short time."[15]

After some time Captain King, late commander of the Neptune, arrived in Nassau and made a sworn protest before Governour Rogers against Captain Vane for the outrages committed against his vessel at Green Turtle Cay. Captain King declared that on the 30th of August, 1718, he had sailed across the South Carolina bar with three other vessels bound for England when a brigantine gave chase. In two hours' time, Vane, with trumpets blaring, black flag flying, and guns blazing, seized the Emperour and the Nep-

tune. Being informed that the other two vessels carried only pitch and tar, Vane decided to let them go but detained the captain of the *Neptune* aboard his brigantine. Vane, his quartermaster Calico Jack Rackam, and his crew, which may have included Anne Bonny and Mary Read disguised as men, robbed and "'rifled as they saw fit.'" After a brief consultation the pirates decided "'to carry the ships *Neptune* and *Emperour* with their crews, to Green Turtle Key, on Abbaco....'"

About four days later John King "'fell sick of a violent Fever'" and Vane permitted him to return to his own ship. Once again the pirates held a meeting. Captain Vane and most of the officers "'were for taking what they wanted'" and allowing the two vessels to go "'about their business.'" The crew, however, looked to the practical side of the issue. Without these ships which could be kept ready to sail, they would be too vulnerable while cleaning their own vessel at Green Turtle Cay. Logic won out and the three vessels arrived at Green Turtle Cay 12 September 1718. There the pirates careened the brigantine for about three weeks, and then bid bon voyage to the captains of their prizes and set sail. When Vane saw a sloop come in the harbour, he dropped anchor again and spoke with Commander Nicholas Woodall. The sloop had brought ammunition and supplies and some of the crew went aboard Vane's vessel. Woodall and the rest of his crew had determined to go back to Providence to accept the king's pardon and would escort the *Neptune* if Captain King wished to go there instead of England.

Angered by the news of conditions at New Providence brought to him by Captain Woodall, Vane and his crew voted the next morning to let the *Emperour* get underweigh but to "'maroon and destroy the *Neptune*, which they did with cutting away the mast, Rigging, Sails, Beams and firing a Gun, double loaded with shot down the Hold....'" Evidently Woodall had suffered a change of heart; Vane ordered his crew to load Woodall's sloop with rice, pitch, tar, deer skins, sails, rigging and other things and the next day "'they all sailed together as Pyrates.'"

When Captain Hornigold and Cockram came into Green Turtle Cay that same day, King apprised them of what had happened. That night Hornigold sailed out after Vane and in three or four days lost Vane but managed to capture the sloop *Woolfe* and Nicholas Woodall.

Vane returned a second time to Green Turtle and plundered the *Neptune* again. Vane threatened Captain King "'that if he offered to touch his Prize he would burn her, and him in her, if ever he catched him again,'" then sailed away a second time.

Three weeks later Hornigold and Cockram returned with five sloops "'sent by the Governour to save what Goods they could out of the *Neptune*.'" King abandoned his vessel and went to New Providence, where in consultation with the governour it was concluded to "'fit out the *Willing Mind* with Guns and Men, enough to stand an Engagement with Vane, and sell the *Neptune*....'" George Hooper purchased the *Neptune* and on 15 November 1718 the *Willing Mind* sailed from New Providence, to arrive at Green Turtle Cay the 19th and take the damaged goods out of the *Neptune*. Finding the *Neptune* to be in better shape than they had thought, they brought both ships to Providence; the *Neptune* got in safely but the *Willing Mind* struck on the bar and sprung a leak.

After the *Willing Mind* had been unloaded, it was discovered that it had not only lost a piece of its main keel on the bar but was iron sick besides. With the *Willing Mind* disabled, Vane and his corsairs safely cruised the Bahamas for some time, touching at Eleuthera where they looted all the provisions they could carry away.[16]

Vane, finally captured in the Bay of Honduras, was taken to Jamaica and tried on 22 March 1721. Among his many other crimes he was charged with seizing the sloop *John and Elizabeth* two leagues from Abaco on 29 March 1718 while it was on route from St. Augustine to New Providence. Near Crooked Island he had also attacked the merchant sloops *Betty, Fortune* and *Richard and John*, and about two leagues from Long Island had stolen away the brig *Endeavour*.

Vane often subjected his prisoners to cruel tortures in order to learn where the ship's money was kept; but although there are many testimonials of this kind in the colonial records nothing of this nature appears in the trial. On Wednesday, 29 March 1721, Charles Vane was executed at Gallows Point, Port Royal, Jamaica. A "worthy gentleman" who witnessed the pirate's execution told Daniel Defoe that Vane "betray'd the Coward when at the Gallows, and died in Agonies equal to his Villainies. . . ." His body "was afterwards hung on a Gibbet in Chains at Gun-Key" very near Plumb Point where the calico-clad remains of his former quartermaster, embalmed in tar and hanging in the same manner, had wasted away.[17]

In November Governour Rogers felt "too weak" to try to execute pirates in Nassau and had to send three criminals to England by the ship *Samuel*. He did however confine ten other pirates aboard the *Delicia* while he decided whether or not to brave an insurrection and try these pirates himself.[18]

Rogers had trusted John Augur, Phineas Bunce, and others to go on a trading voyage to procure breeding stock for New Providence. James Carr, formerly a sailor aboard the man-o-war *Rose* and a favourite of Rogers, had been appointed supercargo for the voyage.[19] On the night of 6 October at Green Cay off southern Andros, Phineas Bunce and Captain Augur distracted Carr and Richard Turnley by drinking beer and engaging in lively conversation while Dennis McKarthy, another conspirator, slipped below and secured the arms. Bunce had admired Mr. Carr's silver-hilted weapon and asked to see it. He then proceeded to march about the deck, flourishing the cutlass over his head and bragging of his former piracies, and once even struck Carr a stinging blow with the flat of the blade. Before the second keg was out, McKarthy signalled Bunce that the mutineers below were armed and ready to attack by singing " 'Did not you promise me, that you would marry me.' " Defoe reported that the following took place:

> Bunce no sooner heard them, but he cry'd out aloud, "By G—d that will I, for I am Parson," and struck Mr. Carr again several Blows with his own Sword; Mr. Carr and Turnley both seized him, and they began to struggle, when Dennis Macarty, with several others, return'd from the Cabin with each a Cutlash in one Hand, and a loaded Pistol in the other, and running up to them said, "What; do the Governor's Dogs offer to resist?" And beating Turnley and Carr with their Cutlashes, threaten'd to shoot them: At the same Time firing their Pistols close to their Cheeks, upon which Turnley and Carr begg'd their Lives.[20]

They took all three vessels, stripped Turnley, Carr, and Captain Greenaway and several others and put them in a boat with oars and very little food and marooned them on Green Cay.

From time to time the pirates returned to the island to torment the marooned sailors, beating any that they could find. Soon the abandoned men took to the bushes whenever anyone came near. The pirate fleet moved on and at a salt pond at Exuma engaged Spanish privateers commanded by a man called Turn Joe. Irish by birth, Turn Joe had once been a privateer on the English side, and now "acted by Virtue of a Commission from a Spanish Governor." Turn Joe put the wounded pirates, including Bunce, aboard one of the English sloops and allowed the forced men to sail the vessel back to New Providence.

Rogers resolved to hang Phineas Bunce the next day, but the prisoner died of his wounds in the night. The governour then "sent for John Sims a Mulatto Man, who had a two mast Boat in the Harbour fit for sailing," laid in provisions, and sent him to rescue the men stranded on Green Cay. Once on the island Sims feared that Carr and the others had perished, for no one answered his calls. Turnley finally recognizd him and scrambled down from a tree top to greet him; it had been seven weeks since the pirates had first set them ashore.

Meanwhile Hornigold gathered up the mutineers who had been put ashore at Exuma by the Spaniards.[21] Thirteen in all had been imprisoned and three had died of their wounds. On the 9th and 10th of December, Governour Rogers, strong now that Hornigold had shown such faithfulness, convened the Admiralty Court "by virtue of his Commission as Vice Admiral of these Islands."

The court consisted of William Fairfax (Judge), Robert Beauchamps, Thomas Walker, Captain Wingate Gale, Nathaniel Taylor, Captain Josias Burgis, and Captain Peter Courant. John Hipps pleaded that he had been a forced man by virtue of Phineas Bunce using "much threatening language against him." Hipps was acquitted but the nine others were condemned and sentenced to hang on Friday, 12 December 1718.

At the "top of the Rampart, fronting the Sea" the governour erected a gallows on which a black flag snapped in the stiff ocean breeze. The prisoners mounted a stage supported on three barrels lashed together and were allowed three quarters of an hour to be spent in singing the psalms. Governour Rogers enclosed a "Brief Account" of the pirates he executed that day and sent it along with the trial proceedings to the Lords Commissioners.

The first, John Augur, a man of forty years, who had accepted the king's grace and the governour's trust and betrayed both, took the small glass of wine offered to him and drank to the "Good Success of the Bahama Islands, and the Governour." William Cunningham, who had been Blackbeard's gunner, "was seemingly penitent and behav'd himselfe as such."

Dennis McKarthy mounted the stage with the agility of a prizefighter, which indeed he had been, and was dressed like one, being "adorn'd at Neck, Wrists, Knees, and Capp with long blew Ribbons. When on the Rampart [he] lookt Cheerfully around him, Saying he knew the time when there was many brave fellows on the Island that would not Suffer him to dye like a dog." He kicked off his shoes "saying he had promised not to dye with his Shoes on and . . . he exhorted the People who were at the foot of the Walls to have Compassion on him," but the audience, outnumbered by the military, dared not make any attempt at rescue.

William Dowling, of about twenty-four years, had spent a "considerable time amongst the Pyrates and of a wicked life, which his Majesty's Act of Grace would not reform. His behaviour was very loose on the stage, and after his death, some of his acquaintance declared he had confessed to them of his having Murder'd his Mother before he left Ireland."

William Lewis, age thirty-four, had been a "hardy Pyrate and a Prizefighter, Scorn'd to shew any Fear to dye, but heartily desired Liquors enough to drink with his fellow sufferers on the Stage, and with the Standers by," to which William Ling, also condemned, replied that "water was more suitable. . . ."

Thomas Morris, about twenty-two, had been an "incorragable Youth and Pyrate" and was "dressed with red Ribbons in the same manner as McKarthy." He openly said "we have a good Governour but a harsh one, and a little before he was turn'd off, said aloud that he might have been a greater plague to these Islands, and now wisht he had been so." Although he said he had never been a pirate before, the sullen George Bendall, age eighteen, had "all the Villainous Inclinations that the most profligate Youth could be infected with."

The crowd expected Rogers to pardon all the pirates, but he reprieved only one, then ordered the provost marshal to haul away the barrels. The stage fell and all eight pirates dangled simultaneously.[22] George Rounsivil, the man reprieved by Rogers, sailed for a time with Captain Burgess who, as a member of the court, probably petitioned the governour for the boy's pardon. George Rounsivil proved worthy of Rogers' compassion. Later, on a privateering expedition commissioned by Governour Rogers, their vessel was driven upon the rocks to the southward of Green Cay and broke into pieces. Rounsivil and five others had abandoned ship in a canoe, but when the boy saw Burgess standing upon the sinking deck of his vessel. Rounsivil begged the others to return and save their captain. When they refused, saying one more would surely sink the canoe, Rounsivil "jump'd into the water, and swam to the Vessel, and there perished with his Friend since he could not save him."[23]

The governour also hoped the hanging of the eight pirates would be an example to the rest of the reformed pirates still in Nassau. Woodes Rogers continued to reprieve pirates long past the extended period of grace because he believed it would be better to receive pirates to help him defend the island against the Spanish than to hang them indiscriminately.[24]

The announcement of imminent war with Spain had been the burr under the saddle of the New Providence inhabitants. Rogers wrote to Secretary Craggs that "the people did for 14 days work vigorously, seldom less than 200 men a day, but nothing but their innate thirst of revenge on the Spaniard could prompt them to such zeal. . . ." Rogers had also generously "supplied the men with provisions and liquors whilst at work;" this gesture also may have contributed to their "zeal."[25]

However, this spurt of energy on the part of the Nassauvians was short lived and in May Rogers once again complained to the council:

I hope your Lordships will pardon my troubling you with but a few instances of the people I have to govern ... these wreches can't be kept to watch at night and when they do they come very seldom sober and rarely awake all night, though ... I punish, fine, or confine them almost every day. Then for work they mortally hate it. ... [They] live poorly and indolently with a seeming content and pray for nothing but wrecks or the pirates, and few of them have an opinion of a regular orderly life under any sort of Government and would rather spend all they have at a punch house then pay me one tenth to save their familys and all those dear to them.[26]

On 7 July 1719 the Spanish treasure galleon *San Pedro* sank off Rock Point at the southwest tip of Abaco but the Spanish had not made an attempt on Fort Nassau.[27] Frequent alarms of Spanish invasion and pirates "robbing all around us" had discouraged "people of substance" from settling in the Bahamas. Nassau had a good fort now with fifty guns mounted and Rogers could muster 250 men in case of enemy attack.

People were still leaving the island and of the four hundred men there were scarcely two hundred left. With his privateers coming and going, Rogers reported there was "no real strength to the place" and with the enemy so close at Cuba they would know when "we are weakest" and "surprize us." Rogers asked the Council to send two hundred men for the garrison and stated that a small cruiser "manned out of the garrison" would "do more service than all the men of war in these parts to prevent piracy."[28]

By February, 1720, Rogers had prepared New Providence for enemy attack as best he could. "All the best men that liv'd at Eleuthera and Harbour Island are here and I have taken guns from the fort at Harbour Island and we resolve to defend ourselves here should Commodore Vernon not see the Spanish in their passage. ..."[29]

The Spanish *Armadillo* sailed through the Florida Straits to attack New Providence from the north. Two large warships, the *Principle* and the *Hercules*, sat too deep in the water to be any threat to Nassau. But on 24 February, Francisco Cornejo, commander of the frigate *S. Josef*, with three small warships and eight sloops, flaunted their Spanish colours near Nassau Harbour. The *Delicia* with its thirty-two guns and the twenty-four gun *Flamborough* under Captain Hildesley sat ready in the harbour, but Cornejo did not hazard a direct attack. The frigate and sloops cruised along Hog Island to the east and the west. Late in the night on the 25th two courageous black sentries hotly repelled a landing party to the eastward, and if the Spanish tried to land at the west, a militia of stalwart ex-pirates eagerly waited to "blow their heads off." The attack degenerated into a very minor assault, but Spanish vessels lurked in waters near the island and worried Rogers for some time.[30]

Soon after this pitiful engagement the war ended. Rogers felt the colony had been abandoned by the mother country, for he had received no official news from home for many months. The small fortune he had fought to win during his privateering days had been spent. Mr. Buck and his partners had expended £90,000 and could give no more and Rogers had no money left to pay the garrison. His health had badly deteriorated through worry and depression and on 6 December 1720 he sailed for Charleston. His six week stay there offered no peace but the cool air enlivened him. Late in January, South Carolinians, through turbulent protest, had effected a change from the Proprietory to Crown government. In February Rogers returned to the Bahamas but only to prepare for passage to England. In April he sailed again to Charleston and from there home to Bristol where he arrived late in the summer of 1721. While the memorials of grateful Bahamians attested to the governour's service to colony and crown, they could not pay his creditors and Woodes Rogers, soon locked in legal battles, found himself forced into bankruptcy.[31]

7

The Return of Rusty Guts

Governour Phenney arrived in Nassau 13 November 1721, along with Mrs. Phenney, who was destined to be the ruination of her husband's government career. What he lacked of his predecessor's charisma, Phenney perhaps made up for in military skill. He set to work repairing the hastily built Fort Nassau and finally constructed a little church.

At the moment of his arrival the governour directed his garrison chaplain to record the births, deaths, and marriages of the inhabitants. The *Fulham Papers* refer to a "List of Persons baptized by Thomas Curphey in 1721 'when 'tis feared he had no ordination.'" The Papers also include a letter from Governour Lawes of Jamaica to the S.P.G., naming Thomas Curphey an impostor. (See appendix A.)[1]

Curphey clung to his position and may have returned to England to finish his studies and receive Holy Orders, for the List indicates marriages performed by magistrates in the "Absense of ye Minister." In 1724 he returned, newly ordained, to carry on his work.[2]

The List, which contained the marriage of William Fairfax, a name which no longer survives in The Bahamas, also marks the beginning of the Curry line whose numerous descendants grace these islands today. John and Kozia Curry of Harbour Island christened their children Rowland (1721), Sarah (1721), Katherine (1724), and Elizabeth (1726); all of these christenings appear in the List.

The List included a number of names familiar to any historian of the Bahamas. A son was born to John "Cochrem," reformed pirate, who with Hornigold had chased Charles Vane and captured Phineas Bunce and his lawless band of mutineers. Edmund Carr, who married Anne Carter, might have been kin to the James Carr who was marooned by Bunce on Green Cay. Robert Rounsenel, buried in 1724, may have been related to the George Rounsevel who sacrificed his life for the man who saved him from the gallows. Sarah Darvil married Thomas Bullard 24 June 1726. Her brother John Darvil of Eleuthera had been among the pirates who took the Spanish launch in 1715. Although the total prize was 11,000 pieces of eight, he bequeathed to his "belov'd Sister Sara Darvill one gold ring, 4 Pewter Spoons and one Pewter Bassin and one Iron Pot forever.'"[3]

Among the few black people included on the List, several of Governour Phenney's Negroes were baptized. John Thomas, along with the other respected inhabitants of Harbour Island, signed a petition on 7 February 1725/26 beseeching the governour for assistance in rebuilding their small fort. The governour knew of the fortification, for in his reply to queries from the Board of Trade in 1723 he mentioned that "There is a small Thing called a Fort at Harbour Island but out of repair. . . ."[4]

Another petitioner and noted inhabitant of Harbour Island, Nathaniel Force, was the father of Joseph, age nineteen, and Anna, age twenty, who were baptized by Thomas Curphey when he visited Harbour Island on the 20th of October, 1724. William Thompson, Justice of the Peace, Richard Thomson, member of the "Council for these Islands," and other Harbour Islanders certified that they had witnessed this baptism. They also testified that the two young people were the children of "Nathaniel and Sarah Force, the Father a Negro and the Mother a Mulatto, both Free People. . . ."[5]

Nathaniel may have been a descendant of William Force, co-conspirator in a plot to cut off and destroy the English in Bermuda. On 2 November 1656 the court condemned nine men and executed the two leaders of the plot. William Force, condemned as an accessory, was taken to the gibbet at Herne Bay and although tortured by the threat of hanging refused to confess his conspiracy. The governour was forced to reprieve him and banished Force to Eleuthera along with all the rest of the free Blacks. A proclamation was issued on 6 November 1656 ordering that all free Negroes, men and women, were to be banished from Bermuda "never to return."[6] Bermuda lost a valuable inhabitant by banishing William Force, but that island's loss was Harbour Island's gain.

According to Governour Phenney, inhabitants increased during his term of office. In 1723 people migrated from Bermuda to the Bahamas on a regular basis to build vessels.[7]

In 1725 the governour entertained the noted artist and naturalist Mark Catesby who, contrary to Woodes Rogers' experience, found the Bahamas "blessed with the most serene air," the wholesomeness of which "induces many of the sickly Inhabitants of Carolina" to retire to the islands "for the Recovery of their Health."[8] Besides New Providence, Catesby visited Andros, Abaco, and Eleuthera. The governour believed Harbour Island "had a better plot of ground than Providence." Although seafaring people, the inhabitants were "inclined to improve the land."[9] Catesby described the three kinds of plantation land in the Bahamas, noting that the soils he observed were not only rocky as they had been reported to be, "but in reality entire Rock, having their Surface in some Places thinly covered with a light Mould," which time had reduced "to that consistence from rotten trees and other Vegetables" and covered "with a perpetual Verdure."

> The black Land is at the Declivity of narrow Valleys and low Places, into which it is washed from the Ascents above them; the Corruption of Vegetable Matter which lye in some Places several Inches deep, of a dark Colour, light, and fine grained; This Soyl is very productive the first two or three years.

The red soil he described as "tolerable productive," and found light-coloured, sandy soil which usually joins the seaside best for Indian corn. "Between piles of loose rocks" inhabitants could plant yams, potatoes, and melons "which fructify beyond imagination."

The following observation would later catch the eye of the defeated but indomitable loyalist planter. "Cotton grows on these Islands without cultivation, in the worst barren Places, it is here perennial, and is said to produce Cotton inferior to none in the world."[10] Loyalists did not heed Catesby's comment that the black soil would be productive for only two or three years; that they would have to learn for themselves.

"Bahamians," observed Catesby, "rove from island to island" and "content themselves with fishing, striking of turtle, hunting Guanas. . . ." Another animal the inhabitants hunted was the Bahama Coney, a kind of wild brown rabbit whose ears, feet, and tail resembled those of a rat but which tasted more like a pig. It was probably a descendant of the prehistoric hutia.[11]

The green turtle, so-called because its fat is greenish in colour, came from Cuba and the continent and feeds on turtle grass. In 1725 Bahamians exported them to Carolina where they were esteemed "for the Delicacy of their flesh." Catesby was curious enough to inquire as to the most common method of taking the hawksbill, loggerhead, trunk, and green turtle. He was told that the fisher must pursue the turtle until it tires and sinks to the bottom where he can strike it with a "small Iron Peg of 2″ long" which fits into a "socket at the end of a staff 12′ long." The striker pierces "the shell through with the iron Peg which slips out of the Socket, but is fastened by a String to the Pole." When struck, the turtle submits and swims to the top of the water where the fisher slips a noose around its neck.

Brasiletto was already scarce in 1725. Catesby reported that the largest trees had already been cut and that the largest remaining were only two to three inches thick and eight or nine feet high. The dyewood, a main source of industry for the Bahamas, was now on the decline. Mark Catesby also observed that Abaco in particular was "much visited for hunting, fishing and the Plenty of excellent Timber, and other useful woods."[12]

It was, however, the problem of the ownership of Abaco that plagued the governour for several years. After government deserted the Bahamas in 1703, the Lords Proprietors had sold the island of Abaco, along with wrecking, salt panning, fishing, and other valuable island patents.[13] In 1724 Governour Phenney wrote that "Mr. Ruchier, formerly Governour of Bermuda, and Mr. Nicholas Trott [Jr.] of these Islands" continued "to solicit their Attorneys here to demand in their names, Abacoa, Hog Island, the Exumas, together with the sole property of braziletto wood and salt;" but it seems that neither gentleman could produce authentic copies of the original assignments from the Lords Proprietors.[14]

At this time Abaco was still coveted for its whale-fishing patents. Samuel Buck, Woodes Rogers' partner, reported to the Council in 1720 that Abaco had fresh water and wood fit for shipbuilding. Also, "Seals come at one Season of the Year in great plenty and some Sperma Caety Whales."[15] At the 16 May 1726 Council meeting, Mr. Spatchers, pursuant to instructions to "find out a proper Place to kill

Whales in order to encourage the Trade and Industry of the Inhabitants" reported that:

> ... among the Northern Keys of Abacoa there is a Place call'd Marsh Sound, within which there is a convenient Harbour about thirty Leagues from hence where the Whales most frequent going into the Shoal Water thereabouts to wean their Young. And of his own Knowledge confirm'd ... the usual time for killing the Whales is from October to Aprill ... great Guana Key is the most proper Place on which to build a Workhouse for the Trying of the Blubber &c.[16]

Two Nantucket whaling sloops experienced an unexpected adventure in Abaco, probably at Marsh Harbour. While riding at anchor, the whalers sighted a vessel off the mouth of the harbour, signalling for assistance. One of the whaling captains took to the boat with a crew and rowed out to the ship. When the captain climbed aboard, an officer put a gun to his head and commanded him to pilot the ship into the harbour. The captain prudently obliged and when the vessel anchored where a point of land "lay between her and the sloops," the whalers were allowed to return to their sloop.

The Nantucket captains conferred and concluded that pirates controlled that vessel and held the former captain prisoner in the cabin. They decided to invite the pirate captain, his officers and passengers to dinner aboard one of the whaling sloops. The invitation was accepted and this somewhat naive pirate arrived with his boatswain "and the man seen in the cabin." As the dinner progressed, the pirate became uneasy and when he proposed to return to his vessel, the whalers seized and bound him.

The man representing the passengers revealed himself to be the rightful captain and told the whalers the story of his misadventure. The vessel had left Bristol, Rhode Island, bound for the coast of Africa on a slaving voyage. Mutiny had occurred shortly after the slaves had been safely landed in the West Indies and a return cargo of sugar had been taken aboard. The mutineers had told their captain that they intended "to become pirates, a business at that time quite thrifty and promising."

The whalers told the rebellious boatswain if he would return to his vessel with the pirate captain in irons and help to recapture the ship, they would do all they could to clear him in the eyes of the law. They also told him a man-o-war was within two hours' sail and they intended to find it and get assistance, then signal him.

Once they had determined that the boatswain had no intention of doing what he promised, one of the sloops weighed anchor and stood toward the pirate vessel. When the sloop looked as though it would pass on one side, the mutineers shifted all their guns to blast it when it sailed by. The whalers, alive to their scheme, suddenly changed course to sweep by the other side and had sailed out of range by the time the pirates had had time to reshift their cannon.

The sloop sailed out of sight of the pirate vessel and after an appropriate length of time returned and signalled that the man-o-war had been secured although, in fact, it had not. The sloop steered boldly toward the vessel. Thinking that an armed force was aboard the sloop, the pirates made for the shore in their boats. The whalers soon apprehended them and brought the ship and the criminals into Nassau where they received a bounty of $2,500. The novice pirate captain was hanged.[17]

Since New England whalers frequented Abaco, Trott and Ruchier pushed to secure their rights. However, the contention remained unresolved, at least for Nicholas Trott who in 1728 petitioned the Council, claiming for his late father Hog Island and half of Exuma as well as a number of lots in Nassau. Mr. Ruchier either won his claim to the island of Abaco and possibly the other half of Exuma or gave it up.[18]

Preserving royal patents, although a major concern of the governour's, was not his biggest problem. By 1728 an avalanche of complaints against the outrageous behaviour of Mr. and Mrs. Phenney fell on the London Commission. A Mrs. Vere appeared before the Board of Trade in August to state the nature of her grievances against the governour's wife. She testified that Mrs. Phenney had private control of all the shop-keeping on New Providence and had even lured away one of her indentured servants "before his time was up." Furthermore, the outraged Mrs. Vere accused Mr. Phenney of bullying juries and threatening magistrates. She also alleged that the governour had used unlawful restraint to keep her in the Bahamas during a time when settlers from Bermuda fled home "because of Mrs. Phenney's ill usage."[19]

Little did Governour Rogers know when he petitioned for an Anglican chaplain in 1718 that William Thomas Curphey would be instrumental in his being reinstated as governour of the Bahamas ten years later. The priest supported Mrs. Vere's accusations that Mrs. Phenney held a monopoly on trade in Nassau and that she charged inflated prices and discouraged all others from trading there. Along with others called in to confirm Mrs. Vere's statements, the chaplain argued the need for a more "orderly civil government and for a Bahamian House of Assembly." Curphey believed that the governour himself was of good character but that Phenney ought not to have permitted such excesses in his wife's behaviour. After hearing both sides of the matter, the Commissioners voted to dismiss Captain Phenney and re-appoint Captain Woodes Rogers governour of the Bahamas, this time with a respectable annual salary. (See plate 18.)[20]

In 1728 the Bahamas adopted Rogers' motto for the colony: *Expulsis Piratis Restituta Commercia*. The governour had personally expelled most of the pirates from Nassau at least, and during his second term of office more trading vessels were built and launched in an effort to restore trade. Rogers had built a snow, the *Providence*, and manned it to protect traders and salt rakers.[21] Rogers disembarked in Nassau 25 August 1729, only a month after a devastating hurricane had swept the island. Phenney had attended to the outer defences of the fort but the buildings badly needed repair inside. When fired to salute Rogers' re-entry to government, the cannon virtually tumbled off their rotted blocks.

Besides ridding the island of the Phenneys and remounting some fifty cannon, the Assembly which met 29 September 1729 became a source of growing tension on the island. In November, the Assembly passed two acts, one to encourage the plant-

PLATE 18: Hogarth painted the Rogers' family portrait before the governour sailed to the Bahamas for his second term. In this detail Rogers sits next to Fort Nassau under a shield bearing his personal motto *Dun Spiro Spero:* "While I breathe, I hope." The globe beside him represents his circumnavigation, and the vessel resting at anchor in the harbour is probably the faithful *Delicia.* His son William Whetstone Rogers stands holding a chart of the Island of New Providence. (Courtesy of The National Maritime Museum, London.)

ing of cotton and the other to encourage foreigners and strangers to settle in the Bahamas.[22]

By February, Rogers was exhausted and longed for a sea voyage. He once again embarked for Charleston to recover his health. There he enlisted the services of the Reverend Mr. Guy, missionary at St. Andrew's in Carolina, to replace Thomas Curphey who had left the island several years before.

Mr. Guy arrived 12 April 1731, a month before the governour returned, and took up his ministry at the quaint little Nassau church.[23] Bryan Little describes the garrison chapel:

> It was of the simplest architecture, with a nave and porch, a small chancel ending in an apse, and a pleasant little cupola capped by a gilded vane; the plain interior must, one feels, have greatly benefited from the rich crimson of the new cushions and hangings brought over by Rogers.[24]

In the two months Mr. Guy spent among the inhabited islands of the Bahamas (New Providence, Harbour Island, and Eleuthera) he baptised 128 people, most of them children; performed marriages; visited the sick, and administered the Blessed Sacrament twice "but had but 10 communicants each time." After Mr. Guy's departure, the President, Council and principal inhabitants sent a Memorial to the S.P.G., stating that they had built with their own private funds "'a commodious church capable of containing upwards of 300 people'" and had provided a "convenient house for a clergyman of the Church of England" with £40 per annum for his support. The Reverend William Smith was appointed missionary to New Providence and the other inhabited islands of the Bahamas; he arrived in Nassau 20 October 1733.[25]

Woodes Rogers returned to Nassau in May, 1731, and ordered the first census to be taken for the Bahama Islands. Rogers enclosed this census, dated 15 September 1731, in his 14 October correspondence to the Lord Commissioners of Trade and Plantations, along with an account and description of the Bahamas.[26]

Of the 1,388 inhabitants, New Providence had the largest population: 633 Whites and 409 Blacks. Eleuthera had 142 Whites and 35 blacks; and Harbour Island, 160 Whites and 9 Blacks. According to Rogers' account, "Abacoa was uninhabited." (See appendix B.)[27]

Most of the Palatines, who had kept the village of Nassau in provisions, had gone off to other colonies. The disappointed settlers from St. Kitts felt Rogers had unwittingly led them to believe that Bahamian soil was fit for the large scale cultivation of sugar. It was not, and most of them sailed away.[28]

Woodes Rogers continued to hold onto his hopes for a better Bahamas until his last breath. On the 15th of July, 1732, the spirit of this inveterate sailor embarked on its final voyage.

8

"Out of the Frying Pan"

Governour Richard Fitzwilliam arrived in Nassau in June, 1734, but was recalled to London early in 1738 to answer charges laid before the Privy Council by a few outraged Bahamians. His Mrs. Phenny-like behaviour had angered assemblymen and merchants, driven judges and jurymen into states of nervous prostration, and set inhabitants quaking in their shoes. He is reputed to have tacked to the church door a notice ordering a census and threatening with imprisonment and whipping those who failed to send in returns.[1] His high-handed arrogance won him little support.

Reverend William Smith's " 'thin congregation' " fattened when Fitzwilliam obliged the soldiers to attend church regularly. This edict probably did not endear the governour to the hearts of the garrison troops, who were already embittered because they had received no supplemental pay for duty in the American colonies as had their fellows in Jamaica. In 1736 the company mutinied.

Oldmixon recounts the "battle" which occurred a little after eight on the evening of 27 March 1736. In order to "facilitate their Dissertion" several soldiers knocked down a corporal, seized the fort gate, surprised the guards at their posts, and took possession of the garrison. One of the sentinels escaped over the fort wall and raced to inform the governour, who was "drinking a Glass of Wine with two or three Gentlemen" at the time. The governour "snatched up a Sword," ordered his personal guard to follow him, and "ran down to the Fort," no doubt brandishing his weapon over his head and trusting that his awesome presence would be sufficient to stop the mutiny.

Nearing the gate, the governour called ahead to one of his sergeants to secure the gate. A half dozen muskets answered him; the governour returned their fire. A shot from the next volley from the wall struck a servant's arm "and many Places through his Clothes, and the Centinel close at his left Hand received a mortal Wound whereof he soon died. . . ."

When "the first battle" was over, the mutineers had "secured all the Arms and Ammunition in the Fort" and begun to fire "the great Guns at two or three Vessels in the Harbour" in order to force them "down near the Fort" so that they could seize one. They also blasted the governour's house.

When Fitzwilliam's efforts to collect enough inhabitants to storm the walls failed, he resorted to his wits. He sent a detachment of inhabitants under the command of his surgeon, Mr. Stewart, to guard the magazine, located about a mile east-ward of the town. Here, out of sight of the fort, a Mr. Charles had anchored his schooner. The governour loaded powder and shot aboard the schooner, placed thirty-five inhabitants under the command of Captain Walker and Mr. Sam Law-ford and commanded them to be ready to set sail at a moment's notice.

By this time the "Mutineers had seized a small Sloop in the Harbour" and "a Party of them had broke open the common Jail and taken out a French Seaman (committed a Week before for endeavouring to carry off some Soldiers) to be their Pilot. . . ." Their attempt to kidnap the governour to insure their safe passage away from the island failed. The mutineers were further repulsed at the magazine, which they intended to blow up. Breaking open a provision store instead, they equipped themselves and their sloop, nailed up some guns which were directed at the harbour's mouth, and set sail about three o'clock in the morning.

Unseen by the mutineers, Captain Walker kept their sloop in sight all night. The surprise at seeing his schooner at daybreak "bred such confusion" among the de-serters "that they were soon taken without any Damage or Loss on either side."

The next day every man of them was convicted and sentenced to death, but only twelve of the most notorious, together with the French pilot, were forthwith exe-cuted, the latter at the masthead of his own vessel. The "poor Wretches declared upon their Death, that they intended to spill no more Blood than might happen in their own Defence, and that their View in attempting to take the Governour, was only to secure him and thereby their own Escape. . . ." They maintained that their only "design" was to get away from the Independent Company at Nassau "where the Pay is scarce sufficient to support human Nature."[3]

Southey reported that Governour Fitzwilliam was praised for his "moderation upon this occasion," however, Paul Albury observed that it was a "sad reflection that Fitzwilliam found it necessary to hang more people during a tranquil period than Woodes Rogers did while performing the monumental tasks of suppressing piracy and repelling invasion."[4] Fitzwilliam's successor, John Tinker, seemed to be struck from the same mold. Peter Bruce, a military engineer at Nassau in 1741, reported that on several occasions the governour had remarked that he would never meddle in any private quarrel, for if one was killed he would simply hang the other.[5]

Tinker governed for twenty years through prosperous times for the Bahamas, occasioned by two wars and the start of a third. Southey commented that in 1736 the Bahama Islands had begun "to look like an English settlement, and the face of af-fairs in this part of the world was entirely changed." He mentioned that the town of Nassau had been rebuilt, that Eleuthera now possessed a small fort and had raised a company of militia, and that Harbour Island boasted a larger fort and their planta-tions had grown "more considerable."[6]

War with Spain broke out again in 1739, presumably over Jenkins' ear; but the real cause was the larger question of trade in the West Indies. Late in December of 1738 Parliament enacted a duty on all sugar and sugar products (including rum) made on non-British plantations and imported to British Islands. This duty was in-tended to encourage subjects to trade exclusively among the English colonies.

Spain maintained that " 'the English have been wrong in supposing that the subjects of his Britannic Majesty have a right to sail to and trade in the West Indies; [they] only have permission to sail to their own islands and plantations. . . .' " His Catholic Majesty made it clear that vessels seen going or coming from Spanish coasts were subject to confiscation.[7]

The Spanish *guardas costas* frequently confiscated brasiletto wood on the false yet stubborn insistence that it grew only on their islands. By 1725 Bahamians had cut down nearly all the dyewood on New Providence and cruised other islands in search of it. In 1738 a Mr. Wimble attended the Board of Trade, petitioning for compensation for the loss of his brigantine the *Rebecca*. He stated that he had been forced into government service by the late Woodes Rogers and had lost his vessel while cutting wood at Abaco.[8]

According to John Crowley, geographer to His Majesty in 1739, the *guardas costas* lay in wait at two locations in the Bahamas to intercept English vessels from New Providence bound for England. Lurking about Hole in the Wall, Spanish ships could pounce on vessels using the Northeast Providence Channel between Abaco and Eleuthera to ride out to the open sea. Memory Rock off West End, Grand Bahama, the other Spanish trap at the mouth of the Gulf of Florida, offered the English mariner little better than Hobson's choice. Usually ships kept near the Bahama coast to avoid the winds and currents that set on the Florida shore. By so doing a vessel could escape the hazards of the Gulf Stream but just as it entered the "high road homeward," it was sure to meet a Spanish ship and find itself indeed "out of the frying pan, into the fire."[9]

Trade then provided the real motivation for war and Mr. Jenkins' ear, an excuse. Notwithstanding, the commissary's list in May 1728 showed fifty-two British vessels "attacked, taken, or plundered by the Spaniards" and "in each case the master and crew were used with great barbarity."

A *guarda costa* boarded Captain Jenkins' vessel and when the Spanish did not find any contraband, they tore off one of the captain's ears and bid him "carry it to his King and tell him they would serve him in the same manner should an opportunity offer." One of the members of the House of Commons asked Jenkins "what he thought when he found himself in the hands of such barbarians." The captain presented his ear to the Parliament and answered. " 'I recommended my soul to God, and my cause to my country!' "

There are always two sides to every war. Southey reported that Jenkins had attacked some Spaniards while they were fishing one of their own wrecked galleons off the coast of Florida, had driven them off and had seized the salvaged money. Spain had demanded satisfaction and got it.[10]

During the war, Nassau served as a base for privateers, much to the consternation of a certain Reverend Mr. Smith. Under Fitzwilliam's government, he had "failed to obtain an allowance from the assembly for a school-master" in spite of the fact that there was " 'no place in his Majesty's American Dominions where one was more necessary.' " In 1735 the S.P.G. provided funds for a school in Nassau but the opening was delayed "owing to the difficulty of finding teachers." Finally Mr. Smith installed one Mr. Michel in his classroom. In December, 1739, however, Captain Hall of Rhode Island arrived "with a Spanish prize of between £3,000 and 4,000"—sufficient to induce Mr. Michel to quit his school and go privateering with the captain.[11]

Privateering continued as the War of the Austrian Succession overlapped the War of Jenkins' Ear. Peter Henry Bruce, sent out from England to fortify the islands against Spanish attack, arrived with Governour Tinker 21 April 1741 and stayed until 5 January 1745.[12] His *Memoirs* provide an invaluable account of contemporary life in the Bahamas as well as an obviously biased character sketch of Governour Tinker and his cronies.

His first confrontation with Governour Tinker occurred in passage when Tinker discouraged the captain from boarding a Dutch vessel. Everyone on board, except the governour, agreed that if they were to examine the ship, it would prove a lawful prize Bruce's estimation of the governour's judgement sank to a new low when he learned of the safe arrival of the Dutch vessel at the Spanish port of Cadiz with £130,000 sterling aboard.

The call of "Breakers!" interrupted a rare cheerful moment of the soggy voyage. Captain Townsend raced to the deck, "ordered helm a lee," some sail shifted, and "when the ship was about, one might easily have thrown a stone from the stern upon the rocks of Abbaco;" very luckily it was a fine moonlit night. In the morning when they crossed the bar at Providence, there was a sudden storm whose thunder caused "such a terrible noise" that the passengers could not hear the cannon salute from the fort even though it was directly opposite. Some people considered this ominous: perhaps Bruce should have.[13] At first the engineer enjoyed his new island home and delighted in the large grove of orange trees which formed part of the garden attached to his house. He watched with wonder as lime seeds "flung carelessly into the ground" matured into full bearing small trees within two or three years. A myriad of other fruits and vegetables enjoyed "quick growth" as well, and flowering shrubs and plants "are so aromatic, that they perfume the air to a great distance."

Sometimes the flamingo appeared in flocks of two or three hundred. Other wild fowl were plentiful, as were green parrots and hummingbirds. Bruce names a variety of good eating fish and his account is the first to name the Bahamian shellfish, the "conque [conch]." His journal does not exclude other less lovely creatures which infested the island, such as the "plague of numerous vermin or insects"—namely cockroaches, mosquitoes, and sand-flies—which tormented inhabitants night and day. Bruce comments on the wild cinnamon and the sweet-scented bark of the Winteriana which the Bahamians exported to the Dutch islands.

Providence, Harbour Island, and Eleuthera constituted the only inhabited islands at this time and settlers consisted of "English, Scotch, Irish, Bermudians, mulattos, free negroes, and slaves." Of the total of 2,303 persons, most resided in Nassau, only 240 in Harbour Island and Eleuthera combined.[14]

The engineer found Fort Nassau in a "ruinous" condition:

... the barracks, which were built of wood, were ready to tumble down, and there was no other building within the fort; the powder magazine was a house which stood at some distance from it, exposed in such a manner that any body might set fire to it. I found no more than sixteen guns mounted upon very bad carriages; the rest were all scattered up and down, and some buried within high water mark in the sand, some of which were spiked up, others rammed full of stones and sand; the carriage trucks and shot were also dispersed, so that with much difficulty I collected them together: the inhabitants made use of great part of them for ballast in their vessels. Having got them all collected in one place, I drilled those that had been nailed up, cleaned the whole from rust, and proved them by firing. I had now fifty-four guns of six, nine, twelve, and eighteen-pounders, fit for service, and mounted them on the new carriages which came out of the store-ship from England.[15]

Since the entrance at the east end of the harbour was scarcely a gunshot in breadth, Bruce decided to build the new fort at this strategic and favourite landing place of the Spanish. On the 10th of June the governour laid the foundation stone and named the fort, Montagu, and the sea battery, Blasden's Battery.

Bruce marvelled at the native building materials, especially the stone which when first raised from quarry could be cut easily, but when exposed to the air for only a short time turned "hard as flint." The mastic wood used for the palisades proved as "hard and heavy as iron." By the end of July 1742 Bruce had completed the fort and battery. The sea protected two sides of the fort and the mastic palisades the other two. The fort held a "terrassed cistern, containing thirty tons of rain water," a barracks, a guard room, and a bomb-proof magazine.[16]

With the back door to the island secured, Bruce could now turn his skills to the repair of Fort Nassau. Governour Tinker, pleased with Bruce's work, wrote Lord Montagu to tell him so. However, one night when a tavern dispute between Bruce and Lieutenant Stuart "began to grow warm," the "governour absented himself" when he should have taken Bruce's side.

The next morning Bruce looked out his window and saw Stuart, "armed with sword and pistols," riding back and forth in front of his house. Upon inquiry, Stuart replied that Bruce must have forgotten the challenge he had offered him the night before. Surprised, the engineer retorted that he remembered no such challenge but would dress and meet him now "wherever he pleased." Stuart hastily replied that if Bruce did not remember issuing the challenge it was too late now. Wishing Mr. Bruce good morning, he went home.

A few hours later, Bruce was walking along the bay and when he got "opposite the governor's windows," Stuart came up to him and knocked him down. When he recovered, Bruce struck the lieutenant with the edge of a stick he had been carrying, laying open the man's cheek "from his ear to his mouth." Judge Rowland and several other inhabitants who had witnessed Stuart's "treacherous insult" separated the men. The governour confined both men to their houses for a fortnight. He never questioned Bruce about the circumstances of the altercation, but he visited his friend Stuart every day.

The two weeks' confinement put a stop to work on the fort and the inhabitants clamoured for Bruce's release. The governour sent for him and told him that Stuart had admitted his wrongdoing and had agreed to apologize in public. Bruce, who was equally outraged at the governour's own behaviour, reminded Mr. Tinker that he had been practically "assassinated in his own sight" and had expected redress, not confinement. Bruce told the governour that he no longer felt safe in Nassau and proposed to leave the island. Since Tinker had "certain intelligence of the determination of the Spaniards to invade the island," he could not allow Bruce to go off but ordered him back to work on the fortifications at once. The governour gave his word of honour that once Fort Nassau was put in a "Posture of defence," he would allow Bruce and Stuart to duel somewhere off the island if Bruce promised not to molest Stuart until then. Bruce agreed "and proceeded with the works again with the utmost diligence; but never without my sword and pistols, thereby to prevent my being attacked again in such a villaninous manner."[17]

The engineer was destined to lock horns with another inhabitant. Garrison surgeon Dr. Irving had decided to build a new house and "thinking everything he did was lawful, went to the fort and ordered several of the labourers to go to his house and dig a cellar." When the overseer tried to prevent the doctor from taking his tools and men away from the fort, he was "miserably beaten." The poor man found Mr. Bruce who sent him "all covered over with blood" to Judge Rowland to enter a complaint. He had no sooner arrived when Irving came up behind and beat the overseer again, this time "before the judge's face." As soon as he heard what had happened, Bruce went directly to the governour, who answered "with his usual cant that he would not concern himself with private quarrels." However, he sent for Dr. Irving who in the governour's presence ranted and raved, threatening "death and destruction to any one" who presumed to enter a complaint against him. This so "nettled the governor, that he sent him prisoner to the fort; telling him, at the same time, that it was not for the complaint laid against him, but for the want of that respect due to his person. . . ."

Upon an application from Scott and Stuart, the other two members of the triumvirate, the governour released Dr. Irving that same day. That evening while Mr. Bruce was sitting in the company of the parson, the collector of customs and others, his servant came to him and told him that "Dr. Irving and one Cuthbert were swearing death and revenge against me and my overseer; and that they were waiting for me with loaded pistols before their door, which was next to mine." This alarmed the other gentlemen but Bruce, well knowing "all bullies to be cowards," decided to call the doctor's bluff. Rejecting all other company except that of his overseer, Bruce "proceeded home with cocked pistols and "coming to Irving's door," found the doctor skulking behind it. The next day Bruce informed the governour of what had happened, only to have Mr. Tinker give his usual response.

The sudden death of the newly arrived garrison chaplain Mr. Hodges on 5 July 1743 "gave rise to a variety of speculation" among the inhabitants; and Bruce again began to "entertain serious thoughts of quitting the island." A letter from a friend compounded his fears. His friend had discussed Bruce's intention to leave the island with the governour who had remarked that he would allow no one to depart the island. Tinker reminded Bruce's friend that "he was king in this government and if he gave orders to kill any man whatsoever, his officers were to obey him. . . ."[18]

Matters went from bad to worse. The Assembly voted to discontinue the governour's salary so Tinker dissolved the Assembly. The governour naturally suspected that Bruce, a member of the Assembly, had had something to do with his losing his salary, but Bruce had remained neutral in the vote and had withdrawn from the Assembly. Meanwhile island intrigue thickened.

In a conference the governour upbraided a Mr. Moone for associating with "persons disaffected to his government." Mr. Cox, Captain Petty, and Mr. Bruce were specifically named. The governour further stated that he "hoped it would be in his power to hang up two or three of them very soon." Under oath, before the Council, Governour Tinker also threatened to "hang up some of the inhabitants;" and an opportunity "soon offered itself for his excellency's gratification." A soldier was condemned and executed for stabbing his sergeant. While cutting brasiletto in the woods, a black man shot and wounded an overseer who had mistreated him and his fellow worker. The governour hanged the man and his innocent companion "to bear him company." At this point an extremely nervous Captain Bruce stepped up his work on Fort Nassau and towards the end of December, 1744, both the fort and sea battery that he had had to rebuild "almost from the foundation" were completed.[19]

While Bruce prepared for his departure to Carolina, Captain Jelf of the sloop of war *Swallow* arrived at Nassau in a boat with his officers. He had embarked from Charleston to return the two brass mortars and the quantity of bombshells which the Bahamas had lent to General Oglethorpe for his expedition against the Spanish at St. Augustine, when the *Swallow* "was cast away upon the rocks of Abaco." Imagine his surprise when Bruce locked eyes on the very same pilot who had almost wrecked him on those very same rocks. Captain Jelf had intended to carry Bruce to Charleston on his return voyage but "was very glad to take his passage" with Captain Bruce in the sloop he had hired for the trip.

When Bruce learned that Lieutenant Stuart intended to go Abaco "to bring what could be saved from the wreck of the *Swallow*, I sent my overseer with an open letter to him, demanding his attendance at Abaco, to give me satisfaction for the treacherous insult I had received from him. . . ." However, the governour refused to grant Stuart the permission to duel at Abaco. Bruce reminded the governour of his solemn promise but Tinker, "well knowing himself as much to blame as the other," gave him an absolute refusal. Bruce knew Stuart had to journey to Charleston in order to settle a law suit and finally Stuart agreed to confront him there.

On the 5th of January Bruce departed Nassau on the sloop *Pelham*, newly built of mahogany by Florentine Cox, and arrived at Abaco "where the wreck lay" the next day. It took several days to collect Captain Jelf's crew "who were dispersed all over the island." The passage to Charleston was attended by fine weather and the *Pelham*, crowded with 120 men, was attended by "a number of sharks."

Captain Cox, a native of Bermudas, who are esteemed the most dexterous fishers in the world, caught upwards of a score of them in a day: his method was by hanging out a rope, with a noose at the end of it, through which he hung a piece of beef; when the shark approached the beef, it was pulled forward through the noose, so that the shark in pursuit of it was slung by the tail, which is large and broad, and in that manner was pulled on board. . . . As the young are good eating, we brought them on deck, and cut them up for the people, who were thereby plentifully supplied with fresh provisions, which was a fortunate circumstance, as we had not provisions for such a number; but it is a common saying that a Bermudian will never die for want at sea if he is provided with fishing tackle.

Under the threat of mutiny by some of the Irish sailors aboard, Cox was forced to attempt the bar of Charleston at night and struck bottom. In the morning a twenty gun vessel met them and secured the mutineers in iron. The *Pelham* arrived safely on the 22nd of January. Bruce waited in Charleston five or six months but Stuart never arrived there. Stuart probably considered it better to lose his suit than to lose his life.

The mortars, shells, guns, anchors, sails and rigging which had been recovered from the wrecked *Swallow* had been carried to Providence. While in Charleston Bruce had been "credibly informed" by letter that the wrecked munitions from the *Swallow* had been sold to the Spaniards.[20] Thus, in irony, Peter Henry Bruce's *Bahamian Interlude* ends.

With the commencement of the Great War of the British Empire in 1758, Bahamians prospered not only from legitimate privateering but also from illegal trade, the former against, and the latter with, their old enemy the French. Philadelphians and traders from other northern American ports carried on illicit traffic with the French through the Spanish port of Monte Christi on the northern coast of Hispaniola. Bahamians pocketed their ill-gotten gains as vessels passed through their islands on the way to Hispaniola.[21] New Providence, frequently ripe for clandestine profiteering, was particularly vulnerable during the period between the death of Governour Tinker in 1758 and the arrival of William Shirley, former governour of Massachusetts, in 1760.

The war, generally known on the Continent as the Seven Years War, started as a worldwide contention between England and France. The struggle for territories in North America was labeled the French and Indian War. Spain did not officially enter the battle until 1761 when it allied itself with France.

French geographers of the period never failed to attack Great Britain for its unlawful claim to the Bahamas. Jacques-Nicholas Bellin in his *Déscription Géographique* maintained in 1758 that even if there were settlements of Spaniards and French in the Bahamas, "it is certain only the Spaniards frequented" those islands. "Therefore it is not right that the British pretend they are theirs."[22] Since Bellin referred to the French settlement at *Lucayoneque* (Abaco) in 1565, he went to some trouble to describe the island. Bigger than Eleuthera, it had a strange elongated shape "forming coves and meanders where little ships can anchor" once they passed through the reefs. The island stretches from south to north about twenty leagues then "makes an elbow" and spreads itself west ten leagues. "The southern point is noticeable by the rock escarpments in which one perceives an opening which seems to be the entrance of a cave. The English maps mark it and name it Hole in the Rocks, *Trou dans les roches.* It serves as a point to recognize this entrance as the best way to go to Providence."[23]

Even though war ended in 1763 in favour of Great Britain, the French attempted to take possession of the Turks Islands in 1764. These salt islands, named after a kind of cactus which grows there and resembles a fez, had received French threats ten years earlier. The French continued to reject British claims to the Bahamas. Buzen de la Martiniere, French geographer to Philippe V of Spain, published in 1768 all six volumes of his *Le Grand Dictionnaire Géographique* in which he flatly stated that the *Lucayes* situated in the "northern part of the Antilles are almost all deserted." Thomas Shirley, who succeeded his brother as governour of the Bahamas in 1767, submitted a report in December of 1768 that the population of New Providence alone numbered 2,350 people; Harbour Island held approximately 350, Eleuthera 400, and about 30 people had lately gone to settle Cat Island.[24] It seems that the French geographer had dipped back into early Spanish history and his statements regarding the settlement of the Bahamas reflect that he had stayed right there. "Herrera says that the Spanish live in some of them. Linschot says they are all uninhabited. Baudrand assures that today they belong to the natives of the country. The English pretend that they belong to them."[25]

The Treaty of Peace concluded at Paris in 1763 put an end to war and established Great Britain as the strongest colonial empire. Not only did England maintain control of the strategic Bahamas, but it won new territories in North America. Spain ceded East Florida to Britain, but after a bitter civil war in America twenty years later Great Britain would be forced to exchange East Florida for the Bahamas.

9

The American War of Independence

The Peace of Paris in 1763 threw the Bahamas into yet another economic slump. In March, 1765, Great Britain devised the Stamp Tax to defray the cost of the French war and provide funds for defence in the American colonies. Whitehall, secure in the belief that the colonists would see the good sense in the legislation, was surprised by the violent protests which followed. Americans simply were not having any taxes, or tea either, for that matter.

Shortly after Townsend introduced the duty on British imports and almost six years before the actual dumping of 342 cases of East Indian Tea into Boston Harbour, Richard Moss arrived in the Bahamas to take up his ministry at Harbour Island. His ensuing personal dilemma in no way compared with the enormity of the current political upheaval although both reached crisis proportions at about the same time.

In 1761 the notable Governour William Shirley issued a report to the S.P.G. which prompted the society to send an additional missionary to serve at Harbour Island. Shirley pointed out that a minister stationed in Nassau had difficulty reaching the seventy families on Eleuthera because they were "dispers'd in settlements along the coast." Although the sixty families in Harbour Island lived "all upon one Spot," the priest could visit only twice a year:

> ... Disuse of publick worship the remainder of the Year [is such] that the good Effect of his Administration there cannot be lasting enough to imprint much sense of Religion upon their minds, so that these two Islands may well be reckon'd among the dark corners of the Earth without little hope of ever being much enlighten'd whilst they continue in their present state, and this must be the case, so long as there shall be but one Minister resident within the Bahama Islands.[1]

Moved by the genuine need and perhaps by the eloquence of Governour Shirley's rhetoric, the Society, in 1767, sent out the Reverend Richard Moss to enlighten "the dark corner of the earth" called Harbour Island. There he held divine service "'under the tamarind trees'" until the church of St. John's opened 16 March 1769.[2]

In April Richard Moss had sufficient knowledge of his congregation to report to the Society that the Harbour Islanders blessed his ministry; of the 438 inhabitants "I cannot say that six persons on the Islands are guilty of swearing, and only two . . .

break the Sabbath." Of the 586 Eleutherans, however, the Reverend could give only this "lamentable account:"

> ... the Eleutherans both men and women and children to a man, Magistrates not excepted, are profane in their conversation. The first rudiment they teach their children is to curse their mother and father, and by the time they can speak plain they are very perfect in that art.

Other than profanity, Mr. Moss did not specify the nature of the "many other sinful habits and heathenish practices" that were "in use among them."

His greatest obstacle to reforming these people was the great difficulty of visiting them, for the minister had to travel to Nassau and sometimes wait as long as three weeks for passage back to Eleuthera. The settlements on the island began in the north at Governour's Bay (the probable landing place of the First Adventurers), continued southward along the lee side of the island and included The Bluff, The Current, Governour's Harbour, Palmetto Point, Savannah Sound, The Bullard, Tarpum Bay, and Rax [Rock] Sound.[3]

Once the people of Harbour Island learned that they were not required to contribute to the financial support of their minister, they became fond of Mr. Moss and he of them. In 1772 Moss wrote "The work goes well at Harbour Island. One of the communicants there becomes very useful, reads prayers on Sunday in my absence; his name is Richard Curry."[4] The next year Mr. Moss wrote the Society asking whether it would be good to encourage Mr. Curry in the ministry. The minister recommended Curry by describing him as:

> ... a serious, sensible man ... exemplary in his life and conversation, of good report among the Brethren, reads much for his own instruction, knows English tolerable well, but has almost gone thro' all my books.

In the same letter Mr. Moss felt it necessary to explain why he had baptized so many children since January, 1773. The situation reflected the hard times experienced by the islanders between wars. Many people had fled their homes in New Providence, Bermuda and other islands from sheer want and had come to the uninhabited islands of the Bahamas "to seek their bread." When fourteen "coloured children" were brought to Mr. Moss from Cat Island, he "baptized them without any hesitation."[5]

In March, 1775, Moss informed the Society that "times are so bad with us, on account of this Rebellion in America" that he could write home only once a year "by the Providence vessels;" Carolina was closed off entirely. Any vessel which arrived there must remain. In that same letter Mr. Moss assured the Society that he would observe the "kind caution" they had recommended in the matter of Mr. Curry's reading prayers and sermons in his absence.[6] This slight disagreement in church policy did not disturb the Society as much as the news that the Reverend Mr. Moss had one wife in Ireland and another in Bristol, England. As the first shots rang out at Lexington and Concord, Mr. Moss had some serious explaining to do.

In a statement sworn under oath the 30th of June, 1780, Richard Moss informed the Society of his marital dilemma. Told in his own words, "The True and Circumstantial Narrative" takes on all the improbabilities of a Smollett novel.

Although he was thirty at the time, Moss stated that his "youthful indiscretions" had thrust him into an undesirable marriage with a Mary Robinson, who had threatened to expose his character. After the ceremony Richard had discovered Mary's "strategem to draw me into a mire" and left her, "never intending further to compleat, or solemnize the nuptials, or burden myself with her." It seems the nuptials had already been sufficiently solemnized and Mary had been left with the burden so, on the supposition that he might be the father, Mr. Moss "made some provision for the infant." Shortly thereafter Mary Moss wed a Westchester man and had another child by him. When he died, she married a Mr. Burk in Dublin, "by whom she had a son who has long since married and settled in Liverpool as a shoemaker." Mr. Moss stated that under these circumstances he considered himself divorced not only in religion but in law, and under the advice of some clergy he felt he "was at liberty to alter" his condition. In 1752 he married Hannah Johnson, who blessed him with six children. After thirteen years of "conjugal Felicity," she followed three of their children who had already gone to their reward.

His search for the right woman to care for his family definitely turned up the wrong one when he married the widow Sarah Bachelor of Bristol "on Christmas day 176-." For a time they "lived together in conjugal happiness;" but when the minister learned of his appointment to Harbour Island, he foolishly delegated the lady to act as his sole attorney, and she deserted his children and mismanaged his affairs. The situation became even worse when Sarah Moss found out about her husband's Irish wife from that woman's son, the cobbler, who had recently come to Bristol. Sarah Moss "denied her marriage by atrociously setting up false witness" against Mr. Moss. Her actions were "so wicked and artful" that she managed to get back her widow's pension of £20 which she had forfeited upon her re-marriage and demanded that Moss send her the whole of his salary in the name of Bachelor. Worse yet, continued Mr. Moss, "she has in my decline of Life accomplished her diabolical Intentions by prevailing on the venerable Society to listen to and credibly believe her patch'd up story." In a final plea, the Reverend Mr. Moss beseeched the Society to grant him a hearing.[7]

Moss's sworn statement was sent to the Society with petitions from New Providence and Harbour Island attesting to his good character. The Providence petition was signed by leading citizens and members of the Council and House of Assembly. The Harbour Island document states that for the past thirteen years Mr. Moss had exhibited "an upright manner of living" and had been an excellent example to his parishioners. It was signed by the principal inhabitants including many by the surnames of Sanders (Saunders), Russel (Russell), Roberts, Sawyer, Albury, Sweeting, Pindar, and Thomson (Thompson). Richard Curry signed as did other Currys.[8] As he had promised to do in his "Narrative," Richard Moss served the Society in Harbour Island until his death on 23 October 1784 at which time he was upwards of seventy years of age.[9]

During the Revolutionary War, Moss served his king as zealously as he did his church. The clergyman managed to get a letter off to England by the ship *Charlotte* late in April, 1777. In it, Moss told the Society how the American War of Independence had made some Harbour Islanders rich and others, including himself, miserable. "We are so unhappy here as to have our Harbour made into a place of Trade for the Americans; their ships and other vessels are always... trafficking with the gentlemen of these islands for salt." On Sunday, some American captains heard Mr. Moss pray for the king and that night took him out of his house, put him aboard a privateering vessel and threatened to take him to America. Moss concluded his letter with a desperate assertion: "God knows how long anyone will be safe who does not join with America."[10]

The American threat must have been not only terrifying but also disappointing to the Bahamians. After all, they had expected that sort of rough treatment from Cuba but not from their friends in North America. Pioneers to both American and Bahamian settlements had emigrated about the same time, for somewhat the same reasons, and up to this time had fought common enemies and enjoyed uninterrupted trade. American colonists shipped provisions to destitute Eleutherans and provided refuge to Bahamians fleeing the ravages of war. Stout island timber supporting buildings at Harvard College was tangible evidence of Eleutherans' gratitude.

Inhabitants from New Providence, Eleuthera, and Harbour Island constituted the native Bahamians who, after 1783, were referred to as Old Inhabitants or derisively called "conchs" by some loyalist refugees. Their survival instinct remained unmatched in Bahamian history. The Loyalists would soon come and soon go, but these hardy adventurers would remain. Their tenacity is most evident in the Out Islands and especially Abaco, which was abandoned by perhaps ninety-five per cent or more of the loyalist emigrants and later resettled by enterprising Harbour Islanders.

Native Bahamians were stubbornly fixed on a way of life which centered on the sea, and only starvation would force them to plant the land to any appreciable degree. The American Congress authorized privateering on the 19th of March, 1776. A Nassau clergyman, the Reverend Mr. Hunt, wrote in May that Bahamians were alarmed by armed American vessels cruising among the islands waiting to intercept "their little trade." To Bahamians that "little trade" with the American colonies meant survival. Bahamians carried turtle and fruit to the continent chiefly in order to buy provisions. The closing of American ports put a stop to trade, and islanders had to turn "to cultivating the lands more than usual."[11]

The Revolution had reduced Bahamian inhabitants to "little above a starving condition." Perhaps this is best demonstrated by the fact that the "'best bread' that could be obtained in Harbour Island 'even for the blessed Sacrament' was 'made of Tree Roots.'"

During the war, Americans needed quantities of salt to preserve food for their troops on the march. They naturally came to the Bahamas for salt as they always had and the Harbour Islanders readily obliged them. Trade meant provisions for starving islanders. It is difficult to sustain patriotism when hungry. Furthermore, historically, Bahamians never mixed loyalty, or anything else for that matter, with business.

American vessels pestered the islands and their crews, who passed their life "'in dancing all night and gaming and drinking all day,'" attempted to corrupt the people, turning them from King George and all government. A Bahamian knows, however, when to display sovereign fealty; and the night the Americans tried to carry away the Reverend Mr. Moss, it was probably the loyal inhabitants of Harbour Island who thwarted their efforts.[12]

At daybreak 3 March 1776, the American war touched Bahamian shores. In the first major operation of the Continental Navy, Commodore Esek Hopkins led a raid on Nassau. (See plate 19.)[13] What constituted a first in American history was old hat in Bahamian history: Nassau had been invaded before and was just as ill-prepared this time as it had been before. When one lives on a remote island where governmental petitions for fortifications and troops are seldom even answered, let

PLATE 19

In the first major operation of the American Continental Navy, Commodore Esek Hopkins led a raid on Nassau, taking the fort as well as capturing the governour as hostage. (From James Thatcher's *Military Journal*, Boston, 1827.)

alone acted upon, it is necessary to keep one's sense of humour above all else. Perhaps this is why the following contemporary account of the American Invasion of 1776 exhibits "a touch of comic opera."[14] Knowledge of things military exposes the writer as a member, perhaps even an officer, of the Independent Company.

Hopkins put to sea 17 February 1776 and ordered his fleet of eight vessels to rendezvous at Abaco from whence the commodore planned to fall on Fort Nassau. Governour Montfort Browne had been apprised by letter of their arrival as early as August, 1775, when General Gage warned him that American ships "were fitting out to attack New Providence and seize the military stores there." In replying to the general's advice, Browne reminded Gage that he, not the general, was commander-in-chief of the Bahamas. Seven days before the actual attack Captain Andrew Shaw brought Governour Browne the news that a naval squadron was making ready at Cape Delaware to sail to the Bahamas. Two days before the invasion Captain George Dorsett arrived from Abaco expressly to report that the American fleet approached those islands. When the American fleet reached Hole in the Wall they seized two New Providence vessels and native sailors "were impressed as pilots."[15]

The pilot at Nassau Harbour was entitled to be surprised when he sighted seven sail of ships that Sunday, the 3rd of March, but the news certainly should not have caught the governour with his pants down. However, when Mr. Farr knocked on the governour's door, Browne

> ... came to the window in his [night] shirt. The Pilot told him that the American fleet had appeared off [the coastline]. The Governor then asked him what was to be done? The Pilot answered he did not know, without his Excellency would get a fast sailing vessel and send away the Powder that was in the Magazine. The Governor replied, "Farr, I thank you for the hint; You are in the Right; go down to Major Sterling and tell him not to suffer Chambers to sail till I have seen him, and I will be down the Hill directly."

The governour summoned his council and "ordered 4 guns to be fired, tho' he was expressly told that the firing of 2 was the proper signal for an alarm." Mr. Gambier, "so lame with Gout he could not walk," did not arrive at the fort until seven A.M. As the ailing man dismounted, the governour addressed him:

> "Mr. Gambier, the Fleet is off, what is to be done?" Mr. Gambier answered that before he could advise what was to be done, he should beg to be inform'd what had been done. The governour replied, "Nothing; had we not better send away the Powder?" Mr. Gambier said in his opinion that ought to be the last thing parted with. . . .

They did resolve to send Mr. Chambers out to reconnoiter the enemy, but it was blowing fresh and there was a great swell so he could not beat up to the enemy and therefore returned. A detachment was sent to secure Fort Montagu, a militia roll was called, and arms and ammunition were inventoried. Two of the four guns at Fort Nassau broke their carriages upon firing the warning; the account of the fort's condition was sufficiently disturbing to have set Peter Henry Bruce reeling in his grave.

Before nine o'clock the governour left the fort, "saying that he would just go home and make himself a little decent." About ten o'clock an enemy sloop headed for the East End; Browne ordered a detachment of thirty men up to Fort Montagu where the officers discovered that "there was not a Barrel of Powder or a length of Match Stuff in that Fort." All the military stores were back at Fort Nassau.[16] The enemy "landed in whaleboats" and "there being no body to oppose them, between 300 and 400 men possessed themselves of the House at New Guinea."[17]

Soon after this, Lieutenant Burke . . . had been sent from Fort Montagu with a strong party to oppose the Enemy's landing and Captain Walker . . . had been ordered to support him with a body of Volunteers. . . . The Governor, without consulting the Council or calling a Council of War, Ordered the Guns at Fort Montagu, excepting two, to be spiked up, and leaving only two Men in the Fort, with orders to fire those two Guns as the Enemy might approach, and then to spike them up and quit the Fort, suddenly retreated towards Fort Nassau, being joined in his retreat by the detachments under Captain Walker and Lieutenant Burke. To make the more haste, seeing a horse saddled he mounted and rode off to the Government House where he remained near two hours.

Instead of retreating to Fort Nassau, many of the inhabitants retired to their homes "to provide for the security of what is so dear to Every man." Reverend Mr. Hunt, however, seemed to have had his house in order, for he "went on with the duty of the church in the usual manner. . . ."[18]

The governour returned to the fort and about four P.M. Lieutenant Burke, who had been "dispatched by the Governor to the Rebels," returned with the news that the rebel commander had come for "the Powder in the King's Forts." He and about 250 to 300 armed men had taken Fort Montagu and were preparing to attack the town and Fort Nassau.

Around eight o'clock the governour called together the Council, officers, and principal inhabitants to advise him on "what would be most proper to be done." Since the condition of the fort offered no defence, they advised him to evacuate the fort and "send away the Powder." About midnight the powder was loaded aboard Chambers' vessel and at two A.M. he sailed with it to St. Augustine.

The account went on to say that during all this time the governour was again absent. The Council took it upon themselves to order Major Sterling to command the militia and march against the enemy. Just then the governour showed up complaining that "a Violent fit of Cholick [colic]" had detained him. Leaving Messrs. Gambier and Atwood, "who were both lame," in charge of Fort Nassau, he placed himself at the head of the militia and "march'd to Fort Montagu." Nearing the fort, the governour "halted and drew out of his pocket some Nails" and handed them to Mr. Thomas Hodgson to give to his blacksmith. When that gentleman asked the governour what the nails were for, Browne answered that "they were for Spiking up the Guns of Fort Montagu." "God," replied Mr. Hodgson "if that is to be the case I don't know what business we had here." They stood there in the road wondering what they were doing there.

The rebels spent the night at Fort Montagu and the next morning handily took possession of Fort Nassau. The Americans distributed leaflets through the town promising the inhabitants security of their persons and property. Browne disregarded a warning by the council to avoid being captured, and when the rebels took government house they found Browne there.

At the time of his arrest Browne claimed that he was seized, collared and dragged like a "felon to the gallows in the presence of a dear wife and an aged aunt, both near relations of the Earl of Dartmouth, who were treated with such abuse and such language as could not be heard at Billingsgate."[19]

Commodore Hopkins lingered in Nassau for at least a fortnight to load military stores before carrying the governour and his other hostages to America. Browne complained that rebel officers drank all his wine and liquors and helped themselves to whatever else they wanted.[20] Later Browne accused and subsequently tried to remove from office some government officials who had "elegantly entertained" Hopkins and his officers. Many Bahamians sympathized with the rebel cause and Browne stated that some inhabitants, including one officer of the militia, had actively served with the rebels. The governour further charged that some Bostonians living in the colony were "'licentious, poor, haughty and insolent'" and "'neither life, liberty or property was safe among them.'" British troops evacuated Boston in March of 1776, making these Bostonians the earliest loyalist refugees of the Revolutionary War.

Although in the contemporary account of Hopkins' Raid, Browne's character is suspect, he had previously reported the "pathetic condition" of the island's defences and had urged the Crown to purchase the Bahamas, a petition which had been consistently rejected since the early 1700s. If colonists could own their land, Browne felt the habitual crimes of wrecking, smuggling, and perjury might subside.[21] Later, American loyalist refugees could not be granted land in the Bahamas until the Crown had purchased the islands from the Lords Proprietors in 1787.[22]

On the voyage back to America, Hopkins' fleet failed to capture the *Glasgow*, His Majesty's vessel of twenty guns. Whatever praise the American Commodore might expect for the bloodless capture of Fort Nassau was dimmed by the embarrassment and censure at the escape of the *Glasgow*.[23] Also Hopkins' primary objective to seize the king's powder had been foiled, however accidentally and humourously that affair had proceeded. Perhaps if the islanders had not been so intimidated by the American force and had offered some resistance, Fort Nassau might not have fallen into enemy hands. If one British warship could battle and outmanuever an entire fleet superior in size, number of men and of guns, the Bahamians under proper leadership and with a modicum of organization could have put on a brave show. An account of the naval expedition in the *Boston Gazette* indicates that the American troops might also have been disabled by illness. When Hopkins sailed from Philadelphia on the 17th of February, 1776, the crews of four ships in his fleet "were infected with Small Pox."[24]

In America Browne indignantly commented that he was exchanged for "'that rebel who calls himself Lord Sterling.'" After his release he managed to get his military career in hand and raised troops to fight in the Siege of Rhode Island.[25] In August, 1777, the governour was apparently in no hurry to return to the Bahamas, for he spent time at his plantation at White Cliffs in West Florida. With the naturalist William Bartram, Browne explored a region called White Plains which stretched along the Mississippi River. Fertile sections of the plains held rich, black soil "surrounded and intersected with Cane brakes and high forests of stately trees."[26]

Montfort Browne had retired to this place after his stint as lieutenant governour of West Florida (1767-1769) and had returned there while governour of the Bahamas in November, 1775, "to recover his health." He probably suffered from a bout of colic, which, real or imaginary, brought on suddenly by something he ate or by the stress of office, seemed to cause his untimely disappearances. Once while lieutenant governour of West Florida, Browne had publicly had to refute a report that he had been "'suddenly carried off by a most violent Fever at Mobile.'"[27]

Governour Browne returned to Nassau late in 1778 with four companies of invalid troops. The Hopkins Raid had thrown the islands "into a distracted state" and left the people "in a deplorable situation." Mr. Hunt further reported that Americans "threatened and insulted" the colony "almost everyday."[28] The minister wrote again in June, 1777, that Nassau had recently been "attacked by two armed vessels from America" that, in coming to take a British vessel out of the harbour, had threatened to burn the town. Mr. Hunt admitted wryly that it was "disagreeable as well as dangerous to have shot flying among our houses."[29]

Despite the date assigned to it, this brief report by Mr. Hunt may actually refer to Captain Rathburne's two-day invasion of Nassau in January, 1778. The former lieutenant on the Hopkins expedition, now captain aboard the *Providence*, had so lightened his vessel giving chase to a British brigantine and sloop that he had had to put into Abaco to make a scaling ladder, after which delay Rathburne set sail for New Providence. Paul Albury recounts how Rathburne dropped anchor outside Nassau Harbour at midnight, 27 January 1778, stole ashore with twenty-eight men and finding a chink in the fort palisades, took the fort. The next morning townspeople awoke startled "to see the American flag flying from Fort Nassau and its guns pointing menacingly at the town."[30]

Some inhabitants probably welcomed Governour Browne back to Nassau; some of the officials, however, were probably not as enthusiastic to see him. Browne insisted on administering the oath of allegiance to the inhabitants. He accused Lieutenant Governour Gambier and the Council of issuing licenses to Bahamian vessels to carry on open trade with the rebels. In turn the Council accused the governour of cowardice on the day of Hopkins' Raid. While governour and council bandied censures, the French at Cape Francois prepared to attack New Providence. The governour refused to do anything about defence until he received an apology for "'so false, so malignant and so malicious an attack.'" He called for the dissolution of the House of Assembly because they refused to transact any business with him.[31]

Although allegations on both sides were serious, the Board of Trade decided that the charge that the governour abandoned Fort Montagu to the Americans was severe enough to warrant recall. Browne "won partial vindication from the Privy Council in 1781 but was not returned to office." In 1782 Montfort Browne went to America and was not heard from again.[32]

On his arrival in Nassau 21 March 1781, John Maxwell was met with news of an impending Spanish invasion. He immediately sent a letter to General Clinton and Admiral Arbuthnot in New York, imploring their assistance. Clinton could spare only 170 men, twenty-five of whom were unfit for duty. When they eventually arrived 15 April 1782, two full years after Maxwell's request for aid, the number of the Nassau garrison rose to 223 men.[33] Clinton was willing to oblige Maxwell in regard to his request for cannon; however the frantic governour had failed to specify the number he required. The wheels of military preparedness came to a halt once again while letters passed from New York to Charleston to Nassau and back again to Charleston.[34]

At daybreak 6 May 1782 the Spanish Army, consisting of three frigates and sixty sail of transports with 2,500 troops aboard, invaded Nassau. Despite his efforts, Governour Maxwell would be hopelessly outnumbered. Their commander Juan Manuel de Cagigal, governour of Havana, demanded the surrender of the Bahama Islands "upon honourable terms" at nine o'clock.

Maxwell tried to stall in the hope that aid would miraculously appear. At four P.M. the governour dispatched Captain Hunt to inform General Leslie at Charleston of his desperate situation: three British frigates "would relieve me. I am in haste."[35]

At least one of the frigates "under sail before New Providence" was an American vessel. At six P.M. the same day, Cagigal sent a message from aboard his ship, the *South Carolina*, to Governour Maxwell, giving him twelve hours for consultation. Since the strength of the country was off the island, privateering, the thirty-three members of Maxwell's war council agreed to surrender.[36]

The next morning Maxwell surrendered Nassau for the last time to the Spanish. The articles of capitulation proved to be quite civilized compared to past treatment of Nassauvians by the Spaniards. By these articles Governour Maxwell would deliver up all the Bahama Islands together with artillery, powder and forts "to the troops of His Catholic Majesty." The British garrison would be allowed "to march out with all the honours of war, Arms Shouldered, Drums Beating, Colours Flying," and embark for any port in Great Britain or America in possession of His Britannic Majesty, Bermuda, or any of His Majesty's islands in the West Indies except Jamaica." The governour would be permitted to send a flag of truce to New York with the capitulation and would not be considered a prisoner of war after he landed with his troops at a British port.

Inhabitants desiring to leave would have eighteen months to settle their affairs. After that time they would be required to take an oath of allegiance to Spain but would not be forced to take up arms against Great Britain. Furthermore, islanders were allowed "free exercise of their religion."[37] The Reverend Mr. Barker, "the only missionary left in the Bahamas," withdrew, leaving Nassau residents without an Anglican priest and no one with whom they might freely practice their religion. A survey of the inhabitants on the Bahama Islands at the time of capture showed 2,750 at New Providence, 500 at Harbour Island, 450 at Eleuthera, and 250 at Long Island, Exuma, and Cat Island.[38]

In the months to come, a number of Bahamian Loyalists crowded into St. Augustine along with American Loyalists from Savannah. By December, the East Florida town literally burst its limits to accommodate even more American Loyalists evacuated from Charleston.

It is perhaps significant to mention that some American Loyalists resided in Nassau before the Spanish invasion of 1782. A few worked as government officials, some merchants traded among the islands, and perhaps even a few planters, sensing defeat, migrated early to join their relatives in the Bahamas.

James Wright, Baronet, Governour of Georgia, submitted to Whitehall a list of officers in His Majesty's Province of Georgia and their present places of residence in March of 1779. The Commissary George Baillie, Esquire, was registered as "trading between Georgia and the Bahamas to get food and supplies from the Bahamas during the war." One of the resolutions passed by the Bahamas House of Assembly in January, 1780, accused Governour Browne of not prohibiting "'the Exportation of Provisions'" which was the usual practice "'when the island was threatened with famine.'"[39] Perhaps this trade with Georgia precipitated their censure. Although Browne's loyalty to his king was certainly unquestionable, one wonders what benefit the people of the Bahamas derived, if any, from his trade with loyalist Georgia.

In the same document, Wright named two Loyalists who did not hold office in Georgia but had been driven from the Province by the rebels and were now residing at Providence in the Bahamas. John Mullryne and George Barry, who figured prominently in Bahamian politics after the Peace, had lost all their civil rights and were labelled traitors by the Georgia Act of Attainder of 1778.[40]

George Barry's memorial illustrates the all too familiar horror story of the plight of a loyalist refugee. Born in Barbados, George Barry had migrated to Georgia from Jamaica. In August, 1775, Barry signed an oath of allegiance to King George. During the war rebels stole a considerable number of his cattle, confiscated his estate, burned his property, and took him prisoner. They carried him some distance before releasing him; then Barry went by raft to the king's ships and on to St. Augustine. In 1778 he came to the Bahamas and was in Nassau when the Spanish attacked. His name appears on the list of inhabitants who bade farewell to Governour Maxwell on the 10th of May, 1782. Barry retreated to East Florida, but in 1783, at the Peace, he was in England. In February of 1784, it is recorded that his wife and family were in New York. Barry himself returned to Nassau on 5 February 1785, and in October of the following year he succeeded Parr Ross as Receiver General of the Islands. The Honourable George Barry died in Nassau in 1789.[41]

James Babbidge, secretary of the Bahama Islands, who was taken hostage by Hopkins in 1776, had been quartermaster of His Majesty's 15th Regiment of Foot at Pensacola before he had come out to the Bahamas with Montfort Browne. His memorial states that upon his return from West Florida, where he had travelled on business, he was seized in Nassau Harbour on 7 March 1776 by "one Whipple of the Rebel Fleet," robbed "by those pirates," and carried to a prison in Connecticut, possibly the Simsbury copper mine where Americans entombed captive Loyalists forty yards beneath the surface of the earth where no light and very little air ever reached. It was seven months before he was allowed to return home to New Providence. Before the rebels would release him, Babbidge had to sign a statement before Governour Jonathan Trumbell of Connecticut, stating he would not take up arms against America on his parole.[42]

The "Rostrum of Civil Officers," recorded on 8 May 1782, lists as Crown Interpreter a Nicholas Martin Almgreen who may have been a German soldier stationed at West Florida before coming to the Bahamas with Montfort Browne. He married Elizabeth Tucker, eldest daughter of Rush Tucker of Exuma, on 27 June 1780. After the war, Almgreen retired to his Exuma estate, "Mt. Gottenburgh," where he died in 1792.[43]

A shrewd merchant from West Florida, John Miller, submitted claims against the Spanish government, stating that his brigantine *Unicorn* was totally independent and not in any way connected with the capitulation of the Bahamas; yet it had been detained until its captain had been "discharged as a prisoner of war." Miller also claimed the loss of the brigantine *Regulator* and his expenses while he sweltered in Morro Castle prison in July of 1782. His loss of the ship, together with his losses in England and in Charleston while his papers were held up in Cuba and his cargo rotted, amounted to 77,986.6 Spanish minted dollars.[44] Later his rivalry with the Panton, Leslie Company brought him close to Governour Dunmore and perhaps into collusion with William Augustus Bowles in his efforts to destroy Panton, Leslie stores in Florida.

During the Spanish occupation, Don Antonio Claraco acted as governour of the Bahamas. The farewell address delivered to Governour Maxwell from the loyal inhabitants on 10 May 1782 best expressed the Bahamians' feeling at the prospect of living under Spanish domination. After thanking Maxwell for his zealous, unwearied efforts to put the islands in a state of defence, they concluded on a note of hope.

> Sorry We are, for your Excellency and for our Selves, that a vastly Superior Force has rendered our Mutual Endeavours ineffectual, and wrested out of your Hands all the Bahama Islands. . . . We can only Console ourselves with the Hopes of seeing the British Standard again Erected in these Islands; and in that case, Shall be happy to see Colonel Maxwell return to his government.[45]

Nearly one year later their hopes became reality.

10

"The World Turned Upside Down"

Loyalist! Rebel! Tory! Whig! In any dispute, there is always plenty of name-calling and the "Sons of Liberty" battled the "Sons of Despotism" to wring independence from the "tyrant" King George; yet Loyalists wondered about the quality of life in a country governed by the victorious "Sons of Licentiousness." (See plate 20.) However refined it may be to refer to the Tories as those "other Americans," the definition which appeared in a New York journal is more direct and certainly more honest: "A Tory is a thing whose head is in England, and its body in America, and its neck ought to be stretched." On whatever side and by whatever name, American colonists were allied by blood, manners, language, laws, religion, and commerce.[1]

Since loyalty formed a part of the British religious teaching, Anglicanism became the bedrock of Loyalism in America. "Discipline, order and hierarchy in the Church supported discipline, order, and hierachy [sic] in the State." Most Angelican ministers remained ardent Loyalists. After the Declaration of Independence, the various states required inhabitants to abjure the king and swear allegiance to the union. The oath posed a difficult choice for Anglican ministers who, at their ordination, had sworn an oath of personal allegiance to their monarch. "Now they must forswear themselves or abandon the performance of their priestly office." Sometimes a priest's choice carried dire consequences. In 1774, a drunken mob attacked the Reverend Mr. Peters, his family, and some Loyalists called Peterites. They stripped off the clergyman's gown and clothes, hung some of the women up by their heels after tarring and feathering them, and wretchedly abused others, marking them with excrement in the sign of the cross.[2]

Loyalists, who numbered one-half of the approximately two and a half million colonists, loved America as much as the so-called patriots who used them as "scapegoats for every ill that beset the state." Loyalism grew from the seed of conservatism and devotion to Great Britain and to the monarch into an attitude of mind. Its expression in America was a slow process because, "like all true conservatives when confronted by the inevitability of change, these men [and women] wanted to put it off as long as possible." In June, 1775, one Loyalist wrote candidly, "'we at present are all Whigs ... until the arrival of the king's troops.'"[3]

Pessimism and fear dominated Loyalists' actions. Early in the war fear drove some of them to England. The American artists John Singleton Copley of Massachusetts and Benjamin West of Philadelphia, for example, resumed their profession

PLATE 20

The choice of loyalty to King George or allegiance to the union of American colonies posed a difficult choice for many, especially for Anglican ministers who at ordination had sworn to support both their king and their church. (Courtesy of the Marquess of Zetland.)

and increased their fame in Great Britain. For the many lonely and some even starving American Loyalists the cool reception of Londoners told them that England was not their home, America was. By then, a few had become obsessed with the fear of dying and being buried in England.[4] One patriot shared their fear; for in 1774, a South Carolina newspaper reported that one Phillip Billes had died in England, leaving a sizable fortune "to two gentlemen Relations, on [the] Condition of their seeing him buried under the Liberty Tree in the Town of Boston, New England."[5]

After Cornwallis's defeat at Yorktown, the Tory future held only doom and gloom. New York Loyalists beseeched the king "not to withdraw his Royal Protection," for that action "would render the Calamities and Distresses of your Majesty's American Loyal Subjects *absolutely insupportable, absolutely Ineffable*." They reminded King George that the throne was the "pillar of the English Constitution" which "breathes nothing but Liberty, Equality and Impartiality."[6]

Loyalists may have been traitors to the rebel cause, but the Revolutionaries were legally the real traitors. America was a Crown colony and as such, all Americans owed allegiance to King George and to Great Britain. From the patriot's point of view, however, loyalty to the tyrant king constituted treason, and Loyalists would be forced to be free of him, like it or not. As one Loyalist wryly commented, " 'which is better—to be ruled by one tyrant three thousand miles away, or by three thousand tyrants not a mile away?' "[7]

Loyal not only to their king, most Tories "sincerely regarded the British constitution as the best possible form of government." The concepts of equality, liberty, and property the patriots did not apply to Loyalists, only to patriot free holders, an attitude which automatically excluded most women and Blacks, who were already aware that equality was a myth. The Revolutionary Congress refused such basic rights as freedom of speech to Loyalists.[8] Wherein lies equality when patriots could persecute Loyalists for expressing their opinion?

Both sides resented the inequitable and patronizing attitude of Great Britain to "her colonies." Yet, independence did not become an issue until early in 1776 and certainly was not the original object of the Revolutionary War. The ultimate result of the war was separation. In fact, "at no other time in history has a nation ever acquired such a vast, rich, strategic tract of land in so short a period of time."[9] And the cause?

> Will not posterity be amazed, cried a Tory writer, when they are told that the present distraction took its rise from a three-penny duty on tea? Will they not call it a most unaccountable frenzy and more disgraceful to the annals of America than that of witchcraft?[10]

Loyalists "ridiculed the idea of boycotting the whole world in order to get rid of a threepence duty on tea" and said that the remedy was "'ten thousand times worse than the disease. It was like cutting off your arm to remove a sore on your little finger.'" (See plate 21.)[11]

The historian Sabine submits that essentially the conflict grew out of a commercial dispute. England's object was to "break up the contraband trade of the Colonial merchants with Holland and her possessions to give her own East India

PLATE 21: The tax on tea which precipitated "The Boston Tea Party" was only one cause for complaints of injustice by the "Sons of Liberty," although it is certainly the most celebrated. (From John Frost's *Heroes and Battles*, Philadelphia, 1845.)

Company the supply of the Colonial markets." Just how this merchant-crown dispute mushroomed into civil war cannot be so simply stated. Nor can Loyalists and patriots be classified in terms of rich versus poor or merchant versus farmer. The factors are too complex to allow such simplification.[12]

One scholar estimated that sixty percent of the executive Loyalists came from elite family backgrounds compared to a mere thirty-one percent of the Revolutionary executives. One arrogant Loyalist demeaned the Whigs by referring to them as "'flaming patriots without property or anything else but impudence.'" Some Tories were royal officials, landed aristocrats, wealthy merchants, and other professionals; but the military ranks swelled with Loyalists from the "conservative masses, of no trades and all trades, of all grades of wealth, education and social position." Perhaps John Adams had this latter group in mind when he spoke of Revolutionary America as being one-third Whig, one-third Tory, and one-third mongrel. One scholar inferred from the diary of the wife of the prominent Philadelphia Loyalist Joseph Galloway that no great enmity between Whig and Tory existed in the upper circles of Philadelphia life. "The gap between loyalists and patriots seemingly widened, as one descended in the social scale."[13]

Unfortunately not many Loyalists, male or female, were as inclined to put pen to paper as was Grace Galloway. This paucity of written material accounts for the difficulty in determining which of the Americans of the period, were in fact Loyalists. As one historian queried, "Is a leading Loyalist one who left papers?" Lorenzo Sabine comments on his problem in collecting information on the Loyalists:

> ... men like the Loyalists who separate themselves from their friends and kindred, who are driven from their homes, who surrender the hopes and expectations of life, and who become outlaws, wanderers and exiles—such men leave few memorials behind them. Their papers are scattered and lost and their very names pass from human recollection.

His two-volume work contains biographical sketches of many northern Loyalists, most of whom migrated to Canada where climatic conditions enabled their descendants to preserve the materials they did have. Lydia Austin Parrish spent twelve years of her life searching the scant, faded, mildewed, scorched, and bug-ridden Bahamian records for exiled Loyalists and keenly felt the urgency of her work.[14]

Except in the case of a few obnoxious Loyalists, loyalism was inconsistent and often determined more by self interests than by idealistic motives. Loyalists often changed sides conveniently according to whatever military power happened to control their district, whereas others chose to fly rather than to fight. Like James Babbidge, Peter Van Schaack signed a parole promising to "'neither directly or indirectly do or say any thing to the prejudice of the American cause.'" He took the oath of allegiance to the rebel cause in order to be with his wife, but at the same time wholeheartedly believed himself to be a British subject. Later he wrote "'In civil wars, I hold there can be *no neutrality; in mind* I mean. Every man must *wish* one side or the other to prevail. The ruling powers, therefore, have a right to consider every person, who does not join them in the action, as averse to them in opinions. . . .'"

"Scottish merchants at Wilmington, North Carolina," wrote Governour Martin, "are compelled to join in sedition by appearing under arms at the musters . . . although they are still at heart as well affected as ever." Augustus Underwood, a Georgia gentleman who eventually migrated to Abaco, was found guilty of treason by the Amercement Act of 4 May 1782 and was compelled to serve in the Continental Army for two years or to the end of the war, whichever came first, yet he emigrated as a Loyalist after the Peace.[15]

For Blacks, attachment to the loyalist cause meant freedom. What began as a threat became a promise—a promise that would be almost impossible to keep. Royal Governour John, Earl of Dunmore, decided to wage the kind of war that would hit aristocratic Virginia landowners hardest.

> The whole country can easily be made a solitude; and by the living God, if any insult is offered to me, or to those who obey my orders, I will declare freedom to the slaves, and lay the town in ashes.

He made both threats a reality. In November of 1775 he ordered the seaport of Norfolk burned and issued a proclamation offering freedom to "'all indentured Servants [and] Negroes'" willing to bear arms in His Majesty's troops. Slaves and convicts from Virginia and North Carolina rushed to his side. Each recruit in Lord Dunmore's Ethiopian Regiment proudly wore a uniform boldly stamped with the words "Liberty to Slaves." This cry was the black Loyalists' answer to Patrick Henry's personal declaration. "I know not what course others may take; but as for me, give me liberty or give me death." In spite of his personal sentiments, however, Henry called Dunmore's action "fatal to the publick safety."[16] Mr. Henry might have done well to consider that civil war is also fatal to the public safety.

In 1779, another proclamation issued by Sir Henry Clinton, Commander-in-Chief of His Majesty's forces in North America, promised "every Negroe who shall desert the Rebel standard, full security to follow within these lines, any occupation which he shall think proper." Clinton forbade "any Person to sell or claim right over any Negroe [that is] the property of a Rebel who may take refuge with any part of His majesty's Army." Historian Catherine Crary estimated that 100,000 slaves escaped behind British lines during the Revolution.[17]

After the war, Dunmore advocated the abolition of slavery. Both Tory and rebel owners terrorized Blacks by abducting them from New York and East Florida. Many Blacks fled to Indian country and joined the Seminoles. It is estimated that between 10,000 and 35,000 loyal black refugees emigrated to Nova Scotia, England, the Bahamas, and the West Indies.[18] The buffeting received during and after emigration drove many black American Loyalists to leave the disagreeable climate of Nova Scotia and seek a final refuge at Sierra Leone, "the mountainous tropical peninsula on the western coast of Africa." Shipboard disasters and disease reduced their numbers and only 270 of the seven hundred original settlers arrived at Sierra Leone in May, 1787. The unfamiliar discomforts of the rainy season there claimed even more lives. Few survived the return to a place where only years before their mothers and fathers had been captured and, somehow enduring the horrors of the Middle Passage, had come to America – a full turn of the wheel. This nucleus of black American Loyalists built the port of Freetown where their descendants have "made distinctive contributions to African Nationalism."[19]

Women experienced a degree of freedom in that, unlike Blacks, they could choose their occupations. Besides the usual number of dressmakers and milliners, colonial women worked as bakers, cutlers, brewers, joiners, fish-curers, chair-caners, soap-makers, tallow chandlers, rope-makers, blacksmiths, coach-makers, tanners, whalers, and printers. Very few women, however, owned property outright. A register of voters for March, 1775, in Worchester, Massachusetts, lists only three women.[20] In New York, Mrs. Charles Inglis, Mrs. Susannah Robinson, and Mrs. Mary Morris had their property forfeited by a new state Bill of Attainder which passed into law 22 October 1779. In 1783 Mrs. Inglis, wife of the Rector of Trinity Church, risked her life to appear in person at a property sale in Charleston where she presented proofs of personal ownership but could not prevent the sale of her home. Loyalists' property sold that day amounted to £120,000 (pounds sterling).[21] Many of the women were ardent supporters of the crown. Wealthy loyalist women of New York City presented the brig *Fair American* to the British as a New Year's gift in 1779, but by 1783 the celebrated privateer, which had served the British so well during the war, was again offered for sale.[22]

In spite of the fact that women were not expected or encouraged to have political opinions, some served as active Loyalists. The civil war pitted father against son, brother against brother, and husbands and wives also found themselves on opposing sides. Some women, like Grace Galloway, used the political situation to free themselves from already troubled marriages. She remained in Philadelphia when her husband and daughter returned to England. Separation from her daughter distressed her greatly, but still she stayed to fight for her small fortune. Although in a constant state of despair, she continued to hope that Great Britain would emerge victorious from the war. Her optimism was not shared by many; for in August, 1779, she wrote: "everybody has given up ye Cause but women...." The war enabled other women to lead more active and adventurous lives. In Charleston, Louisa Wells continued to operate the *Royal Gazette* while her father Robert Wells was in England. Lorinda Holmes worked as a courier for the British as did Elizabeth Henry whose Whig husband put her out of the house. Elizabeth Gray, caught delivering a letter to General Burgoyne, was tried as a traitor and imprisoned for ten months. Posing as a peddler, Ann Bates, a Philadelphia school teacher, worked successfully as a British spy. The spirited Flora McDonald on her snow-white horse addressed the Scotch-Irish Loyalists of North Carolina in Gaelic, inspiring them to bravery at the ill-fated battle of Moore's Creek Bridge.[23]

Loyalist women were accused of treason, imprisoned, and exiled; Jane McCrea, the daughter of the Reverend James McCrea of New Jersey, was murdered. Although loyalist men and women endured the same abuse and hardships, Mary Beth Norton's research confirms that no woman died or went insane because of the distress of war and banishment.[24] Although relatively few men committed suicide because of the misfortunes wrought by the Revolution, those who did had George

Washington's approval. The general wrote his brother from Boston after the evacuation of that city in March, 1776:

> ... all those who have acted an unfriendly part in this great contest, have shipped themselves off. . . . One or two have done what a great number ought to have done long ago, committed suicide.[25]

In March, 1788, London's *Morning Chronicle* published the following "Case of Great Distress" to solicit donations for the relief of "the now destitute Mrs. Finlayson and her children." Her story was but one example of the devastating emotional stress caused by banishment, the common plight of Loyalists during and after the Revolutionary War:

> Henry Finlayson, a Silversmith in Savannah, Georgia, was a sober and diligent Man and lived creditably with his family when the Troubles began in North-America. Being zealous in Support of the British Government, he, with many others, was banished by the prevailing Party, never to return under Pain of Death; whereupon he took Refuge with his Family in East Florida.
>
> Upon the Reduction of Savannah by His Majesty's Troops, he returned home with his Family; and being again obliged to remove by the Evacuation of Georgia, he carried his Family to Charlestown, which was also abandoned in December, 1782.
>
> In the Course of his Removals, he had bought a Vessel in which he had embarked his Family and their whole Property, once more for East-Florida, where the Vessel was wrecked upon the Bar of St. Augustine and every Thing lost. This unfortunate Family were not many Months in St. Augustine, until the Cession of that Province to Spain drove them to Sea for the fifth Time, in extreme poverty. They got to the Island of Dominica; but by this Time, poor Finlayson, quite overborne with Misfortune, became incapable of working for the Support of his Family, and soon after his Reason forsook him. In this deplorable Situation, his Wife, Ann Finlayson, found Means to get her children and insane Husband to London where he was received into Bethlem [Bedlam] Hospital; and she, with her Five Children, were allowed Twenty Pounds a Year by the Commissioners for the Affairs of the Loyalists. After having been about Fifteen Months in Bethlem, Henry Finlayson was dismissed, and incurable. In this State was the poor Woman and her Children obliged to live with him in a small Room at No. 1 Bull-Inn-Court, Strand, opposite the Adelphi, upon the above-said Allowance and such small Additions as a few of her Friends amongst the Loyalists could produce for her.
>
> St. Luke's Hospital and the Parish Workhouse were in vain applied to; neither would receive the wretched Man. The Urgency of the Case obliged the latter to furnish him with a strait Waistcoat; but, having found Means to disengage himself from it, he, on the 19th of last Month, with a Knife, put a Period to his Life! Here, with Grief it is remarked that there are too many instances amongst the People of his Description who have finished their ill-fated Career with their own Hands! Many more have been taken off by Despondency.

In consequence of this news account, small donations were left at the Carolina Coffee House and other places, enabling Mrs. Finlayson to pay off her debts and "to reclaim her cloaths, and other articles from Pawn."[26] Boosted by this temporary assistance from exiled American Loyalists in London, Ann Finlayson found a way to support herself by applying for a government post in Nassau. Undaunted, she emigrated once again, to the Bahamas where for forty years she was in charge of the public buildings. Mrs. Finlayson died in Nassau at the grand age of eighty-eight.[27]

John Bartlam, a despondent Charleston potter, quietly gave up the ghost in 1781. His Camden property had been confiscated and the whole of his personal estate amounted to £9.8.10. He had had his share of problems before the Revolution, when he had borrowed £90 from Robert Daniel in 1766; by 1768, damages for nonpayment mounted to upwards of £200. In October, 1770, the *South Carolina Gazette* had announced the opening of Bartlam's "Pottery and China Manufactory in Old Church-Street." He advertised that his "Queen's Ware" was equal to any imported china and that with the "proper encouragement" he could "supply the demands of the whole Province."[28] He struggled along with his business but fortunately died before American troops took over Charleston in December, 1782.

Mary Bartlam may have gone to East Florida when Charleston was evacuated and remained there until after the Peace. In her 1783 claim, dated St. Augustine, she listed a house and lot in Camden, three town lots also in Camden, ten head of cattle and one horse taken, but not paid for, by the British Army, and a Negro boy "who followed the British Army"—a total of £525. In 1788, she pursued her claim in writing from Charleston where she was "working for her living." At Camden, she, like many wrote ". . . the people in my old district are very cold to me, on account of the part my late husband and my self took in the War, and I could not go home. . . ."[29]

Whether Mary Bartlam stayed in Charleston or later emigrated to the Bahamas is not known and the relationship between this Mary Bartlam and the John Bartlum of Abaco who married Mary Curry, also of Abaco, on 18 July 1803 has not been determined,[30] but it is possible that the family is the same, allowing for differences in orthography over the years. John Bartlum, Jr., born at Green Turtle Cay, Abaco, 3 November 1814, married Sarah, the daughter of William and Eliza Lowe of the same place. In 1847, Captain Bartlum moved his family and his New Plymouth house from Green Turtle Cay to Key West, Florida, where it stands today.

The daily efforts to protect life and property compounded emotional stress caused by the uncertainty of the future of the Loyalists in America. The provincial congresses and committees of safety had the power not only to search and disarm, to arrest, to sentence to prison or hard labour, and to confiscate and black list, but also to impose the death sentence or, in some cases, to commute it to banishment.

In North Carolina, those who came down to consult the governour about their safety were "intercepted, searched, detained, abused" and feared for their lives if they dared utter a word against the proceedings of the committee. Governour Martin and other Loyalists had been forced to take refuge on a sloop of war in Cape Fear River.[31] Punishable crimes ranged from drinking tea or drinking to the king's

New Method of MACARONY MAKING, as practised at BOSTON in NORTH AMERICA

PLATE 22

A 1774 cartoon shows a British official being turned into a "macaroni" or fop by the donning of a suit of tar and feathers, an indignity suffered by a number of Loyalists. (From *The American War of Independence, 1775-1783*, courtesy of The British Library.)

health all the way to passing information to the enemy. The committee used every possible deceitful method to spy into Loyalists' affairs. The famous Pennsylvania Black List contained "490 names of persons attainted of high treason." Some of the accused established their innocence; other were pardoned while most never returned to the state. Two obnoxious Loyalists who remained behind after the evacuation of Philadelphia were hanged.[32]

The dank Simsbury Copper Mine, aptly renamed Newgate, provided a horrible alternative to hanging. Confinement in its cavernous depths claimed many lives. Here, William Franklin, last royal governour of New Jersey and illegitimate son of the notable patriot Benjamin Franklin, was shut away from light, air, and the lovely Connecticut landscape. He had come close to negotiating a separate peace with England that might have aborted the Revolution. Taken from his dying wife whom he never saw again, Franklin was confined at Simsbury early in the war. In 1813, he was disowned by his father who never forgave him for his part in the Revolution. William Franklin died in London in exile.[33]

Loyalists saw little difference between the orderly congress or committee and the disorderly mob. The atrocities of the first American civil war could have equalled those of the French Revolution, which followed soon after, but thankfully did not. Mob violence in New York City never reached the frenzied pitch it would in Paris, and a wholesale blood bath was averted. Wasting the countryside, destruction of property, plunder, rape, and murder ran rampant through the American colonies. Coupled with these usual ravages of war were the barbarities of civil war: branding, whipping, ear cropping, and hamstringing. Nothing pleased the patriot mob more than to see Tories burned in effigy, stripped and ridden out of town on a sharp rail, or clothed in feathers and paraded through the streets in a dung cart. (See plate 22.)

The origin of tarring and feathering reaches as far back as the Crusades. The statutes of Richard I stated that if a man were convicted of stealing, his head "shall be close shaved like a Prize Fighter . . . melted Pitch poured upon him, and then he shall be covered with Feathers, that he may be known to be a Thief. . . ." Sabine quotes an old saying, "man is a two-legged animal *without* feathers."[34] Patriots inflicted this cruel torture with such regularity that a Loyalist was known not only by the feathers he wore but also by his butchered hair and raw skin, the result of his efforts to remove his suit of fine feathers.

The "excesses of Patriotism, when attaining power, have been too frequently productive of a tyranny more dangerous in its exercise, and more lasting in its effects, than the despotism which it was invoked to overthrow." Each state legislature passed laws against disaffected persons.[35] The severity of these punishments depended to some extent on the concentration of Loyalism in the various districts. According to Catherine Crary:

> The Loyalists were probably strongest in New York, weakest in Virginia. In South Carolina and Georgia they may have been a majority. In Connecticut and Pennsylvania they formed small but active blocks of opposition; in Delaware, Maryland, and New Jersey there were troublesome pockets of dissidents.

With one-half the population Tory, New York ranked as the most loyal of all the colonies. Phineas Bond estimated that at the end over 100,000 Loyalists were exiled and two out of three New York claimants were soldiers, the "arch-test of loyalty" for the commission.[36] So many New York Loyalists were merchants that "their exile in 1783 was impossible." Isaac Low, President of the New York Chamber of Commerce, was a delegate to the First Continental Congress until he balked at independence. Thousands more than can be accounted for may have managed to remain outwardly neutral but loyal in their hearts. To Esmund Wright, a "Loyalist was in essence a man or woman with a strong, if sometimes a quiet, devotion to the Mother Country and to the Establishment."[37]

New York City remained a British stronghold and a sanctuary for persecuted Loyalists for the seven years of the Revolution. The city filled with refugees arriving from North Carolina in 1776, from Philadelphia in 1778, and from Savannah and Charleston in 1782-83 when Rivington's *Gazette* reported 250 sail of ships arrived in New York from Charleston as the result of the evacuation of that city.[38]

A few days after the British takeover of New York on 15 September 1776, upwards of nine hundred inhabitants of Queen's County, hotbed of Toryism on the island of Nassau in the Province, presented to General Howe a public testimony of their "unshaken loyalty to our most gracious Sovereign and Zealous attachment to the British Constitution."[39] The New York Loyalists' Declaration of Dependence, dated 28 November 1776, was signed by 547 people. One of the signers, Richard Harris, received a grant of land on Abaco. Another, John Jones, may have accompanied his indentured servant Thomas Grisswell to Abaco in August, 1783.[40] Another John Jones who deserted the rebel artillery in February, 1780, may have been the one to emigrate to Abaco. He gave out some startling intelligence to the British at Staten Island which demonstrated colonists' attachment to their regional provinces and seemed to forecast the prevalent attitude in America's second civil war.

"The Southern Troops and New Englanders hate each other as much as enemies can." Rebel soldiers from the South were not allowed near British lines for fear they would defect. Since coming to winter quarters 2,000 men had deserted the Continental Army. He had not heard about the British takeover of Charleston because "no bad news [was] ever suffered to come to camp." Jones had, however, witnessed an act of savage cruelty. A major in Maxwell's brigade "gave two soldiers a gallon of whiskey to skin two Indians from the hip downwards." Later boots were made of the skins.[41]

Anticipating the arrival of the American army into the city, in November, 1783, rebel printer Mr. Claypole published the following notice in his *Pennsylvania Packet*. Mr. James Rivington re-ran the article in his *Royal Gazette*, soon to be the *New York Gazette*, leveling a bit of humour at himself in the face of the Loyalist defeat.

> The subscriber begs leave to inform the several Printers in America, that he hath lately imported from England a large Quantity of TYPES in cases, consisting solely of the letters R,E,B,E,L, of all the sizes useful in printing. Had the war continued, he should by no means have been induced to part with these types, having such constant use for them at his own press; but his majesty's late gracious speech in Parliament, having rendered the aforesaid letters not so much in demand as heretofore, he is willing to dispose of them on equal terms, and will take continental loan office or army certificates, the financier's notes or American bank bills in payment.
>
> N.B. Many hundred weight of the above letters, worn out in his majesty's service, to be sold for the value of the metal only. Enquire of JAMES RIVINGTON.[42]

While the printers bandied gibes, Gilbert Forbes, Jr., frantically prepared to settle his affairs in order to leave New York for Abaco. His father had had a narrow escape at the hands of patriots, and he was not about to tempt fate by being in New York when Washington's army marched into the city. In 1776 Gilbert Forbes, Sr., was one of two gunsmiths arrested for complicity in a complicated conspiracy "to murder all of Washington's staff officers, seize him [the general], blow up the magazines, arm all loyalists and capture the city upon the arrival of the British." This daring action is known simply as the Hickey Plot because the matter seems to have been dropped after Sergeant Thomas Hickey, one of Washington's personal guards, was convicted of mutiny and hanged 28 June 1776.[43]

The execution of the young officer was preceded by many anxious days for Gilbert Forbes. Early one May morning, a party of rebels forced their way into his house "in the Broad-way," rushed up the stairs, broke down the door, seized him, and demanded his keys. Captain Labatteau conveyed Forbes "to an apartment in the New Gaol" and delivered to the Provincial Congress the culprit's papers, which "threw great light on the designs of the conspirators." The copy of an association entered into on 13 May 1776 "revealed the conspirators to be loyal subjects of George III," intent on frustrating enemy operations. They pledged themselves to secrecy and swore never to reveal the other conspirators even under penalty of death. The signatures on this document had been erased. Another letter reminded Mr. Forbes that he had promised to have rifles and guns "ready by Saturday night." Still another letter states, "we have hopes that the tyranny of our cruel talk-masters" who "plunder our barns and enter our houses" will "soon be ended." If we are "to be slaves, let us be so to the lion, and not to the lousy, dirty vermin of New England."

Mr. Forbes was brought before the Committee and told that his "heinous crime did not entitle him to a trial" but the council would show mercy if he confessed. Gilbert Forbes answered in a "faltering voice" that he did not intend "any harm against my country." Mr. Mulligan shouted that he was involved in a "hellish conspiracy." Committee president, Mr. Peter Livingston, calmly advised him to plead guilty and to make a confession. Forbes reiterated his innocence and asked to be tried by a jury of his neighbours. When asked if he knew about the letters, Forbes said they had been left by a friend but refused to give the man's name. When asked if he were Whig or Tory, Forbes replied that he was for peace. The obstinate prisoner was put back in jail.[44]

David Mathews, mayor of New York, testified that he had met Governour Tryon aboard the *Duchess of Gordon* where the colonial governour had taken refuge. The mayor's mission had been to obtain permission for Lord Drummond to go to Bermuda. As he had left the vessel, Tryon had put a bundle of paper money into his hand and told Mathews to give £5 to the prisoners in the jail but to give the rest to Gilbert Forbes for guns he was making for him. Back in New York, a friend of the mayor advised him not to pay Forbes right away so that in case of discovery the mayor could say he had not paid the money. During the days following, Forbes met with Mathews several times and pressed him for his money. Mathews advised Forbes to get out of this business before he was hanged. During his conversations with Forbes, the mayor learned that the gunsmith had already smuggled the guns aboard the king's vessel. He also mentioned raising a company and a scheme to take possession of one of the batteries and cut down King's Bridge.

A William Forbes, tanner and currier, admitted that he, Gilbert Forbes and a sergeant of Washington's guards, had administered oaths of secrecy to a man named Mason and two or three soldiers who advised Gilbert about how best to get aboard the governour's man-o-war. William Forbes could not recollect the sergeant's name, but said he was a "middle-sized, fresh complexioned" Englishman.[45]

Other witnesses testified that at a dinner at the Sergeant's Arms at which Mr. Forbes was present, the men were overheard plotting to murder General Washington and all the Livingstons. (See plates 23 and 24.) A Mary Gibbons from New Jersey conspired with them to execute the plot. Washington "maintained" her at a house near Mr. Skinner's at the North River and the general had often come there "late at night in disguise." Also intimate with Mr. Clayford, one of the loyalist conspirators, Mary gave him letters taken from Washington's pockets. Clayford copied them and Mary Gibbons replaced them before Washington awoke. Clayford also told his fellow conspirators that Mary would help them kidnap Washington, but the others thought that too hazardous. Mr. Clayford was eventually sentenced to death and an order was

PLATE 23 (Above): A loyalist plot to murder General Washington did not come about, despite the connivance of a Mary Gibbons, who was intimate with both the general and one of the loyalist conspirators.

PLATE 24 (Above, right): Robert R. Livingston was also marked for death in the abortive plot to kill Washington and his associates. (From James Thatcher's *Military Journal*, Boston, 1827.)

issued for his speedy execution. The minutes do not indicate whether or not the Committee followed through with his hanging, and by August trials of other prisoners were deferred. The fate of Gilbert Forbes, New York gunsmith, is unknown. Gilbert Forbes, Jr., signed a petition with other subscribers from Maxwell Town, Abaco, which appeared in the *Bahamas Gazette* 28 March 1785, publicly denouncing Governour Maxwell.[46]

Loyalist influence was so strong in Georgia that only five of the ten parishes sent representatives to the provincial congress to appoint delegates to the First Continental Congress, and those elected refused to serve.[47] Colonial records list the names of loyal Georgians whenever a rebel action provoked their response or a penalty was levied against them. Loyalists who objected to the resolutions of 10 August 1774 are listed as are those who signed the Oath of Allegiance to His Majesty in 1775. Loyalists lost their civil rights through the Georgia Act of Attainder in 1778 and suffered by reason of the Confiscation-Banishment Act of 1782. Finally after the Peace that had secured Loyalists the right to return to their homes, 286 inhabitants of Georgia were declared banished.[48]

The *Royal Georgia Gazette* published a notice in May, 1781, to recruit troops for a regiment of horse. Upwards of fifty Loyalists had been murdered in the back parts of the Province and the Council urged loyal inhabitants to take the king's shilling and help fight the rebels. James Simpson, Agent for South Carolina, returned from England in

1780 to find only misery and distress in the "rich and flourishing Country" of Carolina which he had left. "Numbers of families who four years ago abounded in every convenience and luxury of life, are without food to live on, Clothes to cover them, or the means to purchase either."[49]

Governour James Wright wrote the Earl of Cornwallis that the cruelty of the rebels was so shocking that most of the people had taken to the swamps "for Shelter against these Worse than Savages, who say they will Murder every loyal Subject in the Province."[50]

In Thomas Brown the king had a soldier to equal the savagery of a hundred rebels. Brown sailed from Whitby, England, and arrived in Savannah in the autumn of 1774 with seventy-four indentured servants. In 1775, another colony of seventy-five persons joined him. Settling them all on twelve different tracts amounting to 5,600 acres, he built one house for himself, as well as thirty-six farmhouses, and purchased stock. In one of his memorials Brown described himself as a planter near Augusta.[51]

Brown became obnoxious early in the war by refusing to sign the oath of allegiance to America. In 1775, 140 armed rebels surrounded his house. Brown shot the rebel Captain Chestly Bostick but shortly thereafter six or eight men overpowered him, struck him on the head with a rifle, knocking him senseless, inflicted six or seven other wounds, and generally treated him "with every species of cruelty the most barbarous imagination would suggest." The rebels scalped him in three places, tied him to a tree, and burnt the soles of his feet.[52] In Augusta the rebels "presented him with a genteel and fashionable suit of tar and feathers," then paraded him in a dung cart down to Mr. Weatherford's for the night. He made his escape to the South Carolina backcountry where he persuaded three hundred men to take up arms for the king. His Company of King's Rangers was also known as the East Florida Rangers and the Carolina Rangers.[53] This zealous Loyalist and intrepid soldier rose quickly to the rank of lieutenant colonel, fighting in seventeen actions and receiving fourteen wounds, three of which were dangerous. In 1779 Brown was appointed Superintendent of Indian Affairs for the Creek, Cherokee, and Catawba Nations.[54]

At the Siege of Augusta in 1778, Brown's reputation of valour was tainted by a wretched display of vindictiveness. With serious wounds in both thighs he held out against the rebel commander, Lieutenant Colonel Elijah Clark, before being forced to retreat and leave behind his wounded. Brown hanged thirteen rebel prisoners in the stairway of the Mackey House, four more in other parts of the house, "and several others were turned over to the Indians" to be burned alive.[55]

At the evacuation of Charleston, Brown's corps was ordered to St. Augustine. After the Peace, Brown emigrated to the Bahamas where he was granted over two thousand acres of land on Abaco. He spent much of his time deeply involved in Bahamian politics in Nassau. About 1789 he attempted to move his plantation to the Caicos but was shipwrecked on the way.[56] His Caicos grants amounted to over six thousand acres. On 11 September 1789 he married Hetty Farr on Grand Caicos. Four years later he applied for a grant on St. Vincent where he remained until his death. In April, 1806, his wife died there, and on 4 July 1818 his only daughter, Susan Harriet, was married there to Allan MacDowell, Esquire, M.D. Colonel Brown died at "Calisqua" on the

Island of St. Vincent "at an advanced age" on 11 July 1825. The *Royal Gazette* stated that he had commanded the British American Regiment of King's Rangers during the American Revolutionary War "evincing on every occasion a zeal and bravery surpassed by none of the commanders of the royal armies."[57]

The war in the South produced other fierce fighters like Thomas Brown. Sabine felt the nearly equal division of parties bred resentments that pitted "neighbor against neighbor, until it became a war of extermination."[58] Loyalist military leaders like Richard Pearis, "Bloody Bill," his cousin Robert Cunningham, and David Fanning were just as much at home in the unbroken wilderness of rivers and forests as was Francis Marion, the "Swamp Fox," who crouched in the mire waiting to pounce on them. The guerilla warfare in the Carolina backcountry had none of the tidiness of the Seige of Charleston or any of the other major battles of the Revolution. The backcountry potato, hemp, and tobacco farmer was a world apart from the lowcountry rice and indigo planter. "Although the vast majority of farmers in South Carolina may not have been open Loyalists," yet the moderately wealthy, predominately Ulster-Scot upcountry farmer "comprised the largest single group" among loyalist claimants.[59]

Colonial Charleston, the centre of the Province of South Carolina, was perhaps the richest seaport in all the British Dominions. In 1775 as many as 350 sailing vessels rode in the harbour at any one time. The rice barons exported thousands of barrels of rice, mainly to Portugal. That same year the outbreak of war caused bereaved Charlestonians to curb their luxurious and extravagant mourning practices. The *Country Journal* reported that at the funeral of Solomon Legare, relatives "appeared in their usual dress with the Exception of a Hat-Band or black Ribbon" and the practice of giving scarves or gloves was dispensed with.[60]

To the opulent planter and merchant classes of the tidewater area, the backcountry folk served as a buffer against Indian attack and a counterbalance to the slave population in Charleston. An item in Mr. Timothy's paper shows a striking difference between the lowcountry and backcountry planter. Its intent, however, was to strengthen the resolution of the South Carolinians not to purchase anything not made in the colony. The article described a gentlemanly backcountry planter who came to town from one hundred miles away as "suitable well dressed," yet every piece of his clothing had been made on his plantation "except his hat, which was made in his neighborhood."[61] One might reflect upon which Loyalist would be better prepared to face the wilds of Nova Scotia or the barren Bahamas.

The Carolina backcountry looked to be the "promised land" for four hundred Loyalists who, in 1778, were forced to find shelter in the dense woods.[62] Despite loyalist sentiments among Scottish highlanders, independent backcountry farmers proved difficult to recruit to the British standard, hence the encounter at Moore's Creek Bridge and the Battle of King's Mountain ended in loyalist defeat. Perhaps backcountry South Carolinians should be regarded as loyal rather than Loyalist, for it was commonly known they were numerous there but extremely difficult to identify.

A man could be a Loyalist one day and a rebel the next, depending upon the expediency of the situation. Fear as much as principle created Tories. So also did greed and ambition among those who believed the rebel cause would never succeed.[63]

The 1776 Petty Jury List of the backcountry town of Ninety-Six and its district contained names of four hundred Loyalists. An association "for extirpating the rebellion restoring real liberty, and maintaining peace and good order" was signed by a "considerable number of inhabitants" of the Orangeburgh district in 1780. They resolved to aid "the re-establishment of the British government in this once happy, but now distracted, country." In spite of these declarations of loyalty, after the Seige of Ninety-Six in 1781, one Loyalist leader expressed his disappointment at the "defection of the inhabitants of South Carolina." He called them "a perfidious people, whose allegiance to the British government neither promises could bend nor oaths secure."[64]

The Regulators in North and South Carolina were the earliest revolutionaries in America. In 1767, the *South Carolina Gazette* reported that "gangs of Villains from North Carolina and Virginia" had for some years past infested the back parts of the southern Provinces.[65] Because of the lack of backcountry courts, associations were formed in a kind of desperation to dispel villains. Coming on the heels of the Cherokee War of 1760-1761, this vigilante activity soon blossomed into the War of Regulation which ended in the Battle of Alamance, 16 May 1771. The grand Jury of the District of Newbern called North Carolina Regulators "wicked, Seditious, Evil Designing, and disaffected Persons" who "refused to pay their public taxes" and have gone about the countryside "destroying and pillaging the Houses of such Persons who were obnoxious to their Ringleaders."[66]

In South Carolina, a number of inhabitants between the Santee and the Wateree Rivers "assembled in a riotous manner" and burnt houses of some persons reputed to be harbourers of horse thieves. Lieutenant Governour Bull ordered a new regiment of militia formed to suppress "those licentious spirits . . . assuming the name of Regulators" who have, in defiance of government, "illegally tried, condemned, and punished many persons. . . ." The powerful Regulators punished magistrates who tried to bring some of their members to justice. Mr. Mayson, Esquire, Justice of the Peace for Ninety-Six, was seized, taken from his house, tied under the belly of his horse, and dragged eighty miles.[67] The Reverend George Micklejohn preached against the North Carolina Regulators in the presence of Governour Tryon. The firebrand backcountry itinerant preacher, the Reverend Charles Woodmason, championed the Regulator movement in South Carolina. As spokesman for their cause he penned the "Remonstrance," which illustrated in Swiftian fashion the plight of the backcountry citizen.[68]

One might expect the backcountry Regulators to take the Whig side and government officials to join the Tories in the Revolutionary War, but this was not to be the case. This issue alone might have established proof of the loyalty of Colonel Joseph Curry, Magistrate for Craven County, although no documented proof can be found; but there is not enough substantial evidence to indicate that the majority of anti-Regulators were Loyalists. Joseph Curry craftily gave out the appearance of attachment to the Regulator cause while maintaining his office and loyalty to government. Had he lived through the American War, he might have been expected to make only expedient moves. Curry family tradition states that this Joseph Curry of South Carolina is the antecedent of the Benjamin Curry who married Mary Curry 15 April 1792. Although there were three Benjamin and Mary Currys in the Bahamas at the same time, this Benjamin, of Green Turtle Cay, Abaco, whose will was lodged 28 March 1826, is believed to be the ancestor of many of the Bahamian Currys, some of whom later migrated to Key West. (See appendix C.)[69]

Loyalty, by no measure a clear-cut issue, developed slowly and painfully throughout the events of the conflict and in many cases Loyalists did not make their final decisions to take up the king's standard until the eleventh hour. Early attempts to avert war had failed. Lieutenant General and Governour of New York William Tryon wrote the Earl of Dartmouth in August, 1775, urging a change of policy toward the American colonies, but never received an answer.[70]

The battles raged on in Lexington-Concord. Breed's or Bunker's Hill, Moore's Creek Bridge, and New York, but it was not until 1778 that Loyalists moved from the periphery to the centre of the war.[71] After the Declaration of Independence, nothing "so amazed the loyalists" as the Treaty of the French Alliance, signed 6 February 1778. Loyalists attacked the treaty on the fact that Whigs had taken up with a Catholic ally. The following gibe appeared in Rivington's *Gazette:*

> Since Dr. Franklin has ceded Canada and Florida to the French and Spaniards, it is to be hoped that he will give New England to the pretender and make the Pope Archbishop of North America and that the whole continent in the end may go to the devil.[72]

In spite of the Alliance, the tide of war seemed to undulate in favour of the Loyalists for a while. The British repulsed the rebels at Savannah and forced them to retreat into Carolina. D'Estaing, compelled to re-embark his troops at Savannah, met with severe storms that shattered his fleet but managed to arrive in France, dangerously wounded, with his own vessel and two other ships.[73] In June, 1779, Spain declared war on Great Britain, Charleston fell to the British in May, 1780. Loyalists then suffered defeat at King's Mountain and finally Cornwallis surrendered at Yorktown, 19 October 1781, where

> The military honours which had been denied the Americans at the fall of Charleston were now denied the British. They marched out of Yorktown with colours cased, and, according to tradition, to the ironically appropriate English air of, "The World Turned Upside Down."[74]

11

The Losers

Sir Guy Carleton, Commander at New York, issued the orders for the evacuation of Georgia and South Carolina in 1782 and also directed the final exile of Loyalists from New York and East Florida after the Peace in 1783. (See plate 25.) The Georgia House of Assembly under Governour James Wright protested the evacuation of Savannah scheduled to be completed with the final departure of British troops 11 July 1782. The town had "been put into a good posture of Defence at an immense expence to the Inhabitants." Even the governour's Savannah plantation adjoining the town common had been "pulled down as necessary for His Majesty's Service during the Siege of Savannah by the French and rebels."[1] The hardships of defending Savannah had plunged many inhabitants into "utter ruin," and they were now "reduced to the Melancholy Alternative, either of leaving the Province, in a destitute Condition, to pine under Want in a Strange Country or else stay behind and fall into the hands of their inexorable enemies." Having heard of the expected evacuation of East Florida, the House urged General Leslie to "Keep Possession of East Florida, as an Asylum for the Loyalists."[2]

Many loyalist families were encamped at Tybee Island to await evacuation, and some died on that island from the heat and bad water. Some perhaps even suffered the terror which had surrounded Alexander Wylly's escape to Tybee during the first rebel occupation of Savannah in 1776. The Wylly family had emigrated to Georgia from Belfast, Ireland, in 1750. Alexander had signed the oath of allegiance to the king in 1775; his brother Richard was a rebel. Alexander's marriage to Susanna Crooks had produced two sons, William and Alexander Campbell Wylly, who later served as captains in the King's Rangers and after the Peace maintained interests in Abaco and Long Island and held important government positions in the Bahamas. Their daughter Susanna eventually married John Anderson, a strong Loyalist from Georgia, who also emigrated to the Bahamas.[3]

In 1776, Alexander left behind considerable property and houses in Savannah and retreated to Tybee with his wife, his young daughter and all the personal effects they could carry. A "dangerous disorder" confined him to his island home. Since a few British vessels had entered the Savannah River, he felt his family would be safe on Tybee until the time of evacuation. Soon after he arrived, a party of rebels landed on the back part of the island and stole all their effects, returning to set fire to the house on three different occasions. Each time Alexander's wife and small daughter

PLATE 25

Sir Guy Carleton, Commander at New York, issued the orders for the 1782 evacuation of Georgia and South Carolina as well as for the final exodus of Loyalists from New York and East Florida after the Peace in 1783. He was honoured by having the settlement at Abaco named for him. (From Arthur Bradley's *Colonial Americans in Exile*, New York: Dutton, 1932.)

extinguished the flames. The band took Alexander prisoner, a capture that must have inevitably resulted in his death had not their commanding officer intervened and demanded Wylly's release. "Destitute of all the comforts of life" and now with no means of subsistence, they fled to East Florida, "reduced to the greatest extremities." Alexander Wylly died in December, 1780, and Mrs. Susanna Wylly believed "his Death was hasten'd by the troubles."[4]

Lt. General Alexander Leslie keenly felt the misery of the Loyalists. In a supposedly secret letter to Sir Guy Carleton 11 June 1782, he commented that the impending evacuation of St. Augustine would be a particular hardship because "many Families have retired to East Florida to be quiet and live in Peace." Since he had no king's ship at Charleston, he had had to send Carleton's evacuation orders in triplicate to Georgia and to St. Augustine, a procedure which may have caused the resulting leak of information before the formal announcement when two privateers nearly captured the fishing boats he used as dispatch vessels.[5]

The evacuation of Savannah was in progress, but the evacuation of Charleston had not even begun when the rumours of the proposed evacuation of East Florida spread. Florida inhabitants then in Charleston immediately sent a memorial to Leslie. These overwrought proprietors informed the lieutenant general that their lands in East Florida had been settled and cultivated by over fifteen years of hard labour and at an expense of £300,000 sterling. Governour Tonyn had already issued several proclamations stating that East Florida had been reserved as an asylum for refugees. The province was important for naval stores; the Loyalists feared that vacated, St. Augustine would fall into the hands of the enemy and a "Nest of Privateers would not only annoy our Gulf trade from Jamaica," but would cut off communication with Europe.[6]

By the end of June, Leslie still had not taken any steps toward the evacuation of Charleston and the people doubted it would ever take place. He had sent Lt. Col.

Balfour to New York to inform Carleton of the "miserable state of the Loyalists" in the southern provinces. Carleton had denied Leslie's request to return home to England; he was needed in Charleston to supervise the evacuation of the southern districts. Leslie wrote Carleton: "I am very much run down, my Country had got [its] full share out of me and the moreso from over-anxiety for the benefit of the public." In this correspondence he sent along a list of points that required Carleton's consideration. "*If* this town [Charleston] is to be evacuated, what will be done with the sequestered Negroes under the charge of Mr. Cruden, and employed in the different regiments?" (Emphasis added.) His choice of words suggests that Leslie also did not believe the British would leave the city. He next asked Carleton what he should do about the many Blacks who had aided in the Siege of Savannah and Charleston and had served the military as guides, "and from their Loyalty" had been "promised their freedom." Carleton would be confronted with similar problems less than a year later at the evacuation of New York.[7]

By early August preparation for the evacuation of Charleston had begun. A notice appeared in Robert Wells' paper informing the people of the "expected withdrawal of the King's troops." Any inhabitants who desired "to remove with their families and effects to the Province of East Florida" were to notify the Quartermaster General's Office.[8] Charles Ogilvie and Gideon Dupont, Jr., went to New York to present Guy Carleton with an incomplete return of "the number of persons and quantity of effects to be removed from Charlestown," a tally that by the 13th of August numbered 4,230 white men, women, and children and 7,163 Blacks with 20,955 tons of merchandise. Because of the uncertainty regarding which port would be retained by the British government, most of the people were at a loss as to where to go and refused to commit themselves to any specific location. Of the estimated 11,393, a few were with the army, 989 had chosen Jamaica and 1,588 were bound for St. Augustine.[9]

On 10 September Ogilvie and Dupont submitted a memorial to Carleton on behalf of loyal inhabitants and British merchants whose "ruin must be sealed by the approaching evacuation of Charlestown." They asked Carleton to suspend the move until the spring for several reasons: to facilitate trading interests in Great Britain, to allow for recovery of the sick troops, to harvest the crops, to allow merchants to satisfy their creditors, and to secure asylum in the West Indies.[10]

The evacuation proceeded in spite of all entreaties. There seemed to be a fairly even distribution of people arriving in New York and East Florida. John Winniett, inspector of refugees in both places, reported a return of 2,165 white and 3,340 black refugees in New York a month before the final evacuation of Charleston and 2,428 Whites and 3,609 Blacks in East Florida.[11]

Rivington's *Royal Gazette* in New York published "some particulars respecting the dereliction of Charlestown" which took place 14 December 1782. After describing the orderly departure of British transports, Mr. Rivington alluded to the plight of those who might have been left behind. It was his understanding that General Leslie had insisted, and that the Revolutionary Army had agreed that "no corps of the country militia would be permitted to enter the town until the expiration of ten days after the British troops had left it, by which time it was presumed that those merchants whose embarrassments compelled them to remain in the town might get their property secured."[12]

This agreement was not honoured, however; although perhaps the militia had nothing to do with the despicable tortures perpetrated on those "embarrassed merchants" and other Loyalists who remained behind, but the situation of the exiles was so horrible that one New York historian found it difficult to describe adequately:

> ... There were old grey-headed men and women, husbands and wives with large families of little children, women with infants at their breasts, poor widows whose husbands had lost their lives in the service of their King and country, with half a dozen half-starved bantlings taggling at their skirts, taking leave of their friends. Here, you saw people who had lived all their days in affluence (though not in luxury), leaving their real estate, their houses, stores, ships, and improvements, and hurrying on board the transports with what little household goods they had been able to save. In every street were to be seen men, women, and children wringing their hands, lamenting the situation of those who were ... leaving the country, and the more dreadful situation of such who were either unable to leave, or were determined, rather than run the risk of starving in distant lands, to throw themselves upon, and trust to, the mercy of their persecutors, their inveterate enemies, the rebels of America.
>
> Their fears and apprehensions were soon realized. No sooner had the evacuation taken place at Charleston than the rebels, like so many furies, or rather devils, entered the town, and a scene ensued, the very repetition of which is shocking to the ears of humanity. The Loyalists were seized, hove into dungeons, prisons and provosts. Some were tied up and whipped, others were tarred and feathered; some were dragged to horse-ponds and drenched till near dead, others were carried about the town in carts with labels upon their breasts and backs with the word "Tory" in capitals written thereon. All the Loyalists were turned out of their houses and obliged to sleep in the streets and fields, their covering the canopy of heaven. A universal plunder of the friends to government took place and, to complete the scene, a gallows was erected upon the quay facing the harbour, and twenty-four reputable Loyalists hanged in sight of the British fleet, with the army and refugees on board. This account of the evacuation of Charleston I had from a British officer who was upon the spot, ashore at the time and an eye-witness to the whole.[13]

On the 20th of January, 1783, the "Preliminaries to a General Peace between Great Britain, France, Spain, Holland, and the United States of America" were signed at Paris. A general armistice was declared and "hostilities by sea and land were to cease" on the 20th of February in Europe and on the 20th of March in America, 1783. None of the articles touched the issue of the American Loyalists, but the losers may have had one sympathizer among the American peacemakers. Captured on the high seas, Henry Laurens of South Carolina had been confined in the Tower of London during the last three years of the war. In deference to the father, Charleston's *Royal Gazette* announced the death in battle of Henry's son John, a lieutenant colonel in the rebel army, and referred to Henry Laurens as a man of honour, a gentleman who "constantly condemned every oppressive measure adopted against the Loyalists."[14]

In a sketch of the principal stipulations of the peace treaty, Great Britain acknowledged the "absolute, unlimited and unconditional Independence" of the "Thirteen United States of America" and ceded East Florida to Spain.[15] At the end of the French and Indian War in 1763, Spain had ceded Florida to England. At that time the province was divided by the Royal Proclamation of George III. "The part between the Apalachicola and the Mississippi Rivers, extending as far north as the 31st parallel, was called West Florida, with Pensacola as its capital, while the land east of the Apalachicola up to the St. Mary's River became known as East Florida, with its capital at St. Augustine."[16] The German traveller Schoepf described the St. Augustine bar as "dreadful." He said the Spanish had been wary "to fix the capital of a colony behind a sand-bank which cannot be crossed except at great peril." Sixteen vessels arriving from Charleston "bearing refugees and their effects went to pieces" on that bar, and many lost their lives.

Around about the town of St. Augustine, where "almost every house had its little garden of splendid orange and lemon trees," poor fugitives had built cabins thatched with palmetto leaves. These unfortunate refugees would suffer most by the changeover. "What little property they could save, most of them have fixed here in lands and houses, which they must now again give up. For of all these residents few doubtless will be willing to exchange a mild British rule for the Spanish yoke, even was there no question of religion."[17]

In spite of provisions sent from Charleston to St. Augustine, there was a shortage of food. Plays were staged for the benefit of the distressed Loyalists. Turmoil prevailed as refugees continued to pour into the province. Regiments returned from campaigns in Georgia and the Carolinas, and "large delegations of Indians came and went." Thieves robbed passengers on the public roads and plundered houses.[18]

Formal battle ceased in America at the time prescribed by the treaty, but hostility continued long after. Considerations on behalf of the Loyalists were difficult to negotiate into the treaty. Article V provided for the restitution of confiscated property, much of which had already been sold. On 13 June 1782, a five hundred acre parcel of land in Georgia belonging to Alexander Wylly was sold to a Thomas Stone and a house and lot on the bay in Savannah owned by William and Alexander C. Wylly brought the state £355. Some of Alexander McKee's land in Kentucky was granted to Transylvania University. "In New York alone over $3,600,000 worth of property was acquired by the state. . . ."[19]

When it became certain that the American states did not intend to observe Article V of the treaty, Parliament appointed a commission to inquire into the losses of the Loyalists.[20] Degrees of loyalty were put into classes:

The first was those who had performed exceptional services on behalf of Great Britain. The second class was of those who had borne arms against the Revolution. The third was of uniform loyalists. The fourth, of loyalists resident in Great Britain. The fifth, of those who took the oath of allegiance to the Americans but afterwards joined the British. The last consisted of those who bore arms for the Americans, but afterwards joined the British forces.[21]

Soldiers fell into the first three classes and were highly compensated by the commission on top of the half pay voted the military by Parliament in June of 1783. There would be no compensation for the inhabitants of West Florida because it had been conquered by Spain in war "Whereas East Florida had been given over in a time of Peace."[22]

Egerton's analysis of the individual cases reveals the miscellaneous character of the claimants. Landed aristocracy and ex-colonial governours stood side by side with mechanics and liberated slaves. There were a few fraudulent claims and some prevaricators even protested that ill health required them to leave America. The claims of "poor but still canny Scotsmen" were numerous, but most claimants were just ordinary people.[23]

The twelfth and final report of the commission, dated 15 May 1789, showed a total of £3,033,091 for 3,225 claims, figures slightly higher than the report of 10 June 1789, which appeared in the *Bahamas Gazette*. The number of individual claimants from the province of New York was the largest at 941; Delaware presented the fewest, 9. Champion claimants were John Penn, Sr., and his son. The commission awarded them £500,000 against a claim of £9,444,817 in a perpetual annuity of £4,000 per annum. Many Loyalists received nothing and carried an "almost universal feeling" of "deep resentment against what they believed to be a "great betrayal" on the part of Great Britain.[24]

Privileges secured in Article V allowed Loyalists to return to their respective states, there to remain twelve months "unmolested." Although the sixth article stipulated that "there shall be no future Confiscations made, nor any Prosecutions commenced against any Person or Persons for or by reason of the Part which he or they may have taken in the present War; and that no Person shall on that account suffer any future Loss or Damage, either in his Person, Liberty, or Property,"[25] violence broke out in every quarter of America.

Not only was there a "disregard of the articles of peace," wrote Guy Carleton, but "barbarous menaces" were perpetrated by "committees formed in various Towns, Cities, and districts, and even at Philadelphia, the very place where the Congress had chosen for their residence. . . ." Americans from Georgia and Carolina invaded St. Augustine to recover "their plundered negroes." West Florida Loyalists rode into the South Carolina backcountry and plundered "a number of Negroes, horses and other effects. . . ."[26] Some members of the committee had gone into New York City to hunt down Loyalists, and panic gripped the city. One Loyalist wrote that "a universal despair and frenzy prevails within these lines." In New York Harbour, Loyalists retaliated by seizing the colours of an American vessel. Carleton issued a proclamation warning loyal inhabitants that any riotous, disorderly breaches of the peace would be "punished with the severity due the offense."[27]

Loyalists attempting to return home were whipped, jailed, tarred and feathered, banished under pain of death if they returned, and even murdered. Rivington published a brief "Hint to Loyalists" about a soldier returning to South Carolina who had a "promise of safety and written protection" but was executed. In July, 1783, General McArthur at St. Augustine wrote to Carleton that "A young man named Maxwell well known to us all here was lately murdered in his house near Savannah." The reason—"no other offense than the inexplicable one of being a Tory."[28]

Lydia Austin Parrish asked:

> ... why were our American forebears so merciless ... in the treatment of their defeated neighbors and for that matter, toward the Southerners after the War Between the States? ... We seem to have forgiven Germany and Japan ... Are we growing more civilized, or is there something in civil war that brings out traits which transcend our essential decency? It may be that nothing is expected from our enemies whereas too much is expected from our friends.

Many Loyalists loved America as fervently as did the patriots.[29] Although thousands of inconspicuous Tories remained in the United States, many ardent lovers of America were forced to "quit the settlements they had acquired, and be conveyed like transports [convicts] to cultivate the deserts of Augustine and Nova Scotia."[30]

One American private in the Philadelphia militia spoke out against forced expatriation. In the first place "perpetual banishment" violated the treaty. "We cannot be at peace with a nation and at war with any of her subjects." Several of his remarks struck at the core of the issue.

> If they revolted from America we revolted from Great Britain. . . . With what face can we, who have resisted the claims of the British crown, go to any part of the British Empire? . . . What right have we to punish their loyalty (pardon me for not stating it disaffection, because their King's title was of a prior date to ours)? . . . Why should it be more criminal for them to be true to their Allegiance than for us to be true to ours? . . . I should be the first to anathematize myself, if I put down every man a knave or scoundrel who thought differently from me either in religion or politicks. When the prize is won, and the war over, all animosity ought to cease.[31]

But animosity continued to delay the departure of Loyalists. Carleton refused to "leave [behind] any of the Loyalists that were desirous to quit the Country, [to be] a prey to violence they conceive they have so much cause to apprehend." Between 80,000 to 100,000 Loyalists emigrated. Most New York Tories went to England, Nova Scotia, or Canada. Nicknamed "Nova Scarcity" by the Whigs, Nova Scotia began to receive large numbers of exiles during the summer of 1783. The place proved too cold for some southern Loyalists who later migrated to the Bahamas. William Wylly was one and Dr. Charles Bode, ancestor of Eugenia Bode who married W. E

Armbrister, was another. Charles Bode served as surgeon to the Hessian grenadiers in America throughout the Revolutionary War. At the Peace, he "went with the Loyalists" to settle in Nova Scotia and came to the Bahamas in 1787. He died a respected member of the Nassau community on 20 November 1823.[32]

Jamaica was expensive and overcrowded and as yet the Loyalists had secured no permanent refuge in the West Indies. Like the petitioners to Governour Martin in North Carolina, the intrepid Andrew Deveaux, Jr., believed that "eight years' experience is sufficient to teach us, that we have every thing to fear, and nothing to expect from the British Empire, but what springs from our own... generous exertions...." At his own expense, Deveaux fitted out an expedition to recapture Nassau and take the Bahamas from the Spanish. This adventure, "probably the last military action of the Revolutionary War," ended in Loyalist victory.[33]

A vessel from Havana appeared off the St. Augustine bar and reported that accounts received there gave out that Providence had been taken "by a force consisting of 500 regular troops, 1500 Loyalists, and 400 Indians."[34] Not all news accounts exaggerated the numbers of Deveaux's force. The *Edinburgh Advertiser* reported a force of only 350 "mostly undisciplined and badly armed" men. Rivington's *Gazette* got closer to the correct number at three hundred.[35] Nor can it be said that the Spanish vessel at St. Augustine reported inflated figures to save face. Governour Claraco at Providence reported only what he *thought* he saw. Colonel Deveaux had tricked him.

The contemporary account of Lt. Col. Roderick MacKenzie described the ruse. When Deveaux landed his modest force at the eastern end of Nassau, it appeared to the Spanish that a large and dangerous force had invaded. Deveaux made so many trips back and forth to his vessels, each time seemingly returning with boatloads of men, that the Spanish spiked their cannon and abandoned Ft. Montagu. Some troops were dressed like Indians, their war whoops designed to strike terror in the heart of any Spaniard, and long bundles of bound together sticks (fascines) used in strengthening ramparts, looked like men. On each return trip, the troops crowded in the bottom of the long boats ready to pop up again. One can imagine their embarrassment when the Spanish realized they had been taken by an army much inferior to their own.[36]

If Andrew Deveaux, Jr., had not been famous for such tricks, the account would be hardly credible; but Colonel Deveaux had a reputation for cunning. He had escaped from a rebel prison in Charleston and invaded the parlor of his cousin Robert Barnwell, who had captured him, pointing what appeared to the near-sighted gentleman to be a rifle and demanding his parole. Barnwell capitulated in the face of a spyglass that young Deveaux had picked up when he entered the house.[37] But practical jokes sometimes backfire as Deveaux discovered at Nassau.

In Deveaux's own words this is what happened:

About two hours after I had taken possession of the fort [Montagu], his Excellency Governor Claraco sent out a flag, giving some trifling information of a peace. I supposed his information entirely for the purpose of putting off time and amusing me. . . .[38]

A prankster expects treatment in kind so Deveaux resumed hostilities and on 18 April 1783 Claraco surrendered the town of Nassau. The Spanish governour had told the truth, however; nine days earlier England and Spain had signed a treaty that restored the Bahamas to Great Britain.[39]

This ironic turn of events should not diminish the brilliant military strategem of Colonel Andrew Deveaux, native Carolinian, whose Royal American Forresters took the Bahamas back from the Spanish and proudly raised British colours over Nassau. General McArthur sent the news account from the *East Florida Gazette* to Carleton. Although the story is somewhat inaccurate, the spirit of the event comes through. "Major Deveaux of the Beaufort Militia, with a handful of ragged Militia and five privateers from this place [St. Augustine] took Providence, where were 500 Spaniards, 70 pieces of cannon and 6 gallies; but unluckily he was nine days too late."[40]

Deveaux, however, was loath to share the honours of the exploit. This upset one participant while another officer wanted no part of the business when he learned that Deveaux's action had violated a peace. When informed on 21 April by a vessel from St. Thomas that peace between England and Spain had been proclaimed in Antigua, Captain Wheeler renounced any claim to the capture of the island.[41]

On 1 April, Deveaux's expedition left the St. Augustine bar with about sixty-five or seventy Loyalists, thirty of whom had been raised by Col. David Fanning.[42] On the 8th two brigs, the *Whitby Warrior* of sixteen guns commanded by Captain Wheeler and the *Perseverance* of twenty-six guns commanded by Captain Dow, rendezvoused with two small armed vessels at Hole in the Wall, the southwest bay of Abaco. From there Deveaux went over to Eleuthera to enlist Bahamian Loyalists for his enterprise. Between Captain MacKenzie, detached to Eleuthera, and Captain Higgs of the Harbour Island militia, about 170 additional men were recruited, bringing Deveaux's force to about three hundred men. Fifty fishing boats were also added to the fleet "for no other purpose than of deceiving the enemy."[43]

Robert Rumer of Harbour Island felt particularly "injured by Mr. Deveaux's misrepresentation" in taking the "whole of the meritt to himself" and failing to mention Rumer's own zealous and active part in the expedition. Rumer also tried to get financial redress from England for his own expenses.[44] His memorial to Lord Sidney, 25 April 1786, gives the names of the Harbour Islanders who fought with Deveaux. Some of these Bahamian Loyalists later received individual grants of land from Lord Dunmore and most were included in a six thousand acre grant on Eleuthera later granted by the government to those who had aided Deveaux.[45] Samuel Higgs, captain of the Harbour Island militia, and Joseph Currey, who may have been the captain in Col. Fanning's regiment, signed Rumer's memorial. Gideon Lowe, captain of the *Carpenter's Revenge*, probably joined Captain Wheeler's Sea Forresters, doing his part for king and country.[46]

On the 12th, the American-Bahamian fleet captured the schooner *Harriet* from Port Washington, North Carolina, informing Deveaux that no intelligence had been received there concerning a peace. On the 14th, at daybreak, Deveaux and 160 troops landed and took Fort Montagu. At the same time, Major Archibald Taylor with part of the crews from the armed brigs (about sixty men) boarded the three Spanish ships in the harbour.[47]

At the taking of Fort Montagu Deveaux smelt "a match on fire" and, suspecting the Spaniards' intentions, confined two prisoners inside the fort while he and his troops stood outside. Soon the two Spaniards found the fuse which led to the magazine and two mines. After the news of the "trifling peace," Deveaux waited two hours, then requested the surrender of the garrison. Claraco refused to surrender but agreed to confer with Deveaux. They established a truce which the Spanish governour had no intention of keeping.[48]

Ignoring the brief truce, the Spanish began a heavy cannonade on Society Hill. Under this fire on the 16th, "a party of Negroes" under Mr. Rumer's command performed the labourious task of dragging seven cannon up the hill, and "mounted them in embrasures cut out of the solid rock."[49] It was on this battery, which was within musket-shot of Fort Nassau, that Deveaux hoisted English colours the 18th of April, 1783.[50] Without interruption from that day to this, the British flag has flown over the island.

Col. Deveaux held the governour and five other Spanish officers hostage until certain British merchants and New Providence inhabitants who had been imprisoned in violation of the capitulation of 1782 were released from Morro castle in Havana. Awaiting further instructions from England, Deveaux took former members of the Council and formed a Board of Police to govern the islands.

In his June 6th letter to Sir Guy Carleton, Deveaux ended his version of the siege of Nassau by reminding the commander that he was "an American and a loyalist" who had sacrificed a considerable fortune in South Carolina for his attachment to the crown, and had saved just enough from "the wreck of my lost fortune" to support "this expedition" which has "unfortunately proved too late." Deveaux was not just boasting when he told Carleton that he was known to practically every commander in the southern district.[51] Both he and his father had served as guides to Major General Prevost during his march to Charleston in 1779. After the siege, Lord Cornwallis had appointed Andrew Jr. to captain a regiment which he was to raise himself and called the Royal Forresters.

Colonel Deveaux's father married Catherine Barnwell and lived at Beaufort, South Carolina, where Andrew Jr. was born. In 1767, two warrants for surveys in Colleton County totalling 4,450 acres in the name of Andrew Deveaux appeared in the Council Records.[52] This was only a part of the Deveaux holdings in the Carolinas, but their South Carolina property was confiscated and at the evacuation of Charleston Andrew Sr. went to East Florida. He later emigrated to Cat Island where he had a thriving plantation of "Georgia cotton without bugs."

Andrew Jr. probably inherited his fighting spirit from his father. This story about the elder Andrew was related to Mrs. Parrish. The spunky old gentleman had wearied of privateers raiding his Cat Island plantation so he built a rampart at Gun

Bluff and installed some guns there. On the next pirate raid he was ready and directed the attack while strutting up and down on top of the rampart:

> A well placed shot however, knocked him over and toppled his cocked hat. 'You damn Yankees!' he yelled, as he picked himself up and, waving his sword, continued the work of encouraging his gunners. When [Deveaux's tiny army] made a shot that was too close for safety, the pirates gave up and pulled off.

After he left Nassau, Andrew Jr. maintained a residence in England but visited the islands often. On 22 April 1792 he moved to New York where he married socialite Anna Maria Verplank. He died on 11 July 1812 from lockjaw incurred by a fall and was buried at Red Hook in Duchess County, New York. His father, who was with him the last week of his life, died 23 December 1814 on his Cat Island plantation.[53] The *Bahamas Gazette* eulogized Andrew Sr. as a man of a "very capacious mind, and proved of extreme service to the community ... by his knowledge in several useful arts. He was esteemed as one of the best planters in the Bahamas and was a model of industry and inflexible honesty."[54]

Holding Col. Deveaux in great esteem and overjoyed at their rescue, 110 grateful Nassauvians signed an address to the colonel on 22 May 1783. They too lamented, for his sake, "that the expedition had not been undertaken some weeks sooner" so that he could have been reimbursed for his expenses. However, they had no doubt that the colonel would "meet with a gracious reception from His Majesty, and receive from his royal bounty rewards adequate to your faithful and generous services."[55]

A warm reception from His Majesty was not guaranteed, however; the Spanish were incensed and there were many repercussions. Don Claraco complained loudly to Robert Sterling, the president of the Board of Police, that since Nassau had been taken from him during a time of peace, he wanted restitution of government house stores and the ex-governour's snow, the *Queen of Angels*. Later it was discovered that Deveaux had made no inventories and had kept the snow for his own use, making recompense to Spain difficult.[56]

Unzaga, governour of Havana, sent a letter to Deveaux in August, demanding the return of the Bahama Islands to Spain so he could render them up again to Great Britain as he had been instructed to do before Deveaux had so rudely interfered.[57] When Robert Hunt returned from his Havana prison sometime in September, Deveaux departed for St. Augustine, leaving Mr. Hunt to deal with the problem.

On October 24th, a Captain Andres arrived in Nassau in an American vessel which had found him shipwrecked on the coast of Florida where he had had to leave part of his troops. His force thus reduced in strength, Andres still had the courage to demand that Hunt turn the island over to him. Hunt categorically refused, writing Carleton that he hoped he had done the right thing, but he did not think he should deliver up "these islands at a time emigrations from America were taking place when they seemed to afford the only asylum for these unhappy people."[58]

12

Homeward Bound

Many American Loyalists looked to Abaco, seized by Loyalists during Deveaux's recapture of Nassau, as their new home. The Spanish ex-governour of the Bahamas relayed startling news to the governour of Havana:

> Some families from Florida have taken possession of Abaco Island, seizing the plantations which the people of Providence have there, and it is said that they expect daily the arrival in the islands of many more Florida people.[1]

A look at this and other evidence shows that any refugees coming to the Bahamas before the arrival of the first group of New York evacuees to Abaco early in September, 1783, were actually Bahamian Loyalists returning home.

Rumer's memorial lists those soldiers who were present both at St. Augustine and at Harbour Island during the preparations for the Deveaux expedition that seized Abaco and Nassau. Among those who testified to the vigilance of Robert Rumer during the action were Richard Sweeting, Samuel Higgs and William Lyford, native Bahamians.[2]

There was no urgency to evacuate East Florida at this particular time, but Bahamian Loyalists who left Nassau during the Spanish occupation may have been anxious to return home. General McArthur wrote to Carleton 20 May 1783, "A number of the *old inhabitants* of this Province [East Florida] and *of the Bahama Islands* have given in their names, some to go immediately to Britain (47), others to Jamaica (85), and Providence (90)." (Emphasis added.)

Most refugees did not want to leave St. Augustine and those who had determined to leave did not know where to go. While rumours circulated that Great Britain might exchange Gibraltar for Puerto Rico and the Floridas, there was hope.[3] By June 16th, McArthur announced that the refugees to Jamaica and New Providence would sail "in a few days." The vessels for England were readying but would wait "in case the gentlemen *going* to Providence return with a favourable report." These gentlemen were visiting the Bahamas specifically to study the soil and look at ungranted land, matters crucial to planters. Governour Tonyn could not encourage settlement there. He wrote Townshend that "Providence and the Bahama Islands are mere rocks, fit only for fishermen and the Inhabitants live chiefly by wrecking."[4] Land in the Bahamas, whatever its condition, could not be formally granted until Great Britain had purchased the islands from the Lords Proprietors, a transaction as yet incomplete.

On 25 June, Carleton received a memorial from four hundred New York refugees who desired to settle on Abaco, and on 14 July he ordered Lt. Wilson to the Bahamas with detailed instructions to find the best harbour, inspect "the face and nature of the country, soil and produce, and state of cultivation. . . ." As the island of Abaco was reported to be more fertile than Providence, he was to extend his inquiries and "report on that Island . . . in the most particular manner."[5] Unfortunately these orders did not reach Wilson in St. Augustine until 12 September. By then the first group of New York Loyalists had already arrived on Abaco.

Like the refugees at New York, Lewis Johnson had also heard much about Abaco and had made a special effort to visit the island in July, 1783. He found a "narrow slip of land running along a Bay for about 8 miles with not more than 200 acres vacant" of what he estimated to be a total of 1500 acres of land. The best soil was disappointing and the people were ignorant of cultivation because they had not "as yet turned their minds that way." Bahamians never visited the surrounding cays "with any other view than Wrecking, Turtling, and cutting Timber." On the whole Johnson felt that it was doubtful that any more than eight or ten Blacks could be profitably employed on any one plantation he had seen. The notes written in the margin of Johnson's report were probably put there by President Hunt. The commentator remarked that only rice plantations employed more than twenty-five people on any one settlement and felt that although Mr. Johnson was a man of the "strictest honor and Veracity, other gentlemen are now on the Islands for whom Accounts of Soil may be Daily expected, who are very proper judges."[6]

Since he had not yet received Carleton's new orders, Lt. Wilson sailed to the Bahamas on the 20th of July and confined his investigation almost exclusively to New Providence. He returned to St. Augustine on 30 August with a report which fell "far short" of Carleton's expectations. The gentlemen, a "Committee of Prospective Settlers" from St. Augustine, also submitted an unfavourable report.[7] Neither Johnson's, the committee's, nor Wilson's first report reached Carleton before the Loyalists from New York had departed for Abaco.

Sometime in April Carleton had received final orders to evacuate New York, and the processing of loyalist exiles continued through the month of November, 1783. (See plate 26.) In a letter to the President of Congress dated 17 August

PLATE 26

New York City, its skyline dominated by Trinity Church, remained a loyalist stronghold until the final evacuation in 1783.

Carleton stated that in spite of his orders to accelerate the evacuation, "the violence in the Americans . . . increased the number of their countrymen to look to me for escape from threatened destruction." These "terrors" have of late been such that "almost all within these lines conceive the safety both of their property and of their lives depends upon their being removed by me, which renders it impossible to say when the evacuation can be completed."[8]

On June 25th, a committee representing upwards of four hundred Loyalists "already Engaged to Settle the Island of Abbaco" applied to Sir Guy Carleton for:

> A small Military Force . . . to Protect them against the Deprivations [sic] of Evil minded Persons, a Few Canon, Amunition &c. for their better Defence . . . a Vessel to carry a few Horses, and Horned Cattle; and as Saw Mills cannot be Erected on the Island, request that Crosscut, and Whip Saws may be furnished, for the purpose of Clearing the Lands, also Two Setts of Tools for Black Smiths, and some Coals.

Thomas Stephens, John Davis, Henry Smith, John L. Pintard, and Thomas Victor signed the request and enclosed a sketch of Little Harbour, their intended settlement. The committee also enclosed the following relatively accurate description of the island:

> The Island of Abbaco . . . is Blessed with a good Harbour, and well secured by Nature, with 18 Foot of Water on the Bar, and within the Harbour 24 feet Water.
>
> The Island abounds with Timber, Fir, Madeira Wood, Mahogany, Fustick, Lignum Vitae, Brazeleto, Logwood, and Sundry Woods fit for dying. The Soil is Capable of Producing all the West India Produce &c.
>
> The Utility and Advantage that may arise in Settling and fortifying Little Harbour is well known to all the Navigators in that part, all Ships or Vessels from Havana and South America, especially the Galloons [sic] on their returning come within Seven Leagues of the Island. The said Island is Key to all the Bahamia Islands, being the First Landmade, and a place of Resort for Whalers, who catch a Number of Spermacita Whales of[f] the Island and cut them up there. There is also Timber on the Island of Red Cedar large enough to Build Ships of Three Hundred and fifty Tons, which are cutt of[f] the Island, by People of the neighbouring Islands, and Supplies the Windward Islands with Cedars for Building Vessells, Mahogany &c.[9]

The brief mention of the soil indicates that the main interest of these four hundred people would not be planting; many in fact were soldiers. Three days later Richard Blake, as chairman of the committee, recommended to Carleton that he appoint as agents for the group Captains Thomas Stephens and Patrick Kennedy of the Pennsylvania and Maryland Corps respectively, "whom the prospective settlers have long known and under whose direction many of them served occasionally in the defence of Pensacola. . . ." The memorial further stated that these Loyalists at New York had had the understanding that "your Excellency has been pleased to declare

your purpose of accommodating them to grants of Lands in the Island of Abbaco"
and that they had reason to believe that "near One Thousand Persons" from St.
Augustine would join them.

The memorialists had some knowledge of the Florida exiles and stated that
many "are shipwrights, above thirty are masters of vessels, that they own small vessels convenient for the navigation of those islands." Most of these Florida Loyalists
had been driven from their settlements at Pensacola and had made new ones at St.
Augustine "from which they have been exiled." They "therefore, most earnestly en-
treat your Excellency's attention to the *Security* of the grants" because they fear
being driven out of Abaco "to seek a further Asylum in other parts of the Empire."[10]

There were several reasons for this New York-West Florida tie. In 1775 Royal
Proclamation had established West Florida as a haven for refugees. Between 1775
and 1781 hundreds of emigrants not only from the nearby southern colonies but
from New England as well flooded the Province. Troops captured by the Spanish at
the Siege of Pensacola were first taken to Havana, then sent to New York.[11]

An advertisement that appeared in both the June 28th and July 7th issues of
Rivington's *Gazette* may have lured some planters to Abaco but they were ulti-
mately disappointed. This was an outrageous description of the Bahama Islands
resurrected from something called the "Political Essay, concerning the State of the
British Empire." Although some of the statements are accurate, the description on
the whole is misleading in that the writer greatly embellished the facts. His unfortunate readers were perhaps more eager than discerning.

> The Bahama Islands are very considerable ... all accounts that we have
> had of them render their great fertility beyond a doubt; and the extraordinary
> flavor of their Pine Apples, and other spontaneous fruit which far exceed any
> other in that part of the world, added to their climate, which is excessively
> favourable, and never reached by the least frosts, leave upon the whole, little
> doubt but that Sugar, and all other West-Indian commodities might be pro-
> duced in them in great perfection; ... The truth is they are not half discovered;
> some, which are known, are quite uncultivated and uninhabited, though blessed
> with as fruitful and luxuriant a soil as any in the World, as appears plainly by the
> richness and fragrance of the spontaneous growths: By many accounts, even
> the famous Tinian itself does not exceed some of these beautiful Islands of
> which yet we have left so many details.
>
> The Island of Albico ... is among the most fruitful in produce, and the
> most important to the British Government, and wants only inhabitants, and a
> small degree of cultivation, to render it as flourishing as any of the West-India
> Islands. [12]

During July and August a few vessels came to New York from the Bahamas, and
some of these may have been commissioned to help carry exiles to Abaco. The
Gazette advertised that the brig *Loyalist*, under Master Isaiah Valleau, bound for
Nova Scotia, was "new, well found and fast sailing." If the *Loyalist* was otherwise
engaged in August, perhaps Valleau captained another vessel and went to Abaco at

some point; for he received a forty acre grant on Man-O-War Cay in 1789. The Schooner *Nancy*, under Captain McDougall, arrived in New York in July, bringing turtle, limes, oranges, logwood, lignum vitae, and "Mahogany bedsteads in the ruff." The *Nancy* may have carried some of the August departures to Abaco and was also listed as available for the November group of exiles. At some time between the 9th and 13th of August, the schooner *Rover*, under Captain McKenny, arrived from Abaco.[13]

On July 5th, the *Gazette* ran the Abaco advertisement again and included one additional enticement to fishers. "Vast quantities of delicious TURTLE are caught on the Banks [of Abaco] . . . within . . . a hundred yards of the Island. Great Number of Whales are taken. There were 14 sail of vessels about three weeks ago, successfully employed in the Whale Fishery; they cut up the Blubber on the Island."

This issue also "informed the public" that:

> . . . upwards of Fifteen Hundred Loyal Inhabitants from St. Augustine and other parts of East-Florida have actually engaged to join more that Two Hundred Families, which [at] last are on the point of immediate departure from this port, with every accommodation necessary to establish a Settlement upon the aforesaid Island of Abaco. The last meeting of the Subscribers in the City of New-York will be held this Evening, at Mr. John Davis's, at the Sign of Lord Rodney's Victory, North-River.[14]

On 10 August Brooks Watson, the Commissary General, informed the adjutant general that "a Number of Loyal Americans amounting to near a Thousand Souls . . . [were] about to embark for Abbaco. . . ." He requested the authority to ship six months' provisions and to pay a commissary to oversee their issue on the island. Watson recommended Philip Dumaresq for the position at seven shillings sixpence per day. Mr. Dumaresq was a clerk in his department "with a large Family rendered destitute by heavy losses at Boston, whence this Family have been driven."[15]

At best, records regarding American Loyalists are scant. Generally information is available only because a problem or catastrophe resulted in heated correspondence or newspaper headlines. In the case of the departure of the first American Loyalists for Abaco, meticulous records were kept because of the issue of the black refugees. The seventh article of the Provisional Treaty expressly prohibited "carrying away any NEGROES, or other Property of the American Inhabitants. . . ." Carleton had to take a stand and since he was responsible for *all* Loyalists who sought refuge within his lines, he stood by the Blacks. Carleton's decision quelled some fears, yet Boston King, a black Baptist preacher, recalled the anguish and terror "when we saw our old masters, coming from Virginia, North Carolina, and other parts, and seizing upon their slaves in the streets of New-York, or even dragging them out of their beds."[16]

Many Blacks had come to the city "in consequence of Royal Proclamations promising them Protection and Liberty." Carleton believed that "no minister can by a Treaty disannull those Proclamations." Moreover, it would be "inhuman to the last Degree and a base Violation of Public Faith to send those Negroes back to their Masters who would beat them with the utmost Cruelty. Accordingly, such Negroes as came in by Virtue of those Proclamations are permitted to go *wherever they please*." (Emphasis added.) Carleton proposed that Washington appoint commissions to inspect all embarkations and take "an account of all Negroes that go away." Any complaints by Americans would be referred to "future discussion" and compensation would be granted if warranted. This inspection of embarkations resulted in a certified register called the "Book of Negroes." (See appendix D.)[17]

On the 21st and 22nd of August respectively the "ship *Nautilus*, Mr. Kildare Williamson, commander," and the *William*, transport, John Coom, Master." departed New York bound for Abaco. With good weather they would arrive in about ten days.

Of the eighty adult Blacks going to Abaco, sixty-six had surnames, and twenty-two claimed to be free by birth, governour's certificate, or manumission by gift or by purchase. One Joseph Scott stated that he was born free and had worked as a carpenter in Charleston. A man named Tom had escaped from Cape Francois. Another man, Joseph Paul, and his wife sailed with their three children aboard the *Nautilus*. At the time of embarkation Paul told the inspectors that he had purchased his freedom from Lawrence Cartwright of New York, and Susannah, his wife, had likewise purchased her freedom from a Mr. Brown, also of New York. Joseph Paul's religious work in the Bahamas demonstrates a valuable contribution made by this black Loyalist. The Methodist minister, Mr. George Huxtable, wrote that Joseph Paul had been converted to Methodism when "that mighty man of God, George Whitfield, was preaching in America."[18] At the time of embarkation the Pauls were indentured to Captain Patrick Kennedy but although the terms of these indentures are unknown, the Pauls may have stayed in Abaco less than a year. Samuel Kelly visited Nassau in 1784 and may have been referring to Joseph Paul when he remarked:

> The inhabitants of Nassau were dissipated in the extreme, and from night revels many had injured their health. I saw little appearance of any religion, but heard that a man of colour frequently preached to the eastward of the town under a large spreading tree.

The Reverend Mr. Huxtable wrote that a congregation of three hundred gathered with Paul "every Sunday afternoon under the shade of the magnificent tamarind tree." Under Paul's leadership, a little church, "at the corner of Augusta and Heathfield streets" was built by Blacks after working hours and on beautiful moonlit nights. Paul's church, a solid stone structure which could seat three hundred people, was the "first Methodist Church ever built in the Bahama Islands." Joseph Paul was also the first master of the Associates School, the first private school for Blacks in Nassau.[19]

Over half the number of Blacks (44) scheduled to embark from New York stated that they had "left" their owners during the war. The number of years these people had absented themselves in order to gain their freedom had ranged from two to seven years, yet next to each of the eighty names were recorded the "names of

persons in whose possession they are now." One of the commissioners who super-
vised the embarkation wrote a certificate of freedom for two of the refugees. "The
Bearers, William Willis and Hester his wife, both free Negroes, are inspected and
passed." The document was dated New York, August 22, 1783, and signed by
William Armstrong. The "Book of Negroes" describes William Willis as a "stout
lusty man" of thirty-nine, who stated at the inspection that one Joseph Pente of New
York had given him and his wife their freedom "ten years agoe." In spite of this certificate, both William and Hester were indentured to John Cameron at the point of
departure. Later William Willis had to repurchase his wife from Cameron for £25.[20]
Since Carleton had allowed free Blacks to emigrate to Nova Scotia unindentured,
why he bound those going to the Bahamas and the exact terms of their indenture are
not known.

Most of the thirty-one white persons "possessed" only one or two Blacks. The
term ownership must have carried a loose connotation here, for it appears that over
eighty percent of the black refugees were free, a statistic which may also give an indication of the cause of the 1788 Abaco slave revolt.

There is every reason to believe that the thirty-one Whites embarked on those
transports, but there is no absolute proof of this since the passenger list consists of
Blacks only. There may have been other white refugees on those transports as well
and other vessels may have gone in the convoy. It is certain others left for Abaco at a
later date.

Four Blacks listed as belonging to one Cornelius Blanchard embarked on the
William August 22nd but Blanchard did not sail with them. He arrived in Abaco a
month later aboard the *Charlotte*. Rivington's *Gazette* of 13 September 1783 advertised the following:

> For ABACCO and PROVIDENCE, the Brigantine CHARLOTTE, to sail in
> eight days from the date hereof: For Freight of Passage, apply to Mr. John
> Davis, at the sign of Rodney's Conquest, Bottom of Little Queen-street, on the
> North-River, or to the Master on Board, lying at the same Wharf.
> September 12.   Peter Carter [Captain][21]

Eight days from the 12th would have been the 20th. The *Charlotte* set sail on the
21st and although no embarkation appears in any of the New York newspapers, this
date is confirmed by a later document. In April, 1785, Cornelius Blanchard delivered a memorial to Lt. Governour Powell "in behalf of the poor Inhabitants settled at Carleton upon the Island of Abaco." He explained that Guy Carleton had
"appointed him Captain of a Company of Loyal refugees . . . whereupon your Petitioner accordingly left New York on the 21st of September, 1783, and arrived at
Carleton the place of his destination." By coordinates indicated in later documents
Carleton must have been located at Black Point or what is now known as Treasure
Cay, Abaco.[22]

Since Carleton was the destination of the *Charlotte*, it is reasonable to assume
that it was the destination of the *Nautilus* and the *William* as well. It is unlikely
Blanchard would have sent his people ahead unless he planned to join them later.

PLATES 27 and 28
In these two original oil paintings Alton Lowe has personified both the Loyalists and their "people" in the symbolic persons of two women, one of whom looks to the sea as the other looks to the land. (Courtesy of the Albert Lowe Museum.)

The question remains—why did the first four hundred Loyalists of the 25 June memorial change their minds? Despite all the utilitarian and advantageous reasons for "settling and fortifying Little Harbour," the site seems to have been rejected by the prospective settlers even before Wilson submitted his report. The person who accompanied Wilson and McArthur to Abaco in February, 1784, remarked that, leaving Spencers Bight, "we dropped down to Little Harbour—Lieutenant Wilson intended to Survey that place But the depth of Water in the Bay not answering His Expectations he only Sketched off the Harbour." Later, Loyalists from East Florida settled near there at Spencers Bight to the north and Cherokee Sound or Eight Mile Bay nine miles south of Little Harbour.[23] Later documents prove that Captain Thomas Stephens, one of the signers of the 25 June Memorial, became agent for this first group and desembarked at Carleton. Whether or not he came on the transports in August or on the *Charlotte* in September is not certain. The only certainty is that Carleton was the first settlement established by Loyalists who embarked from New York August 21 and 22 and arrived at Abaco about the 1st of September, 1783.

There may have been more than 127 refugees in this first group of American Revolutionary War exiles to arrive in the Bahamas. What is most significant is that sixty-six of them were black Loyalists. What did these people think about, and what did they do during that month while they waited for the others to arrive? In such a

desolate place, the full realization of exile must have struck many of them. They had been marooned, or so it must have felt to them. These refugees tramped over Black Point where the rocky terrain wore down their shoe leather as black thoughts wore down their spirits and stamina. (See plates 27 and 28.) Perhaps some black and white settlers pulled together and at least tried to move some of the rocks and began to plant. The disputes at Carleton may not have begun until after the arrival of the *Charlotte* with its more affluent passengers who could afford to emigrate in a private vessel as opposed to government transport. Also, Cornelius Blanchard who arrived in the *Charlotte* stated that "on their arrival, not finding the country so fertile as had been expected, certain commotions arose...."[24]

John Harding, agent for the loyal inhabitants, wrote a letter dated "Island of Abaco, Carleton Town, October 1, 1783" probably the very day the *Charlotte* arrived. The memorial to Sir Guy Carleton from these angry, depressed, and seasick refugees "Most Humbly Sheweth

That your Memorialists find themselves in want of many necessaries that cannot be obtained at any Price, and they find it will be impossible for them to clear the Land, Plant it, and Reap the Fruits of their Labour Sooner than Twelve or Fourteen months, therefore Prays your Excellency will be pleased to

Grant them the following small request of an addition Six Months Provisions, a few rolls of Osnaburgs, a Thousand pair of Military Shoes, some nails (6 casks) for building of Houses, a Cross-cut saw (for 6 Families) . . . a few whip saws (12), some medicines as the People are Landed very sickly from the Ships . . . .[25]

This memorial was probably sent by the brig *Charlotte*, which would return to New York after stopping at New Providence.

Meanwhile, back in New York, the list of civil prisoners grew longer; the chief crime, robbery. On 11 October Thomas Willet submitted to Guy Carleton a memorial "in behalf of the Loyalists whose names are annexed" stating that:

. . . your memorialists are obliged from their attachment to their Sovereign and Mother Country to quit this place and seek refuge in some place where they may enjoy that freedom that will shortly be denied them here, that for that purpose they have pitched upon the Island of Abbacco as the place of their residence. . . .[26]

Henry Welfling may have been one of the Loyalists who contracted to go to Abaco with Willet's group. He submitted an individual memorial to Carleton on 20 October 1783. In it, Welfling explained that "on account of the active part he had taken in behalf of Government, [he] was obliged to leave his home and possessions in Philadelphia as early as the year 1778 and take refuge in this city." Being far advanced in age and with an aged wife to support, he had returned to Philadelphia at the end of the war "in hopes of being permitted again to reside there, but was thrown into confinement where he remained until *Ten Weeks after* the arrival and publication of the Provisional Articles of Peace, and was lately ordered away by some of the lawless Committee in that city." (Emphasis added.) This destitute old man declared that he "has not in the least Degree been troublesome or an expence to government" but needed help now because he intended "shortly to go to Abico, one of the Bahama Islands, with his family."[27]

On 21 October Carleton sent a letter to Major General Mathew in the West Indies. "A number of loyal Refugees have lately removed from hence to the Bahama Islands and I expect more will go there from East Florida in the course of the Winter." Carleton explained that he had sent all the provisions he could spare and requested that Mathew send more, "rum excepted," from the islands under his command to General McArthur at New Providence.[28]

At a "respectable meeting of Loyalists" at John Davis's house on Monday, the 28th of October, a third group drew up a memorial on behalf of 509 persons who desired to emigrate to Abaco and nominated Samuel Hake to be chairman of the group.[29] Since this group of Loyalists was the last to embark at New York, it is possible, at this point, to estimate the total number of Abaco emigrants from New York.

On 10 August, Watson reported that "near a Thousand Souls" were *going* to Abaco. Thomas Stephens signed a "Return of the number of Loyalists *gone* to the Island of Abbaco as Per Returns left in the Commissary General's Office." He reported a total of 941 people: men—217, women—118, children over ten years of age—95, children under ten years of age—108, servants—403.[30] Unfortunately, this document is undated. Since Thomas Stephens' name appeared in the memorial of the first group of Loyalists and since 941 is "near a Thousand," these numbers may represent the first group alone. This number would include persons who sailed aboard the *Nautilus*, the *William*, and the *Charlotte* as well as Thomas Stephens himself, who was at Carleton by October 1st, but would exclude Willet's undisclosed number and Hake's group of 509 people. Mary Moseley stated that "All told, 1,458 loyalists embarked at New York for Abaco, according to an official return of the Commissary-

PLATE 29: On 21 September, 1783, the brigantine *Charlotte* sailed for Abaco from the bottom of Little Queen Street on the North River, New York City. The *Hope* proposed to sail from Little Water Street in the East River on about 4 November. (Courtesy of the New-York Historical Society.)

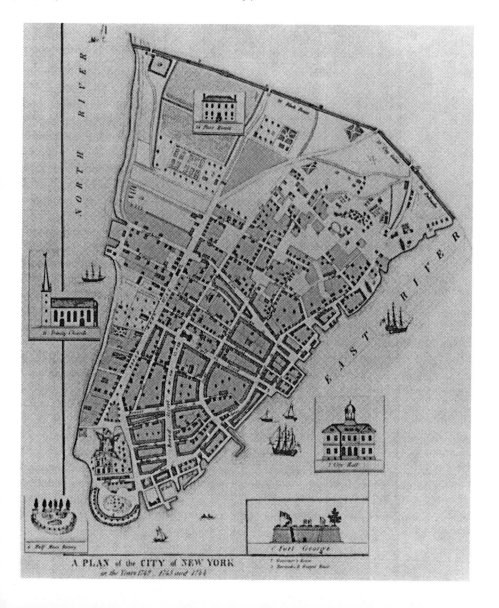

A PLAN of the CITY of NEW YORK
in the Years 1742, 1743 and 1744

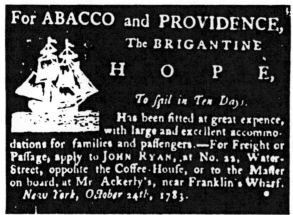

For ABACCO and PROVIDENCE,
The BRIGANTINE
H O P E,
To fail in Ten Days.
Has been fitted at great expence,
with large and excellent accommo-
dations for families and paffengers.—For Freight or
Paffage, apply to JOHN RYAN, at No. 22, Water-
Street, oppofite the Coffee-Houfe, or to the Mafter
on board, at Mr Ackerly's, near Franklin's Wharf.
New York, October 24th, 1783.

PLATE 30
Advertisements such as this
one in the *Royal Gazette* of 25
October 1783 were common as
Loyalists sought transport to the
Bahamas. (Courtesy of the
New-York Historical Society.)

General, dated two days before the British troops evacuated that port [23 November 1783];" however, this particular return cannot be found among the British Head-quarters Papers. Stephens' number of 941 and Hake's 509 add up to 1,450, only eight short of Moseley's figure. If Willet's group included only eight people, he may have joined Hake's group after Hake's number had been submitted, bringing the total to the same figure of 1,458.[31]

Looking back at Stephens' return of 403 "servants," it becomes clear that in-spections were made only on the government transports, not on chartered vessels; however, the possibility of Loyalists smuggling Blacks out of New York cannot be dis-counted.

Because refugees embarked as vessels became available, fixing the dates of de-parture becomes difficult. In his 30 October communication to Guy Carleton, Hake en-closed a list of vessels that *"can be* chartered for Abbico viz:" Schooner *Christian* Captain William Kennedy (65 tons), Brig *Hope* Captain Ryan (120 tons), Brig *Char-lotte* Captain Carter (90 tons), Schooner *Felicity* Captain Victor (100 tons), Schooner *Nancy* Captain Ridley (85 tons), Schooner *Two Friends* Captain Trotter (80 tons), Ship *Elizabeth* Captain Johnson (250 tons), Schooner *De Lancey* Captain Thomas Brown (75 tons). [32]

In an advertisement dated 24 October, Rivington's *Gazette* announced the sailing of the Brig *Hope* in ten days. "For freight or passage apply to John Ryan, at No. 22, Water-street." (See plates 29 and 30.) Perhaps Willet's group and some of Hake's people were prepared to sail on the *Hope's* proposed departure date of 4 November. Many refugees still had to settle their affairs and time was running out. John Davis, at whose house the respectable meeting of Loyalists was held, entered a notice in the 25 October issue of Rivington's *Gazette* that he intended "to leave this city very soon" and desired all concerned to submit claims and pay their debts to him. The houses and lots of William and Thomas Smith would have to be auctioned at public vendue on 10 November if they were not sold before then. The schooner *Felicity*, "a remarkable fine vessel," was offered for sale November 1st. Perhaps Captain Victor had to sell his boat in order to settle his debts before emigrating to Abaco.[33]

Rivington's *Gazette* announced that a meeting for all Loyalists who intended to settle at Abaco would be held at 11 o'clock on Wednesday, November 5th. Alexander McGee and John Martin, two Abaco emigrants, were asked "to call at No. 32 Queen Street" to pick up papers left at the Board of Claims. The *New York Morning Post* carried this final notice:

> All those Loyalists, who intend to settle at the island of Abbico, are requested to attend the Board appointed by his Excellency the Commander in Chief at the City Hall this morning from Eleven to Two o'clock, November 7, 1783.[34]

On 12 November the Commissary General advertised for "all persons having square-rigged vessels to Let, for Great Britain, the West Indies, Bahama Islands or Nevis" to send an account of said vessels to his office.[35]

About this time some of these future Abaco Loyalists had time to play politics amid the hustle and bustle of the final evacuation of New York City. On 30 October, George Shaw, William Kennedy and Thomas Victor made a statement that they were unaware of the erasement of Mr. Hake's name as chairman of their committee from the memorial which was presented to Carleton in behalf of the Abaco settlers.[36] Mr. Hake explained to his friends and "the respectable public" that Captain John Davis had recommended that Joshua H. Smith, Esquire, draw up the memorial because Smith's brother was the Chief Justice and would recommend their petition to Carleton. The committee agreed. The next afternoon Mr. Hake and Captain Shaw called upon Mr. Smith to find that Captain Davis had already delivered the document, "unopened," he said, to the Chief Justice, and then had taken it directly to headquarters. The next morning when the committee called upon Major McKenzie for an answer, Mr. Hake "discovered the erasement of his own name." When questioned in the presence of the committee, Joshua H. Smith admitted that he had erased Mr. Hake's name but gave no reason for so doing.[37]

Business of the "utmost consequence" requiring his "immediate attendance in England" prevented Samuel Hake from emigrating to Abaco with the others. The committee, on behalf of the Abaco settlers, wrote a letter, published in Gaine's *Gazette* on Monday, 10 November 1783, thanking Mr. Hake for the work he had done to assist their departure:

> Sir,
>
> The great attention which you have paid to the suffering Loyalists in general . . . and to the intended emigrants to the Island of Abbaco, impelled with gratitude, this Committee takes the earliest opportunity of returning our unfeigned acknowledgements for your persevering, in rendering all those advantages which his Excellency the Commander in Chief has most happily coincided with our most sanguine expectations. And though it is with reluctance that we cannot have your immediate agency in this object, in consequence of your receiving recent accounts from England that your personal attendance is required, not only in your own private concerns, but conjoined with the interest of the suffering Loyalists.

Permit us to assure you, in your absence that we shall anticipate the pleasure of an early period, when you will resume the agency, and with hearts animated with the warmest friendship, we have the honor to be, in behalf of the Committee, with the highest esteem, Sir, your most obedient Servants.

Samuel Hake, Esq.   [Signed] George Shaw, William
New York   Kennedy, Thomas Victor.[38]

On 12 November, Rivington published the same letter, followed by Mr. Hake's "sincere wishes" that the settlers might succeed in their enterprise and enjoy true liberty in the Bahamas. "I promise myself the pleasure, in the course of a few months, of participating with you."

In that same issue William Kennedy, who had obviously not read the letter he signed, announced "to the intended Inhabitants of Abbaco" that he thought he had signed a letter of thanks to Sir Guy Carleton and not to Mr. Hake.[39] Whatever difference this made at such a crucial period in their lives will never be known. This sort of political bickering is indicative of future outbursts of temper which characterized their brief stay on the island of Abaco where these exiled Loyalists liberally exercised their freedom of speech.

Captain Kennedy may have had legitimate complaints against Mr. Hake or the letter may have simply struck a raw nerve. Although 221 people signed an address to the "ability as well as the Invincible Loyalty of Samuel Hake Esquire," not everyone felt the same way concerning his character. The son of an eminent clothier, he had been called a busybody, a fraud, even a damned scoundrel, but his loyalty to Great Britain had never been questioned. At the risk of his life, Hake carried to General Clinton through enemy lines an address signed in behalf of 2,300 Loyalists.[40]

Samuel Hake married the daughter of Robert Gilbert Livingston and probably used his father-in-law's money for his own failing business. It was Hake's brother-in-law who called him a damned scoundrel and accused Samuel of treating his wife cruelly. If this was true, Hake may have had cause for regret. In 1777, his wife Helena met a horrible death at Rynbeck, the Livingston family estate on the North River. Samuel had thought his family would be safe there with his father-in-law while he returned to England, but a party of rebels came at night and set fire to the house. When Helena and the childred tried to flee, the rebels drove her back inside although the children managed to escape.[41]

Several days after his controversy with Mr. Hake, Captain Kennedy and the *Christian* probably sailed to Abaco with a boatload of refugees. It is hoped that Carleton completed the evacuation of Loyalists and troops from New York ten days after Kennedy's departure; for on 25 November, "American troops marched from Harlem in Bowery Lane and took possession of the City." (See plate 31.) Mr. Rivington gratefully reported the tranquility of the procession which "Proceeded down Queen-Street, and through the Broadway, to Cape'sTavern." After dinner, the company drank a series of toasts, the first of which was to the "United States of America." The eleventh,"May America be an asylum to the persecuted of the Earth," obviously did not include their own American Loyalists.[42]

PLATE 31: Despite their hope that America might be an "asylum to the persecuted of the earth," rebel sympathies were not extended to the Loyalists, shown here evacuating New York City with British troops in Howard Pyle's painting.

13

"Double, Double, Toil and Trouble"

Governour Patrick Tonyn proclaimed on 29 April 1783 that the evacuation of East Florida "probably will not be effected during the course of the summer, as there are no accounts of the definitive treaty of peace being signed." But, any inhabitants" who may not be employed in agriculture, and are desirous of taking the earliest opportunity of departing," should submit their names and destinations to the Secretary's Office.[1]

In the Province of East Florida confusion reigned. Tonyn, while beseiged with petitions to implore Great Britain to keep the Floridas, tried to provide for the refugees still pouring into St. Augustine as well as to evaluate Loyalists' estates for claims. Hordes of transients from Georgia and South Carolina invaded the city to steal Blacks. The troops mutinied and several were killed in an aborted attempt to burn the barracks, plunder the town, take the fort, arm the Blacks, and kill every white man that opposed their efforts to keep the country. The soldiers had vowed to die rather "than be carried to Halifax to be discharged. . . ."[2]

Indian hatred for the Spanish ran deep and stretched back over two hundred years to the time of the bloody tyrant Hernando de Soto. If the "Great King" would not send ships for them too, the Indians were resolved to fight. "We will not submit, nor will we welcome the Spaniards, who were the murderers of our grandfathers. . . ." Cowkeeper and other Indian chiefs swore vengeance "against the King that gave away their country," and when the English left they were determined to kill every Spaniard who "sets his head out of the Lines of the town." Claraco relayed to Governour Ungaza at Havana rumours he had heard in Nassau that the Indians in East Florida were killing ten to twelve English every day "because they are turning over the Province to the Spanish." Also some three thousand Loyalist refugees had "rebelled." Tonyn requested that Colonel Brown, Superintendent of Indians, remain in East Florida until the final evacuation. The Indians felt betrayed by Great Britain and many desired to leave with their loyalist friends. Carleton opposed their leaving and was perhaps mistaken in his belief that "the Bahamas were poorly adapted to their mode of life."[3]

On 22 August 1783 Commander Carleton sent to General McArthur instructions for the disposal of troops, outlining the advantages to those who chose Nova Scotia. He had no objection, however, to soldiers being discharged at St. Augustine or in the Bahamas. "Some refugees from this place have gone to make an establishment" on Abaco and Cat Islands. However, he could not give them any encouragement because he knew nothing of the "tenure of the lands" or if the king had any land to grant there. The Royal Artillery must remain in East Florida until the completion of the evacuation, but McArthur was ordered to New Providence as soon as the troops disbanded in order to take command of the Bahama Islands until a governour arrived. Carleton expressed his intention of recommending McArthur for that appointment.[4]

The Definitive Treaty of Peace between England and Spain, signed at Paris, 3 September 1783, gave Governour Tonyn eighteen months from its ratification to evacuate East Florida. At least ten thousand Loyalists would emigrate, perhaps more. When evacuation had been completed, Tonyn believed as many as four thousand refugees "'passed into the interior parts of America among the mountains'" and reported that 1,033 Whites and 2,214 Blacks had emigrated to the Bahamas.[5]

Problems increased, delaying transport. A group of lawless men calling themselves *banditti* presented even a worse threat now that the troops were leaving. McArthur wrote Carleton on September 15th suggesting to him that the garrison on the way to the Bahamas stop in St. Augustine and remain there until the final evacuation. Little did he know that the final removal of Loyalists would not be completed until September, 1785, or that those troops would be needed in Nassau to check the disorder caused by the rush of loyalist refugees into that town.

In this same correspondence McArthur enclosed an anxious plea from the East Florida inhabitants. Now near the end of their tether, Carolina and Georgia refugees impoverished by one evacuation could see no light of fortune at the end of this one. Even if money dropped out of the sky, "to freight bottoms to convey them away . . . *neither the Bahamas nor Nova Scotia will suit persons with large gangs of Negroes.*" Nor was there any hope of being allowed to return to their former homes. Now with the withdrawal of troops they had no choice but to sacrifice themselves to "Murder, Rapine and Plunder." Was this to be the reward for their loyalty? With these sentiments, the lieutenant governour, the Council and House of Assembly, and principal inhabitants of East Florida wished their general "every happiness and prosperity."[6]

Lord North's final orders, dated 4 December 1783, regarding the evacuation of East Florida reached Tonyn and on 7 February 1784, he published a proclamation assuring the Loyalists that "a considerable quantity of Shipping" would be supplied for their removal. Tonyn also announced that the purchase of the Bahama Islands had been proposed to Great Britain so that grants of land could be made to those who chose to move there. Removal from East Florida should be accomplished by 19 March 1785 although Article V of the treaty also provided for an extension if the Spanish governour approved.[7]

Before the arrival of the Spanish governour in East Florida, a congress with the chiefs of the Creek and Chickasaw Indians was held at Pensacola on 31 June 1783, with Governour Miro of Louisiana and Lt. Col. Arthur O'Neill, Commandant of Pensacola, presiding. Through an interpreter, Lt. Gov. Miro told the chiefs "'that peace had taken place between their old friends the English and the Great King, His Master, but that the English from the bad fortune of war had been obliged to give up to him all the country bounding the sea as far as Georgia; and that the Great King had ordered him to tell the Great Chickasaw and Creek Nations that he wished to be on good terms of friendship and trade with them.'"

One of the chiefs replied to the "little King of the Spaniards" that:

> ... they acknowledged no nations their superior; and never would be under either the Spanish or French, [n]or the undutiful children termed the American government; that notwithstanding their beloved brethren had begot undutiful sons, whose ingratitude had caused the mountains to tumble on their aged parents' head, and had obliged them to quit their Red Brethren for a while; yet the steady Chickasaws and Creeks never would forsake them. That they had no obligations to be on good terms with the Spaniards....

However, the chiefs had no objection to trading with the Spanish if the goods were English-made and delivered by English traders. The governour assured them that trading would be carried on under those conditions. Then he asked "if in the event of war between the Spaniards and the English might the Great King, His Master, depend on the friendship of the great Chickasaw and Creek nations?'"

At this, one of the Creek chiefs named Mad Dog, "a very sensible man and brave warrior, started up, his eyes darting fire and his countenance distorted with rage, and in a most vehement tone of voice" desired the interpreter to say:

> No ... No ... No! Our beloved brethren the English saw us born, they have nourished us from our infancy and have ever been our faithful and steady friends. They taught us to make war and discovered to us the blessings of peace. They clothed us when we were naked and fed us when we were hungry. They fought for us and with us and we with them. They never deceived us nor shall we deceive them. Tell him all this and tell him further that the rivers shall sooner cease to run and the trees of the forest to grow than the Chickasaws and Creeks desert their friends the English.

This "spirited Expression" drew tears not only from some of the Englishmen, but also from the governour who let drop "a sympathetic tear that spoke more effectively than all the studied ornaments of language." The governour told Mad Dog that he applauded "his steadiness to his old friends" and asked only some share in that friendship.[8]

On 12 July 1784, Vincente Manuel de Zespedes took possession of St. Augustine with proper ceremony, witnessed by a "considerable number of loyal British subjects" who were still in St. Augustine awaiting an opportunity to emigrate.[9] Some of those Loyalists refused to leave East Florida and even contemplated a major military action to insure their stay.

Near the end of October, John Cruden, as president of the British American Loyalists "still in East Florida," sent two memorials; one to Zespedes asking for a grant of land "Lying betwixt the St. Johns and St. Marys Rivers" and the other to John Maxwell, Governour of the Bahamas, requesting "a quantity of provisions." Both petitions outlined their dreadful alternatives of returning to our Homes, to receive insult worse than Death to Men of Spirit, or to run the hazzard of being Murderd in Cold Blood, to Go to the inhospitable Regions of Nova Scotia or take refuge in the Barren Rocks of the Bahamas where poverty and wretchedness stares us in the face, Or do what our Spirits cannot brook ... renounce our Country, Drug the Religion of our Fathers and become Spanish Subjects.

To Maxwell, the Loyalists concluded that rather than accept any of those wretched alternatives, "we will die with our Swords in our hands for we are almost driven to despair." Maxwell replied that Cruden should advise his associates to embark immediately. When they arrived in the Bahamas, each would receive six months' provisions and land to cultivate for their immediate needs until permanent grants could be made. Cruden went to the Bahamas but stubbornly refused to relinquish his dream. From Nassau he wrote Zespedes and proposed restoring Canada to France. With Spain as Britain's ally, the American Loyalists would fight to regain their "own Country." Zespedes wrote Cruden off as a "restless soul" and a somewhat fanatic visionary.[10]

During the final months of the evacuations ex-Governour Tonyn had not only the machinations of John Cruden to contend with but those of Governour Zespedes. What free Blacks the banditti had not carried off, the Spanish governour had managed to seduce into slavery. The *Bahamas Gazette* reported an incident reminiscent of earlier insidious tactics perpetrated by Spaniards on the equally unsuspecting Lucayan Arawaks:

We are informed that in compliance with Governour de Zespedes' proclamation a number of free negroes have given their names and places of residence to Mr. Secretary Howard. About a month since upwards of 50 of the unfortunate wretches were ordered to the lighthouse ... under pretence of being employed on the King's works; but were the same day put on board a Sloop which immediately proceeded to sea, and was said to be destined for Havana.[11]

A month before the expiration of the evacuation period, some British subjects petitioned Tonyn to ask for an extension and Zespedes granted the refugees an additional six months. By mid-September, 1785, the last transports from East Florida arrived in Nassau, and on 13 November Patrick Tonyn set sail for England. Zespedes believed that the "real reason" for Tonyn's delay in East Florida was that he was expecting to be appointed governour of the Bahamas.[12] Considering the dispute which erupted almost immediately between the American Loyalists and Governour Maxwell, Tonyn might have made a more compatible choice. Like the New York Loyalists in Abaco, East Florida refugees seemed to arrive in Nassau anxious for a fight.

Whitehall confirmed Carleton's appointment of Brigadier General McArthur to the temporary government of the Bahama Islands. He was ordered to Nassau to make military arrangements for the defence of the island and to govern until Maxwell arrived. McArthur did not arrive in Nassau until 12 January 1784, his delay

caused by repairs to his vessels and contrary winds. Nassau was tranquil; Governour Maxwell and most of the Loyalists from East Florida had not arrived yet.
McArthur found the situation at Abaco tense, the riots there a preview of those
which would take place in Nassau by the summer.

McArthur reported that the New York colony "sent in September last" had
been on shore only a few days when "dissention [sic] got among them."[13] Besides the
emotional stress of the war and exile, and the physical discomforts of sea travel,
further unrest may have been caused by mosquitoes, sand flies, and "stinging
doctors."

According to Lt. Wilson who accompanied McArthur, the refugees from New
York had settled on the "very worst part of Abaco, and appear to have attended
more to politics than to Agriculture." Since their arrival "in August 1783" they had
been so "engaged in trifling disputes and Party-Work, that no steps had been taken
towards cultivation until the arrival of Brigadier General McArthur. . . ."[14]

McArthur informed Lord Sidney that "this dissention rose by degrees to such a
height, they were on the point of taking Arms against each other." The general had
examined the matter carefully: "each party produced a number of affidavits in their
justification which are too voluminous to trouble your Lordship with."[15] McArthur
digested the whole and reported the episode to Sidney this way:

> . . . it appears that some of the people refusing to work at the provision Store, a
> Court of enquiry was ordered. Three of the absentees made apologies which
> were admitted, two refused to appear and three of them treating the Court with
> insolence and contempt, irritated the Officers so far [that] they sentenced them
> and the two who refused to appear to depart the Island in fifty-two hours. A great
> majority of the people justly alarmed at this violent proceeding signed an asso-
> ciation to defend the five men, threw off the Authority of all the Militia officers
> which Sir Guy Carleton had at their own recommendation appointed, and chose
> a Board of Police, consisting of three men to direct all the affairs of the
> Settlement.
>
> Captain Stephens of the Pennsylvania Loyalists, whom these people chose
> for their Agent before they left New York, does not appear to have Acted with
> much prudence or temper, having withheld the Commissions of two Militia
> Officers and assumed the entire Command,[16] in which the Militia Officers
> acquiesced, supposing he had a Commission, as he ordered the Court of en-
> quiry and approved of the sentence.
>
> Sometime thereafter apprehending his person in danger, he armed his
> servants and negroes and seized two reputable inhabitants, keeping them
> prisoners a night in his own house. Next day they refused to be released, not
> thinking their persons safe while he was at liberty. Two of the Militia Officers
> became his sureties that he should not go out of his Town-lot till released by
> proper authority, where he [Stephens] remained from the 13 November till re-
> leased by me on the 9th of February. The party in opposition to the officers hav-
> ing heard a Detachment from the garrison of St. Augustine was coming to sup-

port the Officers, quit the Settlement and retired to Marshes Harbour, six leagues South East of Carleton, where they have laid out a Town, and are well employed in clearing land and erecting habitations. The soil and water there are better than at Carleton, and Harbour safer though not so deep. (See plates 32 and 33.)[17]

After spending some time in each settlement "admonishing the inhabitants," McArthur formed a Board of Police at both places and "the parties being now some distance from each other, I am hopeful all animosity will cease."

McArthur decided to leave in Nassau the captain and twenty-one men of the 37th Regiment which he had brought from St. Augustine "lest the New York Colony should prove refractory." The Loyalists at Carleton and "Marshes" Harbour numbered "658 souls." McArthur reported that six hundred souls brought from East Florida at the expense of government, and fifty who came at their own, lived in two settlements near the south end of Abaco.[18]

PLATE 32: This 1784 "Plan of the Settlement and Harbour at Carleton on the Island of Abaco" was surveyed and drawn by Lt. John Wilson, Acting Engineer at St. Augustine. (W.O. 78/803-3, courtesy of Public Records Office, London, Photograph by Stanley Toogood.)

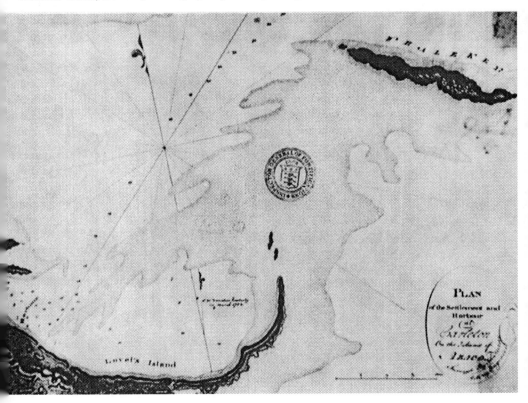

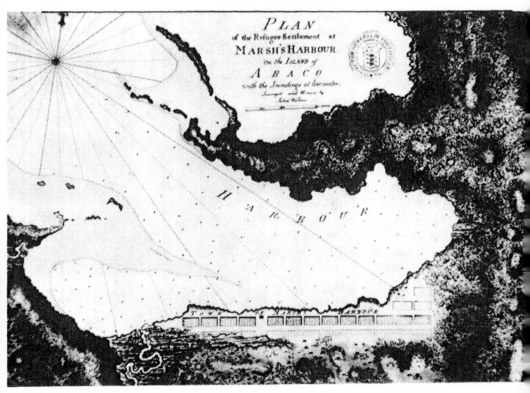

PLATE 33: This "Plan of the Refugee Settlement at Marsh's Harbour, with the soundings at low water" shows Maxwell Town, also surveyed and drawn by Wilson in 1784. (W.O. 78/807-4, courtesy of Public Records Office, London, Photograph by Stanley Toogood.)

Lt. Wilson reported that the soil at the East Florida settlements of Spencers Bight and Eight Mile Bay was better than that at Carleton and Marsh Harbour; but, on the whole, he submitted that there were no "extensive tracts of land fit for cultivation anywhere in this Island. Generally the soil was composed of nothing more than vegetable bodies rotted on the surface of the rocks." This unfavourable report may have discouraged any further settlement of Abaco by East Floridians.[19]

Another gentleman went along on this trip and became friendly with the pilot of their vessel, William Roberts, who furnished him with the names of thirty cays "covering the East and North side of Abaco," many of which were large and had good planting land. Captain Joseph Smith of the King's Rangers, some discharged soldiers, and two or three families were happily settled at Spencers Bight and believed the soil would "yield equal to the Expectations." About nine miles south of that settlement "is a Reef Harbour fit for small Vessels." This is the Cherokee Sound and Eight Mile Bay area mentioned by Wilson and is the other East Florida settlement, where "the negroes of Lt. Col. Brown are settled."[20]

Besides Captain Smith, other King's Rangers had grants of land in and around Spencers Bight: Charles Fox Taylor, Conrad Pennybaker (Drummer), John Cornish (Quartermaster), Major Alexander C. Wylly, Captain Donald Cameron, and Captain Richard Pearis, "once more turned adrift in a wide and inhospitable world."[21]

This same gentleman also had an opportunity to explore some of the land in the northern part of Great Abaco. At the request of Mr. Stephens and Mr. Barclay, he visited a place called Cocoa Plumb Creek. According to his account, after the disputes at Carleton, many Loyalists dispersed in two directions, southeast about twenty miles to Marsh Harbour and northwest about nine miles to Cocoa Plumb Creek. Impressed with the pine land around the new settlement, Mr. Barclay told the gentleman that the pines were even larger toward the northwest end of the Island. Barclay had explored the soon-to-be settled area around Cedar Harbour as far as the small passage which separated Great from Little Abaco. (See plate 34.)[22]

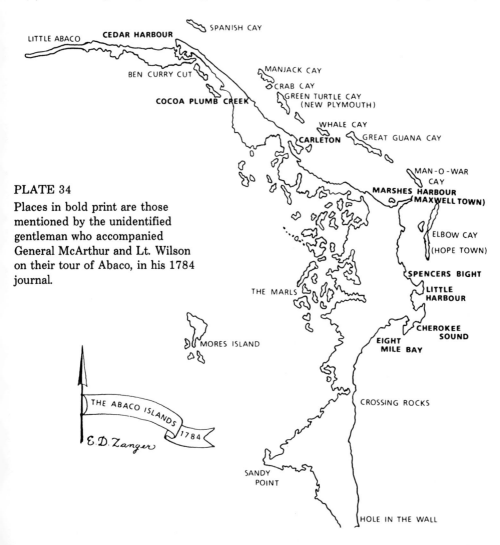

PLATE 34

Places in bold print are those mentioned by the unidentified gentleman who accompanied General McArthur and Lt. Wilson on their tour of Abaco, in his 1784 journal.

About the time of McArthur's arrival, some Loyalists had already made arrangements to leave the Bahamas. William Walker was in the process of negotiating with General Lincoln for grants of land for himself and other Loyalists on St. Vincent. Anxious to receive a response to his letter of 10 February, Walker advised Lincoln to send his reply by St. Christopher or Antigua in order "to catch the trades." In spite of his hurry to leave the excellent climate but poor soil of New Providence, Walker was probably still in Nassau on 5 March when the *Gazette* reported that twelve hundred armed Caribs "were annoying" settlers on St. Vincent.[23]

Like Walker, Philip Dumaresq found the climate on Abaco "delightful," but the soil so shallow "'that in the dry season the sun heated the rocks underneath and burned up any vegetables that had been planted.'" Since their arrival, there had been a terrible drought. He also reported that:

> ... Guinea corn, potatoes, yams, turnips and other garden produce would grow very well, together with such fruits as oranges, limes and plantains, and that cotton would thrive; but he complained that settlers were all poor, had not the strength to do much, and that he had seen no fresh meat, except pork, since his arrival, but poultry, he said, could be raised in plenty. The abundance of wild grapes convinced him that good wines might be produced, and he was told that indigo could be cultivated successfully.[24]

Philip Dumaresq had been among those who moved from Carleton to Maxwell Town where he, his wife and five children lived on his commissary pay. Although reduced in circumstances now, he had been a successful Boston merchant and his wife Rebecca had been "tenderly brought up" to every luxury. (See plate 35.) In a letter to his father-in-law Dr. Sylvester Gardiner, a wealthy Boston Loyalist, Dumaresq wrote that the "earlier occupants of the island did not welcome them with cordiality." Governour Maxwell and General McArthur treated him with great politeness and the governour had appointed him a magistrate at Maxwell Town "to keep him from being 'insulted by the Abaco blackguards.'" The question here is not the treatment of the snobbish Mr. Dumaresq, but the identity of those Abaco blackguards? None of the accounts report any settlers on Abaco prior to the arrival of the New York colony, August/September 1783. Wilson included an official census taken in May, 1782, before the Spanish occupation. Besides the 2,410 people on New Providence, Harbour Island, and Eleuthera, there were 189 inhabitants on Long Island, Exuma, and Cat Island.[25] Could they have been the Florida people who seized the island with Deveaux, the New England whalers, the squatters Mr. Whittleton mentioned, or Eleutherans who had fished for turtle, ambergris, and wrecks on Abaco for over 125 years and considered the island their own?

Although Wilson's second report confirmed other reports that the Bahamas were rocky islands with shallow soil, he did second Mr. Dumaresq by making mention of a few people who had become wealthy on cotton production, and he devoted two pages to the proper cultivation of cotton. This crop seemed to be the hook that

PLATE 35: A miniature of Philip Dumaresq and a crayon portrait of his
wife, Rebecca Gardiner, by John Singleton Copley, display traces of a
Bostonian arrogance which perhaps explains why the Dumaresqs were not
welcomed by what the governour called "The Abaco blackguards."
(From Alfred Jones' *The Loyalists of Massachusetts*, London, 1930.)

dragged over any reluctant East Floridians and cotton production in the Bahamas
did thrive for a while. According to Brig. Gen. McArthur, the sixty-one souls from New
York at Cat Island were "doing well;" Oswell Eve wrote to a friend in London that his
"expectations are entirely answered on this island." He told of another Pennsylvania Loyalist who had lost everything and, saddled with debt besides, went to Long
Island with a half a dozen Blacks to plant cotton and so acquired an even larger
fortune. Robert Hunt reported to Lord Sidney that the southern islands, particularly Long Island, Cat Island, and the Exumas, were capable of producing great
quantities of cotton wool whereas Abaco and the northern islands "may be found
proper for the culture of vines."[26]

In England at this time the wheels of government turned swiftly in some areas,
inched along in most, but never spun. John Maxwell reminded Lord North on the
21st of October, 1783, of the necessity of putting the Bahama Islands in "an order of
regulation, which from its present state of confusion cannot be done too soon." He,
in fact, was ready to leave as soon as he received instructions. In December,
Whitehall raised the pay and made a few appointments to put the civil and government officers in the Bahamas on a "more respectable footing" but still did not give
Maxwell leave to take up his commission.[27]

An anonymous American Loyalist in Nassau accused Maxwell of having "slipt
off from England" without any instructions from the Crown and established himself as governour "by a bare proclamation" which read "whereas *I* have thought
proper to take upon *me* this Government etc." This Loyalist acknowledged that
Maxwell was the man intended for the job, but many of the governour's enemies believed him to be more of an "usurper or Imposter than a legal or lawful governour."[28]

Since there had been trouble in Abaco when he arrived, Maxwell anticipated
the same in Nassau. He informed Lord Sidney that he had assumed the government
on 27 March 1784 and that the New York and St. Augustine refugees "have re-

paired to several of the principal islands. On Abaco they have laid out a town, which they have called Carleton. It must be a difficult task, I imagine, to please so dissatisfied a people . . . ."[29] He would not have to imagine for long.

Part of Maxwell's problem with the Loyalists stemmed from England's tardiness in sending aid. Bahamians had gone years sometimes without even a note, but to the thousands of hungry new refugees such neglect was intolerable. The American Loyalist wrote:

> Nova Scotia we see has been more early and particularly attended to, and as these Islands were also long ago held out as a *Land of Promise* and an Asylum to the Unfortunate, several Thousand of Emigrants of various Colours and Professions from the American Continent have within these last twelve months arrived, and more are still coming in here to Settle. But as yet no sort of Attention either from the Crown or Parliament has been paid to this Country since the Peace.

A total of 1,190 barrels of provisions sent by Governour Mathews of Barbados arrived in the *Two Brothers* some time late in February 1784.[30] But with so many refugees these supplies did not last long, and sometimes there was nothing on hand for the new arrivals.

The loyalist writer somewhat sarcastically referred to His Majesty's "eminent and humane bounty" in sending the transport *David*, which after a safe passage from Cork, Ireland, wrecked on the Nassau Bar on or before 17 May 1784. In October of 1783, Whitehall had requisitioned those tools, clothes, and salt provisions for twelve months for "those unhappy settlers" in the Bahamas.[31] If only His Majesty could have seen those even unhappier faces seven months later as they watched those long awaited goods sink before their very eyes.

Maxwell set about salvage proceedings but had to inform Lord Sidney that losses were heavy. He also sent along a petition from the Loyalists asking for more provisions. Another British government ship, the *Earl of Effingham*, with provisions and tools for the American Loyalists, did not arrive until almost a year later.

By June, the salvage operations on the *David* had been completed. Maxwell took one-fourth to cover government expenses and distributed the rest among the refugees. The remaining ironmongery and dry goods were dispersed to Loyalists on 15 June 1784. The return gives an indication of the islands settled by Loyalists at this time and the percentage of Loyalist population on each. The largest allotment of three-twelfths went to New Providence, two-twelfths for Exuma, Cat Island, and the New York Division at Abaco, and one-twelfth for Eleuthera, Long Island, and the Florida Division of Abaco. Items distributed consisted of paint, a variety of locks and tools, corn mills, frying pans, compasses, bolts of "oznaburg," thread, and hats.[32]

The responsibility of providing for so many people placed Governour Maxwell in a "damned if I do, damned if I don't" situation all during his hectic year as governour. Off and on he considered making Nassau a free port, and he was forced at times to allow the importation of Indian corn in American bottoms and to prohibit the exportation of provisions. Loyalists were opposed to the free port because

Americans would be the principal gainers. Both temporary solutions to the food shortage problem angered Loyalists; they rioted against the first and smuggled their goods in defiance of the second. Although loyal to Great Britain, Bahamians had carried on trade with America even during the Revolution. Their survival depended on trade with America. The Loyalist riot in the summer of 1784 made no sense to the Old Inhabitants.

Maxwell wrote Lord Sidney concerning what he called the two classes of Loyalists. The first consisted of the peaceful farmers who had settled for the most part on the Out Islands; the second, and much closer to home, were the officers, merchants, and those who intended to return to America "when they have made their peace there. Nothing can satisfy these people." They always demanded provisions, land, and employment immediately upon arrival.[33]

Because of the wreck of the *David*, Maxwell had permitted Americans to supply Nassau. The "lawless set" of Loyalists attempted to tear down American colours from the ships in the harbour. Like Carleton, Maxwell considered this action a "monstrous offence" and on 4 June issued a proclamation warning inhabitants that if there were any further "riotous proceedings" or insults against the American flag, they would "answer at their peril." He also ordered masters of American vessels to stay aboard on Sundays in order to prevent further incidents in town.[34]

The proclamation stopped the riots and Loyalists amused themselves by "writing libels." The following broadsheet was disrespectfully circulated under the heading "A Proclamation by Governour Maxwell:"

TO BE SOLD

Any day when Loyalists are out of town looking for lands a Quantity of Beef & Pork (not a Word of this to any of the Committee) for the very plausable purpose of paying Expenses . . . that I may touch a Commission and the old Inhabitants of this Town (who I commonly call damned Villains behind their Backs) may come in for Snacks.

Maxwell requested a garrison of his own or the help of the Navy because he believed the Loyalists meant to overthrow his government.

To Patrick Tonyn, he wrote that "the gentlemen Loyalists have been a little riotous." He also mentioned that he was obliged to hire a secretary because of a "stiff finger," which may have been caused by shaking it too vehemently at the Loyalists or by a chigger, both equally irritating. The postscript confided to the ex-governour that Maxwell had not heard one word from the home ministry since his departure from London 19 December 1783.[35]

As Chairman of the Board of American Loyalists, James Hepburn circulated a handbill calling a general meeting to be held at Mr. Johnston's house 29 July 1784. (See plate 36.) John Wells, publisher of the *Bahamas Gazette* and secretary at that meeting, sent a letter to all the Out Islands. The committee desired each island to elect a deputy to meet "with the Select committee of the Loyalists" at Nassau on September 1st. Since the resolution opposed the governour, Thomas Willet, Magistrate at Maxwell Town, Abaco, refused to call the meeting to elect a deputy. In-

THE peculiar Situation of the
Loyal Refugees, now in
the Bahama Islands, requiring their
steady and united Exertions to preserve and maintain those Rights and
Liberties, for which they left their
Homes and their Possessions; it was
agreed upon by the following
Gentlemen, viz.

James Hepburn   Robert Johnston
Philip Moore   John Wells
Peter Dean   Alexander Ross
Alex. Dryfdale   George M'Kenzie
Lewis Johnston   J. M. Tatnall
W. Henry Mills   William Moss, &
George Leitch   Robert Moodie,

to request a General Meeting of
the Loyalists from the Continent of
North-America, at Mr. Johnston's
House, next Door to the Printing
Office in George-ftreet, on Thurf-
day the 29th inft. at Ten o'Clock in
the Forenoon.
                JAMES HEPBURN,
                          Chairman.
Naffau, July 26, 1784.

PLATE 36:
In July of 1784, James Hepburn,
Chairman of the Board of
American Loyalists, circulated
this handbill to call a meeting
to rally opposition to Governour
Maxwell. (CO 23/25 f. 148
courtesy of Public Records
Office, London.)

stead, he decided to go to Nassau and see for himself what was going on there. He witnessed what he described as every species of disloyalty, licentiousness, and anarchy. On Sunday, 21 August, rowdy Loyalists stood opposite the church door with drums and beat the "Rogues's March" until they drove out all the people. Having possessed themselves of the church, they amused themselves with ringing the church bell at 11 o'clock at night, "as if the town had been on fire!"[36]

The meeting of the Loyalists held on 1 September resolved that "Governour John Maxwell has evinced himself to be an inveterate and determined enemy of the American Loyalists settled on the Bahamas, and has by his conduct greatly re-tarded and obstructed the settlement and population of these Islands." For example, according to Stephen Haven, Governour Maxwell had refused to allow Haven and Messrs. Hepburn and Johnston to practice law in the Bahamian court. This may have been done in spite of, or because of, a letter of recommendation from Patrick Tonyn approving Hepburn's work as council member and the king's Attorney General at St. Augustine.[37]

After Maxwell refused to speak with the Committee of Loyalists, Hepburn and Johnston invaded the Court, spewing a "torrent of Billingsgate language" at Chief Justice Thomas Atwood. These "two strangers from St. Augustine" scurrilously dis-puted the authority of both the court and the governour. Since Atwood could not control the situation, Maxwell closed the court indefinitely in early September. Once more Nassau was a scene of riot. Since magistrates were afraid to perform their office, Maxwell was without military, naval, or civil aid. The anonymous Amer-ican Loyalist described Justice Atwood as a "Goose of a Fellow" and the governour as "ignorant, illiterate and Avaricious, full of a low Duplicity of Conduct and really uncapable of well governing a private Family, much less so large a Body of People as the Bahama Islands now contains. . . ."[38]

Maxwell compromised and appointed a few Loyalists as magistrates, but they all refused to accept the offices. On 20 September, the Board of American Loyalists signed a petition to the king calling for the removal of John Maxwell and stating that he had taken the government upon himself, oppressed the Loyalists, refused to seize American vessels, and publicly declared that he had come to this country only to make money. In a letter to Lord Sidney the committee requested him to beseech the king to appoint a governour who would serve the interests of the American Loyalists, someone with the "distinguished merits and obliging disposition of Governour Tonyn."[39]

In November, Maxwell had the support of some Loyalists who disapproved of the action of the Board of American Loyalists as illegal and unprecedented in a civil government. Of the forty-five Loyalists who signed, twelve were from Maxwell Town and one man, Isaac Stansbury, was from Carleton, Abaco. (See plate 37.) By early December Maxwell had dissolved the House of Assembly. During the election, rancor amongst the contending parties increased. The Old Inhabitants, termed

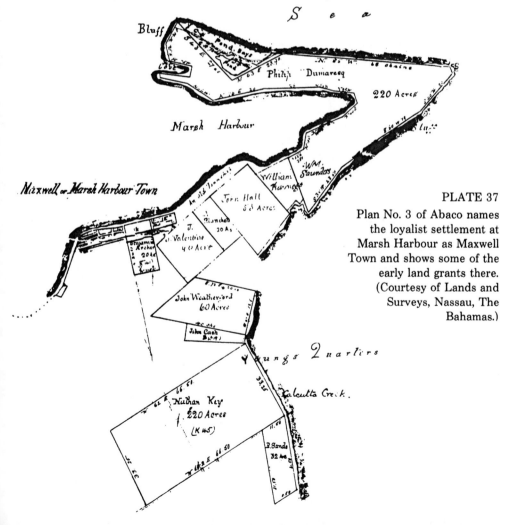

PLATE 37

Plan No. 3 of Abaco names the loyalist settlement at Marsh Harbour as Maxwell Town and shows some of the early land grants there. (Courtesy of Lands and Surveys, Nassau, The Bahamas.)

Conchs, and the new settlers, termed Refugees, were near to violence. On the 1st of February the House of Assembly met and prorogued the same day. Some seats were contested. Hugh Dean, William Kennedy, and James Ridley were returned for Abaco and James Hepburn for Cat Island. On 21 March Governour Maxwell sailed for England and on 2 March subscribers from Maxwell Town, Abaco, supported public disavowal of their governour. Some of the signers included Samuel Isaacs, Alexander McGee, Henry Smith, John Valentine, Duncan Taylor, John Forbes, and Gilbert Forbes, Jr. Mathew Arnold, partner of John Valentine, tombstone maker in Maxwell Town, does not appear on the list. Considering his famous surname, it would be fascinating to learn on which end of this political seesaw he sat.[40] William Haynes and Robert Linton had signed the 1784 address supporting Maxwell.

The final document concerning the Maxwell affair is an interesting one. It is a list of persons from New Providence "who have cause to deprecate Governour Maxwell's return to this Country, as the Greatest Evil that can possibly befall these Islands." In a last attempt to vindicate himself, Maxwell pointed out to Lord Sidney that most of the signers were "Clerks, Apprentices, Discharg'd Soldiers, Paupers, and Vagabonds." Next to the names of some of the associates, these remarks were written: James Hepburn, President, "formerly a retailer of Gin and Whisky in North Carolina;" John Wells, printer "formerly of the Silk Stocking Company at the Siege of Georgia in the Rebel service;" John McKenzie, "a nobody, having nothing;" James Fulford, "a blind Beggar in the town;" George Outlaw, "a discharged Soldier;" and Soloman Glass "has not a Farthing."[41]

Maxwell turned the government over to Lt. Governour James Powell, a Loyalist from Georgia. Although charming, this new governour did not have enough of Mr. Tonyn's "obliging disposition" to suit Mr. Hepburn. Powell warned the President of the Board of American Loyalists that he would hold him personally responsible for any further breaches of the peace. The hard-spirited Mr. Hepburn replied that "'he was not afraid of any power here etc. . . . .'" When the governour asked Hepburn to explain his behaviour of the past few months, this rude but energetic and athletic man grabbed his hat and "'skipped down 46 steps in a jump and a half.'" The violence had subsided. Although he did not "expect to sleep on a bed of Roses," Powell hoped he could lessen the prejudices between the Loyalists and Old Inhabitants and unite them in a common interest, that of encouraging industry. Cotton thrived and the whaling business once again held promise. Bermudians had already established a whale fishing company but could not prevent American encroachment.[42]

Smuggling was an intolerable trouble. The illicit practice originated from the "former precarious and irregular supplies of the country." Powell requested a shallow draft vessel to cruise about the islands, particularly Turks Island, Harbour Island, Eleuthera, and Abaco "where most of this vile traffick, so injurious to the fair Trader and his Majesty's Revenue is carried on with impunity. . . ." The request was made in March but by October Powell still had no cruiser. Goods smuggled into Abaco and to other Out Islands were brought to Nassau in small craft and "sold at noon day by auction."[43]

If allegations that Maxwell had come back to the Bahamas to make money were true, it is possible that he may have been involved in this Out Island smuggling business and in that way had won the support of some Abaco Loyalists. At a time when trade with America was so hotly contested, an advertisement appeared in the *Gazette*: "Wanted:" a thirty-five to sixty ton vessel to load at Abaco for Charleston. The next year, another curious entry appeared in the *Gazette*. About eight p.m., 2 July 1785, a Captain Wallace in the sloop *Norman* spoke to a "Brig that hailed from Africa, bound to Abaco and Rhode Island.[44]

The House of Assembly was back in session by 4 April with twelve members absent. Peter Dean and John Petty protested that since the House had been dissolved last February, many Out Island members had to attend to business and could not return. As a result "Andros, Abaco, Exuma and Cat Island (whereon are nearly one-half of the people that compose the whole body of the Inhabitants of the Bahamas) are entirely unrepresented." Five persons were charged with not having been duly elected and their seats had gone undisputed. According to the Dean petition, there were only seven out of twenty-five members in the present house whose seats were undisputed.

Mr. O'Halloran made a motion that the protest be burned by the common hangman. The motion to expel Dean, Petty, and James Moss, the signers of this protest, was unanimous. Another motion made by O'Halloran, seconded by Mr. Rumer and agreed upon unanimously, was as follows: that James Hepburn, George Miller, and the three delegates from Abaco, Hugh Dean, William Kennedy, and James Ridley, having withdrawn themselves from their duty and neglected to attend these sessions, be expelled. This house also voted to suspend for a time Woodes Rogers's "act for the encouragement of Foreigners and Strangers settling on these Islands,"[45] believing such encouragement to be superfluous.

A general meeting of the American Loyalists on 9 May at the house of William Panton resolved that since "we do not consider ourselves represented" in the house, an address would be submitted to the lieutenant governour calling for the dissolution of the present assembly as "illegal and unconstitutional."[46]

Loyalists continued to pour in from East Florida. Tonyn sent a fire engine, bells, and pews from the church of St. Augustine, which the Spanish government had declined to purchase, on to Nassau. He proposed to sail to England in the *Cyrus* but forgot to knock wood when he told Lord Sidney that "not a single accident has happened by the Marine [at sea]." In September, 1785, the *Cyrus* sprang a leak on St. Marys Bar. Tonyn sent an express vessel to the Bahamas to inform transports there to return to St. Augustine. The express wrecked on Abaco, but the master, carrying Tonyn's dispatches, reached New Providence.[47]

Lack of provisions was still a problem for Governour Powell. In trying to discourage emigration, he had perhaps singled out the very settlers who had the sustaining qualities of the native Bahamians. He wrote to Tonyn:

> I understand a large number of back Country Loyalists may be expected by the next Transports that arrive here. These Islands are by no means calculated for these people, who mostly subsisted on the Continent by Hunting, and

like Arabs removing their habitations and Stock from one place or province to
another, and therefore could Your Excellency order them to Nova Scotia or
some other Province on the Continent. . . .

Tonyn appreciated Powell's situation but could not discourage settlers once they
had made their choice. He hoped rather that by their "persevering industry they
may perhaps rise to opulence and wealth although wading through a dilemma of
embarrassment, distress and Poverty."[48]

These last divisions of transports from East Florida sailed in rough weather.
The *Bahamas Gazette* announced the arrival in Nassau of the ship *Sally*, Captain
Croskill from London, "so long looked for here, last week put into Hurricane Harbour in Abaco, after a tedious passage of near eleven weeks." The *Sally* carried some
important passengers: Josiah Tattnall, Esq., Surveyor General, and Mrs. Tattnall;
Mrs. Wood; Miss Colleton, daughter of deceased Sir John Colleton; and Miss Carolina Gordon, daughter of late John Gordon Esq. of Charleston. All had taken refuge
at the tiny inlet near Little Harbour, Abaco.[49]

Throughout the month of July the weather had been erratic. The *Gazette* of 2
July reported that "we have had a continued succession of light winds and calms, accompanied with heavy rains. A small vessel from Abaco that arrived here last night,
was thirteen days on the passage." During the week of 11 September the last division of transports arrived from St. Augustine. A week later, on September 21 and 22,
a hurricane hit the windward Bahamas, and some effects were felt in Nassau. The
ship *Hope* lying off Russell's shipyard was "driven from her mooring and carried a
sloop belonging to Mr. Armstrong of Abaco with her. At 12 o'clock on Thursday she
was seen driving before the wind out to sea." The *Hope* was found wrecked, but Mr.
Armstrong's sloop returned undamaged.[50]

The storm struck violently at Harbour Island, Eleuthera, Abaco, and Long
Island, causing great damage to crops and building. Among the eight vessels lost was
one belonging to Captain Wylly of Abaco. On 29 September the Council received
petitions from Harbour Island, Wreck Sound, and other settlements on Eleuthera
and from several settlements on Abaco "representing the alarming situation to
which they had been reduced by the late Hurricane." The Council authorized the
purchase of flour for their immediate relief.[51] But even after the hurricane the
weather remained destructive; the 10 December *Gazette* reported:

> About four weeks since a decked boat on board of which were Captain
> Kidd, Dr. Isaacs, Mr. John Cameron and some others sailed from Maxwell in
> Abaco for this place. From some clothes which were known to be Mr. Camer-
> on's, several mahogany logs, and a keel of a small vessel, having lately drifted
> ashore at the Bluff on Eleuthera, there is every reason to fear she was lost in a
> violent gale of wind a day or two after she left Abaco.[52]

The year ended with the safe arrival of the last refugees from East Florida and the
horrible death of several of the first arrivals.

14

"When the Hurly-Burly's Done"

Every misfortune which visited Nassau in those days, even the death of James Powell on 6 February 1786, was indirectly blamed on the refugees. Dissension subsided and General McArthur believed it would "dwindle away" unless Mr. Hepburn, "the soul of that faction," returned from his plantation on Cat Island to "reanimate it." This semi-ceasefire was occasioned by the temporary lack of a governour with whom to wage war. Although President Brown lacked a governour's authority, he refused to be pushed around by either party.[1]

When three church wardens of unsavoury character prevented the remains of Lt. Gov. Powell from being buried in the sanctified ground of the church yard, Brown exercised his ecclesiastical power by shutting up the church for four weeks. Robert Rumer, one of a small faction of Loyalists that Brown labeled the "Refuse of America," had teamed with an Old Inhabitant, the drunken council member Mr. Boyd, and a Mr. Ferguson in that "brutal affair." From Brown's point of view, Ferguson stood in the middle of a social quagmire by reason of the fact that he had arrived in the Bahamas in 1770, too late to be an Old Inhabitant and too early to be an American Loyalist. Ferguson had been an inoffensive drummer and tailor until, by fortunate circumstances, he acquired both property and arrogance.[2]

Besides the usual petitions for provisions and grants of land to Loyalists, the Old Inhabitants sent a memorial requesting aid from Great Britain to pay house rents, which had increased since the influx of new inhabitants. The Out Island smugglers sailed in armed vessels and "lived in a state little short of actual piracy and Rebellion." This clandestine piratical behaviour irked the collector of customs but may have brought a smile to the lips of one ancient Nassau woman who recounted stories of the days of Blackbeard and piracy in the Bahamas. "Still sound in Mind and Memory," she declared that "she had not seen such happy days since. . . ."[3]

George Barry informed Anthony Stokes, agent for the Bahamas, that the inhabitants of "Abaco, Exuma, Cat Island and Eleuthera" were shipping cotton and dyewood to America "in American Bottoms" and were smuggling teas, wine, and brandy into Nassau. Irate Loyalists on Exuma petitioned President Brown. At least four hundred American vessels had carried away salt from Turks Island "without making the smallest acknowledgement to the Colony." These were the very same Americans who had robbed Loyalists of their fathers' inheritances by taking their property and banishing them. One Loyalist saw the same Boston patriot who had imprisoned him during the war bartering on Exuma for cotton and brasiletto.[4]

Some of the smugglers on Abaco and probably on Eleuthera may have been getting their wood from lands other than their own. A group of influential absentee Abaco proprietors complained:

> The subscribers have information that frequent trespasses have been committed upon their lands, situated at Cedar Harbour, on the island of Little Abaco, [and] take this method to warn the inhabitants of the adjacent islands against such practices in future, as they are determined to punish the aggressors with the utmost severity.

The subscribers were Josiah Tattnall, Surveyor General; Lt. Col. Thomas Brown; Thomas Stephens; Thomas Forbes, member of the House of Assembly for Abaco, Nassau merchant, and member of the merchantile firm of Panton, Leslie and Company; and Edmund Rush Wegg, Attorney General for the Bahamas. A letter from Abaco reporting that "all things flourish" probably came from the Spencers Bight or Eight Mile Bay settlement where the schooner *Sally* delivered freight "at reasonable rates."[5]

The New York division at Maxwell Town was busily engaged in shipbuilding. In January John Chrystie advertised for ship carpenters to go to Maxwell where a "fine new vessel" was to be built for him by Mr. Faggo. The vessel, named *Maxwell*, launched at Abaco 3 August arrived in Nassau 7 October, and set sail from Exuma to Charleston in December of 1786.[6] Besides the ship *Maxwell*, other large vessels were built at Abaco between 1785-1788: the 155 ton snow *Recovery*, schooners *Dolphin, Resolution, Fair Abaconian, Ulyses,* and *Eliza*, and the sloops *Huaebras, Carleton,* and *Two Friends.* Ironically, the *Fair Abaconian,* returning from Savannah in April, 1789, was "lost on Abaco."[7]

During these interim months without a governour, prices in the Bahamas doubled. Exports rose and imports skyrocketed. American refugees were estimated to number anywhere from four thousand to seven thousand. Whatever their number, Loyalists' greatest preoccupation besides experimenting with Anguilla cotton was speculating on Britain's choice of their next governour. Rumours arrived from various quarters to enliven coffee house conversation for months. The *British Chronicle* of 15 March 1785 declared that "Lord Dunmore is certainly appointed Governour of Jamaica." Advices from England received in Antigua mentioned the appointment of Dunmore as governor of Bermuda and that the Bahamas and Bermuda were expected to be formed into one government. Jamaica's *St. Jago de la Vega Gazette* of 22 June 1786 reported that Brigadier General McArthur had been appointed governor of the Bahamas in place of John Maxwell who had resigned; but on the 26th of August, 1786, advices from London arrived in the *Mary,* announcing the appointment of the Earl of Dunmore as governor of the Bahamas.[8]

Almost a year before he arrived in Nassau, Dunmore had petitioned Lord Sidney for a small vessel as "indispensibly necessary" in order to carry out his duties as governor of the Bahamas. Early in the American Revolutionary War, rebels had

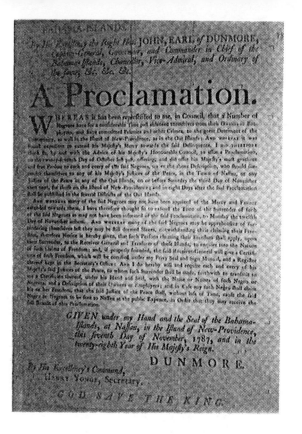

PLATE 38
Although this proclamation of Lord Dunmore's offered a general pardon to those fugitives who would surrender themselves, many who left their loyalist "owners" found themselves "freed" into the custody of the governour's friends. (CO 23/27 f. 78, courtesy of Public Records Office, London.)

forced his lordship to seek refuge aboard the British ship at Norfolk. Once again he would be prepared for rebellion; the irritating flaws in his character would, in fact, provoke it. Avaricious, narrow-minded, indiscreet, obstinate and violent are among the terms applied to the Earl of Dunmore. His "proclamation relative to Negroes" and especially his refusal to dissolve the House of Assembly antagonized the Loyalists beyond the point of endurance.[9] In most instances Dunmore's actions in regard to the Negro Court, to smuggling, and to land grants were motivated solely by greed. His methods were illegal, and only fear of losing control of the government kept him from dissolving the General Assembly.

Loyalists had been hijacking free Blacks from America and were selling them to the French at Hispaniola. Many Blacks, protesting their illegal bondage, had absconded and committed crimes against the peace both in Nassau and in the Out Islands. The day after his arrival Dunmore issued a proclamation offering a general pardon to fugitive Blacks who would surrender themselves, promising an inquiry into their claims of freedom. (See plate 38.)

There was some question as to the legality of Dunmore's Negro Court and to the sincerity of his motives as well. Certainly some Blacks received certificates of freedom, but many were lured to the court to be legally stolen from their loyalist "owners" only to be enslaved by one of the governour's friends.[10] This kind of deception was perhaps more intolerable than the institution of slavery itself because the ordeal compounded the misery of the black petitioner by completely disregarding his feelings in the matter. Since Blacks constituted the bulk of loyalist "property," this law was meant to hit hardest at them. Some retaliated with a vengeance.

In Nassau "five or six gentlemen with swords and pistols went in the night to the House of a free Mullatto woman with seven or eight children, broke open the doors . . . beat the poor old woman, cut in the head one of her daughters and otherwise abused and alarmed the rest of the family. . . ." Hearing their "cries of Murder." Dunmore sent some of his servants to protect them. Young J. M. Tattnall, searcher of customs, who was one of the men arrested, swore "he would burn every house belonging to the free negroes in that quarter of town."[11]

Incidents in Abaco had grown to riot proportions. In April, 1785, Cornelius Blanchard informed Governour Powell that after the first commotions subsided, the people began to make a trial of the land, "but no sooner did they begin to reap the fruits of their Industry, than a Number of Negroes had taken the wood, and have robbed the places, that they have now no support left." John Ferguson of Spencers Bight offered a twelve dollar reward for the return of a runaway "mulatto Fellow known by the name Jem." He also forewarned all persons from "harbouring, employing or *taking him off*" the island of Abaco. (Emphasis added.)

By November, the Blacks on Abaco had taken up arms. Dunmore wrote Lord Sidney:

> I am just now informed from the Island of Abacco that numbers of the outlaying Negroes went about with muskets and fix'd Bayonets, robbing and plundering. That the white Inhabitants had collected themselves in a body, and having come up with the Negroes had Killd, wounded and taken most of them Prisoners, three of the latter they immediately executed.

When Dunmore's proclamation reached them, some of those who had escaped surrendered themselves.[12]

The transport *Mercury* which had brought Dunmore had been fitted out to carry home the 37th Regiment, but McArthur had not received his orders to embark, a circumstance which he thought fortunate "considering the daring behaviour of the negroes on Abaco." Neither he nor Dunmore felt the troops should leave until replacements arrived. As it turned out, Dunmore would detain the troops and the transport almost two years to assure his own personal protection, at a cost to government of close to £4,000. Unlike General McArthur, Dunmore did not fear a black uprising but rather a loyalist revolt, which seemed about to take treasonous shape in the ensuing months.

Dunmore found the House prorogued until 1 November and at the advice of his council further prorogued it to 4 December. This was the same "packed" house in which the few elected Loyalists refused to sit during Maxwell's government. William Wylly, sometime Attorney General, full time devil's advocate, stated that loyalist discontent was well founded. Because the Loyalists constituted at least one-half of the population and did not share in the legislation, they were "galled by the perversion of public justice" and claimed that the present House was illegal. From the votes given in Wylly's *Short Account*, the six losers in the Nassau districts had called for a scrutiny. Without even bothering to open the polls or take "any step whatever to *reduce the greater number of votes to the lesser*, the Provost Marshall simply declared those losers "duly elected." When the six winners appeared at the opening of the Assembly to demand their seats, they were "thrown out." Others left in protest. After this incident, Loyalists were elected to replace those vacant seats but refused to sit in the "improperly constituted assembly."

Abaco had one empty seat. On 4 December 1787 the Assembly summoned Thomas Brown, duly elected member for Abaco, to take his seat. Mr. Brown sent reasons why he could not come. The Assembly commissioned William Wylly to go to Abaco and address the inhabitants. Wylly declined to accept the commission, stating as his reason "if the Governour wished him to get a broken head, he could not have fallen upon a better expedient."[13]

A new writ returned Dr. Robert Scott for Abaco in January, 1788; he said "the nature of his business prevented him from taking a seat." Thomas Brown and Thomas Forbes were returned for Exuma on 5 February. The Assembly resolved to fine them for not taking their seats. The struggle continued for yet another year. On 5 February 1789 Colonel Thomas Brown defeated Alexander Murray, Lord Dunmore's son, for a Nassau seat, a major victory for the Loyalists. Some inaccuracies appeared in the writ for Abaco and another election was held. Thomas Forbes, duly elected for Abaco, took his seat on 9 March 1789.

While all this was going on in the House, Dunmore was barraged with memorials from inhabitants of Nassau, Exuma, Long Island, Abaco, and Cat Island to dissolve the Assembly. The governour rejected every one. Dunmore singled out the Abaco memorial as originating with the loyalist party in Nassau, who procured the seventeen signatures from Abaco. This memorial reflects a legal mind and could have been the work of Hepburn or Johnston. The memorial stated that Loyalists constituted a large proportion of the inhabitants, possessed a considerable part of the property, and had in three years "rescued the Bahamas from insignificance and demonstrated their value and importance to the Trade and manufactures of Great Britain." Yet they were altogether unrepresented in the legislature and in this plantation colony "there is scarce a Planter or Merchant or an American Loyalist in the Lower House of Assembly." The Abaco memorialists felt themselves "subject to laws they have no share in making." Most of these laws appeared to them to be absurd, contradictory, impolite, and even repugnant to the acts of British Parliament. Nothing short of a dissolution of the present incompetent body which "has been sitting for 3 years" would please them.[14]

Some of the Loyalists connected with Abaco were in Nassau at the time and signed a memorial there. Dunmore sent it along to Lord Sidney with derogatory remarks written next to most of the names. Hugh Dean "formerly a pedlar" had been a proprietor of a dry goods establishment in New York city before he emigrated. Another well-respected merchant, Thomas Forbes, Dunmore called a "shopkeeper." Many Abaconians had been soldiers and being one himself Dunmore could not say much against them; but he seemed to hold labourers in particularly low esteem: Thomas Brown "Lt. Colonel of Provincials on half pay; John McGillivray, John

McFarlane, and Silver Crispin "soldiers from Abbacoe;" Anthony Friar "laborer, formerly a soldier;" Seth Freeman "Carpenter from Abbacoe;" James Armbrister, "Taylor, formerly a Soldier;" John Lovell "journeyman soldier;" John Fergusson "formerly a taylor and Deserter from his Majesty's Navy, now a trader." Dunmore labeled the noted shipbuilder John Russell a "ship carpenter" besides suggesting that the man must be an enemy to Great Britain because "he keeps his wife and Property in Carolina." Lord Sidney backed the governour by replying that he did not think it "expedient" to dissolve the House of Assembly at this time.[15]

In a private correspondence to Lord Sidney on 4 March, Dunmore wrote that "the malcontents of this colony have again set their engines to work . . . to obstruct every measure of government in these Islands." Dunmore named Thomas Forbes, James Hepburn, and Robert Johnston as the three most dangerous members of the loyalist party. The only reason the governour acknowledged for Loyalists' wanting a majority in the House was to "pass acts allowing them to keep Free slaves which they abducted from America and sold to the Spanish and French." Dunmore believed "in his heart" that "had we a war with America tomorrow, the Loyalists . . . would be those I should have the greatest reason to fear. . . ."[16]

The political situation had reached a crisis. By mid-June Dunmore would close the courts and declare the Bahamas in a state of rebellion, proclaiming martial law and shipping Chief Justice Matson off to England to "explain the state of the colony" while he shut himself up in his own house for protection. All this commotion resulted from Mr. Wylly's calling Mr. Matson a "damned liar" in the public street. What could, at most, be considered a breach of good behaviour, Matson took as "fresh proof of the Determination of Party Violence." The matter went to court when governour and council ordered Mr. Wylly arrested and, according to Wylly, accused him of plotting treason against the state. One judge accused another judge, who had been drunk for seven years, of having surprised him into signing an illegal warrant for Wylly's arrest. Since Mr. Matson never appeared to accuse him of anything, Mr. Wylly had to be discharged.

For a minor personal dispute to balloon almost into revolution is ridiculous. Nevertheless in August, 1789, over a year after the incident, Wylly published a pamphlet in England partially to vindicate his character and partly to clarify his side of the incident. He sought an audience with the Secretary of State, desiring to explain in person because his dispute with Mr. Matson "had caused so much injury to the colony at large."[17]

William Wylly, native of Georgia, had come to the Bahamas in 1787 from New Brunswick, where, as a member of the Council, he had avoided all party connections and had decided to remain neutral in the Bahamas. When the addresses for dissolution came in and were rejected so contemptuously, Wylly had heard that it was because Dunmore and Mr. Matson had come from England "to crush the Loyalists." With two or three others they conspired to revive political party distinctions "which had worn out" under President Brown's administration. Wylly accepted the post of Solicitor General without pay in the hope it would lead to something better. At that time Mr. Matson suggested to Wylly that he should choose a political party.

PLATE 39
As Director General of the Creek Nation, the controversial William Augustus Bowles, an ally of Lord Dunmore, presented a colourful picture in his Indian garb. (From J. Leitch Wright's *William Augustus Bowles: Director General of the Creek Nation*, courtesy of the University of Georgia Press.)

Wylly declined. Later, Wylly felt he had been ill-used by Dunmore and Matson in regard to an appointment in the Admiralty Court because he had not "taken a party." Insulted, Wylly resigned as Attorney General. On 1 April 1788, the day when, as Mr. Matson put it, "he was accosted by Mr. Wylly on the street," Mr. Wylly reminded Mr. Matson of their conversation some four months before and put the question to him in front of Mr. Forbes, who was the only other person there. Mr. Matson responded that he remembered having asked Mr. Wylly to take command of a militia but denied he had ever advised him, or anyone, to take a party. At that moment, Mr. Wylly admitted, "I certainly did, coolly and deliberately, whisper in his ear, 'Sir, you are a damned liar.'"

For Wylly right was might and the real test of truth lay in the law. When Wylly brought action against Mr. Matson for his false arrest, the Chief Justice played "hide and seek" for a while, then with the governour's assistance "ran away to England." It was then that Dunmore decided to shut down the courts and represent the colony as being in a state of rebellion. In this scandalous manner, Wylly stated, were "the interests, the reputation, and the laws of a valuable Colony sacrificed, by the arbitrary mandate of a Madman, to serve the infamous purposes of a knave."[18]

There happened to be in Nassau at that time one William Augustus Bowles, a colourful personality and controversial character, who from later activities appears to have been on very friendly terms with Lord Dunmore. (See plate 39.) It is perhaps a little too curious that on 9 April 1788, only a week after the Wylly incident, Bowles, under oath, swore that a loyalist faction in Nassau and Abaco was plotting independence from Great Britain.

Young William Bowles had fought with the Maryland Loyalists during the

Revolution. For a time he had taken refuge with the Creek Indians in West Florida and had even married the daughter of one of their chiefs. He had endeared himself to the Indians as their "Beloved Warrior" and became a controversial figure in international politics as Director General of the Creek Nation. The tall, handsome William Bowles must have posed a striking character on Bay Street when outfitted in his Indian dress complete with a turban stuck with feathers, arm bands, and other ornaments. Besides being a daring and resourceful soldier, he was a portrait painter, an amateur chemist, a flutist, and an actor.[19]

Bowles allied himself with Lord Dunmore and John Miller, rival merchant of the Panton, Leslie Company which had been "marked out for destruction" by them. Allegedly, Dunmore borrowed armaments from the Fort Nassau magazine and Miller's company financed a secret expedition, the sole objective of which was to raid one of Panton's stores on the St. Johns in September, 1788. George Welbank, one of the captains on this raid, had known Bowles in New York before he emigrated to Carleton in the *William* on 22 August 1783.[20]

Dunmore, of course, denied supplying Bowles with arms from the king's stores but admitted to sending two Irish convicts to Baltimore with him and giving three Indians some "trinkets." In the only extant issue of the *Lucayan Herald* (19 August 1789) Bowles swore that Lord Dunmore and Mr. Miller had had nothing to do with his recent trip to Florida. He stated that his purpose for going there was to settle some destitute Bahamians on Creek lands and that he had no designs on Panton's St. Johns store; in fact, he said that he had saved the storekeeper's life. According to Bowles's statement, those false accusations were wrung out of a few thieves in their party who had escaped to the Spaniards at St. Augustine. The facts are otherwise.[21] The falseness of Bowles's testimony must be emphasized here because he charged a fellow Maryland Loyalist, John Barclay of Carleton, Abaco, with treason. In another statement sworn, curiously enough, before John Miller on 9 April 1788, Bowles testified that in February of 1787 he had met John Barclay in Georgia. When Bowles informed Barclay of his intention to visit the Bahamas, Barclay urged him to call upon Messrs. Johnston, Hepburn, and Cruden, leaders of the strong loyalist party. According to Bowles, Barclay showed him some letters from Cruden which outlined the facility of rendering "the Bahamas independent from Great Britain. They would then open their Ports to all the world" and derive greater profits from the salt ponds.

When Bowles asked how the Bahamas would defend themselves against Great Britain, Barclay replied that England would not even consider the islands "an object worth contention." If opposed, Colonel Cruden, former superintendent for the sequestered estates in South Carolina, had worked out a plan to mobilize troops. Barclay had been appointed to gain the support of the inhabitants in Abaco and a day would be appointed for them "to rise and possess themselves of the Government;" when he had left Abaco, however, "things were not sufficiently ripe to put their scheme in execution."

Although approached many times by Mr. Barclay, Bowles said he had refused to join the party whose object was to "overturn the King's government." Bowles had arrived in the Bahamas by April, 1787, and "having much leisure" had observed the loyalist faction in Nassau. After a year it seems he was convinced that everything Barclay had told him was the truth. "There has been and is now a design to wrest this colony from the Dominion of Great Britain."[22]

It is more than coincidental that Mr. Bowles should wait until the moment of the Wylly-Matson controversy to come forth with this startling declaration. Perhaps in this, as in the later nefarious action against the Panton, Leslie Company in Florida, Bowles served as Dunmore's pawn. In his secret and confidential testimonial to Lord Sidney, Mr. Matson carried Bowles's testimony a step further. The United States, lured by the "easy supply of salt," would aid the American Loyalists in their scheme to make the Bahamas independent of the mother country.

If Dunmore wanted to stir up more trouble in order to give the appearance of rebellion, he knew how and where to go to do it—Abaco. The governour had squandered more of the colony's funds by hiring a small schooner, the *Shearwater*, for his personal use. In it he sent Samuel Mackay to Abaco to seize smuggled goods and to bring back "Rebel property Negroes."

Eric Williams perceptively asserted that "West Indian History, conceived in monopoly, was reared in smuggling." Suffice it to say then that Abaco played a small part in the development of West Indian history. Even as late as 1825, an American newspaper gave an account of vessels wrecked by a June storm and "among the vessels named is one of the *Abaco smugglers*"

> ... the sloop *Stranger*, Child, from Green Turtle Key, Bahamas bound to New York, cast away on Currytuck beach, during the gale of the 4th. The cargo, consisting of old copper, brazeilleto, turtle, fruit and conch shells, has been chiefly saved, and will be sold by the commissioners of wrecks.

The *Gazette* had further comment: "This smuggling trade with Abaco, Harbour Island and North part of Eleuthera ought by some means to be put down, for it tends so much to the injury of the Revenue, when the country is considerably in debt."[23]

On it goes, and so it happened on a Sunday, 4 May 1788, that Mr. Mackay with a company of armed men, surrounded the plantation house of Mr. Richard Pearis at Spencers Bight, and demanded entrance to his cellar where allegedly smuggled corn was stored. When Mr. Pearis asked to see his authority, Mackay babbled something about a deputation from Mr. Baker, a naval officer, and waved a letter showing Dunmore's large, bold signature but refused to read or allow anyone else to see the letter. Philip Dumaresq, magistrate, refused to assist Mackay when he learned he had no writ of assistance, and Pearis would not give him the key. Mackay placed Pearis and his family, along with his guests Messrs. Pengree, Edwards, Wilson, Forbes, Armstrong, and Captain Smith, under house arrest while he broke open two of the stores and seized in the king's name 401 bushels of Indian corn.

Pearis wrote to a friend in Nassau that Mackay had nearly caused a riot before he left Spencers Bight that Sunday.

> This Man has likewise spread such Confusion among our Negroes, that some of my Neighbours are left without their House Servants, and all have ...

gone to the Woods. Those who have been retaken or come in uniformly declare that they were misled by Captain Mackay and his crew who told them he had the Governor's authority to carry them to Nassau, and that all the Rebel Property Negroes would be made free. A Memorial and affidavits are going down upon this Business. . . .

Pearis was "determined to have satisfaction or quit a Country where such doings are permitted."[24]

The memorial from Spencers Bight stated that upon the encouragement of Captain Mackay some of their slaves went aboard the governour's yacht. The memorialists stopped them from going off with Mackay but afterwards many absconded. Mr. Pearis and the other memorialists stated that they could not "believe it is your Lordship's intention to distress this infant Settlement or to bring ruin and misery upon its Inhabitants."

Dunmore immediately sailed to Spencers Bight, his illegal court in tow. Thirty Blacks came out of the woods to claim their freedom. Twenty-nine of the claimants were "adjudged to be Slaves." Wylly included the Abaco slave revolt memorial and trial in his published *Account* to prove the duplicity of the governour. He chose however, not to include a further damning piece of evidence; for one memorialist testified that Mackay's "Authority" consisted of these words: "'Sir, if you should be in want of any assistance you can get six or eight of the *armed Negroes in the woods* . . . at any rate I wish you to bring down three or four of them. Yours [Dunmore].'"

According to Wylly, there was no rebellion unless "we date a trifling rebellion, which it had been judged expedient to kick up among the Negroes upon the Island of Abaco." On 2 June the Spencers Bight Loyalists thanked Lord Dunmore for the "impartial trial which has been afforded to our Runaway Slaves. . . ."[25]

While Dunmore held court at Spencers Bight, Samuel Mackay patrolled the coast in the governour's yacht *Shearwater* looking to commit fresh piracies. Near Maxwell Town, Mackay fired at William Kennedy's twenty three ton sloop *Elizabeth*, sending one shot whizzing through the main sail and another through the jib. He ordered Mr. Kennedy to "heave to" and asked to see his register.

It so happened that Kennedy had just purchased the vessel from Cornelius Blanchard and had gone to Nassau to make an application only to find that the Customs House was out of blank forms. Once again, Mackay had no writ but informed Kennedy that Lord Dunmore had sent him "for the express purpose of Seizing" his sloop. Kennedy said he had just heard that the governour was at Spencers Bight and would go there now. Mackay promised to wait while Kennedy went to his house to get his papers and clothes, but Mackay pirated the sloop and took it to Dunmore.

Kennedy had to hire a boat to take him to Spencers Bight. When he got there, he was unable to convince Dunmore that his sloop "had done nothing illegal" and was entitled to a register. Dunmore, who would hear no excuses, took the sloop to Nassau and prosecuted it in the Admiralty Court. Since Dunmore had not allowed Kennedy to go to Nassau in his own sloop, it had been sold by the time he arrived there.[26]

Captain Kennedy was advised not to risk court costs by prosecuting Mackay, who had no property, and "no suit could be brought against Lord Dunmore within his government."

On 13 May, just a few days after the corn seizure and slave revolt, Richard Pearis deemed it to his best interest to inform the governour about a memorial "slashing most seriously at your Lordship's conduct." The paper had been circulated at Abaco but had been rejected by Pearis and his friends at Spencers Bight. They had also refused to empower an agent to go to England with complaints. It may very well have been this letter rather than the 6 May memorial which brought Dunmore to Spencers Bight and condemned the runaway Blacks to slavery.[27]

The memorial from Abaco, directed to William Pitt, Chancellor of the Exchequer, stated in strong language the points of grievance: six of the fifteen members of the House of Assembly held their seats by false returns, the public treasury had been "squandered away" and no account made, and an unconstitutional tribunal made up of three bankrupts held court; slaves had been stolen, seizures had been made on Spanish trade, the courts of justice had been shut up, and the Chief Justice had gone off without giving public notice. The governour had given him private transport and had "actually accompanied him out to sea, at the time of said elopement." The Abaco memorialists avowed their determination to carry their complaints "to the foot of the throne" and had empowered an agent to go to England prepared with charges and armed with proofs of their intolerable "oppression."[28]

William Wylly, the agent appointed, arrived in England in October, 1788, to find he had a formidable opponent in Anthony Stokes, colonial agent for the Bahamas. Mr. Stokes had been misinformed and in turn had misrepresented the situation in the Bahamas to Whitehall, thereby causing the Wylly affair to drag on through the summer of 1789. Wylly believed John O'Halloran was the "ingenious writer" of the letters to Stokes.[29] The Georgia Loyalist had married the daughter of an Old Inhabitant and was one of the illegal members of the House of Assembly.

Wylly learned that Stokes had sent a communication to Evan Nepean, Permanent Undersecretary for the Home Department, on 3 June 1788, that a vessel had arrived from Georgia reporting that in the Bahamas matters were in the "utmost confusion." The Earl of Dunmore had been obliged "to keep to his houses and have a vessel in waiting for the sake of his personal safety." Wylly reported that "confusion" was a favourable word in that it described the "natural result of shutting up the courts." Wylly had come to England with petitions from scores of people who had been injured by the corruption in government and the suspension of civil justice on 22 April 1788. In consequence some people had left the Bahama Islands.[30]

Stokes attended a meeting of London merchants who were interested in trade with the Bahamas and reported back to the Committee of Correspondence in Nassau. Wylly had spoken for three hours at a previous meeting, accusing the governour of many oppressive acts including the seizure of a vessel "in person."

To prevent Wylly from spinning out his speech at this particular meeting, Stokes begged the floor. He reminded Mr. Wylly and the committee of merchants that the Loyalists had quarreled with every governour since their arrival. That honest man Mr. Maxwell had been recalled; they had treated Lt Gov. Powell, one of their own, in such a way "as to hasten his end," and had used Mr. Brown and now Lord Dunmore in the same manner. He had been informed that when the Loyalists could not impress their views on the Old Inhabitants, they dragged an old cannon up to a summit overlooking the town and threatened to fire.

Stokes respected Mr. LeMesuier, chairman of the meeting of British merchants, but questioned his judgement in allowing Mr. Wylly to harangue the governour without bringing any formal charges against him. Procedure instructed that complaints against the House of Assembly be put in writing and laid before the governour and council and that grievances against the governour be submitted to the secretary of state. He further urged Mr. LeMesuier to recall what happened in America when London merchants had interfered.[31]

Wylly returned to England in June, 1789, to solicit the secretary of state on behalf of merchants and planters of the Bahamas regarding matters of "general grievance." Fully prepared this time, Wylly presented Lord Grenville with a forty-four page pamphlet stating the nature of the "discontents which prevail in the Bahamas." According to Wylly, a contributing factor was the governour's lack of culture and education and his ignorance of the constitution of England. His principles of government were what one might expect "from a lordly despot of a petty clan." Wylly remarked that Dunmore's private life was as reprehensible as his public one and did not elucidate further on that point, but whoremongering was implied. Wylly requested that Grenville suspend opinion until he had heard "both sides of the question."[32]

Although much angered at Anthony Stokes' attempt "to vilify and traduce" his character, Wylly remarked that the man's "age and strange character must protect him from my resentment."[33] Wylly presented a lengthy letter to clear up any misrepresentations which Mr. Stokes had transmitted to Whitehall. He included a copy of the speech delivered by Governour Montfort Brown to the House of Assembly in 1779 accusing Bahamians of complicity with the Americans while American Loyalists shed their very blood in the cause of Great Britain, Wylly's question was: how is it that the Old Inhabitants are dutiful now and the Loyalists are rebellious "all of a sudden?"

Stokes continued to bring up the Matson business although Wylly had long since been vindicated of that charge. Wylly had prosecuted only to prove to Dunmore that no man "whatever his rank or situation could violate the law." He also said that Dunmore would have stopped his trial but was at Abaco at the time. A report of the proceedings was published in the *Bahamas Gazette*.[34]

Early in September, 1789, Colonel Pearis of Abaco finally got his day in court. He brought an action against Samuel Mackay for armed trespass and a £5,000 damage suit for the seizure of his Indian corn. Since Mackay had acted under deputation of a naval officer who was not a customs house officer, the seizure was illegal. Counsel for the plaintiff argued that Mackay's trespass was an invasion of a British subject's individual rights and as such "one of the most flagrant acts of oppression ever known in any part of the British Dominions."[35] Although dramatically effective, this exaggeration did not put Spencers Bight, Abaco, on the map but it did bring in a conviction.

John Baker, the naval officer, may have been the real victim of Dunmore's raid on Pearis's corn. He had to pay part of Mackay's damages and probably had not received a shilling from the sale of the corn. Baker submitted an account for £400 as "damages given against my deputy Samuel Mackay for the corn he seized at Abico which he brought to Nassau in the governour's schooner and by the governour's order." Baker also submitted a memorial stating that his property in the Bahamas had been detained against these actions.[36]

Dunmore accused Wylly of using the Baker and Kennedy complaints to misrepresent him to the home government. The governour declared that the seizure and condemnation of Mr. Kennedy's sloop were "a matter in which I could not possibly have the least concern whatever."[37] Once again Dunmore claimed his hands were clean. If the Loyalists were to remain in the Bahamas, they would have to learn to be as patient as the Old Inhabitants. Dunmore would be recalled but not until 1797. By that time, how many Loyalists would remain on Abaco to uncork a bottle of madeira to celebrate the departure of Lord Dunmore?

15

More Hurly-Burly

The search for better soil to grow cotton, the primary crop of the American Loyalists, drove refugees from island to island until finally drought, bugs, blight and hurricanes caused them to leave the islands forever. By 1788, Wylly reported that New Providence and the northward islands had not answered their expectation, "for which reason the planters are all removing further South." Islands inhabited at that time were New Providence, Abaco, Exuma, Eleuthera, Harbour Island, Long Island, Cat Island, Andros, and Turks Island. In barely four years the total white population had doubled and the black population had tripled. Brown's report of April, 1789, showed a total of three thousand Whites and eight thousand Blacks.[1]

At Abaco, there were forty-nine white male heads of families, ten planters with ten or more slaves, a total of 198 slaves and 1,837 acres of land in cultivation, although Wylly remarked that the planters on Abaco were "moving off." No Old Inhabitants appeared on the population record and almost half the black population were free: 282 Whites, 384 Blacks, giving a total for Abaco of 666. The cotton planters on Abaco 1 November 1785 were exclusively from the East Florida contingency: Brown, Weatherford, Armstrong, Wylly, Smith, Ferguson, and Pearis. This record notes that Colonel Brown and many of the other planters "are removed" to Caicos Island.[2]

The 1788 crop had been a total failure, but it had been because of the excellent "prospects of the cotton crop" in the Bahamas that planters from Grenada and Barbados were expected to emigrate. The *Gazette* predicted, "should the crop prove as unproductive as the last, the stream of emigration will in all probability be directed *from* rather than *to* the Bahamas." Happily, reports from the Out Islands from October to December again spoke favourably of an abundant cotton crop. Ravaged by the usual hurricanes, the 1788-89 crop was plagued by unseasonable weather as well. To the consternation of the planters, on the last day of February in 1789 snow fell in Nassau "for several minutes." Every possible remedy had been tried to eliminate the destructive worm called the chenille whose "baleful industry" had wreaked havoc in the cotton field but to little avail.[3]

The 1786 news from Abaco that "all things flourish" truly was, by 1789, a piece of intelligence "out of date." On 13 October 1789 Lord Dunmore had sailed to Abaco, the first island of his Out Island tour, only to find that most of the inhabitants had departed: only ten families remained and very few slaves. Although the soil was adaptable to the raising of all kinds of provisional crops, neither cattle or cotton seemed to thrive on the island. On the other hand, the whalers informed him that there was no island in the world better suited to whaling than Abaco. In all seasons of the year whales could be sighted from the shore. Whalers would "run out and kill them in their boats and tow them to shore without the assistance of large vessels." Dunmore believed he could encourage a few Nantucket families to settle on Abaco. Their only fear was seizure of their vessels as "American Bottoms" by customs house officials or His Majesty's ships. Dunmore mentioned in his report that Abaco had seven good harbours for small vessels where fresh water could be found: Carleton, Maxwell, Spencers Bight, Little Harbour, Eight Mile Bay, Fig Tree Hill, and the Crossing Rocks. Material for shipbuilding was abundant and convenient.[4]

In January, 1789, Dunmore purchased from John Ferguson and Joseph Smith nine Blacks and three tracts of land on Spencers Bight and Little Harbour containing 480 acres, with all buildings and improvements. Besides growing cotton, raking salt, and breeding sheep, Loyalists experimented in other forms of cultivation. Brown's committee reported that various grasses, reed cane, and especially the Madeira grape grew in great luxuriance. Wild grapes abounded, particularly on Abaco. Dunmore had planted a few cuttings of Madeira vines in February which were already bearing splendid grapes in July. He believed wine might be made on the island and proposed to encourage a few French Protestant families to settle on Abaco for that purpose.[5]

Powell's proclamation of 5 September 1785 announced the granting of forty acres to every master or mistress, and twenty acres for every white or black man, woman, or child in the household and the waiving of quit rent (of two shillings per one hundred acres) for ten years. Negotiations for the purchase of the Bahamas had begun in 1783 between the crown and the Lords Proprietors and were finally concluded in March, 1787. At last Great Britain had acquired the isles of perpetual June—for a trifling £12,000. Lord Dunmore issued the first official land grants in 1788, seeing to his own interests first. He parcelled out 5,355 acres for himself and 1,173 acres for his son Colonel Murray. When Eleanor Gambier received one grant of four thousand acres on Cat Island, Denys Rolle, obviously unaware of the vast amounts of vacant land available in the Bahamas Out Islands, complained that the lady's grant might "leave little for recompense to the Loyalists and East Florida planters."[6] Thomas Brown's acreage totaled six thousand, making him recipient of the largest single grant, with Abaco land comprising almost a third of it. (See appendix E.)

The almost thirteen thousand acres granted on Abaco were situated primarily on the main island. John Allender named the long narrow cay in Carleton Creek after himself but was never heard of more. A few Loyalists did find good planting on some of the larger outlying cays, those which pilot William Roberts had mentioned to the gentleman accompanying Wilson and McArthur to Abaco in 1784. The grant sheets for 1788-89 list the following: Crab Cay (Kenneth Ferguson), Powell's Cay (John W. Barclay), Little Guana Cay—Hope Town (George Smith, Philip Fry), Bridge's Cay (Martin Weatherford), Monjack Cay (John W. Barclay), Allen's Cay

PLATE 40
Thomas Stephens' plat, dated 6 December 1786 and signed by Surveyor General Josiah Tattnall, is the sole land grant to a Loyalist for Green Turtle Cay. (Book "B," courtesy of Lands and Surveys, Nassau, The Bahamas.)

(Edmund Rush Wegg), Man-O-War Cay (Josiah Valleau), Pensacola Cay (Robert Crannel).

Thomas Stephens rediscovered Green Turtle Cay and probably farmed his 140 acre tract on Gillams Bay. (See plate 40.) Although Stephens died before 26 October 1787, a codicil to his will stipulated that any property he might "be seized, possessed or entitled to" in the Bahamas should go to Edmund Rush Wegg to be held in trust for Wegg's children.[7] This grant probably passed to them. Thomas Stephens had been agent for the first group of New York Loyalists to arrive at Carleton and was the central figure in the stormy period following the initial emigration. Most of the Abaco Loyalists left suddenly without a trace, yet there is a pond on Green Turtle Cay known to this day as Stephens Pond.

Loyalist Margaret Pearis was the only woman to receive a grant on Abaco, but she probably abandoned her forty acres at Little Harbour in 1788 or 1789 to go to live with her father in the western suburbs of Nassau. In September, 1789, her father, Colonel Pearis, and William Jones gave notice in the *Gazette* warning people to keep their goats from climbing over their wall and destroying their "corn and Herbage." On 22 June 1790 her brother Richard married another Margaret, the loyalist daughter of Brigadier General Robert Cunningham, and they moved to Caicos with Colonel Brown.[8] A few years after Colonel Pearis's death, Margaret married Judge William Jones.[9]

Theodora Brown evidently did not apply for a grant at Abaco, but she was living at Spencers Bight in April 1789. The *Gazette* printed a notice that she had loaned Richard Pearis, Sr., £120, payable 15 April, 1789, and she had either "lost or mislayed" the note. But the widow Brown had further difficulties that year: the Blacks at Spencers Bight did not take kindly to re-enslavement. Recorded in the *Votes of the House of Assembly* was a payment of £60 to Theodora Brown for a "runaway Negro who was shot in Arms." Her husband may have been related to Thomas Brown, for she seems to have been part of the East Florida contingent that followed Brown to Caicos. As a Loyalist of some standing she received a grant for five hundred acres on Grand Caicos.[10]

Thomas Brown married Hetty Farr at Grand Caicos where his grants for 1788-89 were upwards of five thousand acres. In November, 1790, Brown wrote to the Honourable William Pitt that "had he bothered to petition at the close of the war he might have been as fortunate as any man who never saw the face of the enemy." His reason for petitioning at this time was that the Spanish government had offered him the post of commandant of troops in Florida with an additional salary of ten thousand dollars as Superintendent General of Indian Affairs. Brown had answered "that in peace or war my principles would never permit me to enter into the service of any foreign power without an express permission from the King I had the honor to serve." Not being on the best terms with the Creek nation, Governour Zespedes needed Brown to exert his influence with the Indian tribes in order to prevent outrages against the inhabitants. The attachment of the Creeks to Colonel Brown remained strong. Although they had never before been to sea, three Creek Indians came to Nassau to see their old friend in April, 1787. In the postscript of his letter to Chancellor Pitt, Brown also petitioned in behalf of another Loyalist who had emigrated to Abaco with him and now resided with Brown at Caicos. Charles Fox Taylor was the son of the third queen of the Cherokees and one Captain Taylor, natural son of the late Lord Holland. The well-educated young Taylor had served as captain and "War Leader" of the Cherokees and would have been "Head King and Chief" by now; but because of his attachment to His Majesty's service, Taylor had abandoned his American family and property "and every view of ambition in his own land." According to Brown, Taylor was a "singular worthy character" who deserved "some mark of His Majesty's favor."[11]

The planters at Caicos petitioned Lord Dunmore for supplies and for the prevention of illicit trade. Besides Thomas Brown and Charles Fox Taylor, the names of other Abaco settlers appear: Joseph M. Moore, Richard Pearis, Jr., John McIntosh, Thomas Armstrong, and John Harding, the agent who signed the letter from Carleton on 1 October 1783.[12]

More Loyalists made their departure from Abaco legally and otherwise. The 26 November 1790 issue of the *Bahamas Gazette* reported that John Mackay, a Nassau huckster, considerably in debt, had gone off "under the cloud of night" in a small sloop. Conjecture had determined that he was destined for Abaco to "take on board a Sergeant Armstrong's family and had gone on to West Florida," but the only direct evidence of John Armstrong's elopement was found in an unsigned letter from Abaco dated 9 November 1790.

John Mackay, John Armstrong and two other men landed at Blanchard's, possibly Maxwell Town. Forewarned of their arrival and in the face of their drawn swords, Blanchard was cautious; they likewise gave evasive answers to his questions. They had sent their boat around to Spencers Bight. Since there was no magistrate on the island, Blanchard alerted Mr. Weatherford and the correspondent as soon as Armstrong had left. Arming themselves, the three islanders went in pursuit but could find neither Armstrong nor the others. The three took out their boat, hoping to intercept Mackay, but were hampered by the dark, the wind and the high seas. At daybreak they returned to shore. Going to Armstrong's house, they found he had already been there and had carried off a boat and anchor belonging to Stuart, the carpenter. On Sunday Mackay returned by another route to pick up Armstrong's family and his effects and sail for Eight Mile Bay.[13]

The cotton crop of 1790 was not a "perfect crop" everywhere in the islands. Planters on Great Exuma and Cat Island watched puzzled as their neglected fields yielded and their laboured ones did not. The total pounds of cotton exported amounted to 940,000. Loyalist Joseph Eve introduced his cotton gin, capable of cleaning eighty to one hundred pounds of cotton a day. West India sheep, called goats by the islanders, multiplied profusely on Exuma. Lord Dunmore was still busily spending colony funds on the construction of Ft. Charlotte and renting a wrecking vessel "to get about in."[14]

In 1791 high winds hurt the Exuma cotton crop; the red bug appeared, and the chenille devastated fields in Nassau, Watlings, Long Island, and Exuma. Cotton was a major concern. According to a Philadelphia planter, the smoke from a burning mound of gunpowder when dew was on the plant would destroy the worm, but no method was entirely successful. Although testimonials from various planters confirmed Eve's claim that his machine doubled the quantity of cotton ginned in one day, the Bahama Islands exported bales weighing only 752,966, a total slightly lower than that of the previous years; however, expectations were higher for 1792.[15]

Although almost phased out of the planting business, Abaco still figured in party politics. The election of a representative to replace Cornelius Blanchard was expected to take place on 24 June 1791. Because of some problem, a select committee of the House of Assembly was ordered to investigate the election. It was declared void, but on 11 October, five months later, the duly elected Philip Dumaresq took his seat. This was neither the first nor the last turmoil over an election in Abaco. Dunmore appointed Philip Dumaresq Receiver General and Treasurer of the General Assembly, a move they would both soon regret.[16]

The 1790-1794 list of land grants shows an exodus to other islands and gives only nine new tracts for Abaco. David Aiken, John Anderson, Daniel Dalby, Thomas Forbes, and George Harkness added one hundred acres to their holdings, and John Harris and Alexander McDonald received grants for the first time. William Wylly obtained two grants, dated 1791, for a total of 750 acres. The fees of £9 which Kenneth and John Ferguson, Hugh Dean, Thomas Forbes, George Smith and William Moxey paid when their grants were audited in 1790 may indicate active holdings on the island. Many of the proprietors formerly associated with Abaco appear on a 1792 survey map of Long Island.[17]

The precarious cotton industry caused many Loyalists to return to America. Beaten by the forces of nature, Loyalists capitulated and some even chose to become Spanish subjects. The Reverend John Richards wrote that a new settlement was to be formed on the banks of the Mississippi and that the Spanish were giving every encouragement to new settlers. In his letter to the S.P.G., 16 December 1791,

Richards enclosed a population report which recorded a total of only 220 inhabitants for the islands of Abaco and Andros combined. The historian Wilbur Siebert wondered how Mr. Richards could have "missed so widely on the numbers at Great Abaco" since nearly three thousand Loyalists had gone there just eight years before; but from evidence of early emigration, it must be acknowledged that Richards was correct. Another Anglican priest verified Richards' figures when he toured the Out Islands and reported in June, 1792, that Abaco and Andros were "almost deserted."[18]

The news from Abaco brought by Mr., Blanchard in the schooner *Lark* in January, 1792, reported that the few struggling cotton planters had had their crop injured last December by cold weather and high wind. Islands to the windward submitted more favourable accounts to exceed any former crop. Joseph Eve's horse and wind machines worked overtime; Eve claimed his gin machine, operated by two boys and a horse, could clean five hundred pounds of cotton in ten hours. By November 1,162,822 pounds of cotton had been exported.[19]

In England, staunch abolitionist Mr. Wilberforce submitted that it was the opinion of his committee that the slave trade "ought to be abolished." In October, the New World commemorated the tricentenary of the European discovery of the West Indies. Cat Island was Christopher Columbus's San Salvador for that celebration. In Paris, revolutionaries revelled in their new-found freedom by butchering the friends of the king and queen.[20]

By proclamation in May Dunmore allowed the importation of corn, grain, rice, and salt provisions in "foreign as well as British Bottoms" and was censured for his action by Whitehall in August, 1793. Importation in foreign bottoms was "contrary to law," particularly in time of war and could only be justified "upon absolute necessity." In July, Dunmore issued another proclamation to restrain the admittance of "French Mulatoes and Free Negroes" into the islands. French royalists from Santo Domingo came to Nassau and were "requested" to "proceed to America."[21]

In order to maintain the "dignity and honor of the governor," Dunmore's salary was doubled; and if the planned French invasion of the Bahamas by Genet and a force from New York had materialized, he might have had the chance to prove his worth. For the very first time in Bahamian history, New Providence was prepared for battle. Ironically, it would never again be attacked by a foreign power.

On 25 November, William and Alexander C. Wylly, Josiah Tattnall, Thomas Forbes, and Hugh Dean gave notice that they had granted permission to Harbour Islanders owning small vessels to cut cedars and other woods on their lands at Great and Little Abaco. In August of 1793 Mr. Tattnall and William Wylly had lost some of their plantation buildings when a devastating storm struck northern Long Island. Another man ventured to say he would not find one of his wind machines where he had left them.[22] One hopes that he had insured them.

Joseph Eve, the Eli Whitney of the Bahamas, charged £4 a year to insure his gins against "the Dread of being blown down in a gale." Without labour but with diligence and a steady wind, Eve's wind machine could gin four hundred pounds a day. (See plate 41.) Inventor, scientist and poet, Joseph Eve epitomized the industrious,

COTTON GIN,

Invented by Joseph Eve of Pennsylvania.

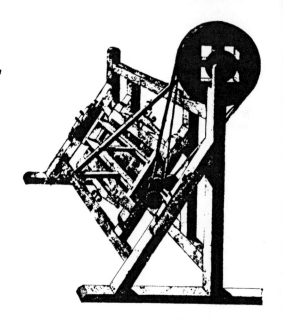

PLATE 41
Joseph Eve's gins
revolutionized the Bahamian
cotton industry. This machine
could be powered by the wind
or by cattle and could gin as much
as 360 pounds per day. (From
L. A. Parrish photo collection,
courtesy of Dr. Thelma Peters
and the Albert Lowe Museum.)

educated, and cultured Loyalist. As a subscriber to the library Joseph Eve worked on a committee to purchase books and in 1800 took over as editor of the *Bahamas Gazette* after the death of John Wells.

Led by talented and energetic men like Joseph Eve, the Loyalist invasion marked the beginning of a new era for the Bahamas. Besides bringing the Bahamas into prominence as exporters of cotton, Loyalists constructed public buildings, established laws, and founded a newspaper, a church and a library.[23]

The Abaco vote for 1794 caused such contention between the House and Dunmore that the governour finally dissolved the Assembly. On 26 September Mr. Haven laid a petition before the House from Richard Pearis, Sr., John Wells, and Alexander Taylor, three candidates in the election held at Abaco on 22 September. The votes at the close of the polls were as follows: John MacKenzie 12, Philip Dumaresq 11, Christopher Fisher 11 for the majority, and John Wells 10, Alexander Taylor 10, and Richard Pearis, Sr. 9, the losers and protestors.

The petitioners claimed that a number of unqualified persons had voted for MacKenzie, Dumaresq, and Fisher. They named Alexander Thomson, John Lovell, and John MacDonald as those who, having no right to vote, had taken oaths of qualification and thereby were guilty of "corrupt and wilful perjury." Thomson had voted as a freeholder based upon a warrant for survey of land; John Lovell had sold all his property. When he came to the poll in the morning, John McDonald was sober and declared he could not take the oath of qualification; however, he had returned about one o'clock, drunk, and swore that the honourable Mr. Miller had seen a grant of lot of land to a Miss Foster, now his wife. He subsequently admitted he knew nothing about the land; in fact there was no such grant.

Christopher Fisher had voted for himself and for MacKenzie and Dumaresq, founding his right to do so upon a "pretended conveyance of land," supposed to be held by Joseph Curry and company, of which company he said he was a member. The petitioners maintained that the majority had been obtained illegally by "nefarious conduct."

The petition was referred to a committee whose findings declared the election void. It was resolved that the governour be requested to issue a new writ of election for Abaco. Outraged, Dunmore dissolved the assembly. The Abaco vote, petition, and resolution provided his lordship with his fifth and sixth reasons for dissolution, but the next year Abaco constituents elected Hugh Dean, Alexander Taylor and James Webster as representatives.[24]

Fort Charlotte was a useless waste of money, and Dundas censured Dunmore for his expenditures. In 1795, the king showed displeasure at the expense involved in keeping so many armed vessels at Nassau but in spite of instructions to stop construction, Dunmore continued work on Fort Charlotte. French privateers cruised the islands, but natural disasters and Harbour Island wreckers, who would soon repopulate Abaco, seemed to have that situation under control. On 17 December three "Harbour Island vessels from Abaco" brought in eighteen Frenchmen, crew of the privateer schooner the *Parisienne*, which had been cast away near Whale Cay. Their guns and military stores were in the hold and they were bound for Cuba to recruit more sailors.[25]

In one of his last official actions, Dunmore tried to help the 1,400 wreckers who were having a problem in the Admiralty Court with improper disposal of salvaged goods. The insurers at Lloyds Coffee House attested to the fact that considerable amounts had been saved to their insurors by the Bahamas wreckers who should be encouraged to continue their work. Dunmore informed the Duke of Portland that Mr. Franks, the Attorney General, seemed determined to destroy "those poor people" by contradicting "established practice in this country for many years respecting wrecking vessels and the property saved by them." If allowed to continue, Franks would "put an end to the wrecking business by which much property and many lives have been saved."[26]

In 1796 Dunmore had lost control of himself and of the Council and Assembly as well; recall was imminent. On one visit to Harbour Island, his favourite retreat, Dunmore's frustrations erupted in violence. John Clear of Harbour Island testified that, without the slightest provocation, Dunmore had assaulted him in public by beating him over the head with a stick.[27]

Even before Dunmore's departure, Mr. Wylly began liquidating Dunmore's household, Philip Dumaresq resigned his post as receiver general, but on 10 March he refused to turn over his books to his replacement James Menzies, alleging he had been advised to keep them. On Mr. Wylly's motion it was resolved that Philip Dumaresq was guilty of contempt and a warrant was issued for his arrest. The next day Mr. Menzies reported he had received some papers but no books because Mr. Dumaresq told him that he had petitioned the governour and Council for a trial and had retained the books for that purpose. He then asked to be discharged from the common jail because of ill health. On 16 March he paid his fees and was released. On 22 August, a house committee examined Dumaresq's books and found that he owed £1,859.18.½.[28]

Dunmore may or may not have been directly involved in Dumaresq's indiscretions, but he had committed many of his own. George Chalmers, agent to the Bahamas from 1792-1823, provided the secretary of state with evidence of Dunmore's corruption. Besides assault, his list of offenses included drunkenness, keeping mistresses (one of whom may have been Mrs. Dumaresq), overspending colony funds, irregularities in granting land, and illegalities in closing the courts, not to speak of quarrels with the Assembly and Council. All of this built a powerful case for a recall which many Loyalists thought was long overdue.[29]

Lt. Gov. John Forbes arrived to take up his post in November, 1796. Early in 1797 England declared war on Spain and William Wylly was appointed Chief Justice. Forbes fell victim to yellow fever during the summer, and President Hunt once again took charge of the interim government. Dunmore's opponents showed signs of renewed anxiety. Since Forbes' commission did not arrive until ten months after the lieutenant governour's death, Dunmore's commission remained in force. Although Dunmore petitioned for reinstatement, the king appointed William Dowdeswell, a young military man, son of the late Chancellor Dowdeswell, who arrived in Nassau late in March of 1798.[30]

Even the Church shared in altercations with Lord Dunmore. In 1795 no salaried person, the Reverend Mr. Richards among the lot, had received a single shilling all year. Perhaps the Council paid for Dunmore's increase in salary by neglecting to pay anyone else. In addition, Dunmore had "'possessed himself of the most ancient burying ground'" on Harbour Island, which he desecrated together with a portion of the glebe, the Church's own land. Another complaint lodged against the governour was that he maintained that laws forbidding incestuous marriages in England did not apply to the colonies.[31]

The Reverend William Gordon, outspoken opponent of slavery, began his ministry at Harbour Island at some time before 7 June 1796, the date when the inhabitants of St. Johns Parish petitioned for his removal. The name of Joseph Curry heads the list of signatures on this petition. The inhabitants complained to Dunmore that Mr. Gordon held passionate and mercenary attitudes in regard to church business and had insisted on having the governour's buildings torn down because they encroached upon the burial grounds. Besides this, a speech impediment produced such a "sluggish manner" in his reading of the service that "it was impossible to understand one fourth part of what he uttered."[32]

In May, 1799, Joseph Curry and the Reverend Mr. Gordon locked horns over the lustful behaviour of a black man named Prince.[33] On 7 May Mr. Charles Russel came to Mr. Gordon, also one of the magistrates on Harbour Island, and accused four black men, one of whom belonged to Joseph Curry, of "having ravished a Negro Wench of his." Gordon immediately sent a warrant to Constable Uriah Sanders to apprehend them, which he did. Gordon questioned the girl, who declared that against her will, she was "enjoyed by all of them." Another black man stated under oath that at a "Negro Dance" on the 6th he had taken this girl under his protection because he suspected that some fellow desired "to entice her to Whoredom." One of the accused men "belonging to Mr. Joseph Ingraham" said she had agreed to be his whore for two shillings and that they had left the party. The other three men followed, overtaking the couple just a short distance off "a most public street in

Dunmore Town." The four men argued about who should enjoy her first and all admitted that they had enjoyed her.

Gordon wrote to another justice of the peace, Mr. Sinclair, to confirm his sentence of thirty-nine lashes "well laid on" as just punishment for these men guilty of such a shocking display of whoredom.[34] With written authorization from Mr. Sinclair, Gordon notified the owners to come forth if they had any objection. Three owners gave their consent and their Negroes were whipped. Mrs. Curry sent word that her husband was off the island and that she would take her Negro by force from the whipping post if Gordon persisted. Angered, Mr. Gordon ordered that Prince be whipped. Hearing this, a not-so-patient Patience rushed into Gordon's room in a rage and demanded her Negro. She was about to lay hold of Prince when Mr. Gordon stopped her. The clergyman and Mrs. Curry scuffled at least until Gordon managed to command Sanders to arrest her in the king's name. Subdued in the face of imprisonment, Mrs. Curry controlled herself and said calmly that she did not think Prince should be whipped until Mr. Curry returned. Gordon agreed to wait and released Prince to Mrs. Curry's custody until that time.

Joseph Curry arrived on the 9th and stormed into Mr. Gordon's room, hot from Mrs. Curry's rendition of the facts in the case, and shouting that "he did not chuse that his Negro should be tried" by Mr. Gordon but by Mr. Edwards in Nassau. Gordon sent Sanders to bring Prince to him. Curry raved on that he would prevent it. Gordon threatened to imprison Joseph Curry unless he put up a bond of £40 and found two other men to bind themselves in £20 each that he would keep the peace until next quarter's court session.

Uriah Sanders returned without Prince; Mrs. Curry, "deficient in honour," had hidden him. Gordon allowed Curry to go home only on the condition that he take Uriah Sanders and certain letters from himself along to Nassau. Before sunup the next day Curry sailed away in his schooner *Betsy* with Prince, but without the constable or Mr. Gordon's letters. A few days later the Reverend Mr. Gordon sent Uriah Sanders to Nassau with a letter to Attorney General Moses Franks.[35]

After he heard that Prince would not be punished, Gordon wrote to Mr. Franks that he was not surprised because Mr. Curry was known to have a great sway over people's minds. He had certainly convinced the governour, and they both probably had a good laugh over Curry's recounting of the incident. Dowdeswell wrote to Mr. Gordon that to his mind Mr. Curry did not deserve "the usage that he met with" from Gordon.[36] As did his grandfather Colonel Curry of Carolina, Joseph probably came to be more in the governour's favour than he would have had the incident never happened.

Later, Gordon asked for six months leave to recover his health. The leave was granted but the governour refused to allow Gordon to return to the Harbour Island parish. "King Curry," as Joe Curry was called in Harbour Island, had seen to that.[37]

The cotton crop began to fail in all the islands around 1797 due to heavy rains, hurricane, the red bug, and the chenille. A valuable cay of 220 acres, probably Man-O-War, which lies adjacent to Abaco, had to be put up for sale. According to the notice the island was interspersed with high hills and valleys." The hills commanded a picturesque view of a number of small cays, Marsh Harbour, and the ocean. The advertisement went on to promise that the rich and fertile valleys would produce large crops of Georgia cotton, corn, and other vegetables, but the promise was unduly optimistic.[38]

Two years later, the cotton crop of 1800 failed so miserably that planters petitioned the government for an inquiry that led to the formation of regulations for cotton planting. William Wylly attributed the failure to various causes: planting too large fields, exhausting the soil by constant tillage, destroying the vegetable bodies by burning fields, and cutting down the woods thereby exposing them to high winds and the sun.[39]

The planters demanded strict regulations be enforced regarding the cultivation of cotton; the Bahamas would cease to be a plantation colony unless some means could be found to stop the emigration of planters whose crops had failed. The government must encourage the planting of coffee, pimiento, or any other tropical crop that had a different yield season than that of cotton. A means of destroying the red bug and chenille must be found. The king must be petitioned to remove restrictions on grants, and fresh lands must be made available without the loss of old grants.[40]

In spite of the reopening of the grant office in 1802, the exodus of planters continued. Circumstances became so desperate for Henry Yonge, Esquire, member of the House, that he departed the island unannounced, leaving behind his debts. Yonge left in a vessel belonging to him but registered in "the name of a woman of colour with whom he is said to cohabit." A strong spirit of emigration" persisted, especially to Georgia and neighbouring states in America. Thomas Brown estimated that more than three thousand Loyalists had emigrated to the southern part of Georgia. Brown extracted comments from a letter from his friend James Moss, second only to himself as the "largest proprietor of slaves" in the Bahamas. Moss stated that Long Island was almost deserted and that many other planters in the Out Islands would have gone by now but for the expectation of fresh grants of land. He and some of his Crooked Island neighbours planned to stay on another twelve months to rake salt. Brown informed officials in Great Britain that unless the administration supported a request of the Bahamas Legislature to allow the exportation of Turks Island salt in American bottoms, all proprietors, with the exception of those at New Providence and Eleuthera, would emigrate from the Bahamas.[41]

Brown's primary reason for making a trip to England at this time was to salvage his own estate on Caicos. The French War on Hispaniola had forced all but four families at Caicos to abandon their possessions and flee to the American states. Because of his particular part in the late rebellion he would not be safe there, but most of his money had gone into the defence of Caicos. By his removal, Brown would have to sacrifice property consisting of eight thousand acres of land, thirteen cotton plantations, and a sugar estate. Brown asked to trade all his holdings on Caicos for a grant of land on St. Vincent.[42]

Nathaniel Hall had been about to embark for Georgia when he heard about an

PLATE 42: In another original oil painting, Alton Lowe depicts
Nassau's St. Matthew's Church, the "elegant little church" which first
opened on 18 July 1802. (From the collection of Claudette Kufter.)

imminent French attack on Nassau. About two to three thousand French troops
from Santo Domingo had assembled at Baracoa on the east end of Cuba. Hall told
Mr. Tattnall that he planned to stay on to give the French "a warm welcome."[43]

The Reverend Mr. Richards wrote the S.P.G. that the French were expected
any minute, that practically the entire island had been armed and that most of the
women and children had been sent to America or to the Out Islands. Richards had
sent his own family to Charleston. He was also concerned for the safety of St. Matthew's, the "elegant little church" which had opened 18 July 1802; but this attack on
Nassau never materialized. (See plate 42.)[44]

After the war, disbanded French soldiers and "other persons of desperate fortune" destroyed plantations and ravaged the Out Islands. Settlements were scattered, but in December, 1804, the House of Assembly resolved to furnish £50 for a person to teach the poor children of Green Turtle Cay so there was habitation on at least one of the Abaco cays which Daniel McKinnon said were visited only by pirates and by turtles looking for a quiet place to lay their eggs.[45]

McKinnon also remarked that there seemed to be "nothing remarkably flourishing in the circumstances of Abaco." One Abaconian, Benjamin Archer, found himself in a state of "absolute want," claiming that his house was beset and burnt, his hogs and poultry destroyed and other "outrages" committed by Benjamin Saunders, Richard and William Sawyer, and William Clear.[46] No grants for Abaco appeared on the list for 1803, but there were still enough freeholders to warrant three seats in the House. The inhabitants of Abaco, however, continued to have difficulty with their elections. The first ballot in 1804 was declared void and the House incurred the expense of £108 to hire Joseph Curry's schooner and crew for two election trips to Abaco. In February, 1805, Alexander Bain, William Kerr, and James Armbrister took their seats for Abaco.[47]

That Abaco was no longer a plantation island is clearly shown by its slave population. In addition to two free black males living on the island, a return of slaves in Abaco in 1805 totalled a scant *fifteen persons*: four men, four women, six children, and one female "between twelve and twenty years of age."[48]

16

"Anything to Make a Living"

Harbour Islanders repopulated the Abacos and intermarried with the remaining few diehard Loyalists. According to Thelma Peters, this remnant of Loyalists was composed of sturdy stock, humbler people than the Southern planters. These Loyalists who had stayed on Abaco had adjusted to "the only practical economy of the Bahamas, one directly or indirectly tied to the sea." Because they had adapted to the Bahamian way of life, these Loyalists "did not alienate the Conchs" as had the cotton planters who had departed.[1]

Together these people established three principal settlements on the windward cays: Green Turtle, Man-O-War, and Little Guana or Elbow Cay (Hope Town). Dr. Peters compares these offshore islands to coastal New England, for the inhabitants possess the same "qualities of ruggedness and resourcefulness often associated with Yankee sailors. Scornful of racial mixtures," these settlers stubbornly refused interracial marriage although, in the case of Hope Town, close intermarriage caused serious degeneration in their physical and mental health.[2]

Harold Lowe, much respected in the village of New Plymouth, Green Turtle Cay, for both his industry and his generosity, has devoted a great deal of time and study to the history of Abaco. He believes that some of the Green Turtle Cay settlers came from Harbour Island and were primarily mariners who farmed as well as engaging in wrecking.[3] He and his brother Floyd share in the heritage of their predecessors, for they reap the harvests of both the sea and the land. Part of the land farmed by Harold Lowe was the two hundred acres on Manjack Cay that was originally granted George Catton in 1806.

Emigration from Harbour Island to the Abaco cays could have started around the turn of the century during the time the land office was closed and Loyalists were emigrating to other Out Islands or back to America. The settlement at Green Turtle Cay was probably fairly well established by 1800, for Richard and Mercy Curry had moved there sometime between 1795 and 1803. Between 1806 and 1808, fourteen new grants appeared on the grant list. The ancestors of Floyd and Harold Lowe appear on the list: Benjamin Curry acquired 122 acres on Crab Cay in 1806 and Gideon Lowe was granted 240 acres at Angel Fish Creek at Rocky Harbour in 1807. Other grants for Abaco were listed in the names of Isaac Rush Tucker, John Hancock Kelly (Man-O-War), James Braynen, Esquire (Great Guana Cay), Benjamin Archer, Benjamin

Saunders, Benjamin Roberts, Jacob Adams (Little Guana Cay), Mathew Lowe, and Ridley Pindar.[4]

In his *Short Account* William Wylly stated that among the fifty-eight families on Harbour Island there were only five surnames: "Roberts, Russell, Saunders, Sawyer and Currie," but he was not entirely correct. Although these families comprised the majority of the population, theirs were not the only surnames on the island. In addition there were such names as Bethell, Albury, Thompson, Johnson, Melone, Pindar, Sweeting, Kemp, and Lowe. All the aforementioned names appear in the last Slave Register taken for the year 1834, but almost none of the original Abaco Loyalists show up in this register.[5] (See appendix F.)

A Georgia Loyalist and drummer in the King's Rangers, Conrad P. Baker, who changed his name from Pennybaker, was a Great Guana Cay planter who consistently registered only one female slave named Ginny or Jenny. In 1828 Conrad gave gifts of land on Great Guana Cay to his wife Margaret, his son Philip and his daughter Nancy. Baker also gave his son a seventeen foot boat which he had built with his own hands in 1825. Alton Lowe's great uncle Oliver Saunders, a man noted for his fine memory, spoke about a loyalist lady with long black hair, named Baker, who had been wrecked off Green Turtle Cay. She could have been either Conrad's wife or daughter.[6]

Uncle Oliver also believed Jacob Adams to be a loyalist name in Abaco, and this particular piece of oral history can be verified. Clark's comprehensive work on the *Loyalists in the Southern Campaigns* confirms that a Private Jacob Adams of South Carolina who began his military career in the Orangeburgh Militia in 1780 went on to join Thomas Brown at the Siege of Augusta in 1781. Imprisoned by rebels during the Siege of Savannah, he was eventually released and fought with Major Bill Cunningham at Ninety-Six in 1782. Further verification of the loyalty and emigration of Jacob Adams appeared in his death announcement in the *Royal Gazette*. He died at Abaco, 30 May 1829, at "an advanced age." The notice stated that Adams was "an honest, industrious man who having fought for his King and country, settled in that island upwards of 40 years ago."[7]

In his study of the "Sanitary Conditions in the Bahama Islands" published in 1905, Clement Penrose included a genealogical chart showing the inbreeding that occurred in the Wyannie Malone family of Hope Town. Since Penrose did not document historical sources, it must be assumed that his information came from oral tradition. The chart shows that Jacob Adams married Wyannie, the daughter of Wyannie Malone, a Loyalist from Charleston who had emigrated to Elbow Cay in 1785; there are no colonial documents however, to verify the existence or loyalty of Wyannie Malone in South Carolina or to verify the death of her son Walter who, according to Penrose, died at Charleston. This does not mean that Penrose's information is false. On the contrary, he talked to people at Hope Town who in 1905 could have had first-hand knowledge of the settlement there.[8]

Loyalist Malones listed in Clark's records are from South Carolina and include a Benjamin and an Ephraim, both privates in the Camden militia under Colonel English and Colonel Ballantyne. Susannah Malone, a widow with two children under the protection of Colonel Ballantyne's regiment, was living as a refugee on James Island. She also received military pay for her son Benjamin, possibly deceased. There was an Ephraim Melone on the muster of Captain James Yarborough's South Carolina Light Horse Company in Charleston in 1782. Perhaps this man was Wyannie's husband or son. The Lewis Malone who signed an oath of allegiance on 15 June 1780 at Charleston could also have been related to her.[9]

Penrose's chart indicates further that Wyannie moved to Long Island, leaving her two sons, Ephraim and David, and her daughter Wyannie to propagate in such a manner that after the third generation inbreeding had caused physical deformities, deafness, blindness, insanity, and idiocy.[10]

Martin Weatherford, a Georgia Loyalist, served under Thomas Brown as "war conductor" to the Creek Indians. Having rendered himself obnoxious to the rebels, he suffered losses of property in Georgia and South Carolina which amounted to £1,692.5. Martin moved from Abaco to Harbour Island to plant on Russell's Island. He died in 1805, leaving a wife Isabella and several children: John, William, Charles, Richard, Caty, Charlotte, and Isabella."[11] Later the family moved to Key West. The Weatherford name has died out in Abaco, except for Man-O-War Cay, but many families on other islands can trace their ancestry back to this strong Loyalist.

Benjamin Archer named one of his sons "James Weatherford," probably after Martin's brother. The *Revolutionary Records of Georgia* 3 January 1783 show permission being granted to a James Weatherford "to send by one of the Flags to East Florida the children of Martin Weatherford."[12] Since James does not appear to have emigrated, perhaps Benjamin Archer chose this way to keep alive a friendship separated by loyalties.

Family tradition holds that a man named Nathan Key served in the British navy and came to the Bahamas sometime after the Revolution. He married Martha Roberts of Harbour Island on 23 January 1798 and received a grant of twenty two acres in 1807 and 220 acres at Marsh Harbour, Abaco, in 1812. He died there 20 October 1850 at age eighty-one. A relationship between Nathan Key and loyalist Philip Barton Key has not been established, but Philip Barton, son of Francis Key and captain in the Maryland Loyalists, had fought at the Siege of Pensacola and gone to England after the war. In 1785, he returned to Maryland and was elected to the General Assembly in 1794. His nephew Francis Scott Key wrote the United States national anthem, the "Star-Spangled Banner," in 1814 while watching the shelling of Fort McHenry from a British prison ship in the Chesapeake Bay.[13]

The John Russell, Abaco planter and shipwright, who registered forty-five slaves in 1834 may have been the son of John Russell, the South Carolina Loyalist and East Florida shipbuilder who maintained a shipyard on Hog Island after the war. John Russell the elder, whom Dunmore accused of keeping his wife and property in South Carolina, returned to East Florida in 1812. The tomb of the younger John Russell at Green Turtle Cay records his birth on 4 June 1770 and his death on 3 November 1840 at Abaco at the age of seventy years.[14]

Besides the Old Inhabitants of Harbour Island, the closely related people of Abaco can trace their ancestry back to these few persons: Jacob Adams and Martin Weatherford, loyalist soldiers, and Benjamin Archer, Wyannie Malone, Nathan Key,

Benjamin and Richard Curry, and John Russell, possibly Loyalists or related to
Loyalists.

The 1834 Slave Register shows that the Abaco proprietors employed their people
at woodcutting, turtling, and wrecking, activities carried on by Eleutherans at Abaco
from the arrival of the seventeenth century Bermudian Adventurers to the present. In
documenting the birth and baptism of little Harriet Eliza Bethel of Cherokee Sound,
Abaco, in 1830, the Christ Church Register recorded her father's occupation as
"planter, wrecker, fisherman or anything else to make a living."[15]

Bahamians did not go to the trouble of alerting vessels to danger by riding up and
down the beaches on a horse with a lantern tied around its neck as was done at Nags
Head, North Carolina. Nor was the practice of putting out false lights to lure ships into
the reefs as widespread as some writers would have it.

At times during the nineteenth century, imports by wrecking exceeded any others,
making wrecking an important industry in the Bahamas. The clergy denounced it as a
nefarious business. Reverend George Huxtable who served the Methodists in Nassau
in the 1850s was amazed at the number of fine vessels employed exclusively in the
salvage business. At times between 2500 to 3000 men went out cruising and "praying
for wrecks." Not all wrecks had natural causes. Huxtable described a circumstance
where a little wrecking schooner would signal a large ship to "heave to." The captain of
the wrecker would go aboard, and in the cabin the two captains would strike a bargain
over a cup of brandy. Sometimes such bargains would be made months before at New
York, Charleston, or other ports of embarkation. As a rule, there was no loss of life connected with the wrecks as used to be the case in Devonshire and Cornwall.[16]

Because salvors received a higher percentage of the value of wrecked goods taken
from a derelict vessel, they might be tempted to kill a lone survivor, but cases of this
kind were rare in the Bahamas. Acts of daring and bravery were characteristic of the
wreckers, and saving lives was always the first order of business. The first man to come
aboard a cast-away vessel became the wreck master and directed the operation. Salvaged goods were taken to Nassau where the Chamber of Commerce arbitrated any
disputes and accounts were settled.[17]

By necessity, wreckers must dwell on coasts so the second wave of inhabitants
settled on the outlying cays, windward of the main of Abaco. Green Turtle Cay soon
became the wrecking capitol of Abaco, and by mid-century wreckers carried salvaged
goods there for disposal.[18]

Frequent storms and the swift, changing currents of the Gulf Passage had plagued
navigators since the first Spaniards had travelled in Bahamian waters. Also, inaccuracies of English charts caused accidents up to the early part of the nineteenth century.
Roman's chart, considered to be the best navigational aid to pilots, was erroneous from
the "Pan of Matanzas [Cuba], and Double Headed Shot Key to the Coast of Florida." A
Spanish chart was dangerously mistaken in showing the islands of Abaco, Grand
Bahama, Great Isaac, and the chain of cays as far south as Orange Cay, a full thirty
miles westward of their actual position.[19]

About 1804 the Nassau papers began to print arrivals of wrecking vessels and list
specified items brought in as "salvaged or wrecked goods." From this year on, the

reports of vessels cast away on Abaco and wrecking vessels arriving from Abaco are staggering. In November, 1804, the schooner *Ann* and the sloop *Three Brothers* arrived from Abaco with wrecked goods from the brig *Samuel* and the schooner *Mars*. The only survivor of the brig expressed gratitude for his rescue but also reported an act of villainy. Before the salvors got to the wreck, "some fellows, settled on one of the Abaco Keys," not only stole what they could lay their hands on but also threatened his life. Two men captured at Abaco around the same time may have had something to do with the villainies against the *Samuel*. On 15 November, the *John Bull* brought in two outlaws named Sawyer and Saunders who had been hiding on Abaco "for some time . . . in consequence of outrages they had committed" there.[20]

Britain defeated the French navy at Trafalgar in 1805, but Nelson lost his life. In a lesser battle Mr. B. Low with the felucca *Shaving Mill* captured a French prison ship and "rescued several negroes" for which action he deserved "the attention of the country." Captain Russel of New York received deserved thanks from the inhabitants of Hope Town who helped lighten his brig *Little William*, which had gone ashore on Elbow Cay. After he got off, Russel gave the people seven hundred dollars worth of dry goods "for their exertions."[21]

Captain Gideon Lowe of the wrecking vessel the *Carpenter's Revenge* arrived in Nassau in May, 1806, with the captain and crew of the American brig *Betsey* and 2,700 pairs of shoes. On the 14th of September, Harbour Island experienced the most severe hurricane known "in the memory of the oldest person there." About 146 houses were demolished, along with the island's entire crop. At the Bogue, Eleuthera, most of the inhabitants drowned, not a house was left standing, and the seventeen survivors who escaped the fury of the storm were stranded on the summit of a hill, surrounded by water and destitute of provisions. The Council purchased supplies from Joseph Curry, Esq., and sent them to Harbour Island for the relief of the inhabitants.[22]

In America in 1807 Aaron Burr, who had killed General Alexander Hamilton in a duel in 1804, was tried and acquitted of treason against the United States. At Abaco, John Weatherford, Conrad (Penny) Baker, Benjamin Archer, and James Braynen warned all persons cruising about the island not to land on Great Guana Cay "under any pretense." Messrs. Braynen and Archer also issued the same warning for Man-O-War Cay, and Mr. Braynen likewise forebade anyone to land at his property at Marsh Harbour except those coming to his house "on business or friendship."[23]

England abolished the slave trade that same year after more than two million "hapless souls" perished in the Middle Passage.[24] When the filthy business had begun early in the sixteenth century, Las Casas had warned the Spanish tyrants that in the long view slavery was always expensive, and the British would find that out. Great Britain would have to recompense owners of condemned slaves from foreign vessels seized in English waters. Because it was necessary for American and Spanish ships to use the passages and Gulf Stream through the Bahamas, damages would be considerable. Government would have to provide for hundreds of men and women seized or wrecked in the Bahamas after 31 January 1808. Since the Bahamas was no longer a substantial plantation colony, the absorption of so many Blacks became a serious problem.

For the people involved, the road to freedom was arduous. It was an especially long one for Flora Thompson, who died at Harbour Island 11 May 1808 at the reputed age of 150 years. Born in Africa in 1658, Flora had been carried to Jamaica as a slave. Later she was sold to a man at Nevis and afterwards brought to Nassau at the time when pirates ruled New Providence. William Thompson purchased Flora and at his death she became the property of his son. At the son's death in 1759, she obtained her freedom. In 1791 Flora received a grant for a lot in Dunmore Town. Seventeen years later, the remarkable number of three hundred people attended her funeral in Harbour Island.[25]

Fast becoming a thriving village, Green Turtle Cay profited materially from services rendered desperate mariners and received public acknowledgment as well. In January 1810, the *Royal Gazette* published a letter from Anthony Frazur, master of the schooner *Laurel* of Philadelphia, which was stranded on Grand Cay, Abaco. He expressed his appreciation for the splendid treatment that he and his crew had received from the inhabitants of Green Turtle Cay and particularly from Messrs. Richard Curry and Benjamin Saunders. The master and part of the crew of the American ship *Orion* likewise received "every hospitality" from Jacob Adams and his family at Little Guana Cay. Squally weather had driven the ship on to Pelican Cay on 28 October; the mate and three seamen had been drowned.[26]

The master of the poor school at Green Turtle Cay had twenty students in 1812; a school had also been established at Guana Cay and "Cherock Sound" had petitioned for a teacher. Perhaps the Abaco magistrate failed to take the census in June, 1812, for Abaco did not appear on the population account with the other Out Islands.[27]

In his address on 5 November 1812, President Munnings regretted to inform the Legislative Council that war had been declared "against our government by a people whose habits, customs, and manners so nearly resemble our own. . . ." In June, the *Gazette* reported that the United States was determined to take possession of East Florida, and on July 4th Americans celebrated what British subjects believed to be the last anniversary of their independence.[28]

Enemy privateers menaced ships in the neighbourhood of Abaco. The schooner *Hussar* embarked at Nassau on 14 March, bound for Bermuda, and was captured on the 15th by the Gallo-American privateer *Liberty*. The passengers and crew were "stripped to the shirt" and marooned on an uninhabited part of Abaco with only three gallons of water. After six days Mr. Benjamin Roberts happened upon them and brought the distressed group to Nassau.[29]

A devastating hurricane hit Nassau in late July and partially destroyed Government House and the greater part of the public buildings and levelled about one-third of the houses. Love Curry, wife of Joseph Curry, Esquire, died 26 July when the fury of the hurricane caused her house to collapse suddenly on top of her. She left three small children and numerous relations.[30]

In July, 1814, all American subjects who were not prisoners of war on parole were required to depart from the colony immediately. American cruisers had stationed themselves between Abaco and Egg Island to intercept European trade with the Bahamas. Near Pear Rock, the 280 ton privateer schooner *Midas*, with a force of eighty to one hundred men, seized and burned a small sloop belonging to a Mrs. Higgs which was returning to Harbour Island from Abaco with a load of cedar. The privateer held part of the crew captive, leaving them at Little Harbour a few days later when the vessel stopped there to fill its water casks. On 19 February 1815, the *Gazette* reported that a vessel spoke with one of His Majesty's ships off Abaco and confirmed rumours of a peace between Great Britain and America.[31] The War of 1812 was over.

On the 18th of June, 1815, the day of Napoleon's final defeat at Waterloo, a young Methodist missionary named Joseph Ward embarked at Nassau in Benjamin Lowe's sloop and sailed for Abaco. He came in response to a request signed by twenty-one heads of families at Green Turtle Cay and some thirty-two years after the arrival of Joseph Paul, the first Methodist preacher in the Bahamas. On the way, Ward passed "Cheriok Sound" and he was invited to Hope Town where inhabitants were also eager "to receive the gospel." Landing at Green Turtle Cay on the 20th, he preached every night to the twenty-four families which comprised the total population of 193 souls on the cay. His lectures must have drawn people from the neighbouring cays because in one month's time the zealous Mr. Ward had converted twenty-nine families, a total of 215 people.[32]

Brother Turton of the Nassau Mission found the Abaco society to be as unstable as he believed the Reverend Mr. Ward to be and compared the mission at Green Turtle Cay to "Jonah's gourd 'that sprung up in a night and perished in a night.'" The cause of the early failure of the Methodist mission at Green Turtle was twofold: the lack of a permanent missionary and the demoralizing effect of wrecking.[33]

Intrepid masters and their colourfully named wrecking vessels busily evaded Cartagena cruisers in their neighbourhood and managed to "save" lives and bring in "stranded" goods to Nassau.[34] Some of the vessels and their masters arriving from Abaco were: *Carpenter's Revenge* (Lowe), *Nelly* (Sweeting), the *Nassau* (Skelton), *Nimble Rake* (Adams), *Centipede* (Saunders), the *Conch* (Baker), *Carpenter's Delight* (Johnson), *Zanga* (Russell), *Good Intent* (Curry), the *Spinwell* (Roberts and sometimes Weatherford), *Fair Bahamian* (Eners), *Sea Flower* (Symmonett), and *Two Brothers* (Thompson). A variety of stranded goods included such items as tools, furniture, nails, saddlery, horses, bricks, soap, candles, fish, lard, flour, chocolate, raisins, wine, and old copper.

In June, 1816, a slaver wrecked on Abaco caused considerable excitement for Green Turtle Cay residents involved in rescue operations, and further turmoil at Nassau when the human cargo arrived there. The year before, Parliament had passed a bill requiring a registration of slaves in the colonies in an effort to control smuggling. A fifteen year struggle over the question would ensue between government and the Assembly. The Bahamian legislature denied the existence of the evils which the registration was to remedy and came to the conclusion that the registration of slaves in the Bahamas was not only unnecessary but absurd. The distribution of slaves on the many Out Islands was spread over a distance of six hundred miles of ocean, making registration impractical when compared to contained colonies such as Barbados and Jamaica. Bound up in this question as well as in the slave trade act were regulations against the removal of slaves from one colony or island to another within the same government. For example one proprietor had to leave a security of £100 per slave at the Customs House prior to removal.[35]

The proximity of the Bahamas to the foreign government of East Florida provided an opportunity for runaway slaves from Florida to seek asylum in the islands. One John Perpall found this to be true when he tried unsuccessfully to recover four slaves, partly his own property, who had arrived in Nassau after running away from his relative Gabriel William Perpall in East Florida. The United States press persisted in accusing American refugees of selling Blacks stolen from America. Lord Bathurst wrote Governour Cameron alleging that the British brig *Moselle* had brought "negroes from Norfolk to Nassau" and sold them. A Mr. Wood supposedly purchased a carpenter for £1000 on or about 13 June 1813 and his lordship requested the Bahamian Council to question the gentleman regarding the matter. James Wood acknowledged the arrival of many foreign agents in Nassau at that time but stated that he had not been in town for the alleged sale and swore that he had never purchased any "American Negroes."[36]

Besides a latent resentment of British government's legislating for the colony, there had in fact been little need for the Bahamas to import slaves at all. Crops continued to fail. Planters strained under the necessity of caring for the "free African indentures" left in the colony as the result of wrecks or seizures, and they could not afford the high prices of labourers after their indentures had expired. Inhabitants feared that they were dangerously outnumbered and that lack of employment might lead to massacre and pillage.[37]

Because the islands lay on the turnpike road between the African coast and the Cuban market, Bahamians saw no relief to the burden and terrors placed upon them from conditions arising from the humane act of abolition of the trade. An 1811 petition from the Council and Legislature recounted that of the 451 slaves which had recently been brought in, three hundred had been distributed as indentures in New Providence and ninety-one had been placed in His Majesty's service. African troops posed a real threat, at least in the minds of the inhabitants. The petition also stated that Africans were not liege subjects and had no legal right to residence in any of the Dominions.[38]

In April, 1816, the *Royal Gazette* printed a startling piece of news brought in by the *Charlotte* which arrived from Isle de Los, Greece, where the captain had been informed that a party of natives from the country attached to Sierra Leone had succeeded in destroying the place. Warriors had murdered nearly all the white inhabitants and several British officers.[39]

It was no wonder that Nassau inhabitants reacted so vehemently in June, 1816, when the Spanish slaver *La Rosa* wrecked near Green Turtle Cay. The vessel had embarked at Bonny in Africa and was bound for Havana with over three hundred slaves when the disaster occurred. All the slaves, together with the crew, were rescued by several wrecking vessels and landed safely at the cay.[40]

Captain Pakenham of His Majesty's brig *Bermuda* proceeded to Abaco to make inquiries and to bring the slaves to Nassau in the event of illegal trade. The *Gazette* reacted adversely and at length, stating in essence that the government had no right to meddle with foreign vessels in a time of peace. The Spanish captain was forbidden to continue and his cargo was seized, brought to Nassau and turned over to the Admiralty Court for adjudication.[41]

Nassau residents immediately expressed to the Council their apprehension concerning "the dangerous consequence likely to arise from the introduction of a further number of native Africans" to the colony. While the Vice Admiralty Court heard the case, William Wylly complained about the incompetence and deafness of Judge Edwards who was not a lawyer and in the past seven years "had heard but one word in ten."[42]

At a meeting to formulate a petition, the inhabitants of Nassau restated their old grievances while wrecking vessels from Abaco had brought in stranded oil, rigging, mahogany and old copper from the wrecked slaver. To their thinking, the crew and slaves of the *La Rosa* should have been allowed to remain at Green Turtle Cay and wait for vessels from Cuba to come for them. The natives referred to the "injurious circumstances" arising from the distribution of Africans in 1811, fearing the kind of bad behaviour from indentured Africans revealed in a report about a Mongolan named Mancanger, who had been wrecked on the Spanish ship *Oviedo* in 1811 and apprenticed to Joseph Curry for fourteen years.

Curry had first employed Mancanger at High Lands in Eleuthera, then sent him to sea for a time. The African had been arrested for thievery and put in jail on several occasions so, in order to free him from prison, Mr. Curry had to promise to take him off New Providence. The African, who had no wife or family, was exiled to Mr. Curry's plantation on Moore's Island. Mr. Curry provided his clothes and a plot of ground for Mancanger to cultivate and he was allowed one day of the week to attend to it.[43]

The inhabitants resolved at that July, 1718, meeting, that if the *La Rosa* Africans should be detained, "*no Inhabitant of these Islands ought to receive one of them.*" In August Pedro Proche, supercargo of the *La Rosa*, was acquitted of having "beaten an African so severely as to have caused his death," and in September the slaves were condemned in the Admiralty Court. In the somewhat ambiguous yet ironic language of the court those three hundred souls were tried for having the bad luck of being enslaved in the first place and the bad or good fortune of being wrecked in the Bahamas and were then "condemned" to freedom.[44]

Facts brought out in the trial showed that the *La Rosa* had embarked in May, 1815, for Bordeaux, France with a cargo of sugar, coffee, and dyewood from Havana. Deterred from landing at Bordeaux by the French Revolution, the *La Rosa* went on to Spain to land the cargo and then sail for Africa. The captain bartered at Bonny for the slaves but was shipwrecked at Green Turtle Cay on his way back to Havana. Saved by wreckers, the slaves received kind treatment and comfortable lodging at the cay; however, a few slaves died and more were taken sick when they were removed to the prison vessel at Nassau Harbour. Close confinement caused even more illness and some died. Since there was "no proof of the Negroes having been unlawfully brought away from Africa," Captain Pakenham's seizure at Green Turtle was ruled illegal and he was required to pay damages to the claimants.[45]

Mr. Murray, collector of customs at Nassau, had the responsibility for the apprenticing of the free slaves. On 16 September he wrote a memorandum to Governour Cameron outlining problems connected with his task. The commandant of the garrison "intimated" that none of the Africans would be taken into the service, leaving the entire lot to be distributed among the inhabitants. Most of the applicants were "poor illiterate people residing upon the Out Islands." Their intention was to employ the indentures in agriculture and salt raking. By order of the Council, no females could be employed in agriculture. Murray had written to Lord Bathurst in April of 1812 about the impracticability of this ruling, but he had not received an answer. Since there were no customs officers in the Out Islands except at Exuma, Crooked Island, and the Turks and Caicos, there would be no one to attend to the welfare of apprenticed Africans. Murray believed that in nine out of ten cases the covenants regarding the indentures of apprenticeship would be broken. The few Nassau applicants intended to send their apprentices to other islands to rake salt, rendering it impossible for the absentee proprietors to perform the covenants in the indentures.

Cameron ordered Murray to go ahead with the apprenticing and follow existing regulations since he had received no instructions to the contrary. Planters at Abaco who received apprentices from the *La Rosa* were: Benjamin Archer, Benjamin and Richard Curry, William Hield, John (shipbuilder) and William Russell, John D. and Thomas Smith, Samuel Sawyer, and Anthony Wallace, a free black man. A total of 221 Africans "in Health" were thus "disposed of" on 24 September 1816. One-fifth of them were issued to Nassau residents in spite of their resolution and the rest went to the Out Islands where Mr. Murray hoped they would learn "habits of Industry," which would be useful to themselves and their families.[46]

17

The High Road to Freedom

Debate over passage of a slave registration act plunged the islands into a state of distraction and ferment which resulted in a power struggle between the courts and the House of Assembly. Solicitor General William Wylly, staunch advocate of justice though sometimes tactless, became the object of contention, and the controversy therefore became known as the Wylly Affair. A decision Mr. Wylly had made in 1816 over three slaves had pitted him against the Assembly.

A female slave named Sue had been brought into the Bahamas from Georgia in 1809 and left in Nassau. Her owner came in 1816, accompanied by another slave named Sandy, and attempted to take them and their child back to Georgia. Sue and Sandy ran away but were soon caught and imprisoned. Wylly seized upon this opportunity to bring action against their owner for unlawful importation. Sandy and the child, Ann, were restored to the owner, but Sue was freed on the alleged grounds that she had been offered for sale.[1]

A seemingly endless clash ensued between Mr. Wylly and the Assembly over the slave registration question. The members of the House believed that the solicitor general should support their opposition to the bill. To them the issue was clear-cut. Slave trade laws had been faithfully executed; there was no slave smuggling; and twenty hurricanes in twenty years had "dampened all ardour" in regard to agricultural speculation. The prices of slaves in Jamaica and Cuba were much higher than in the Bahamas. "None but a madman would think of importing Negroes into the Bahamas where every owner would rather sell, than buy slaves."[2] It is surprising that illegal exportation of slaves was not a major issue at this time.

The House of Assembly, together with agent George Chalmers, conspired to bring William Wylly, the "evil genius of the Bahamas," to his knees. Wylly was anti-slavery and Chalmers was not, and the Assembly suspected that Wylly had been corresponding with the English abolitionists who called themselves the African Institution. The planters were probably justified in accusing the idealistic followers of Wilberforce of not understanding the colonists' needs and problems regarding the slave situation, but they could hardly accuse Mr. Wylly of looking at the issue from a distance. Wylly owned two large plantations on New Providence as well as one on Long Island and was considered to be one of the wealthiest proprietors in the Bahamas. He could attest to the fact that slaves were better treated on the Bahamian cotton plantations than on the hard-driving sugar estates of Jamaica.[3] That kind treatment did not justify the basic and undeniable evil of owning other human beings Wylly recognized, as did Mark Twain when, years later, he waged a subtle battle over the issue in America and sarcastically labelled slaves "baptised property."

In an effort to convince Parliament that a slave register was unnecessary in the Bahamas, a select committee questioned various people on matters relative to the subject. When Mr. Wylly did not answer several questions fully and introduced material unconnected with the inquiry, the committee asked him to reconsider his answers. Mr. Wylly replied somewhat insolently that he was satisfied with the fact that he had spoken the whole truth and declined at that time to make any alteration in his testimony, but later made some revisions. In an extract of a letter to the African Institution, Wylly informed the secretary that the committee had rejected his answers as irrelevant or "going beyond" their questions and suspected that his last statements would be as "unpalatable" as the preceding ones.[4]

One particularly touchy point pertained to the question of whether free people of colour were protected in their persons and property by the same laws which protect white people. Wylly answered it in the affirmative but went on to say that in the criminal court no person "with one drop of black blood" could testify against a white person. He further stated that in 1802 the Assembly had suspended for fifty years an act made in 1756 under George II which declared all persons "three degrees removed in a lineal descent from a white ancestor" to be a White. Since the law had been suspended and not repealed, it had not attracted the attention of His Majesty's ministers and so had escaped the notice of the African Institution as well. Wylly revised his answer to the same question simply by stating that he did not feel that the black man was protected in criminal cases because his evidence was not admissible in court.[5] Wylly's extract did not indicate that he had forwarded any of his answers to the Institution, yet statements such as the foregoing appeared in print in London and found their way back to Nassau.

The Assembly then accused Mr. Wylly of "injuriously and scandalously" misrepresenting the proceedings of the House to the African Institution. The Speaker issued a warrant for his arrest and ordered him to appear before the bar of the Assembly to answer the charge of contempt. Mr. Chisholm proceeded to arrest Mr. Wylly at his plantation at Clifton on 22 January 1817. Gunfire alarmed him as he approached the road leading to the gate where sixteen to twenty black men met him, some of them armed with "flintlocks and bayonets." He was refused admittance, and the next morning he was further inconvenienced when he found that his horse had been stolen.[6]

Wylly's affidavit concerning the events of the 22nd of January stated that he could see no reason why he should allow himself to be dragged fourteen miles to Nassau at eight o'clock at night like a common criminal so he had ordered his gate shut and posted a few guards with rifles but without ammunition. The muskets had been fired off and their report had frightened Mr. Chisholm on the road. Wylly remained close by and overheard the conversation between his guards and the messenger of the House who was refused admittance when he declined to state either his name or his business. Wylly rode off to spend the night at one of his other farms.

The next forenoon Wylly went to town "for the express purpose of waiting upon the House of Assembly" but learned that a second warrant had been issued, this time for his commitment to the common jail. He returned to Clifton. On Friday, he received a message from the governour requesting his appearance at Government House on Saturday, the 25th of January. When he arrived there, Mr. Chisholm, assisted by William Baylis, the Provost Marshal, arrested him for a fresh contempt, that of arming his slaves against the messenger of the House.[7]

In an episode reminiscent of the Dunmore days, the members of the Assembly, close to hysteria, stated their opinion that a spirit of rebellion existed in the colony and that islanders lived in fear, wondering when "the latent and desolating fires of insurrection" would next burst forth. The House demanded that the governour suspend Mr. Wylly from office because of his "most daring, wicked, illegal and indecent conduct."[8]

A writ of *habeas corpus* was immediately issued and the judges released Mr. Wylly on bail since there was some doubt as to whether the Assembly had the power to commit a suspect to jail on a charge of breach of privilege. The Assembly considered the bail unprecedented and illegal and immediately issued a third warrant for Wylly's arrest. At this point Governour Cameron took charge, calling the Assembly's warrants illegal and Mr. Wylly's arrest at Government House an "outrage." The governour dissolved the Assembly by proclamation and suspended Mr. Baylis from his office as provost marshal.[9]

House members and the community objected vehemently and even violently to the interruption of Assembly business. Besides the stoppage of the slave registration bill, the closing of the session posed serious consequences to the public schools, the public works, and the poorhouse. Four days after the dissolution of the House, Solicitor General Wylly was assaulted in the public street by a member of the Assembly who severely horsewhipped him. The committee of correspondence told agent Chalmers that this "piece of violence" had nothing to do with the closing of the House proceedings but resulted from a quarrel of a private nature.[10]

After Governour Cameron was recalled, Chief Justice Munnings supported Wylly; and Whitehall, displeased with the Bahamas Assembly for not passing an acceptable slave registration bill, backed him also. Chalmers called Wylly arrogant and drunk, not from wine but from vanity. The battle continued in the courts throughout the spring. In April, the warrant for Wylly's arrest for contempt was determined illegal, yet in May a motion for a new trial was granted. In July, 1818, a weary solicitor general was still obliged to refute the charges against him and in the *Gazette* explained his conduct at Clifton on that night of 22 January.[11] The debate continued. The Assembly felt it had every right to arrest a member for breach of privilege; the courts ruled otherwise.

Around that time, acting Lt. Governour Munnings dissolved the House again. In the 25 July issue of the *Gazette*, the inhabitants of New Providence expressed their sorrow for the "long chain of evils" which had "grown out of the unhappy and unprecedented interference of the Justices of the General Court of these Islands, with the inherent privileges of the House of Assembly." Abaco constituents did not mince words on the subject either:

> We the undersigned Inhabitants of Abaco, have learned with astonishment and dismay that the business of the General Assembly of these Islands has been once more suddenly suspended and for no other reason than to screen from just responsibility one or two individuals, by whom the people of these Islands and their Representatives in General Assembly have been insidiously traduced, grossly insulted and lawlessly set at defiance.

The fifty-nine signatures represent only sixteen surnames, and most of those trace back to Old Inhabitants.[12]

In 1817, William Wylly reached his sixtieth year and decided to relinquish the office of solicitor general which he had held for eighteen years. In a May petition to the Prince Regent, Wylly stated that he had no desire "to withdraw from His Majesty's service" to which he had devoted his life, but his fear was that "under the present circumstance of the Bahama Islands" it would be impossible for him to discharge his duties as solicitor general. Wylly later removed to St. Vincent where he served as Chief Justice. He died in Devonshire, England, 31 January 1828, and in retrospect the *Gazette* paid him a fine tribute. The eulogy stated that the colony was greatly indebted to "the active and enlightened mind of Mr. Wylly," who had given the Bahamas many of its "most useful Laws and public institutions."[13]

In the interim between the beginning of the Wylly affair and his death, the Assembly passed a census act in 1819, a satisfactory slave registration bill in 1821, and a new slave code in 1824. The slave population increased over this period: three slave vessels from Norfolk bound to New Orleans wrecked on Abaco. Then, on the 4th of May, 1818, the American Schooner *Carolina* ran up on Fish Cay Reef; twenty-four slaves drowned but ninety-six were saved. On 23 March, 101 American slaves wrecked on Abaco arrived in Nassau on the sloops *Maria*, Curry, and the *Carpenter's Revenge*, Lowe. A year later survivors of an American vessel wrecked near Hole in the Wall came to Nassau. In 1819 the slave population in the Bahamas reported in consequence of the Census Act numbered 11,007.[14]

Incidents in Florida caused unrest to spread to the Bahamas. In 1818 Robert Chrystie Armbrister, youngest son of James Armbrister, Registrar of Slaves in Nassau, was executed by Andrew Jackson allegedly for sympathizing with the Indians. He died before a firing squad in Florida, and his friend Alexander Arbuthnot, Indian trader at St. Marks, was hanged. Bahamians were horrified and the English outraged. Later the United States ruled that the American hero had overstepped his authority by executing two British subjects.[15]

All was not peaceful even in nature, for at Green Turtle Cay lightning struck the Methodist mission house, shattering the furniture in the room adjoining the one the minister and his family had left only a few days before. Appropriately enough the clergyman was the Reverend Mr. Turtle.[16]

On 27 September 1822, a "severe gale of wind" damaged plantations at Cherokee Sound so badly that the planters were forced to petition the House of

Assembly for two months' aid to ward off starvation until a new crop could be harvested. The petitioners were named Albury, Bethell, Johnson, Pinder, Roberts, Russell, Sands, Sawyer, and Sweeting, the families totaling 139 inhabitants. The Assembly acted on a motion to pay them £100 by resolving to pay only £40.[17]

That same storm caused a Colombian pirate vessel, the *Mary*, to wreck on Abaco. Despite the fact that pirates constantly annoyed Bahamian vessels, wreckers saved the commander and crew of the *Mary* and carried them to Nassau. The *Mary* had previously been captured near Havana by Lieutenant Stokes of *H.M.S. Iphigenia* as it had attempted to board the schooner *Sarah* bound for Nassau.[18]

Between 1819 and 1823 piracy along the coast of Cuba flourished and every week the newspaper printed at least one account of an atrocity. An editorial in the 5 June 1819 *Gazette*, entitled "More Piracies Still," remarked that the exploits of the famous Blackbeard paled in comparison to the "bold and multifarious Piracies that are every day committed with impunity in our neighbourhood." Generally, these marauders resorted to the barbarous practice of "*hanging their captives*" to extort a confession as to where the ship's valuables were hidden.[19]

Abaco wreckers braved white water to rescue mariners and aid stranded vessels. Sometimes the cargo was worth the trouble and risk and sometimes it was not. Wreckers salvaged only provisions when the American brig *Cicero* with a cargo of ice wrecked on Abaco in June, 1818, and when the brig *Horizon* of Newbury Port wrecked on Fish Cay during the night of 22 November the same year, its entire cargo of hay and bricks was lost. When the American brig *George Washington* from New York wrecked on Green Turtle Cay, wrecking vessels rescued the cargo and carried it to John and G. K. Storr in Nassau. The merchants posted a notice of a sale to be held 26 August 1819. The *Washington's* wrecked goods consisted of rum in puncheons, brandy in pipes and Madeira wine in boxes, along with hats, candles, gigs with harnesses, elegant furniture, and silver and gold watches. Also for sale was the hull of the brig "as she lies at Green Turtle Key, Abaco."[20]

Wrecking was still a major enterprise on Abaco. Uriah Saunders of Green Turtle Cay advertised his new Bahama-built forty-seven ton schooner *Success*, which could be "sent to Sea at a little or no expense." (See plate 43.) On two

PLATE 43
The Bahama-built schooner *Success* was offered for sale in the *Royal Gazette* on 19 June 1819. It was probably used for wrecking, since this was the primary island activity of the day. (Courtesy of the Nassau Library, Nassau, The Bahamas.)

occasions John Russell aided stranded vessels. On 3 March 1822, an American ship, *Rebecca*, "got entangled among the Abaco Keys" in the night and came to anchor. On the next day, Mr. Russell assisted by piloting the vessel safely out to sea. Mr. Russell rescued another American ship when it struck an Abaco reef, passed over it, and came to anchor on the other side. Russell went aboard and piloted the vessel to Nassau.[21]

Even though a headline in the *Royal Gazette* 22 March 1823 announced "Still More Atrocious Piracies," pirates had no monopoly on atrocities; landlubbers occasionally perpetrated deeds as heinous as those usually associated with criminals. A crime of mayhem on Grand Bahama involved Charles Weatherford, probably the son of Georgia Loyalist Martin Weatherford, late of Abaco and Russell's Island.[22] One John D. Smith, with his two daughters, had lived apart from his wife for over a year, on the same island yet thirty miles distant from her. Entertaining "unfavourable suspicions of his wife's purity of character," he and four black men sailed over to the house of Charles Weatherford on the night of 11 March 1824. Weatherford then accompanied them to Mrs. Smith's house. At about eleven P.M. Smith and company broke into the lady's bedroom and found her in bed with a young man named Archibald W. G. Taylor. One of the black men seized Taylor by the throat and dragged him out of bed onto the floor where Smith took a small knife and cut off both Taylor's ears. Smith called out to Weatherford, "I have caught the son of a bitch."

Weatherford shouted back, "Have you cut them both?"

Smith replied, "Yes, I have cut them both."

This testimony by the sole witness, Mr. Taylor, went unrefuted in court and Mr. Smith was found guilty, but the jury recommended mercy. The jury also convicted Charles Weatherford and the black men Dundee, Tom, Peter, and George for "felony as principals in the second degree." Under the sentence of death, all six men were first granted a respite by the court late in May and then were issued free pardons in August of 1824.[23]

This narrow escape from death is perhaps what made Charles Weatherford a fearless man. In 1828, a wild boar that had "for many years infested the island of Grand Bahama" found his way into Mr. Weatherford's house whereupon the man "had the temerity to attack the monster with a hand hatchet." The animal made a desperate rush and ripped the man's leg with his immense tusks. Weatherford succeeded in cutting the boar on the shoulder, an injury which so enraged the animal that it would have killed him but for the timely arrival of his two sons who shot the boar dead. The news article ended with the following particulars:

> This plantation marauder measured 15 feet from the snout to the root of his tail, stood 3 feet high, and netted 260 pounds of pork; he had battled the skill of the hunters for a length of time past, and the destruction of Yams, potatoes and pumpkins is altogether incalculable.[24]

Physical toughness and hardiness of spirit characterized the people of the Out

Islands who continually battled adverse conditions on their farms, in the forests, and on the sea. When Governour Smyth reported on the state of agriculture in the Bahamas in 1832, wind and rain had caused the rich soil, no longer protected by trees or nourished by fallen leaves, to disappear; pineapples would grow only in particular situations and soil, and the quantity of cotton was "trifling." Yet these islands, composed of limestone and formed by the "accumulation and agglomeration of the shells of ages," served the petty farmer's family needs. The governour had taken a "wretched looking tract of land" and divided it among a number of liberated Africans. He now reported that a little plot thirty by thirty-five paces "at this moment" enjoyed "full beauty and vigour" and abounded in Spanish plum trees, sugar cane, guinea corn, pawpaw trees, pumpkins, okra, guava, coconuts, tamarinds, sapodilla, and palma christi.[25]

Abaco pine had been described as superior to that found in the southern United States, and some pieces found on the roofs of old houses were "nearly as hard as horn." The ruggedness of the land made the building of roads into the forests virtually impossible. The practice of burning the woods was most improvident. Many of the Abaco Islands had been destroyed and by 1828 woodcutters had begun to burn parts of Andros. For hundreds of years, woodcutting had been one of the means of support for inhabitants of Harbour Island, Eleuthera, and Abaco, but wood was running short.[26]

Turtling was almost as exciting as wrecking. A turtle of uncommon size, of a type usually found on the coast of South America and Africa, found its way to Abaco and was captured there. Its head and neck were fourteen inches long, its beak looked somewhat like that of a parrot. The mound measured ten feet in circumference and was six and a half feet long; the two fore fins were three feet long and fourteen inches wide and its estimated weight was between eight hundred to one thousand pounds.[27] Such a huge beast had never before been caught.

Navigation routes and weather conditions still provided Abaconian wreckers with perhaps more excitement than they wanted but insured their livelihood through the sale of salvaged goods. In 1817, Mr. De Mayne, a nautical surveyor, took soundings of the bank which "runs out easterly from Hole in the Wall to the south end of Abaco." This bank, on which soundings are from ten to fifteen fathoms, had never before appeared on any charts. The bank measured two to three miles wide and ran out about seven miles from Hole in the Wall. In addition to this bank, Joseph Kirk, master of the brig *Clio*, discovered a rock about ten yards long and not more than three yards under the water off Hole in the Wall. Mr. Blount of the United States made several unjust remarks about Bahamian wreckers in his nautical book, but ironically his book contained misleading sailing instructions which could easily cause wrecks on the islands. As a result an American brig *Plato*, of Charleston, once mistook the east end of Eleuthera for Hole in the Wall.[28]

In 1824, the United States offered to purchase from England "a space of land" at Hole in the Wall, Abaco, to erect a lighthouse to be used for the sole purpose of providing security to navigation. Governour Grant wrote Lord Bathurst that in the four years he had resided in the Bahamas not one British vessel had been wrecked

PLATE 44
John Bartlum of Green Turtle
Cay was a successful wrecker
before he moved his household—
and his entire house—to Key
West. (Courtesy of the Monroe
Public Library, Key West,
Florida.)

on Abaco. He did not see the need of a lighthouse and feared if a "foreign state" should build one, it could easily be converted to a military tower and used against the colony. Anthony De Mayne advised the building of a lighthouse at Hole in the Wall because of its "high commanding situation." In case of war with America a total blockade of American trade to Cuba and the Gulf of Mexico could effectively operate from that station. The British refused the United States' offer and decided they would build the lighthouse, but the structure would not be completed until 1836.[29]

The wreck on Long island of the American brig *Abaco* from New York bound for Nuevitas, Cuba, could be interpreted as a kind of ill omen for Abaco wreckers. Sir James Carmichael-Smyth wrote the Honourable George Murray to urge him to effect changes in duty regulations on wrecked goods. Both foreigners and wreckers complained that seafaring problems had not been considered when framing customs laws. Because of the many distressed vessels in these islands, wreckers should be encouraged in the business, not deterred from it. As the system stood, foreign goods, whether imported or wrecked, were subject to duty. Damaged materials were charged as good; even old iron and copper which must be remanufactured were taxed. Smyth suggested that government change the present system and made recommendations along the lines of the then current American laws. Sums raised by wreckers from the sale of salvaged goods should be duty-free; old iron and copper should be considered raw material and charged at only twenty-five percent, and duty should be diminished on all damaged goods. Smyth apologized for using America as precedent but went on to say that at Key West wreckers were given encouragement. Bahamian wrecking schooners found it more advantageous to fall in with American vessels and sell their salvage to them rather than bring it to Nassau.[30]

On 7 February 1832, John Bartlum of Green Turtle Cay and his wrecking vessel the *Wanderer* arrived in Nassau along with the *Carpenter's Revenge*, under captain Roberts, carrying candles, butter, dry goods, and oil from the line ship *Dewitt Clinton* which wrecked on Elbow Cay. (See plate 44.) In August the brig *Hannah V* from Montego Bay, bound for Quebec, caught fire; the crew took to the boat and arrived at Cherokee Sound where they were treated with "every kindness and hospitality" and then brought to Nassau in the sloop *Amelia* by Benjamin Roberts. In December, 1832, the wreck on Green Turtle Cay of a vessel carrying fifty-three English, Scottish, and Irish emigrants probably caused several days' excitement, especially for the Curry family. Wrecking vessels brought the passengers to Nassau where Governour Smyth housed them in an unoccupied part of Ft. Charlotte barracks. The *Gazette* published their names and occupations which included a shoemaker, a butcher, a cooper, a harness-maker, an engineer, a bricklayer, a baker, a stone mason, and a mantua-maker. Some got employment in Nassau, some went to Jamaica, and the remainder got passage to different parts of the United States.[31]

Before Smyth arrived to govern the Bahamas, the colony had acted on most of the slave reforms demanded by the home government. Although the islanders complied with the slave registration, it worked a hardship on some of them. Benjamin Lowe, eldest son of Gideon Lowe, came to Nassau from Green Turtle Cay in 1825 to attest to his father's return before James Armbrister, Registrar of Slaves. Gideon Lowe had two people employed at Andros and thirteen at Abaco that year and from "disability," that of being "extremely old and infirm," was unable to attend and swear to his return.[32] Out Island farmers brought in their African employees when their period of indenture expired. In 1825, the governour complained to Lord Bathurst that few Africans worked at trades, therefore proprietors hired them out for road work or to planters and salt rakers to do those jobs they would be unwilling to hire out their own slaves to do. Government learned the condition of these indentured Africans from their own statements. Some liberated Africans had been settled on Out Islands and allowed to work patches of ungranted land.[33]

In 1831, the population increased by 165 American slaves. On the night of 2 January, the American brig *Comet* from Alexandria, Virginia, bound for New Orleans, wrecked on Abaco. The *Gazette* reported that upwards of 160 slaves "who were going to be settled in Louisiana and who, together with several other passengers, have been saved from the wreck and arrived here last evening [11 January] in three Abaco vessels. These people will sail in a few days for their original destination, as a vessel has been procured for that purpose." This report was in error. The inhabitants laid a petition before the House of Assembly on the 14th, recommending that the American slaves be restored to their owners. Governour Smyth denied the petition and on the 18th the Assembly voted to investigate the wreck. The *Gazette* of the 15th argued that for the "preservation of the public tranquility" the slaves should be allowed to go on to America. The *Comet* had been travelling on the "High Road of Nations" and should not be detained for having had the misfortune to be wrecked in a "civilized country."[34] Crowded on the three Abaco fishing vessels, eleven Blacks had escaped to shore and sought refuge at Government House. Governour Smyth determined that those eleven would not be taken away as slaves under any circumstances.

The Assembly's committee investigation resulted in the seizure of all 165 American slaves, including a baby who had been born during the voyage. They were taken from the Abaco boats and housed in a barracks on Hog Island until their case could be decided by the Vice Admiralty Court. In reporting the proceedings of the House 27 January, the *Gazette* told its subscribers what they did not wish to hear: bringing foreign slaves to Bahamian shores even by accident was a criminal act. There would be little doubt that the slaves would be condemned and the owners recompensed. The slaves would be "well sold, and the British Nation will have to become the paymaster." The *Gazette* had done some research on that point and came up with the fact that there were several artisans among these slaves, who in New Orleans would bring 1,000 to 1,200 dollars each. The average value of each slave was estimated at £200 for a total of £33,000.[35]

Another touchy issue surfaced during the investigation. Smyth had written to England in April, 1830, requesting a change in the law regarding the removal of slaves from one island to another within the colony. If a proprietor wished to bring his family from an Out Island to Nassau, he would have to obtain written permission from the governour. Since the Bahamas consisted of many individual islands, this regulation was extremely inconvenient.[36] Compliance with this law in the Bahamas bloomed into full absurdity during the investigation of the American slaves.

The House committee probed the question of illegal removal of slaves during the rescue effort. They examined the following people: Isaac Staples, late master of the brig *Comet* of New York, Mr. Stephen Foxwell, late mate, Joseph Curry, master of the island sloop *Sarah*, William Fox, searcher of customs, Nassau, and John Storr, United States Agent for the Bahamas.

The *Comet* had encountered severe weather and had rarely seen the sun or other heavenly bodies to govern its course. At Abaco, the pilot thought he was much farther to windward than he actually was and at ten P.M. grounded on a reef eight to ten miles off the windward coast of Abaco. Before daylight the next morning, island vessels came to their assistance. No lives were lost and everyone was landed with a quantity of provisions and water on Spanish Cay, situated about four miles from the reef. That Spanish Cay could by some fiction of the law be construed as land was absurd. In actuality it was nothing more than an uninhabited and uninhabitable rock. The committee felt it a "monstrous injustice" to punish the inhabitants of Abaco for saving the lives of those shipwrecked people, for surely had they been left on the reef they would have perished. These humanitarian arguments saved the salvors from prosecution.[37]

The Vice Admiralty Court ruled that it would be illegal to remove the slaves from the Bahamas and declared them all to be free. Since England had not as yet passed acts regarding restitution, each party was directed to pay "his own costs." The American agent for the owners of the wrecked slaves intended to take the matter first to Washington, then to England.[38]

The American agent was not the only one angered at the court's decision regarding damages. Smyth had discovered that the trial had not been necessary in the first place. As he was destroying some old papers, Thomas Brown Wylly came across an important paper he supposed had been left in the office by his father. The document, dated 27 August 1818, stated the judgement of Sir Christopher Robinson and the late Lord Gifford that wrecked slaves should be declared free without a trial. The circular letter also containing that same directive from Whitehall, 15 September 1818, had not been among Mr. Munnings' papers when Smyth took over the government. Had he been in possession of those dispatches, he would have freed those American slaves and saved the colony the expense of a trial. The removal of this official dispatch from Government House in 1818 resulted in several costly seizures.[39]

Since the slaves were American, not native Africans, they would not be indentured but were allowed to seek employment as any other free person might. Governour Smyth also recommended to Lord Goderich a claim made by the salvors of $1,650. The wrecking master and the supercargo of the *Comet* had agreed on the price of ten dollars per head for the rescue of the 165 slaves. Since the owners did not recover their slaves, they could not be expected to pay. These 165 American Blacks enjoyed the good fortune of being saved from shipwreck and released from slavery almost thirty-five years sooner than they would have been if the *Comet* had reached New Orleans. In 1832, Governour wrote England that these American Blacks were a "quiet orderly industrious set of people" who appeared "contented and grateful."[40]

Governour Smyth, an ardent abolitionist, meant to enforce the slave code. He encouraged the settlement of Headquarters, the name later changed to Carmichael, and established Adelaide for wrecked African slaves. The governour also provided work on wells, roads, and salt ponds and endeavoured to educate the people, black and white. He built a school for the Africans at his own expense and attempted to elevate Whites to a humanitarian plane which would shield the Blacks "from occasional barbarous treatment." All reforms were designed to lead to the abolition of slavery and colonial Assemblies were advised to make laws now to insure for Blacks the enjoyment of full British citizenship when abolition was effected.[41]

Topping the House of Commons' slave reform platform was the abolishment of the flogging of female slaves. Smyth and the Assembly locked horns on this issue. He wrote home that he would have difficulty getting this "horrid business" abolished by colonial law. A stipendary justice had allowed eight women to be whipped "within sight and almost within hearing of Government House" and one of the women was with child. Because of this incident, Smyth suspended police magistrate Robert Duncome from office. The House continued to argue against this last reform, the "darkest blot on the institution of slavery."[42]

In late January, 1831, the Admiralty Court had seized and condemned five slave mariners from the sloop *Perseverance*, Jeremiah Carey, master. Since the *Perseverance* sailed within the colony only, neither the sloop or the mariners should have been seized. Governour Smyth overruled the court and returned the Blacks to Mr. Carey. The whole town was grateful for this ruling and for the exemption of small vessels and fishers from this law. Smyth deemed it a propitious time once more to bring up before the Assembly the question of the flogging of female slaves. Obviously, the members were not grateful; the House could not agree with Smyth on the issue. Females were more difficult to deal with than males and flogging was considered the only effective punishment. Until some other mode of punishment could be found, they refused to act on this reform.[43]

In spring of 1831, Smyth dissolved the Assembly. One member, a Mr. Wildgoose, had issued a second thirty-nine lashes to be executed upon a woman for saying she had not deserved the first thirty-nine. Governour Smyth brought Wildgoose to trial as soon as he heard that the slender, delicate female had received seventy-eight lashes "by order of this ruffian."[44] The newly elected Assembly of 1832 remained adamant, refusing to alter any laws governing Blacks or to legislate at all while Smyth remained governour of the Bahamas. The members sent complaints home to England, demanding his recall. W. E. Armbrister summed up Governour Smyth's term of office this way:

> Upon assuming the government [Major General Sir James Carmichael-Smyth] set himself at work to correct abuses connected with the systems of slavery which he found in existence. While in many cases slave owners were mindful of their slaves being human beings equally with themselves, and were good and kind in their treatment of said slaves, looking after their health and comfort, there were no doubt others who were harsh and in some cases cruelly so with their slaves. This of course gave rise to a commendable determination of the governour to interfere in behalf of the slaves as against any harsh and unnatural owners. Consequently great opposition soon manifested itself against the governour, and radicals of a most determined type united to make his tenure of office most unpleasant, disagreeable and unsatisfactory.[45]

Recall would not be easy, however; and Smyth retained complete control of the government for a time.

Public opinion in England ran high and the ministry had no choice but to take giant steps towards abolishing slavery once and for all. In spite of repeated warnings from England, the Bahamas Assembly persisted, refusing to pass a bill that would prohibit the flogging of female slaves. Their delay in this reform hastened emancipation.[46]

18

"Free at Last"

The Farquharson Journal of 1831-32 stands as the only extant record of plantation life in the Bahamas. The Farquharson Estate, located on the east side of Watling's Island (San Salvador) between Pigeon Creek and Great Lake, contained about 1,500 acres and was considered the best cattle-producing plantation on the island. (See plate 45.) The Journal describes cows being carried by boat from Snow Bay to French Bay at Sandy Point on the southwest tip of Watling's where they would be shipped. Without Mr. Farquharson's details, the fact that the Bahamas Out Islands employed "cowboys" to "hunt up" cattle would have been lost.[1]

Besides dwelling houses for Mr. Farquharson and his children, other plantation structures mentioned are: a corn house, a cotton house, a cow pen, the mistress's shed, a gin circle, a pigeon pea house, and the lower barn. Ruins of a building with wooden bars in the window stand today. Since Charles Farquharson acted as a magistrate for the island, this barn-style building may have doubled as a jail. Among the many provisional fields worked were Hercules, Blanket (cotton), Lookout, Pumpkin, Thursday's, Sage, the Garden, and Guinea Grass patches.[2] The Journal primarily records daily weather conditions and work activities of the plantation and gives an account in miniature of what a thriving plantation in the late 1700s must have been like. Besides cattle raising and provisional planting, Farquharson's people worked at building houses, thatching roofs, erecting boundary walls, carpentering, mending fences, raking salt, and weeding both fields and the public road. They cut guinea corn but broke Indian corn, gathered peas, picked and ginned cotton, dug yams, made castor oil, and pulled catnip.

Anything vaguely resembling an island event Farquharson handles with cool reserve. Ben Storr's sudden death and funeral is sandwiched between the "old people weeding" and the weather report. The Journal also records the arrivals and departures of vessels, always a major event on an Out Island. In March, 1832, a "wrack" at Graham's Harbour broke up the daily routine for a few days, for the American brig *Enterprise* bound for Jamaica wrecked on Watling's on 9 March. The crew took to the launch, leaving behind their provisions and water, and with hardly an oar drifted to the east side of Cat Island, reaching shore on the 19th. There they met with the sloop *Shearwater* and returned to Watling's but could save nothing from the wreck. Nor did the people of Watling's find anything useful although in this declining stage of the plantation period almost anything would have been wel-

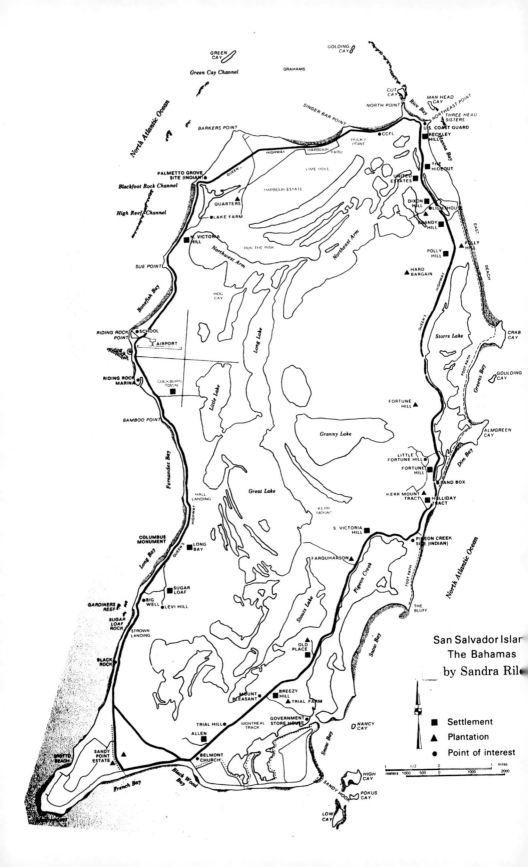

San Salvador Island
The Bahamas
by Sandra Riley

■ Settlement
▲ Plantation
● Point of interest

comed. The brig had split in two and pieces of rigging had been found hanging about the reef, but the cargo had drifted out of the hull. James Farquharson took some people to the wreck for several days but found nothing but "some blocks and a few pieces of rope of very little value."[3]

The world may never know what motivated this ageing and kindly Scot to record life on his Watling's Island plantation so minutely, especially at a time when very little exportation was being carried on. His Journal records that he shipped only twelve bales of cotton and a few boxes of oranges during the two years. When Charles Farquharson died he left a considerable stock that included 46 horned cattle, 250 head of sheep, 7 horses, a few goats and hogs, all valued at £674. Besides 60 gallons of rum valued at £24, his household effects were meager: 12 silver spoons, 1 side board, 1 sofa, 12 chairs, 1 mahogany table, a lot of glass and a lot of books totalling in value only £38.16. A classification of Farquharson's apprentices in 1835 showed that he had the responsibility of caring for fifty-two people.

Charles Farquharson and Kitty Davies are buried side by side on the plantation just down the hill from the main house. In his preface to the Journal, Mr. McDonald referred to an enclosure containing the graves, but they had not been seen until a group of botanists on a field study excursion with the College Center of the Finger Lakes tripped over the tombs in the dense bush sometime in the early 1970s. After two years of off and on searching, the tombs were found again on 1 April 1979. The smaller tomb had been badly broken up but the larger one was intact. (See plate 46.) A year later, one of the islanders burned the field for planting and a subsequent visit showed that both graves had been desecrated by local gold seekers. Two great piles of rocks stood at least ten feet high in the field and what looked like a cobblestone road ran just north of and parallel to the path currently used to approach the plantation yard. Farquharson left a more important legacy, however, which was discovered in 1903 by Ormond McDonald, assistant Justice of Watling's Island, who painstakingly copied the Journal. Realizing its significance as a record of pre-emancipation days in the Bahamas, he entitled the work "A Relic of Slavery." Perhaps even more significant is that not once in his Journal does Mr. Farquharson ever use the word "slave."[4]

Nothing is known of the presumed Loyalist background of Charles Farquharson, who received a two hundred acre grant on Great Lake in 1803. He may have come from Scotland by way of South Carolina, for an Alexander Farquharson had obtained one hundred acres in Craven County in 1756. Dr. John Farquharson, who came to America in 1751, practiced medicine in Charleston and left South Carolina in 1778. A James Farquharson who died in Charleston in 1780 mentioned a brother William, also a physician, in his will. Charles also had a brother William to whom he

PLATE 45: This map of San Salvador (Watling's Island) shows the estates of Burton Williams, Harbour Estate and Fortune Hill, as well as Prince Storr's Polly Hill and Sandy Point. Farquharson's Estate stretches between Pigeon Creek and Great Lake.

PLATE 46
Local historian Elmore Nairn
cleans brush from the cement
grave of Charles Farquharson
on the Farquharson Plantation,
San Salvador (Photograph by
the author.)

bequeathed £200 in his will. However, a relationship between Charles and any of the aforementioned Carolina Farquharsons has not been definitely established.

Charles had three sons, Charles, James, and William, and two daughters, Mary and Christina, all by his "faithful companion" Kitty Davies, alias Dixon. Charles, Jr., is not mentioned in the Journal. William died in May, 1824, when the schooner *Eleanor*, bound for Nuevitas, Cuba, wrecked on Brothers Cays near Ragged Island.[5]

His middle son James assisted in the management of the plantation. Farquharson's Journal records an altercation with a few of the plantation workers that nearly climaxed in a revolt. James struck a man named Isaac with a palmetto leaf for mounting a mule on the wrong side against instructions. Isaac's brother Alick appeared and challenged James with a heavy bludgeon, threatening to strike James with it if James struck Isaac. James provokingly tapped Alick with his walking stick and Alick struck him several times with the bludgeon and would have killed James had not Matilda grabbed hold of Alick's arm. The next morning "every Black soul on the plantation that could walk" assembled; some men carrying clubs and the women carrying sticks. Farquharson had sent for neighbouring proprietors John Dickson and Prince Storr to come to try to reason with his people. Some refused to listen to any advice but did go back to work by noon; however, they carried their clubs with them all day.[6]

On 21 March, the *Traveller* carried three mutineers, Alick, Bacchus, and Peter, to Nassau. Farquharson and his son James embarked for Nassau on 11 April with Matilda and March, also destined for trial at Nassau.[7] On 4 May James Farquharson, "free man of colour," brought five slaves to trial for "mutiny and insurrection." Governour Smyth, suspecting the Out Islanders of punishing their slaves without regard to laws, looked into this case but found the entire matter exaggerated. He thought James Farquharson impudent and could see that he did not wield his father's authority or even the same influence he would have had "if he were his father's legitimate heir." Nor did James have the respect of his people. Alick called him "Jim." Probably much to James's surprise, the court granted light sentences to the Blacks.[8]

Farquharson recorded that he brought back March, Bacchus, and Peter but left Matilda and her child in the workhouse for a time as punishment. Alick would be sold. Charles had gotten permission to take Mary Ann, one of Alick's wives, and her infant child to Nassau to be sold with him.[9] Mr. Farquharson was certainly in no way obligated to go to this trouble and expense to avoid breaking up Alick's family, but consideration and compassion were ingrained in the man's character.

About one month after Sir James Carmichael-Smyth returned to London, James and Charles Farquharson returned to Nassau to testify at the murder trial of Prince Storr, a free black man who managed the estates of Polly Hill and Sandy Point on Watling's. Sancho Storr had died allegedly after Prince had beaten the man with a barrel stave, then hanged him up in a tree by the wrists and ankles and beaten him again with a switch for one-half hour. This was the kind of ill treatment Smyth had so abhorred. However, the Farquharsons, in truth, were bound to testify to the "general correctness" of Prince Storr's character. Fortunately for Mr. Storr a "respectable young lady happened to be present at the most (alleged) severe part of the punishment" and she entirely contradicted the evidence brought against him. The court ruled for acquittal on the grounds of insufficient evidence.[10]

Loyalist Joseph Stout was shot on his Watling's Island plantation, supposedly by a black man who had absconded a few weeks prior to the shooting. Stout, who originally came from Philadelphia, had married Mary Rolph of England and evacuated to East Florida where he was overseer of a 31,000 acre estate on the St. Johns River. Later he had emigrated to New Providence with other Loyalists at the Peace and finally established a plantation called Trial Farm, just south of Farquharson's on Watling's.[11]

On the night of 15 February, Stout's murderer entered his dwelling house and shot him several times in the chest and once through the head. One cannot help wondering the cause of such bitter hatred or whether Mary was witness to "this horrid transaction." Fearless, as many of the loyalist women were, Mary remained at Watling's until her death in 1817.[12]

Burton Williams, probably the largest proprietor on Watling's, signed Mary Stout's estate appraisal. Displaying characteristics indicative of the most intrepid of American Loyalists, Williams battled soil and weather to build a wealthy Out Island empire and struggled through the grueling period of decline in the Bahamas. Burton's descendants continue in the Bahamas; even the ghost of Burton's descendant Tom (One Foot) Williams has been seen wandering about the old plantation grounds at Grahams Harbour, San Salvador.[13]

General Samuel Williams, Burton's father, member of a wealthy family residing at Lynhurst Estate in England, had emigrated to America and lived on the Pedee River in Anson County, North Carolina. Burton was the second youngest of seven sons born to Samuel, who left East Florida with Governour Tonyn and died about 1786 at Portsmouth, England.[14] Burton and his brother Samuel emigrated to the Bahamas after the Peace. In 1788, Burton received a forty acre grant at the north end of Watling's Island on the edge of a swampy area called Run the Risk, just the kind of challenge a man like Burton Williams relished. Brother Samuel was also granted forty acres and their older brother, Major Henry Williams of Brown's East Florida Rangers, received two grants totalling 560 acres.[15]

Henry later moved to Cat Island while Burton and Samuel built the plantation on Watling's. Later, Samuel went to Florida to start a plantation at New Smyrna, leaving Burton owner of the growing Harbour Estate which stretched from sea to lake. On 22 April 1797 Burton married Jane Hartley. In 1804 Burton purchased Alexander Muir's one thousand acre tract for £750 and built another estate called Fortune Hill. Burton also had vast holdings on Eleuthera as well as property in Nassau and served as a member of the House of Assembly for Eleuthera in 1808.[16]

On the evening of 1 March 1814, Burton sailed his schooner *Jason* with fair wind but ill fortune between Rum Cay and Watling's when an American privateer boarded and plundered his vessel, setting fire to it. The Americans "inhumanely butchered" Mr. Williams' favourite stud horse before his eyes, then carried off Burton and five or six black men. On 10 April, the *Gazette* could report only that there had been no word of Mr. Williams since his capture. Burton arrived in Nassau on 2 September after he had been carried by the privateer to Philadelphia, then sent to Charleston and Savannah to be taken with other prisoners to Jamaica. Finally a Jamaica packet had brought him to Crooked Island.[17]

Returning to Watling's, Burton struggled to provide for his five growing boys by working the exhausted soil. In 1820, Burton was elected member for Abaco but never took his seat. He had obtained a grant in Trinidad where the government waived a $2.00 head tax to welcome an experienced grazier. Mr. Williams eagerly emigrated to better soil. Between 1821 and 1822 Burton exported nearly two hundred of his youngest people in the schooner *Midas* leaving behind, at their own request, at Watling's about one hundred elderly folk. Later, when they wished to be reunited with their children, Burton removed them also.[18]

Burton's wife Jane died at Trinidad 1 September 1822 and his son William Augustus Williams married Eliza Hamilton Gloster, the second daughter of Archibald Gloster, late Chief Justice of the island of Dominica on 29 November 1826. Evidently Burton moved easily in Trinidad's social circles, for the governour gave him an elegant gold snuff box which is reputed to be still in the family's possession.[19]

With the coming of emancipation, Burton returned to the Bahamas. In December, 1833, Governour Balfour wrote to England that he hoped Mr. Williams would consent to come into the Assembly because he was a "sensible man" and shared the "same views entertained by Mr. Smyth" and himself. Because of the prejudices involved in effecting a smooth transition at emancipation, Balfour had need of an ally in the Assembly.[20]

Reduced from affluence to poverty, Burton Williams eventually outlived all his sons to die at age eighty-three at Watling's in July, 1852. Any proceeds from the sale of his holdings were to be divided among his eight grandchildren. Mrs. Parrish, indefatigable searcher of island archives, uncovered this story of the death of Burton Williams, "one of the last Loyalists to die in the Bahamas" which Thelma Peters poignantly placed at the end of her dissertation "The American Loyalists and the Plantation Period in the Bahamas:"

> There is pathos in the death of the last Loyalist, Burton Williams. . . . Foreseeing that there might be no tools left with which to dig his grave when he died, he had it dug ahead of time, out of the limestone ridge. His foresight was wise, for when this once energetic and rich man died at an advanced age, a Negro servant had only to shovel away the light leaf mold from the waiting grave, and to do this he used the only tool that was left, the tool that was in common use by all the Conchs before the Loyalists came, a sharpened barrel stave.[21]

One would think after such an energetic life this man should have been allowed to rest atop that hill at Harbour Yard overlooking the north cays of San Salvador, but even this peace was denied him.

The Catholic Church had acquired a portion of the estate and when Father Chrysostom Schreiner, the first Catholic priest to come to the Bahamas, died 3 January 1928, his parishioners buried him at Harbour Yard "on top of Mister Burton's grave" because "it was the easiest way." (See plate 47.)[22] Strange bedfellows indeed and the situation is even more ironic when coupled with Samuel Williams'

PLATE 47

The double grave at Harbour Yard holds both the last Loyalist, Burton Williams, and Father Chrysostom Schreiner, first Catholic priest to come to the Bahamas. The smaller grave at right is thought to be that of Burton's wife, Jane Hartley. (Photograph by the author.)

burial circumstances. When Burton's brother died in St. Augustine during the Spanish occupation, as a Protestant, he was forbidden burial in the Catholic city. His body is buried somewhere on Anastasia Island or Fish's Island as it was called then, for he remained exiled in death as well as in life.[23]

With a stroke of the pen, King William, acting on a bill passed by Parliament, abolished slavery throughout the British colonies on 4 September 1833. Of the sixteen proclamations posted in Nassau, fifteen were torn down. The few Out Island disturbances were soon put down, and 1 August 1834, the day of liberation, passed quietly in the Bahamas.[24]

England had dealt the deathblow to the institution of slavery and now the home government endeavoured to ease the situation by suggesting a period of apprenticeship so that the colonial proprietor would not be totally deprived of his employees or the Blacks immediately deprived of provisional care. Apprentices were classified three ways: agricultural labourers working on land belonging to their employers (predials attached), agricultural labourers working on land not belonging to their employers (predials unattached), and anyone not belonging to either of those two classes (non-predials). The term of apprenticeship was fixed at four years for non-predials, expiring 1 August 1838, and six years for predials, expiring 1 August 1840. In exchange for forty-five hours of work per week, the employer provided the apprentice with the necessities of life, a plot of land, and time to cultivate it. Voluntary work agreements could be made between parties during the term of apprenticeship, a practice which was successfully continued after the end of apprenticeships. By mutual agreement the term of apprenticeship could be terminated prior to expiration. In 1842, two days' work was the usual payment in Abaco for the occupation of slave cottages with small lots attached.[25]

Compensation amounted to £20,000,000 and certain amounts were to be allotted each colony, the total determined by the value of each slave. Bahamians worried that because they had only a few slaves they would not receive their fair share of the money. Inhabitants petitioned the king, explaining that many Blacks had been removed from the colony because of the exhausted soil and that it would be unfair to value their people at the rate of £19.18.93/4 between the years 1820 and 1830. When Whitehall sent out three special justices for administration purposes, the lieutenant governour put them on New Providence, Eleuthera, and Turks Island. He then appointed other special magistrates for each island to oversee the system, to explain rights of employers and apprentices, to settle disputes and to issue any punishments for violations of laws. Joseph Saunders and Thomas Russell were appointed for Abaco.[26]

Donald McLean and Hector Munro, Special Justices and members of the Board of Commissioners for Crown Lands and Woods, visited Abaco in May, 1835. They noted the poverty of the people at Cherokee Sound and did not recommend the village for expanded settlement. Southward along the coast to Hole in the Wall there was no shelter for vessels except at Crossing Rocks. The crown land at Great Harbour, (Hope Town) like the centre of Abaco, consisted primarily of pine barren, destroyed by lightning almost every season. The valuable wood on Elbow and adjacent cays "has been entirely cut down." Five families of formerly indentured Africans lived at Cedar Harbour. The justices allowed them to remain on the crown land there but could not recommend that area for further settlement because of the barren soil and want of a proper harbour. A strong wind prevented a visit to Walker's Cay. Benjamin Russell, a large scale cultivator of the castor oil plant on Grand Bahama, had offered to buy the island for five shillings an acre, but the justices felt the island should be put up for public auction. At least one family should be settled there to assist mariners wrecked on the dangerous Matanilla Reef.

The justices reported that the town at Green Turtle Cay, "situated on the isthmus of land," seemed to be the central place in Abaco for trade because of its "nearness to the American coast and its good harbours for small vessels." The inhabitants they described as "an enterprising and trading people" and although many were extremely poor, those amongst them "in better circumstances possess a considerable number of boats which they have for the purpose of wrecking." Since there was no land other than crown land suitable for cultivation, Green Turtle Cay people found it necessary to take their apprentices by boat to and from their plantations which were located on nearby cays and principally on the main of Abaco. For health reasons the justices felt the governour should stop any further encroachment on the already overcrowded and irregularly laid out town. Adjoining the village was a four acre parcel of swampy land which could easily be filled so that the town could expand in that direction. However, "all improvements of this kind in and about the place seem to be neglected, from the people's minds being directed to wrecking and trading."

Thirty-nine heads of families, mainly apprentices, asked the justices to examine a location in the vicinity of the town where they might build a settlement. They chose a place in the immediate neighbourhood, well sheltered and with a good harbour, and marked off a closed settlement, reserving land for a school and a chapel. Townspeople with houses on crown property were eager to buy the lots. Also under consideration was the purchase or lease of a turtle pond located between the town and the new village: "It is a small arm of the sea, with a narrow and shallow entrance, which could be easily filled up leaving a sluice and gate large enough to admit a small boat." Turtle grass abounded there, enough for a vast number of turtle to feed for twenty years. Mr. Saunders and several other wealthy individuals would "like to get possession of the pond for the purpose of supplying the American market." The justices believed that government should encourage this turtling enterprise as well as the two pineapple estates which had been started with good success last year on the cay.

While at Green Turtle, the justices "manumitted twenty-four apprentices by mutual request." No one had any complaints needing arbitration. They examined the jail and found it satisfactory, but suggested that the wooden partition be torn down and a stone one be put up to better separate the sexes. On their return they suggested to the governour that a jailer be appointed for Abaco, and in 1836, Benjamin Archer was appointed jailer and special constable for Abaco. Because of an increase of theft on Green Turtle Cay, apprentices and manumitted apprentices petitioned the governour to reinstate moderate flogging as punishment for persons of "any class or colour" who might be convicted of theft.[27]

Probably as a result of examining the reports of the justices, Governour Colebrook wrote the secretary of state in England that settlements in Eleuthera, Harbour Island, and Abaco differed from those in other islands. "The proprietors are, for the most part, indigent and illiterate persons who are often without means of maintaining themselves or their apprentices." He also made mention that New Plymouth "had recently been settled on Green Turtle Key."[28]

The governour had taken care to see that the apprenticeship system ran smoothly toward the approaching day of freedom. Governour Colebrook also tried to encourage the free Blacks to seek employment within the colony. The Bahamian Blacks, "Being an enterprising race," were sought by the inhabitants of East Florida who employed them as mechanics, mariners, and wreckers. They were also employed in New Orleans and in Texas "where several lost their lives in the last massacre by the Mexican Army."[29] With so much attention paid to the apprentices and the free Blacks, the African settlements struggled to survive.

One old and destitute sailor at the settlement of Carmichael endeavoured to petition for the reinstatement of his military pension. John Lamotte had served on the *Victory* for seven years, had been wounded three times, and had fought with Nelson at Trafalgar. He had received a pension of £10 upon his release from a Greenwich hospital and had gone to Glasgow. Intending to come to the Bahamas, he embarked on the brig *Surprise* which wrecked off Cape Bogadore where Lamotte was taken as a slave, first to Megadore, then to Algiers, where he was rescued by Lord Exmouth's expedition. On his return to England, his vessel cast away near Plymouth and his certificate of pension "shared the fate of the ship." He was then taken to Liverpool where he got passage for New Providence, but having lost his certificate, he was unable to draw his pension. Almost a year later, England had still not awarded the measly pension to a man who had fought beside their beloved warrior. Further examination of the sailor's history revealed another military adventure. After Nelson's burial, Lamotte had been put aboard the *Conquesdador* which fell in with two French vessels. The British warship passed between them, causing the enemy vessels to fire into each other.[30] Whether this worthy naval veteran ever received his pension is doubtful, but African slaves continued to wreck on Bahamian shores. Of what concern was one when there were so many?

In early February, 1834, the packet brig *Encomium* on its way from Charleston to New Orleans struck a reef at Fish Cay about midnight and bilged within twenty minutes. The crew cut away the mast to lighten the vessel, and most of the sixty-nine passengers and crew, including forty-five slaves, "clung to the wreck" until daylight. Some embarked in a small boat which was twice swamped before it reached shore five miles away. They remained there for four days until Green Turtle Cay wreckers picked them up. Everyone was saved and brought to Nassau in the schooner *Jasper*, Sawyer, and the sloop *Carpenter's Revenge*, Lowe. [31]

George Hayler of the United States consulate in Nassau wrote Lt. Governour Balfour that the forty-five slaves had been interrogated at the police office and were quartered at Fort Charlotte barracks. The owners had chartered another vessel and were ready to embark. They wished to know if there was any impediment to their taking their slaves with them. The governour must have been absent at the time, for acting public secretary C. R. Nesbitt curtly responded that the only impediment he knew of was that "they are liable to be hanged" and every accessory to their removing their slaves to New Orleans "is also liable to the same punishment." Later the governour gave a more polite answer to Mr. Hayler. The forty-five Blacks "are free to remain here or depart where they please."[32]

A few slaves returned to the United States preferring to "bear those ills we have/Than fly to others that we know not of." The rest of the American Blacks stayed in Nassau. Mr. Maddell, master of the *Encomium*, told the lieutenant governour that "either 'Uncle Sam' or 'John Bull' should pay the price of his slaves and he considered them to be well sold." Balfour warned Stanley that if the British government should even entertain the idea of paying masters the value of any slaves who, by touching Bahamian shores, became free, "we shall have all the infirm Slaves of Charleston, St. Augustine, and the neighbouring coast of America sent to this colony and I hardly need dwell on all the inconvenient results of such a scheme."[33]

An article reprinted in the *Royal Gazette*, entitled "Cruelty of the Existing Slave Trade," estimated that at the very least eight to ten "living souls every day of the calendar year are sacrificed to the Mammon of the sugar trade—not by breakers or by tempests, but in summer seas, beneath the bright tropical moon." It is in the "putrid hold of the slave ship where the manacled wretches lie doubled up, chin to knee, sweltering between decks scarcely three feet high, that death doth his regular business. . . ." If a British sail came into sight, the hatches were closed tight and before the crisis of discovery passed perhaps thirty of the "gasping freight" had died of suffocation. If the British cruiser has not been fooled:

> . . . the slave dealer crowds all his sail for flight; the rescuing vessel gains upon him, and capture seems inevitable. Only one chance remains—to baffle the discovery of his crime by destroying all proofs. The time grows short—the English lieutenant bears on—and a gun shot in advance almost sweeps the foam-track of the slaver. Fear gets the better of avarice. The negroes, confined in casks, or laden with a sinking weight of irons, are swiftly lowered into the sea. One splash and one shriek, and all is over. A moment's ripple curls where the sunny water has closed over the dying: then the clear blue deep resumes its calm, and every trace of death and guilt is gone.

Legal evidence thus stifled, the "miscreant triumphs with impunity."[34]

Due to the efforts of the Abaco wreckers, the lives of 150 African slaves were saved when the Portuguese schooner *Washington* wrecked at Cherokee Sound 18 January 1838. Prior to this year, wrecked Africans had been relatively easy to place in Nassau because their period of indenture was longer than the time of apprenticeship. Now with England pushing to release all apprentices in August, 1838, "persons of respectability" were difficult to find. Cockburn managed to place out seventy-nine adults from this wreck. As field labourers for one year, they were to receive food, clothing, lodging, medicine, and instruction so that at the end of the year they would be capable and free to make their own bargains with any employer. The seventy-two minors were placed under deeds of guardianship to the African Board by the chancellor of the colony and distributed to persons approved of by the board.[35]

The Bahamas House of Assembly tried to fight the early manumission of predials, shouting the old argument that the government of the Empire had no right to legislate for the colonies. Regardless of any protest, on 1 August 1838, the expiration date for non-predial indentures, predials were also to be excused from their last two years of apprenticeship. By autumn all African indentures were cancelled and the "last of bonded labor as a general system was done away with in the Bahamas."[36]

Great Britain abolished the system of slavery but could not cure the baseness and ignorance which caused it, nor stem the evils resulting from the jealousy and prejudice now so ingrained in it. In 1841, Major McGregor told Governour Cockburn that he suspected that Bahamians had been conveying away Africans for the "atrocious purpose" of again selling them into slavery. In 1845, Governour Mathew received a petition from some people whose relatives had "been sold into slavery in Florida." There had been more than one instance of this in the past fifteen years. "Bahama vessels with coloured crews have been purposely wrecked on the coast of Florida and the crews ... sold," and in November, 1830, a mariner from one vessel had been put up for sale in Mobile, Alabama, *by an inhabitant of Abaco*.[37]

Emancipation resulted in limited emigration. Governour Colebrook wrote the home government that "many settlers in Abaco who possess sloops and trade with the United States have lately ... speculated in quitting the colony and settling in the continent." Some Currys had already found their way to Key West. On 1 February 1834, the American sloop *Charlotte*, Curry, master, arrived in Nassau from Key West with a cargo of turtle for merchants Greenslade and Forster. The Blue Books show a decrease of seventy-three people in the population of Abaco between 1834 and 1836.[38]

Most Abaconians remained to ply their old trades and experiment with some new ones. In 1834, Lt. Governour Balfour stated that salt and wrecks were the chief source of revenue for the Bahamas. Other sources of colonial wealth were turtle, pineapples, some bark and woods, and a few bales of cotton. With the exception of cotton, Abaco managed to export in all these areas and as the years moved toward mid-century Abaconians speculated heavily in fruit. Bananas, pineapples, and citrus were exported, and by 1849 fruit and salt had become the two staple productions. The cultivation of oranges on New Providence, Eleuthera, Current Island, Abaco, and some parts of Cat Island had happened by accident, but it seemed that nature had designed those islands "for the purpose of orange groves alone." The trees secured their roots in cane and sink holes and were relatively sheltered from devastating storms.[39]

By mid-century the population of Abaco reached about 1900 and could boast a Colonial Secretary and a Receiver General as representatives in the House of Assembly. Wreckers and shipbuilders constituted the majority. Boats built in Abaco were generally smaller than those crafted by Harbour Islanders; however, in May, 1850, the sixty ton schooner *Clyde*, owned by Uriah Saunders, was launched at Abaco. After emancipation, wrecking reached new heights, especially during the years between 1845 and 1870. Green Turtle Cay, the largest settlement in Abaco, rose in prominence, and the language of an address of the New Plymouth inhabitants to the acting Stipendiary Justice Christopher Mardenbrough on his departure shows that some refined and educated people resided there.[40]

The lighthouse at Hole in the Wall, completed in 1836, hindered the wrecking trade somewhat. In 1846, two thousand vessels passed the Abaco Light. Lt. Governour Nesbitt suggested another lighthouse be built at Abaco because the one at Hole in the Wall could not be seen from the north side of the island. In 1847, an American transport vessel carrying 360 recruits to the American Army in Mexico wrecked on a reef near Man-O-War Cay at midnight. "By the exertions of a useful class of persons, denominated wreckers, the men, and part of the officer's baggage were saved, together with the arms, ammunitions and other warlike stores, though in a damaged state." Nesbitt also recommended an improvement in the wrecking regulations.[41]

Current regulations required that the first boat at the wreck must save the lives of passengers and crew instead of taking salvage. The lieutenant governour thought this "unjust and impolite" and feared this rule would cause delay in rescue operations. "No boat wants to be first if he gets no reward for his labour." A too strong dependence on wrecking did not encourage "habits of steady industry" among the inhabitants. Although plundering went hand in hand with the practice, government tried to apply certain checks although they did not want to discourage wreckers because they saved so many lives. Governour Mathew, however, spoke out strongly against wrecking as being "most injurious to the population engaged in it." His successor Governour Gregory supported the wreckers although Mathew had felt that they should "cultivate the soil." In response to an address from the New Plymouth inhabitants on his visit to Abaco in 1849, the governour praised the people for "promoting the Agricultural and Commercial interest of Abaco." Moreover, he praised their esteemed reputation in the "art of ship-building, and the daring qualities of the Abaco mariners—qualities which have largely contributed to the saving of lives from shipwreck."[42]

Churches complained about the demoralizing effects wrecking had on the people. The Methodist missionary at Green Turtle Cay reported that the people there regarded wrecking as a trade and were almost entirely dependent on it for their livelihood. In spite of this attitude, the mission had grown. In 1836, the congregation had numbered three hundred but in 1841 the wooden chapel "capable of containing seven hundred people" was too crowded. On 4 September 1843 the cornerstone was laid, but the new chapel was not completed until 1856. (See plate 48.) Membership dropped in the interim, due to backsliding and emigrations to Florida. Baptists worshiped at four or five places on Abaco and it was not until 1848 that the S.P.G. sent a clergyman to reside at Abaco. The Reverend J. C. Astwood estab-

PLATE 48: The Methodist Church at Green Turtle Cay was begun in 1843 but took 13 years to complete "due to backslidings and emigrations to Florida." Two Carrara marble memorial plaques in the Albert Lowe Museum are all that remain of the chapel which was destroyed in the 1932 hurricane. (Photograph courtesy of the Albert Lowe Museum.)

lished the first Anglican Church in Abaco in a wooden store at Green Turtle Cay, purchased for £73.[43]

Church and government leaders believed that violent prejudice against colour in Abaco caused the emigration to Florida. After struggling to adjust to two hundred years of changing political and economic conditions, the people of Harbour Island and Abaco could not adapt to civil and religious equality. Bitter prejudices influenced every phase of their lives. Considering Abaco's history of troublesome elections, problems in the March, 1837, election came as no surprise. The *Gazette* reported on April 19th that "yesterday, a few hours after the meeting of the House of Assembly, the writ of election for Abaco reached town." George R. Bannister, Robert W. Sawyer, and Henry R. Saunders each had eighty votes and John J. Burnside, Thomas R. Winder and William Gillam each had ten. The official report showed ninety votes penciled in for Abaco with no designation of Whites and Blacks as was given by many of the other islands. A note to this document indicated that the total number of votes had been estimated since the actual returns could not be found. All things considered, the election of 1837 was a suspicious affair at best.[44]

Angered "by a fancied personal slight," Archdeacon Trew diligently worked to secure Governour Mathew's recall. Although unable to get total support in Nassau, Trew successfully received signatures both in Harbour Island and in Abaco. The white Wesleyans were highly irritated at the governour's determination to mingle white and black children in the schools.[45]

Poor, and for the most part illiterate, many Abaconians were jealous of the rising condition of the Blacks. They would allow Blacks to share the dangers of wrecking with them but nothing else. Regarding Blacks as inferior to themselves, many Whites rejected "proffered education" out of excessive pride. Governour Gregory commented in his 1849 report: "There is still prejudice of white toward black. This is especially tenacious in Abaco and Harbour Island, where the white inhabitants will forego the advantage offered by the Board of Education rather than let their children go to school with blacks and coloureds."[46] In reporting to the S.P.G. regarding Mr. Astwood's mission on Green Turtle Cay, Archdeacon Trew called town prejudice a "plague" which not only infested the people but had spread to the government schools, where it "prevailed in its most unmitigated form:"

> The black and white children were most religiously kept asunder. In the New Testament classes, whilst the children read of 'God having made of one blood all nations to swell on the face of the earth' it must have seemed strange even to the little ones themselves, to be thus left to emulate each other within their own privileged or degraded circle.

The effect of such a system could not fail to prove injurious to the moral and social interest of any society. In spite of this prejudice, white and black learned the same lesson in the same class at the Anglican Mission. Trew was pleased to report that the Sunday school numbered forty-five, day school sixty-two and ten "persons of divers grades and complexions" attended the adult school.[47]

The archdeacon submitted acrid remarks, however, about the pew arrangement in the Methodist Chapel. "Divisions and strifes" had arisen which threatened disaster to the settlement and extinction to the entire mission. Although Whites and Blacks had worked side by side in harmony to build the spacious chapel, when it came time to worship "their common Father," disputes arose concerning the seating of parishioners. The Methodist Districts resolved that there should be no colour distinctions in seats. However, in 1847, John Blackwell, missionary at Green Turtle Cay, compromised by allowing the Whites to sit on one side and Blacks on the other. This ruling was condemned by the District Meeting, but in 1848, his successor Samuel Annear was violently opposed and ill treated for trying to enforce the District's regulations. Annear finally had to be removed. A "long season of angry disputation" terminated in the "voluntary expatriation" of some hundreds of the white population:

> The American settlement of Key West on the Florida Coast became henceforth the adopted home of those who preferred the protection of the Stripes and Stars with the negro's depravation, to that of the British Lion with his acknowledged right as a free designer of the world.

Governour Bayley maintained that Key West owed two-thirds of its population "to the violent prejudice against colour which has driven several hundred natives of Abaco, disgusted at the civil and religious equality of the negroes, to take refuge in a community wherein they can gratify their contemptuous dislike, without stint and without reprisals."[48]

Because Key West was an important wrecking town like Green Turtle Cay, many people were prompted to go there. William Lowe even practiced his hand-writing by scrawling "Key West" all over one of the pages of his ciphering book. In preparation for his removal to Key West, William Lowe sold three parcels of Abaco land to Henry Edward Thompson on 3 November 1846. This same year a hurricane damaged many Key West houses and caused a shortage of building materials. Two prominent Green Turtle residents were not discouraged, however. Captains Richard Roberts and John Bartlum dismantled their New Plymouth homes, carried the pieces to Key West, and reassembled the houses. The Bartlum and Roberts' houses stand to this day and provide visitors to Key West with two excellent examples of Bahama-built homes. (See plates 49 and 50.) Green Turtle lost one of its most expert and ingenious shipbuilders in John Bartlum; however, he did not break all ties with the Bahamas and continued to trade with Nassau. On 2 January 1847, the *Pensacola Gazette* reported that a British schooner from Green Turtle Cay had ar-

PLATE 49: John Bartlum's "Bahama House" at 730 Eaton Street, Key West, was dismantled on Green Turtle Cay and reassembled in Florida. The valley between the roof helps to collect rainwater. (Photograph courtesy of the Monroe Country Public Library, Key West.)

PLATE 50
In about 1846, Richard
"Tuggy" Roberts moved
his clapboard house
from Green Turtle Cay
to Key West. Like the
loyalist cottage in plate
12, this house has a New
England flavour.
(Photograph courtesy of
the Monroe County
Public Library, Key
West.)

rived in Key West "with 50 white immigrants who fled the Island in consequence of an insurrection of the free negroes."[49]

Emigration did not end the evil dissension at Green Turtle. On the morning of 26 September 1847, an incident again triggered the people's prejudice. An American schooner ran up on a reef on the back part of the cay and sustained some little damage. When it got off and put into the harbour for repair, rumours circulated that there were slaves aboard. Somehow one young girl got ashore and the black people tried to persuade her to remain with them. Some of the white population intimidated her by saying she would surely starve if she stayed on Green Turtle. At night, she was taken into the house of a white person and dressed in boy's clothes. Her hands and face were covered in a white paste made by a mixture of flour and water. A party of white people walked the disguised slave to the harbour, hoping she might reach the boat undetected. Some Blacks, however, got wind of the deceit and rescued the girl. For several days, continual fights broke out between the white and black residents; heads were broken, assault actions were preferred, and magistrates sent off many cases to the General Court in Nassau for trial. The girl was content to stay, but one morning the Whites succeeded in getting her on board the American vessel which departed New Plymouth with "all her Slaves on board." Archdeacon Trew concluded that this simple narrative illustrated "better than any comment what must have been the social state of that society where such an event could have happened."[50]

The Blacks at Green Turtle Cay fought to free one slave girl. Fifteen years later Americans were to fight a second civil war, this time to free her and her brothers. Once again Americans battled their neighbours, their friends and their kin for the principle of liberty, and in the words of Julia Ward Howe's battle hymn, prayed "let us die to make men free."

CHAPTER REFERENCES

ABBREVIATIONS APPEARING IN THE NOTES

AC: American Claims PRO.
ALM: Albert Lowe Museum, Green Turtle Cay, Abaco, The Bahamas.
AO: Audit Office Series, PRO.
BG: *Bahamas Gazette* (Nassau).
BHP: British Headquarters Papers (Carleton Papers), NYPL.
CC: Christ Church Registers, NA.
CO: Colonial Office, Public Records Office, Great Britain, Microfilm in NA, unless otherwise cited.
CRG: *Colonial Records of Georgia*, Georgia Archives, Atlanta.
CRNC: *Colonial Records of North Carolina*, North Carolina Department of Cultural Resources, Division of Archives and History, Raleigh.
CSP: *Calendar of State Papers*, PRO, NA.
f.:   folio [page] in CO.
GC: Georgia Claims in PRO.
JBTP: *Journal of the Board of Trade and Plantations*, NA.
JHA: Journal of the House of Assembly (Bahamas), NA.
LS: Lands and Surveys, Nassau, The Bahamas.
NA: Nassau Public Archives, Nassau, The Bahamas.
NL: Nassau Library, Nassau, The Bahamas.
NYPL: New York Public (Lenox) Library, Rare Books and Manuscripts Division.
ORG: Office of the Registrar General, Nassau, The Bahamas, NA.
PRO: Public Records Office, Great Britain.
RG: *Royal Gazette and Bahama Advertiser* (Nassau), NL.
RRG: *Revolutionary Records of Georgia*, Georgia Archives, Atlanta.
SCA: South Carolina Department of Archives and History, Columbia, S.C.
SPG: Society for the Propagation of the Gospel in Foreign Parts, also USPG, London.
VHA: *Votes of the House of Assembly*, Nassau, NA.

1: In the Beginning . . . Enigma

1. *Pangaea* in Greek means all earth.
2. Robert S. Dietz, John C. Holden and Walter P. Sproll, "Geotectonic Evolution and Subsidence of Bahama Platform," *Geological Society of America Bulletin* 81 (July 1970):1915.
3. Dietz, pp. 1915, 1923.
4. Dietz, pp. 1923, 1924, 1927.
5. James E. Andrews, Francis P. Shepard and Robert J. Hurley, "Grand Bahama Canyon," *Geological Society of America Bulletin* 81 (April 1970):1061.
6. I wish to thank Dr. Robert Adams, geologist at State University College at Brockport, New York, for his explana-

tion of the geological formation of the Bahama Islands and his informative geological excursions on the island of San Salvador.

7. A Captain Stuart counted the islands, cays and rocks. In a letter to Edward Campbell, Sir Rawson W. Rawson, governour of the Bahamas 1864-1868, states that he compiled the lengthy report because of the lack of information about the islands. The Turks and Caicos Islands are not included in this count. In 1848 that group politically separated from the Bahamas and were taken under the jurisdiction of the governor of Jamaica. When the Bahamas gained independence from Great Britain in 1973, the Turks and Caicos Islands remained part of the British West Indies. Rawson W. Rawson, *Report on the Bahamas for the Year 1864* (London: George E. Eyre and William Spottiswoode, 1866), p. 9.

8. George B. Rabb and Ellis B. Hayden Jr., "The Van Voort-American Museum of Natural History Bahama Islands Expedition," *American Museum Novitates* no. 1836 (28 June (1957):4.

9. *BG,* 28 February 1789, p. 3, NL; Rawson, p. 11.

10. Rawson, pp. 9, 11.

11. *Nassau Quarterly: Mission Paper being Notes of Church* [Anglican] *Work in the Diocese of Nassau, Bahama Islands,* 25 (December 1910):89.

12. William C. Coker, "Vegetation of the Bahama Islands," in *The Geographical Society of Baltimore: The Bahama Islands,* ed., George Burbank Shattuck (New York: The Macmillan Co., 1905), p. 195. This book contains chapters on every phase of island environmental studies, complete with detailed lists of birds and fishes.

13. Mark Catesby, *The Natural History of Carolina, Florida, and the Bahama Islands,* 2 vols. (London, 1754; facsimile reprint ed., Savannah, Georgia, 1974), 2:40.

14. Storrs L. Olson, "Biological Archaeology in the West Indies," Proceedings of the Third Bahamas Conference on Archaeology 18-22 March 1982, *The Florida Anthropologist* 35 (December 1982), (hereinafter cited as BCA 1982 *FA* 35 or if conference paper was not published in the journal, BCA 1982).

15. Columbus was probably not the first European to sail to the West Indies. An unknown Portuguese navigator preceded the admiral. A nautical chart of 1424 in the John Bell Ford collection at the University of Minnesota shows a large red rectangle in the Mid-Atlantic labelled "Antilla." Alvin M. Josephy, Jr., "Was American Discovered Before Columbus?" *American Heritage* 6 (April 1955):16. Phoenician sailors may have journeyed to the New World as early as the tenth, perhaps even the ninth or eighth centuries. John Frye, *The Search for the Santa Maria* (New York: Dodd Mead and Co., 1973), pp. 126-127. Scholars still debate the original landfall of Columbus. The island referred to in this chapter is the present island of San Salvador, formerly Watlings Island, Bahamas. Samuel Eliot Morison, *Admiral of the Ocean Sea: A Life of Christopher Columbus,* vol. 1 (Boston: Brown and Co., 1942; reprint ed., New York: Time Inc., 1962), p. 222. Arne Molander believes that Columbus would have used the more reliable method of latitude sailing which would have brought him to the north end of Eleuthera. Tracing what he believes to be Columbus's northern route through the Bahamas, Molander fixes New Providence, not Rum Cay, as Columbus's Santa Maria de la Conception; Andros, not Long Island, as Fernandina; and Long Island, not Crooked Island, as Isabella. Arne Molander, "The Search for San Salvador," *Journal of the Bahamas Historical Society* 4 (October 1982):5, 3.

16. Brian Edward, *The History Civil and Commercial of the British West Indies,* 2 vols. (London: John Stockdale, 1794), 1:87.

17. Julian Granberry, "A Brief History of Bahamian Archaeology," Proceedings of the Second Bahamas Conference on Archaeology, *The Florida Anthropologist* 33 (September 1980): 83.

18. "Lifeways" is a term created by Shaun Sullivan, "Modeling of Economic Strategies Based upon Analysis of Resources within Site Catchment Areas," BCA 1982. The Third Bahamas Conference was hosted by the Bahamas Archaeological Project (BAP) and held on the island of San Salvador. BAP has been organized expressly for the purpose of making a systematic study of the archaeological remains of the Lucayan Arawaks. This project was initiated through the work of Dr. Donald Gerace, Director of the College Center of the Finger Lakes, Bahamian Field Station, located on San Salvador, The Bahamas.

19. Christopher Columbus, *Journal of First Voyage to America,* (Kettel Translation 1827, reprint ed., New York: Albert and Charles Boni, 1924), p. 23. Mrs. Ruth Durlacher-Wolper has done extensive research in order to uncover the identity of Christopher Columbus. Her study concludes that the explorer was Byzantine from the island of Chios, Greece, that he was a member of the Royal Palaeologus family, and that Columbus's origin had been concealed by Peter Martyr for political and religious reasons. In 1929 the Borromeo letter, written in 1494, was discovered. In it, Peter Martyr makes a secret declaration of Columbus's real identity. Columbus sailed twenty-three years with his kinsman George Palaeologus who was known as "Colon the Younger." The island of Chios was under Genoese rule from 1346-1566 during which time Genoese fashion and architecture influenced Greek culture there. Columbus wrote his secret log in Greek leagues. The two headed eagle appearing in the Palaeologus family crest is found in the crest of Las Casas which may explain why Las Casas had possession of Columbus's original journal. Ruth Durlacher-Wolper, "Who was Columbus?" (BCA 1982, FA 35). See also, Mrs. Wolper's *A New Theory Clarifying the Identity of Christophoros Columbus a Byzantine Prince from Chios, Greece* (San Salvador, Bahamas: New World Museum, 1982).

20. D. G. Brinton, "The Arawak Language of Guiana in its Linguistic and Ethnological Relations," *Transactions of the American Philosophical Society* 13 (1871):441.

21. Columbus, p. 25. It was the custom among the Arawaks to tie a board to the infant's forehead in order to flatten and supposedly harden the forehead against enemy blows.

22. Brinton, pp. 428, 437.

23. Columbus, pp. 25-29. Some of the dry leaves were probably tobacco leaves. Frederick Ober, "Aborigines of the

West Indies," *American Antiquarian Society* 9 (April 1894): 292.
24. Columbus, p. 25.
25. Granberry, p. 86.
26. William H. Sears and Shaun O. Sullivan, "Bahamas Prehistory," *American Antiquity* 43 (January 1978): 6.
27. John Winter, "Preliminary Results for a Cuban Migration," BCA 1982.
28. Brinton, p. 435; Irving Rouse, "The Circum-Caribbean Theory, an Archeological Test," *American Anthropologist* 55 (April-June 1953):188.
29. Brinton, p. 444.
30. Brinton, p. 427; Rouse, p. 197. In recent times, bitter manioc was used to make starch. Only a few people in Abaco know how to extract the poison; most people eat bread made from the sweet manioc or cassava. Interview with Mizpah Sawyer, Boca Raton, Florida, 10 August 1982.
31. Sears and Sullivan, p. 19.
32. Sears and Sullivan, p. 17.
33. Sears and Sullivan, p. 23.
34. Steven W. Mitchell, "Analysis of Tidal Growth Sequences in Populations of *Codakis Orbicularis* (Linnaeus) from the Lucayan Arawak Pigeon Creek Site, San Salvador," *Bahamas Archaeological Project Reports and Papers* (San Salvador, Bahamas; CCFL Bahamian Field Station, 1980), p.4.
35. Mitchell, pp. 13, 14, 17.
36. William F. Keegan, "Settlement Patterns in the Bahamas Region," BAC 1982.
37. William F. Keegan, "Lucayan Fishing Practices: An Experimental Approach" BAC 1982. FA 35.
38. Charles A. Hoffman, Jr., "The Palmetto Grove Site on San Salvador, Bahamas," *Contributions of the Florida State Museum, Social Science Number 16* (Gainesville, Florida: University of Florida, 1970), p. 12-13. The site is actually located in a grove of silver top, not palmetto, palms.
39. Sears and Sullivan, pp. 15-16.
40. Hoffman, p. 13.
41. Sears and Sullivan, p. 13.
42. Richard Rose, "Archaeological Investigations at Pigeon Creek, San Salvador, Bahamas," BAC 1982, FA 35.
43. Columbus, p. 30.
44. Robert A. Curry presents a comparison of island names which appear on old charts, beginning with the one drawn by Juan de la Cosa, pilot to Columbus on his second voyage to the New World. Robert A. Curry, *Bahamian Lore* (Paris, France: By the Author, 1928): 28.
45. Brinton, pp. 430, 437.
46. Figure 4. The total length of the paddle measures 4'2¾" and the crosspiece is 4½" long. The shaft is 2' long and the blade 2'¾" long, measuring 6¼" at its widest point and 1¼" at its narrowest. Theodoor De Booy, "Lucayan Artifacts from the Bahamas," *American Anthropologist* 15 (January-March 1913): 2-5. The petroglyph of this particular paddle is on a piece of the wall, taken from the cave at Rum Cay and now in the New World Museum, San Salvador, Bahamas. The paddle is in The Museum of the American Indian, Heye Foundation, New York City.
47. Sears and Sullivan, p. 17.
48. Sears and Sullivan, pp. 7-8.
49. Granberry, p. 90.
50. Cecil G. Ford MS., pp. 122-123, copy in the ALM: M. A. Gerassimos, 24 September 1982; The artifacts are in the collection of the ALM.
51. Figure 5. The bottle measures 13.5 cm in length, 12.9 cm high and the gourds are up to 7 cm in diameter. Robert S. Carr and Sandra Riley, "An Effigy Ceramic Bottle from Green Turtle Cay, Abaco," BAC 1982, FA 35.
52. Columbus, p. 31.
53. Columbus, pp. 26-27.
54. Columbus, p. 71; Morison, p. 233. A Spanish *legua* measures roughly 3½ miles. Bartolomé de Las Casas, *The Devastation of the Indies: A Brief Account,* trans., Herma Briffault, intro., Hans Magnus Enzensberger (New York: The Seabury Press, 1974), note 7, p. 178.
55. Columbus, pp. 33-34.
56. Las Casas, *Brief Account*, pp. 42-43.
57. Sears and Sullivan, p. 23.
58. Shaun Sullivan, "An Overview of the 1976 to 1978 Archeological Investigations in the Caicos Islands," *The Florida Anthropologist* 33 (September 1980): 131.
59. Columbus, pp. 27-28.
60. Sears and Sullivan, p. 22.
61. Shaun Sullivan, "Astronomical Alignments of Stone Line Formations at Two Arawakan Sites on Middle Caicos Island," BAC 1982.
62. Edward Gaylord Bourne, "Columbus, Ramon Pane and the Beginnings of American Anthropology," *Proceedings of the American Antiquarian Society* 17 (April 1906): 342.

2: "The Flag That Bears No History but Blood and Tears"

1. Henry Christopher Christie, *Blackbeard: A Romance of the Bahamas* (Nassau, Bahamas: Bahamas Publishing Co. Ltd., n.d.), p. 141.
2. Thomas Southey, *Chronological History of the West Indies*, 3 vols. (London: A & R Spottiswoode for Longman, Rees, et. al., 1827), 1:102.
3. Las Casas, *Brief Account*, p. 41.
4. William Robertson, *The History of America*, 4 vols. (London: Printed for Cadell and Davies, et. al., 1808), 1:262-263; Bryan Edwards, *The History Civil and Commercial of the British West Indies*, 2 vols. (London: John Stockdale, 1794): 1:87; Southey, 1:107; Bartolomé de Las Casas, *History of the Indies*, ed. and trans., Andree Collard (New York: Harper and Row, 1971), pp. 155-156. See also Lewis Hanke, *Spanish Struggle for Justice in Conquest of America* (Boston: Little, Brown & Co., 1965).
5. Hans Enzensberger, "Las Casas, or a Look Back into the Future," intro. to Las Casas, *Brief Account*, p. 8.
6. Enzensberger, p. 13.
7. Edwards, 1:89.
8. Las Casas, *History*, p. xxii.
9. Sandra Riley, "Journal IV" (1975-1977), 27 March 1977. Although there is an Army Museum in Honolulu, this particular Army Museum is no longer in existence. The Spanish crucifix is part of the private collection of Mr. Warren Sessler of Honolulu, Hawaii.
10. Las Casas, *History*, p. 155.
11. Las Casas, *Brief Account*, p. 40.
12. Las Casas, *Brief Account*, p. 52.
13. Las Casas, *History*, p. 154.
14. Robertson, 1:262.
15. Robertson, 1:262-263.
16. Las Casas, *Brief Account*, n. 7, p. 178 and pp. 108-109.
17. Las Casas, *Brief Account*, p. 66.
18. Edwards, 1:88.
19. Las Casas, *History*, p. 157. Also Edwards, 1:88 and Southey, 1:107.
20. Las Casas, *History*, pp. 157-158.
21. Robertson, 1:268.
22. Las Casas, *History*, p. 159.
23. Las Casas, *Brief Account*, pp. 109-111.
24. Las Casas, *History*, p. 160; *Brief Account*, p. 40.
25. Las Casas, *History*, p. 161.
26. Las Casas, *Brief Account*, p. 39.
27. Eric Williams, *From Columbus to Castro: The History of the Caribbean 1492-1969* (New York: Harper and Row, 1970), p. 25.
28. Enzensberger, p. 21.
29. *BG*, 9 July 1787.
30. According to Ovieda this tyrant governour was "responsible for the death of roughly two million people." Las Casas, *Brief Account*, n. 16, p. 179.
31. Las Casas, *Brief Account*, pp. 59-60, 18.
32. Las Casas, *Brief Account*, p. 55.
33. Las Casas, *Brief Account*, pp. 138, 43, 80, 137-138.
34. Las Casas, *Brief Account*, pp. 60, n. 12 p. 179.
35. Las Casas, *Brief Account*, pp. 118-119 and n. 47 p. 181.
36. Joseph Byrne Lockey, *East Florida 1783-1785: A File of Documents Assembled, and Many of Them Translated* (Berkely and Los Angeles: University of California Press, 1949), p. 173.
37. Las Casas, *Brief Account*, pp. 84, 57, 58, 65, 56.
38. Las Casas, *Brief Account*, p. 27.
39. A. P. Newton, *The European Nation in the West Indies 1493-1688* (London: A & C Black Ltd., 1933), p. 19.
40. Southey, 1:90.
41. Las Casas, *Brief Account*, p. 27.
42. Arthur Helps, *The Spanish Conquest in America*, vol. 3 (London: n. p., 1904), p. 148.
43. Las Casas, *Brief Account*, p. 38.
44. Ober, "Aborigines of the West Indies," p. 273.
45. Las Casas, *History*, pp. 160-161.
46. *Daily News* (Washington), 13 October 1937; James H. Stark, *Stark's History and Guide to the Bahama Islands* (Norwood, Massachusetts: Plimpton Press, 1891), p. 31.
47. Joshua R. Giddings. *The Exiles of Florida* (Columbus, Ohio: Follett, Foster and Co., 1858), p. 3.
48. Nixon Smiley, "The Lost Tribe of Andros," *Tropic, (Miami Herald)*, 20 February 1972, p. 16.
49. Smiley, p. 14; John M. Goggin, "An Anthropological Reconnaissance of Andros Island, Bahamas," *American Antiquity* 5 (July 1939): 24.
50. Interview with Elmore Nairn, San Salvador, Bahamas, 24 March 1982. See plate 46.

3: The Re-Peopling of the Bahamas and Other Disastrous Accounts

1. The population of the Bahamas in 1871 counted 39,162 people. Mary Moseley, *The Bahamas Handbook* (Nassau, Bahamas: *The Nassau Guardian*, 1926), p. 97. The term "re-peopling" is Miss Moseley's, p. 93.
2. Frederick A. Ober, *A Guide to the West Indies, Bermuda, and Panama* (New York: Dodd, Mead and Co., 1920), p. 69.
3. The Spanish historian Herrera claims Ponce de Leon's voyage happened in 1512. Lawson believes there is over-whelming evidence that the voyage took place in 1513. Edward W. Lawson, *The Discovery of Florida and Its Discoverer Juan Ponce De Leon* (St. Augustine, Florida; Edward W. Lawson, 1946), pp. 22, 24, 44, 45. See plate 6. Bimini is located on the Great Bahama Bank directly across from Santa Marta. Lawson's Map no. 1, "Dead Reckoning of Juan Ponce de Leon's First Voyage to Florida," back flyleaf.
4. Herman Moll, *A Map of the West Indies on the Islands of America in the North Sea* (London, 1721); Another version of the Spanish Convoy system is demonstrated in a supplemental chart produced by the Cartographic Division of *National Geographic*, "Colonialization and Trade in the New World." in Mendal Peterson, "Reach for the New World," *National Geographic* 152 (December 1977): 724A; In 1595 seventeen sail of Spanish ships were lost in the Gulf of Florida, J. H. Lefroy, comp., *Memorials of the Discovery and Early Settlement of the Bermudas or Somers Islands 1515-1685*, 2 vols. (London: Longmans, Green and Co., 1877). Appendix 1, 2:571-572.
5. Southey, 1:160.
6. Woodes Rogers Report, Vernon-Wager Papers, Peter Force Collection, Library of Congress, 6 reels, Reel 2, pp. 155-156; Peter Henry Bruce, *Bahama Interlude: Being an Account of Life at Nassau in the Bahama Islands in the Eighteenth Century* (1782; rpt. ed., London: John Culmer Ltd., n.d.), p. 40.
7. Moseley, p. 20; James Martin Wright, "History of the Bahama Islands, with a Special Study of the Abolition of Slavery in the Colony," in George Burbank Shattuck, ed., *The Geological Society of Baltimore: The Bahama Islands* (New York; Macmillan, 1905), p. 421.
8. Richard Wilson, ed., *Stories from Hakluyt* (New York: E. P. Dutton and Co., 1921), pp. 153-154.
9. Jacques-Nicolas Bellin, *Déscription Géographique Des Isles Antilles Possedées Par Les Anglois* (Paris, 1758). p. 142: Antoine Augustin Buzen de la Martiniere, *Le Grand Dictionnaire Geographique Historique et Critique*, vol. 3 (Paris 1768), p. 920. I wish to thank Olga Michel for translating certain passages of these works.
10. Westminster 30 October 1629, *CSP*, 9:70-71; Moseley, p. 20.
11. Curry, p. 36.
12. Southey, 2:268-269.
13. G. B. Harrison, ed., *Shakespeare: The Complete Works* (New York: Harcourt, Brace and Co., 1948), p. 1471.
14. In Greek mythology Eleutherius is an epithet of Zeus meaning god of freedom. *The Random House Dictionary of the English Language,* unabridged edition (New York; Random House, (1966), p. 461. Eleutheria was an ancient Greek festival commemorating their deliverance from the Persian Armies. *The Random House Encyclopedia* (New York: Random House, 1977), p. 2144.
15. J. P. Kenyon, *The Stuarts: A Study in English Kingship* (London: Fontana-Collins, 1970), p. 75.
16. G. M. Trevelyan, *English Social History: A Survey of Six Centuries: Chaucer to Queen Victoria* (London: The Reprint Society, 1944), p. 211.
17. Curry, p. 40. A reprint of the "Articles and Orders" of the Eleutheran adventurers can be found in Curry, pp. 39-46 and in H. E. Bates and Hilary St. George Saunders, "The Bahamas Story," Nassau 1954, NA, Appendix A, pp 1-10. This unpublished work was commissioned by the Bahamas Government in 1950 and information was gathered primarily from the PRO in London by Jane Bowlinger and Marjorie Napier. Saunders died in 1951 and Bates finished the project. Bates, foreword, Nassau 1954. Mary Moseley perhaps was referring to Mr. Saunders when she told Thelma Peters about a man who came from London to write a history of the Bahamas in collaboration with Bates, a popular English writer. Saunders "lived quite handsomely" on a locally paid expense account but died only a few weeks after his arrival. In the same interview Mrs. Pyfrom said that since Mr. Bates had no deep interest in the history of the colony he was content to throw the notes of his predecessor and the two researchers into readable form. Altogether £12,000 was spent on the project. The committee was not pleased and refused to publish the book. Interview with Mary Moseley held by Thelma Peters in Nassau 28 July 1958. The original copy of the MS seems to have disappeared from the Bahamas House of Assembly. A photostat of the typewritten carbon copy is deposited in the Nassau Archives.
18. Curry, pp. 40-41.
19. Curry, pp. 42, 43, 45. There are no mines in the Bahamas. Gold would have been salvaged from Spanish wrecks. Ambergris, the fragrant secretion of the sperm whale valued by perfumers, often washed ashore. The Bahamas had always been rich in salt.
20. John Winthrop, *The History of New England from 1630-1649*, 2 vols. in 1 vol., ed. James Savage (1825; rpt. ed., New York: Arno Press, 1972), 2:335.
21. Curry, p. 44.
22. Bates, Appendix B, pp. 11-14.
23. W. Hubert Miller, "The Colonization of the Bahamas, 1647-1670," *William and Mary Quarterly*, Third Series, 2 (January 1945): 35-36; In 1646 William Sayle obtained a grant from Parliament. The Independents were banished from Bermuda by Royalists in 1649. Lefroy, 2:10-11.
24. Winthrop, 2:335.
25. Miller, p. 36.
26. Miller, p. 37. In 1899 the original letter of attorney "was in the possession of William N. Manning of Rockport,

Massachusetts, a descendant of Joseph Bowles." John T. Hassam, "The Bahama Islands: Notes on an Early Attempt at Colonization," *Massachusetts Historical Society Proceedings*, Second Series, 13 (March 1899). 4-0.
27. Miller, p. 38.
28. Hassam, pp. 16-58.
29. Miller, p. 39. See also Forster to Somers Island Company in London, 7 September 1650, Lefroy, 2:9.
30. Catesby, 2:51.
31. The arrival of the seventy Eleutheran adventurers in Bermuda was mentioned in the postscript of Forster's letter to the Somers Island Company in London, 20 December 1650 in Lefroy. 2:19-20.
32. Lefroy, appendix 5, 1:726; Miller, p. 36.
33. Lefroy, 2:84, 89, 94-96; Miller, p. 41.
34. Paul Albury, *The Story of the Bahamas* (London: Macmillan Education Ltd., 1975), p. 45.
35. *CSP*, 1:453. According to Lefroy these people had already left Eleuthera, 2:98; Miller, p. 41.
36. *Yachtsmans* [sic] *Guide to the Bahamas*, ed., Harry Kline (Coral Gables, Florida: Tropic Isle Publishers, 1974), p. 190.
37. Miller, pp. 39-40.
38. Lefroy, appendix 5, 1:726.
39. Richard Richardson's sworn statement, 18 July 1658, Lefroy, 2:112; Bates, p. 49; Michael Craton, *A History of the Bahamas* (London: Collins, 1962). The confusion here may arise from the fact that Lefroy mentions that "six attestations are recorded" between 24 June and 18 July 1658 regarding Spanish treasure recovered from "a wreck upon Abaco." But he also states that the "subjoined statement of one of the parties [Richardson 18 July 1658] gives a connected narrative of this adventure, *which does not appear to have any connection* with the expedition of Captain Richard Lockyer in 1656." (Emphasis added.) Richardson's statement may have been inadvertently included with the other five disputes which resulted from the Lockyer expedition to Abaco in 1656. Lefroy, no. 90, 2:112; Lefroy, no. 48, 2: 77-78. Man Island, as it is called on today's charts, is located just off the northeast point of North Eleuthera, just north of Harbour Island.
40. Lefroy, 1:112-113.
41. Lefroy, 2:133; Miller, p. 42.
42. Lefroy, 2:236. Lefroy indicates that there are more statements attesting Nathaniel Sayle's commission. These may reveal the names of other Eleutheran adventurers.
43. Lefroy, 2:235-236.
44. Miller, p. 44. 1666 is also the year of the great Fire of London. Letter from the Bermuda Company describing the fire, 1 November 1666, Lefroy, 2:244-245.
45. *CSP*, 7:56.
46. Miller, p. 44.
47. Trevelyan, p. 213.
48. Maurice Besson, *The Scourge of the Indies: Buccaneers, Corsairs and Filibusters* (New York: Random House, 1929), p. 8.
49. Besson, pp. 6,7.
50. John Esquemeling, *The Buccaneers of America* (Swan Sonnenscheim and Co., 1893; rpt. ed., New York: Dover Publications Inc., 1967), pp. 103-104. The first English edition of the work of the Dutch buccaneer and barber-surgeon John Esquemeling appeared in 1684.
51. Esquemeling, p. 143.

4: Lords, Knaves, and "They That Go Down to the Sea in Ships"

1. A. S. Salley, *The Lords Proprietors of Carolina* (n. p.: General Assembly of South Carolina, 1944), p. 3.
2. *CSP*, 7:147; "Chalmers Papers" v. 1, Bahama Islands: Account of Them from Their Settlement to 1728," a true copy, State Papers Office, Whitehall 25 January 1803, John Bruce, Keeper of the State Papers, NA. (hereinafter Chalmers "Bahamas Account to 1728").
3. Salley, pp. 14-15.
4. *CSP*, 7:147.
5. *CSP*, 7:170; Bates, pp. 59-60; Craton p. 66 gives the date of this wreck as 1770 which contradicts Russell's 1669 date in the *CSP*. Since the wreck occurred in January, these historians may have assumed that the state papers had used the old calendar. In 1666, Sir John Colleton died leaving his share to his son Peter. Salley, p. 16.
6. *CSP*. 7:56.
7. Bates, appendix C, pp. 15-17. This letter first appeared in the Egerton MSS, 2395 F. 472. The date is probably 13 March 1670, prior to the official proprietary grant 1 November 1670.
8. Moseley, p. 16.
9. Miller, p. 42.
10. Bates, appendix I, p. 29. *Homeward Bound* uses Mary Moseley's list of proprietary and royal governours and their dates of office from 1670 to 1924, pp. 103-105.
11. John Wentworth to Governour Thomas Lynch of Jamaica, 23 August 1672, *CSP*, 7:403.
12. Craton, pp. 68-69. In 1672/3 Elizabeth Carter, a Quaker formerly of Barbados, had caused a public disturbance by arguing with a Reverend Edwards while he was preaching at Devonshire Tribes Church in Bermuda. The Council banished Elizabeth Carter and Anne Butler to New Providence aboard the ketch *Francis* and they were forbidden

ever to return to Bermuda. Lefroy, 2:374-379.
13. Miller, pp. 45-46.
14. *CSP*, 9:232.
15. *CSP*, 9:418.
16. Trevelyan, p. 214.
17. John Oldmixon, *The History of the Isle of Providence*, a chapter from *The British Empire in America*, 2 vols., first printed 1708 (London: John Culmer, 1741; rpt. ed., Nassau: The Providence Press, 1966), pp. 12-13.
18. Sir Thomas Lynch to Lords of Trade and Plantations, Jamaica, 29 August 1682, *CSP*, 11:284.
19. Chalmers, "Bahamas Account to 1728."
20. Oldmixon, p. 13; Chalmers, "Bahamas Account to 1728."
21. Charles W. Baird, *History of the Huguenot Emigration to America*, vol. 2 (New York: Dodd, Mead, 1885), p. 200.
22. Stark pp. 143-144; Massachusetts Archives CXVI. 83, 200 in Hassam, p. 15.
23. The Davis petition was filed 12 July 1687, Hassam, p. 16. Hassam's date of Mass. Archives CXXVI, 387 disagrees with the date given in Stark, p. 144. Hassam's date is used here.
24. CO 23/3 f.5, NA.
25. In 1834 many Abaconians made their living wrecking and turtling. See appendix E.
26. Eric Whittleton, "Family History in the Bahamas," *Genealogist Magazine* 18 (December 1975): 189.
27. 2 November 1686, *CSP*, 12:275.
28. *CSP*, 12:326.
29. Commission and Instructions from the Lords Proprietors to Thomas Bridges, governour of the Bahamas, 12 July 1688, *CSP*, 12:570.
30. Oldmixon, pp. 13-17; Chalmers, "Bahamas Account to 1728."
31. The account of the 1692 earthquake appears in Southey 2:161. Nicholas Trott probably built the first Anglican Church in Nassau. After extensive research, Antonina Canzoneri determined that the site was located on the property of Graycliff, the home of the Duke of Windsor when he was governour of the Bahamas 1940-1945. Using a sketch map of the area Miss Canzoneri and Father Irwin McSweeney were able to measure off and pinpoint the site. This church was probably leveled during the Spanish attack on Nassau in 1703, but some of the ruins are visible at the top of a hill there.
32. Oldmixon, pp. 18-19.
33. Oldmixon, p. 20.
34. Bates, pp. 122-123.
35. Oldmixon, p. 12.
36. Herman Melville, *Moby Dick; or, The Whale*, Great Books of the Western World Edition (Chicago: Enclyclopedia Britannica Inc., 1952), pp. 46-47.
37. [John Smith], *The History of the Bermudaes or Summer Islands*, ed. J. H. Lefroy (London: printed for the Hakluyt Society, 1882), p. 89.
38. George Francis Dow, "The Whale Fishery in Colonial New England," in *Whale Ships and Whaling: A Pictorial History of Whaling During Three Centuries* (Salem, Massachusetts: Marine Research Society, 1925), pp. 11, 20.
39. Obed Macy, *The History of Nantucket* (Boston: Hilliard, Gray and Co., 1835), pp. 8, 28.
40. F. V. Morley and J. S. Hodgson, *Whaling North and South* (London and New York: The Century Co., 1926), p. 23.
41. Melville, p. 418.
42. Bates, p. 62.
43. Lefroy, 2:254.
44. Frances Diane Robotti, *Whaling and Old Salem: A Chronicle of the Sea* (Salem, Massachusetts: Newcomb and Gauss Co., 1950), p. 11.
45. J. Ross Browne, *Etchings of a Whaling Cruise*, ed., John Seelye (Cambridge, Massachusetts: The Belknap Press of Harvard University, 1968), pp. 522-523.
46. Melville, p. 209.
47. William Henry Tripp, *There Goes Flukes* (New Bedford, Massachusetts: Reynolds Printing, 1938), pp. 67-73.
48. Dorrell to Ashley, 13 March 1670/1 in Bates, appendix C, p. 17.
49. Browne, p. 521.
50. Richard Stafford, Bermuda, 16 July 1668, Lefroy, 2:265.
51. 25 April 1688, *CSP*, 12:536.
52. Dow, p. 17.
53. *CSP*, 17:447.
54. Randolph to Council of Trade and Plantations, 25 March 1700, *CSP*, 18:136.
55. According to Mr. Elding's letter of 4 October 1699, Governour Webb appointed Elding deputy governour on 14 April 1699, the day Webb left New Providence. CO 23/12 f. 57.
56. Edward Randolph to Council of Trade and Plantations, 11 & 25 March 1700, *CSP* 18:119-120, 135-136; 27 April 1700, 18; 39-40.
57. CO 23/12 f. 57.
58. Craton, p. 90.

5.: The Great Age of Piracy

1. Thomas Smith to Board of Trade, 12 April 1700?, *CSP*, 18.
2. Thomas Walker, 30 January 1700?, *CSP*, 18.
3. Cole to Council of Trade, 17 February 1702, *CSP*, 20:80.
4. Oldmixon, p. 21. The ruins of this church can be seen atop Graycliff.
5. Oldmixon, p. 22.
6. Wright, J. M., *History*, p. 423.
7. *CSP*, 22.
8. *CRNC*, 6:633.
9. *JBTP*, 1:386.
10. *JBTP*, 1:387-388.
11. *JBTP*, 1:398-399.
12. *JBTP*, 1:583-585.
13. Oldmixon, p. 22; 11 June 1708, *JBTP*, 1:504; 29 June 1709, *JBTP* 2:48.
14. Captain Smith, Virginia, 12 August 1710, *CSP*, 25:421.
15. 22 September 1710, *JBTP*, 2:183-184.
16. John Graves, *A Memorial: or a Short Account of the Bahama Islands, 1708, NYPL.* 2:48.
17. Mendel Peterson, *Funnel of Gold* (Boston-Toronto: Little Brown and Co., 1975), p. 360.
18. Lt. Gov. Pulleine to Board of Trade, Bermuda, 22 April 1714, *CSP*, 27:334.
19. Walker, New Providence, 14 March 1715, *CSP*, 28:119.
20. Lt. Gov. Spotswood to Council of Trade and Plantations, Virginia, 3 July 1716, *CSP*, 29:141.
21. *CSP*, 28:119.
22. *CSP*, 28:120.
23. Memorial of Mr. Richard Bereford to the Lord Commissioners of Trade and Plantations, 23 June 1716, *CRNC*, 2:231-233.
24. Spotswood, 3 July 1716, *CSP*, 29:139-140.
25. Vickers' deposition in Spotswood 3 July 1716, *CSP*, 29:140-141.
26. Report of Captain Mathew Musson to the Board of Trade, 5 July 1717, *CSP*, 29:338. The colonial seaport in South Carolina has been spelled Charleston since 1783 and unless the name appears in a direct quotation, the town will be referred to that way. From 1670-1680 the place was spelled Charles Town and from 1720-1783, Charlestown.
27. Daniel Defoe, *A General History of the Pyrates*, ed., Manuel Schonhorn (Columbia, South Carolina: University of South Carolina Press, 1972). Schonhorn's work is the "first scholarly edition of the *General History* and the first to bear Defoe's name on the title page." Joel Herman Baer, "Piracy Examined: A Study of Daniel Defoe's *General History of the Pirates and its Milieu*" (Ph.D. dissertation, Princeton University, 1970), p. 2. Double quotation marks are used when Professor Schonhorn believes Defoe used original documents or direct discourse of eyewitnesses.
28. Defoe, pp. 4-5.
29. Defoe, pp. 244, 221. The small jack on the *Royal Fortune* is the one mentioned here. See plate 14.
30. Defoe, pp. 243-244.
31. John Smith, *A Sea Grammar* (London, 1627; facsimile rpt. ed., New York: Da Capo Press, 1968), p. 58.
32. Smith, *Sea Grammar*, p. 58.
33. Defoe, pp. 95, 587.
34. Defoe, p. 156.
35. CO 137/13, PRO.
36. CO 137/14 ff. 9-16, PRO.
37. CO 137/14 ff. 16A-18, PRO.
38. Defoe, p 6.
39. Defoe, p. 164.
40. Defoe, pp. 159-165.
41. Defoe, pp. 153-159.
42. Defoe, pp. 84-85. Gunner's matches or fuses are lengths of loosely twisted hemp cord which have been dipped in a solution of saltpetre and lime-water. They burned at the rate of about twelve inches per hour.
43. Defoe, p. 85.
44. Robert E. Lee, *Blackbeard the Pirate: A Reappraisal of His Life and Times* (Winston-Salem, North Carolina: John F. Blair, 1974), p. 86; Defoe pp. 82-83.
45. Newton, p. 256.

6: Old Rusty Guts

1. Fleming MacLeisch and Martin L. Krieger, *The Privateers: A Raiding Voyage to the Great South Sea* (New York: Random House, 1962), p. 338. See also chapters 1, 6, and 8.
2. Brian Little, *Crusoe's Captain: Being the Life of Woodes Rogers, Seaman, Trader, Colonial Governor* (London: Odhams Press Ltd., 1960), pp. 178-180.

3. Defoe, pp. 40-41.
4. Rogers to Council of Trade, New Providence, 31 October 1718, *CSP*, 30:272.
5. Shirley Carter Hughson, "The Carolina Pirates and Colonial Commerce, 1670-1740," in *Johns Hopkins University Studies in Historical and Political Science*, v. 12, ed. Herbert Adams (Baltimore: Johns Hopkins Press, 1894), p. 112.
6. Lawes to Council of Trade and Plantations, Jamaica, 1 September 1718, *CSP*, 30:345-346.
7. *CSP*, 30:373.
8. Will of John Graves, Collector of H. M. Taxes, dated 1718, proved 1721, ORG, Book "C" in Bates, appendix D, pp. 18-20. This Thomas Walker, Chief Justice, is the same man who fled Nassau in 1716. He died in 1722, leaving his entire estate to his wife and sons Thomas, Charles and John. His will was dated 21 August 1722 and proved 4 September 1722, "Wills 1700-1750," pp. 15-16, NA. His tombstone can be seen in the garden of an estate called Glenwood.
9. CO 23/13, ff. 271, 287, PRO.
10. Clark Kinnaird, *George Washington: The Pictorial Biography* (New York: Hastings House, 1967), pp. 9, 14, 16; Lorenzo Sabine, *The American Loyalists or Biographical Sketches of Adherents to the British Crown in the War of the Revolution,* 2 vols. (Boston: Charles C. Little and James Brown, 1847), 1:409.
11. *CSP* 30:373, 374.
12. *CSP*, 30:374, 375, 377, 380. Samuel Buck submitted a report contrary to that of Mr. Taylor concerning the Spanish raid on Cat Island. Buck told the Council of Trade that the Spanish had "murdered all the men and carried off the women, children and Negroes." 2 January 1719, *CSP*, 31:2. Richard Taylor however was an eyewitness and Mr. Buck was not.
13. *CSP*, 30:378.
14. *CSP*, 30:376-378.
15. Christopher Gale to Col. Thomas Pitt, Jr., South Carolina. 4 November 1718, enclosed in Rogers 24 December 1718, *CSP*, 31:10.
16. Defoe, pp. 144-147, 620; *CSP*, 30:376.
17. CO 137/14, ff. 27-28A, PRO: Defoe, p. 144.
18. Rogers to Mr. Secretary Craggs, 24 December 1718, *CSP*, 30:437-438.
19. Two sloops, the *Mary of Providence* and the *Lancaster,* and the schooner *Batchelor's Adventure* embarked on this voyage. CO 23/18, f, 76, PRO. Defoe's account of the mutiny of Phineas Bunce, pp. 626-641, is followed by the "Tryal of the Pirates at Province," pp. 642-660. The original transcript of the trial of John Augur and others, held at Nassau, 9 and 10 December, 1718, was submitted by Woodes Rogers and appears in CO 23/18, ff. 75-82, PRO.
20. Defoe, p. 629. According to the testimony at the trial Phineas Bunce, head mutineer, had struck people with the flat of his sword, but the elaborate plan, song, etc., was not mentioned. Today "Bunce" is a monster-type of character appearing in the New Year's festival called the Bunce which is held at Green Turtle Cay, Abaco. It is possible that the character and festival were named after this pirate.
21. Defoe, pp. 627-641.
22. CO 23/28, ff. 76-82, PRO.
23. Defoe, pp. 640-641.
24. Rogers to Mr. Secretary Craggs, 30 January 1719, *CSP*, 31:11.
25. *CSP*, 30:438.
26. Rogers to Council of Trade and Plantations, Nassau, New Providence, 29 May 1719, *CSP*, 31:100-101.
27. "This chart is the latest version of 'Ye Charte of True Location of Sunken Vessels . . . .' listed in *A Descriptive List of of Treasure Maps and Charts in the Library of Congress*. It is larger, contains more locations and information, and is more accurate." Note on back of map in David O. True Collection, University of South Florida.
28. Account of the present state of Providence," Nassau 1719, enclosed in Craggs to Council of Trade and Plantations, Whitehall, 21 January 1720, *CSP*, 31:312-313.
29. *CSP*, 32:31.
30. Little, pp. 193-194.
31. Little, pp. 195-196.

7: The Return of Rusty Guts

1. "List of Christenings, Marriages and Burials," 13 November 1721-1726, CO 23/13, ff. 267-?, PRO. The photo-stated copy appears to be incomplete and for the most part the names are written in Latin. Also included in appendix A are some surnames which appear in the *Fulham Papers* in the Lambeth Palace Library, compiled by William Manross, Oxford, 1965, SPG. The microfilm of the *Fulham Papers* was provided by Irwin McSweeney. Since the "List, 1721-1726" does not always indicate the place of residence, names from two Harbour Island documents are included: On 7 February 1725/6, the Bahamas Council considered a petition from Harbour Islanders requesting assistance to build a fort, CO 23/31 ff. 419A-420, PRO; Harbour Islanders certified the baptisms of Joseph and Anne Force, 20 October, 1724, *Fulham Papers*, p. 47, SPG. By 1722, Thomas Cox had lived on Providence seven years and he believed there were two hundred families living there. Harbour Island and Eleuthera had sixty each, and Cat Island seven families. The minutes of the SPCK standing Committee, St. Dunstans Coffee House, 27 March 1722, notes provided by Irwin McSweeney, SPG. However, Governor Phenney reported twenty-nine families on Harbour Island, and twenty-seven or eight families on Eleuthera, 1 May 1722, *JBTP*, 4:356.

2. Little, p. 204.
3. Bates, appendix F, p. 21.
4. CO 23/31, ff. 419A-420, PRO; *CSP*, 33:402.
5. *Fulham Papers*, p. 47, SPG.
6. Lefroy, 2:94-95, 364.
7. Governour Phenny's reply to queries by the Board of Trade, 26 June, 1723, *CSP*, 33:402.
8. Catesby, 2:39.
9. *JBTP*, 4:356.
10. Catesby, 2:39.
11. Catesby, 2:38, 79.
12. Catesby, 2:38-39, 51, 38.
13. CO 23/14, f. 104; Chalmers, "Bahamas Account to 1728," NA.
14. Phenney to Lord Carteret, New Providence 6 July 1724, *CSP*, 34:131.
15. Samuel Buck to Council of Trade and Plantations, 3 February 1719/20, *CSP*, #154?, 31:?
16. Council Minutes, 16 May 1726, CO 23/13, f. 264, PRO.
17. Dow, pp. 30-32. Dow does not cite the date of this adventure which appeared in the *Boston Newsletter*. "However, the would-be pirates stated that the business was "promising" at that time which would place this incident sometime after April, 1704 (first issue of the *Boston Newsletter*), but prior to 1722, usually considered the end of the heyday of piracy in the West Indies.
18. Council Meeting, 9 January 1728, CO 23/14, f. 76.
19. Little, p. 205.
20. Little, p. 189; 27 August 1728, *JBTP*, 5:425; Little, p. 206-207; 20 October 1728, *JBTP*, 5:430.
21. Moseley, p. 25; Little, p. 216.
22. Little, pp. 210, 213; 4 and 5 November 1729, *VHA* (1729-1753), p. 22. The Bahamas had had an intermittent House of Assembly since the Proprietary patent in 1671. The year 1729 marks the beginning of a royal and continuous House of Assembly. Woodes Rogers' Commission, 29? November 1728, stated that "with the advice and consent of Council and Assembly [he] shall have full power to make and constitute laws, statutes and ordinances." The front oi this document states "The Assembly Established 1728, Constitution of the Bahamas, Chalmers Papers, Reel 1, NA.
23. Little, pp. 218, 211; C.F. Pascoe, *Two Hundred Years of the S.P.G.: An Historical Account of the Society for the Propagation of the Gospel in Foreign Parts 1701-1900* (London: S.P.G., 1901), p. 216.
24. Little, p. 211.
25. Pascoe, pp. 216-217.
26. *CSP*, 38:298.
27. Appendix B is actually two censuses. The first is called the "Particular Account of all the Inhabitants of the Bahama Islands," 15 September 1731, Governour Woodes Rogers, compiled by Eric Whittleton and the second a later, undated census appearing in ORG, Book "C," pp. 166-178. The approximate date of this census is 1740. Antonina Canzoneri and William Holowesko have placed it after 1731 and it is definitely not the Fitzwilliam census of 1734. Betty Bruce, archivist at the Monroe County Public Library in Key West, has done an in depth study of Book "C" and from internal evidence of both the book and the census has placed the census between 1737 and 1740. Craton's assumption that the Book "C" census was the first census for the Bahamas in 1671 is incorrect. Craton, p. 70. The names of the Eleutherans appearing on pages 175-177 of the Book "C" census were printed in A. T. Bethell, *The Early Settlers of the Bahama Islands with a Brief Account of the American Revolution* (Norfolk, England: Rounce & Wortley, n.d.), pp. 77-79. Some of the names have been copied incorrectly from Book "C."
28. Little, p. 220.

8: "Out of the Frying Pan"

1. Craton, pp. 132, 135, 133.
2. Pascoe, p. 217.
3. Oldmixon, pp. 28-30.
4. Southey, 2:260; P. Albury, p. 84.
5. Bruce, p. 36.
6. Southey, 2:260-261.
7. Southey, 2:251, 265-266.
8. John Crowley, *A. Description of the Windward Passage and the Gulf of Florida* (London: Corbett, 1739), p. 13; *JBTP*, 7:238.
9. Crowley, pp. 13, 14.
10. Southey, 2:264-265.
11. Pascoe, p. 217.
12. Bruce, p. 9.
13. Bruce, pp. 17-18.
14. Bruce, pp. 44-49. Bruce may have compiled these figures from a census taken by Governour Tinker around this time which could be the Book "C" census. There are just over two hundred names recorded for Eleuthera in Book "C."
15. Bruce, p. 19.

16. Bruce, pp. 26-27.
17. Bruce, pp. 29-30.
18. Bruce, pp. 35-37.
19. Bruce, pp. 41-42, 49.
20. Bruce, pp. 51-53.
21. Craton, p. 145.
22. Bellin, p. 142.
23. Bellin, p. 151.
24. Buzen, 3:920; 9 December 1768, CO 23/18, ff. 11-12.
25. Buzen, 3:920.

9: The American War of Independence

1. Governour William Shirley's Report to the S.P.G., New Providence, 15 January 1761, USPG, Reel 1, pp. 3-4.
2. *Nassau Quarterly* 16 (September 1901): 60; Pascoe, p. 219. On 2 February 1768 the House of Assembly voted to allot funds to build a church and support the missionary of Richard Moss at Harbour Island, *VHA* (1766-1770):35.
3. Richard Moss was sent to Harbour Island so that he could minister to the nearby Eleutherans. Why he had to travel to Nassau in order to get back to Eleuthera is a mystery. Richard Moss to S.P.G., Harbour Island, 11 April 1769, USPC, Reel 1; Pascoe, p. 219.
4. Pascoe, p. 218; Moss to S.P.G., 10 November 1772, USPG, Reel 1.
5. Moss to S.P.G., 27 May 1773, USPG, Reel 1.
6. Moss to S.P.G., 27 March 1775, USPG, Reel 1.
7. Moss Narrative, 30 June 1780, SPG. Transcript courtesy of Irwin McSweeney; conversation with Irwin McSweeney at Hipoint, Nassau, Bahamas, 6 July 1981.
8. New Providence Petition to S.P.G., n.d.; Harbour Island Petition, 24 June 1780, USPG, Reel 1.
9. *BG*, 30 October 1784.
10. Moss to S.P.G., Harbour Island, 28 April 1777, USPG, Reel 1.
11. Hunt to S.P.G., 13 May 1776, USPG, Reel 1.
12. Pascoe, pp. 219-220.
13. On 5 November 1774 Congress made Esek Hopkins Commander in Chief probably of this particular fleet, not of the entire Navy. Gardner W. Allen, *A Naval History of the American Revolution*, 2 vols. (New York: Russell and Russell Inc., 1962), 1:30. See also "The New Providence Expedition," vol. 1, chapter 4.
14. The following account of the Hopkins Raid by the anonymous author appears in Bates, pp. 268-275.
15. Allen, 1: 96, 95, 97. The fleet consisted of the *Alfred* (24 guns), *Columbus* (20 guns), *Dora* (14 guns), *Cabot* (14 guns), *Providence* (12 guns), *Hornet* (10 guns), *Wasp* (8 guns), and the *Fly* (a dispatch vessel). Stark, p. 71
16. An inventory "taken by Admiral Hopkins of the Fleet of the United Colonies of North America, 4 March 1776 at Fort Nassau" showed twenty-four cases of powder and a quantity of match rope among the many cannon, shells, shot, chain, fuses, etc. Lydia Austin Parrish, "Records of Some Southern Loyalists, Being a Collection of Manuscripts About Some Eighty Families, Most of Whom Immigrated to the Bahamas during and After the American Revolution," collected from 1940-1953, typed MS in Widener Library, Harvard University, copies in P. K. Yonge Library of Florida History, University of Florida, Gainesville, Florida and NA., p. 179.
17. Official records indicate that the American force numbered 270 men. Allen, 1:97.
18. Hunt to S.P.G., 3 May 1776, USPG, Reel 1.
19. Parrish, p. 179.
20. Allen 1: 100; Parrish, p. 179.
21. Bates, pp. 276-278.
22. Wilbur H. Siebert, *Loyalists in East Florida 1774-1785*, 2 vols. (Deland, Florida: Florida State Historical Society, 1929, rpt. ed., Boston: Gregg Press, 1972), 1:193-194.
23. Allen, 1:101-108. John Paul Jones's narrative of the *Glasgow* encounter from the *Alfred's* log appears in Allen, 1: 103-104.
24. *Boston Gazette*, 15 April 1776, in Parrish, p. 179; Allen, 1:96.
25. Parrish, p. 179; Craton, p. 156.
26. William Bartrum, *Travels Through North and South Carolina, Georgia, East and West Florida*, first published in 1791, ed. Mark Van Doren (New York: Dover Publications Inc., 1955), p. 343.
27. Parrish, p. 178.
28. Hunt to S.P.G., 3 & 13 May 1776, USPG, Reel 1.
29. Hunt to S.P.G. 21 June 1777, USPG, Reel 1.
30. Allen, 1:293; P. Albury, p. 99; "We set out 13 stripes flying at the fort." *Rhode Island Historical Magazine* (July 1886) in Allen, 1: 294. "The American Flag . . . first appeared over a foreign stronghold June [sic] 28, 1778 when Captain Rathbone [sic] of the American sloop of war *Providence* captured Fort Nassau, New Providence, Bahama Islands." *The Century Book of Facts*, ed. Henry W. Ruoff (Springfield, Mass.: King-Richardson and Co., n.d.), p. 639, note in "Malcolm Collection," Folder B65.7 (1734-1775), NL.
31. Bates, pp. 280-281; Parrish, p. 181.
32. Bates, p. 282; Parrish, p. 182.
33. The year 1790 given for Maxwell's arrival in Nassau in Parrish, p. 181 is a typographical error; Bates, pp. 283-284.

34. Clinton to Balfour, 13 July 1781, BHP, #3614.
35. Maxwell to Lord George Germain, 11 May 1782, CO 23/25, f. 54; Maxwell to General Leslie, 6 May 1782, CO 23/25, f. 58.
36. Cagigal to Maxwell, interpreted under oath by Nicholas Almgreen, CO 23/25, f. 56; Maxwell to Germain, 15 May 1782, CO 23/25, f. 48.
37. Articles of Capitulation signed by Don Juan Manuel de Cagigal and John Maxwell enclosed in Maxwell to Germain, 15 May 1782, CO 23/25, ff. 50-52.
38. There must have been a reason why Richard Moss was excluded here, but it is not known. Pascoe, p. 220; Return of Inhabitants by John Wilson from Recorder General's Book, BHP, #4705.
39. CRG, 38 (Pt. 2): 150-151; Parrish, pp. 180-181.
40. CRG, 38 (Pt. 2): 150-151; RRG, 1 (1769-1782): 328.
41. CRG. 38 (Pt. 2): 19-21; New Providence Inhabitants to Governour Maxwell, 10 May 1782, CO 23/26, f. 22A; 9 February 1784, AC, 100: 133; GC, 34: #68, #71, and 20 September 1783 #82; 24 November 1783 in GC, Bundle 38: #15; Parrish, pp. 124-125.
42. Parrish, p. 109; 28 February 1777, AC, Bundle 99, #62 and 25 January 1783, #64 and Statement to Governour of Conn. #69. The Simsbury mine was called the Black Hole of Connecticut. Catherine S. Crary, The Price of Loyalty: Tory Writings from the Revolutionary Era (New York: McGraw-Hill, 1973), pp. 216-217.
43. This Rostrum, mainly of old inhabitants, lists a Richard Curry as Justice of the Peace. CO 23/26, f. 25. Nicholas Almgreen died at age forty-eight at Great Exuma. BG, 31 July 1792; Parrish, pp. 60-62.
44. CO 23/26, f. 123.
45. This document includes a list of inhabitants. CO 23/26, ff. 22-23.

10. "The World Turned Upside Down"

1. Claude Halstead Van Tyne, The Loyalists in the American Revolution (New York: Peter Smith, 1929), pp. 263, 192; Leonard Labaree, "The Nature of American Loyalism," American Antiquarian Society 54 (1945): 47.
2. Esmond Wright, "The New York Loyalists: A Cross-section of Colonial Society," in The Loyalist Americans: A Focus on Greater New York, eds., Robert A. East and Jacob Judd (Tarrytown, New York: Sleepy Hollow Restorations, 1975), p. 91; L. Labaree, p. 27; 14 August and 4 September 1774, Peters' History of Connecticut (London, 1781), pp. 414-419 in Crary, p. 91.
3. Parrish, p. 11; L. Labaree, pp. 18, 31, 36, 49; Alexander Clarence Flick, Loyalism in New York During the American Revolution (New York: The Columbia University Press, 1901), p. 76.
4. Sabine, Biographical Sketches, 1:332; Mary Beth Norton, The British Americans: The Loyalist Exiles in England 1774-1789 (Boston: Little, Brown and Co., 1972), p. 70; See also North Callahan, Flight From the Republic: The Tories of the American Revolution (Westport, Connecticut: Greenwood Press Publisher, 1967), chapter 5.
5. South Carolina Gazette and Country Journal (Charleston: Charles Crouch), 13 September 1774, Charleston Country Library and Charleston Library Society, (hereinafter cited as Country Journal).
6. New York Loyalists to Sir Guy Carleton, 18 December 1782, BHP, #6438, ff. 1-4 enclosed in #6437, ff. 1-2. The following subscribers to this petition later touched on Abaco: John Clark, William Curtis, William Gerrard, Samuel Isaacs, William Russel, Captain George Shaw, and John Smith.
7. Kent Britt, "The Loyalists," National Geographic 147 (April 1975): 521.
8. Benjamin W. Labaree, America's Nation-Time 1607-1789 (Boston: Allyn and Bacon, Inc., 1972), p. 211; L. Labaree, p. 54; Flick, p. 61. England has no single written document known as a constitution.
9. Flick, p. 52; Raymond F. McNair, "The Spirit of America," Plain Truth 41 (July 1976): 9.
10. Van Tyne, p. 9.
11. Flick, p. 45.
12. Lorenzo Sabine, A Historical Essay on the Loyalists of the American Revolution, with a foreword by Benjamin Keen (Springfield, Massachusetts: The Walden Press, 1957), p. 47; B. Labaree, p. 212.
13. E. Wright, p. 93; Van Tyne, p. 23; Flick, p. 35; Raymond C. Werner, Introduction and Notes to the Diary of Grace Crowden Galloway Kept at Philadelphia From June 17th, 1778 to July 1st, 1779 (rpt. ed., New York: Arno Press, 1971), p. 34.
14. Comment by Eugene Fingerhut at the Conference on American Loyalists, 6-8 February 1975, St. Augustine, Florida, (hereinafter cited as CAL); Sabine, Biographical Sketches, 1: see preface; Parrish, p. 7.
15. William A. Benton, "Peter Van Schaack: The Conscience of a Loyalist," in East and Judd, pp. 48-50; Governor Martin to the Earl of Dartmouth, 28 August 1775, CRNC, 15:231; CRG, 19, pt. 2 (1774-1805): 152-155.
16. For Dunmore see Egerton Ryerson, The Loyalists of America and Their Times from 1620-1816, 2 vols. (First published 1880, rpt. New York: Haskell House Publishers Ltd., 1970); Van Tyne, p. 99; Jeffrey J. Crow, The Black Experience in Revolutionary North Carolina (Raleigh, North Carolina: Department of Cultural Resources, Division of Archives and History, 1977), pp. 59-61; Special "1776" Edition, Time 105 (4 July 1976): 33.
17. Clinton Proclamation, 30 June 1779, BHP, #2094; Crary, n. 6, p. 429.
18. J. Leitch Wright, "Southern Black Loyalists," CAL; Crary, pp. 427-428.
19. Special Bicentennial Issue, Time 107 (26 September 1789): 33-34; Carole Watterson Troxler, The Loyalist Experience in North Carolina (Zeblon, North Carolina: Theo. Davis Sons Inc., 1976), p. 54.
20. Elizabeth Anthony Dexter, Colonial Women of Affairs: A Study of Women in Business and Professions in America Before 1776 (Boston-New York: Houghton Mifflin Co., 1924), see chapter 3, and p. 188.

21. Flick, pp. 146-147; Extract from a letter from a gentleman at Charleston, 22 June 1783, James Rivington's *The Royal Gazette* (New York) 9 July 1783, p. 3., New-York Historical Society, (hereinafter cited as Rivington's *Gazette*). On 22 November 1783 the name of this newspaper became *The New York Gazette and Universal Advertiser.*
22. Flick, pp. 113-114; Rivington's *Gazette*, 19 April 1783.
23. Grace Galloway, Werner, p. 178; Linda Grant DePauw, *Founding Mothers: Women of America in the Revolutionary Era* (Boston: Houghton Mifflin Co., 1975), see chapter 6; Flora McDonald see Crary, pp. 50-51.
24. For Jane McCrea, see Sabine, *Biographical Sketches*, 2:451; Mary Beth Norton, "Loyalist Women: A Case Study in the Social Impact of the Revolution," CAL.
25. Sabine, *Historical Essay*, pp. 13-14.
26. AO 13/34, f. 495.
27. *RG*, 30 December 1837.
28. John Bartlam died "A British Subject" in 1781, reported by Col. John Marshall on a "List of Returns made by Regimental Commanders" in the Confiscated Estates File, SCA; Bartlam's death is also recorded on a "List of Loyalists" compiled by Leonardo Andrea, Microfilm Roll 55, Caroliniana Library, Columbia, South Carolina; Estate Appraisal dated 3 October 1781 and taken by Mary Bartlam, Administratrix, Charleston County Courthouse Inventories, Vol. 100 (1776-1784), p. 375; "Robert Daniel vs. John Bartlam," Judgement Roll, Box 68, #59, 1768, SCA; *South Carolina Gazette* (Charles-Town; Peter Timothy), 11 October 1770, p. 2, Charleston Library Society, Charleston, S.C. (hereinafter cited as *SC Gazette*).
29. St. Augustine, 27 August 1783, AO 13/95, Part 1, ff. 2A-5; Mary Bartlam to Col. John Hamilton, Charleston, 25 December 1788, AO 13/95, Part 1, f. 7.
30. "St. Johns, Harbour Island, Marriage Register, 14 February 1802-15 December 1819," p. 279, NA.
31. Martin to Dartmouth, 28 August 1775, *CRNC*, 10:231.
32. Van Tyne, pp. 269-270; *Black List: A List of those Tories who took Part with Great Britain in the Revolutionary War and were Attainted of High Treason, Commonly called the Black List!* (Phil., 1802), N.Y. Historical Society. A Captain Ross Curry was stationed in Philadelphia in 1777, p. 10.
33. Willard S. Randall, "William Franklin: The Making of a Conservative," in East and Judd, pp. 56, 70.
34. *Country Journal*, 30 May 1775; Sabine, *Historical Essay*, p. 76.
35. William Gilmore Simms, *Mellichampe: A Legend of the Santee* (New York: W. J. Widdleton, 1864), p. 2; for state laws, see Van Tyne, appendices B and C, pp. 318-341.
36. Crary, p. 4; in New York, see E. Wright, pp. 78-79.
37. For Phineas Bond, see E. Wright, pp. 78-79; for Isaac Low, see Crary, pp. 20-21; E. Wright, p. 89.
38. *CRNC*, 10: 899-900; for Rivington's *Gazette* see Van Tyne, p. 289.
39. Flick, p. 89; Hugh Gaine, *New York Gazette and The Weekly Mercury*, 2 December 1776, p. 2, N.Y. Historical Society, (hereinafter cited as Gaine's *Gazette*). Loyalists whose names appeared in this document and later received grants of land on Abaco are: John Hall, John Martin, John McIntosh, John, Joseph, and George Smith, Thomas North (Nassau), and Jonah [John] Valentine.
40. "Declaration of Dependence," Y1776, MS. Room, N.Y. Historical Society; "Book of Negroes," BHP, #10427 (100).
41. *Documents Relative to the Colonial History of New York*, 8:784-786, Reading Room, NYPL.
42. Rivington's *Gazette*, 8 March 1783, p. 2.
43. For Forbes' conspiracy see Flick, pp. 103-104; for Hickey plot see *Time* (1776), p. 31; Sabine, *Biographical Sketches*, 1:430.
44. *Minutes of the Trial and Examination of Certain Persons in the Province of New York Charged with being Engaged in a Conspiracy Against the Authority of the Congress and The Liberties of America* (London, n.d. [1776]), NYPL, pp. 1-19. hereinafter cited as *Minutes* 1776).
45. *Minutes of a Conspiracy against the Liberties of America* (Philadelphia: John Campbell, 1865, rpt. ed., New York: Arno Press, 1969), pp. 74-76, 78-79.
46. *Minutes* 1776, pp. 20-45; *BG*, 9 April 1785.
47. Van Tyne, p. 88 and Sabine, *Historical Essay*, p. 34.
48. "Objectors" 10 August 1774, *RRG*, 1 (1769-1782): 29, 18-21. The same document appears in the *Royal Georgia Gazette*, 7 September 1774, Georgia Historical Society, Savannah; "Oath of Allegiance" August 1775, *CRG*, 38 (Part 2): 19-21; "Attainder" 1778, *RRG*, 1:326-330; "Confiscation and Banishment Act" 1 March 1778/1782, *RRG*, 1:373-397. Names of Loyalists who later appear in the Bahamas (*indicates those who touched Abaco): Isaac Baillou, George Barry, *Col. Thomas Brown, *Donald Cameron, Peter Dean, Peter Edwards, *Thomas Forbes, Roger Kelsall, *John Martin of Jeckyl Island, *John McGillivray, William Moss, John Mullryne, Simon Munro, William Panton, James E. Powell (Lt. Gov. 1784-1786), *Josiah Tattnall, *Augustus Underwood, Charles, John and Martin *Weatherford, Samuel Williams, *Alexander Wylly, *William Wylly, and Henry Yonge; the "Particular Case of the Georgia Inhabitants," February, 1783, states that 286 Georgia Loyalists were banished but does not give any of their names. This document appears in the back of Copy 2 of the *Case and Claims of the American Loyalists Impartially Stated and Considered* (London: G. Wilkie, 1783), NYPL.
49. *Royal Georgia Gazette*, 3 May 1781; Simpson to Henry Clinton, Charleston, S.C., 1 July 1780, BHP #2877 (1).
50. Gov. Wright to Cornwallis, Savannah, 23 April 1781, *CRG*, 38 (Part 2):506.
51. Dr. Cashin believes this man was the Thomas Brown of "Brownsborough" which was a place due west of New Richmond. Edward J. Cashin, *Story of Augusta* (Augusta: Richmond County Board of Education, 1980), p. 27.
52. Georgia Claims, AO 13, Bundle 34.

53. Thomas Brown was tarred and feathered by Committee order in Augusta, 2 August 1775. See Parrish, p. 184; for King's Rangers see Murtie June Clark, *Loyalists in the Southern Campaign of the Revolutionary War*, 3 vols. (Baltimore; Genealogical Publishing Co. Inc., 1981), 1:49.
54. AO 13, Bundles 34 and 38; Germain, Whitehall, 9 July 1779, *CRG*, 38 (Part 2): 167.
55. Sabine, *Biographical Sketches*, 1: 262. What was thought to be the Mackey House is actually the Harris House. The Mackey House is believed to be located "closer to the Savannah River on a site that can be seen from the front of the Harris House." The Sibley Mill, built in 1880, marks the site. Correspondence from Barbara Harley Johnson, Augusta Heritage Trust, Augusta, 21 August 1981.
56. Brown ordered to St. Augustine, Leslie to Carleton 27 June 1782, BHP, #4916 (2), item 6; Abaco grants CO 23/30; Shipwrecked AO 13, Bundle 34.
57. Caicos grants, Grant Books "M" and "K," LS; marriage to Hetty Farr, "CC Mar. Reg. (1789-1805)," p. 1; wife's death, *RG*, 25 June 1807, p. 3; daughter's marriage, *RG*, 21 November 1818, p. 3; Brown's death, *RG*, 1 October 1825, p. 3.
58. Sabine, *Historical Essay*, p. 34.
59. Wallace Brown, *The King's Friends: The Composition and Motives of American Loyalist Claims* (Providence, Rhode Island: Brown University Press, 1965), p. 225.
60. For Charleston Harbour see Mary K. Armbrister, "Henrietta My Daughter" 1836, Kelsall family genealogy assembled from letters. Mrs. Armbrister died in 1969 and the project was completed by her daughter Mary K. Young, MS in NL Vault B. 57.2 MS 1836; 7,935 of the 12,595 barrels of rice exported from Charleston in 1769 went to Portugal, see *SC Gazette*, 21 December 1769; Funeral customs *Country Journal*, 22 November 1775.
61. *SC Gazette*, 24 August 1769.
62. Crary, p. 281; Tonyn to Howe, St. Augustine, 28 April 1778, BHP, #1133.
63. Crary, pp. 281, 285.
64. Professor Lambert stated that in a civil war any crime against the state could put a person on a list of disaffected persons such as the Ninety-Six district Petty Jury List of 1776. Robert S. Lambert "Loyalism in Back-country South Carolina," CAL: Orangeburg Association, Rivington's *Gazette*, 22 July 1780, p. 3; Siege of Ninety-Six, see Col. Banastre Tarleton, *A History of the Campaigns of 1780 and 1781 in the Southern Provinces of North America* (London: Printed for T. Cadell, 1787).
65. Sabine, *Historical Essay*, p. 26; *SC Gazette*, 3 August 1767.
66. See William S. Powell, *The War of the Regulation and the Battle of Alamance, May 16, 1771* (Raleigh, North Carolina: State Department of Archives and History, 1965; Presentment of the Grand Jury for the District of Newbern, 15 March 1771, James Lowe is on a list of Crown Prosecutions, 11 March 1771, #6, The King vs. James Low and #27 James Lowe, *CRNC*, 8:529-531.
67. Inhabitants of Santee, *Country Journal*, 5 October 1767, #33, pp. 257-258; Gov. Bull, *SC Gazette*, 19 October and 9 November 1767; Mayson seized, *SC Gazette*, 19 October 1767.
68. For Micklejohn see L. Labaree, p. 23; for Woodmason see Richard Maxwell Brown, *The South Carolina Regulators* (Cambridge, Massachusetts: Belknap Press of Harvard University, 1963), pp. 41-42; see also Richard J. Hooker, ed., *The Carolina Backcountry on the Eve of the Revolution: The Journal and other Writings of Charles Woodmason, Anglican Itinerant* (Chapel Hill: The University of North Carolina Press, 1953).
69. William Curry Harllee, *Kinfolks: A Genealogical and Biographical Record, Vol. 2: Fulmore, Curry and Kemp Sections* (New Orleans: Searcy & Pfaff Ltd., 1935), p. 1504, 1610; Benjamin Curry's will is dated 4 October 1825, ORG Book "C-4," pp. 64-65, NA.
70. Crary, p. 4 and L. Labaree, p. 37; Tryon to Dartmouth 7 August 1775, F. 1-38650A, British Museum.
71. John Shy, "The Loyalist Problem in the Lower Hudson Valley: The British Perspective," in East and Judd, pp. 5-6.
72. Van Tyne, pp. 156, 154 and Rivington's *Gazette*, 20 October 1779 in Van Tyne, p. 156.
73. *The Caledonian Mercury* (Edinburgh, Scotland), 25 December 1779, issue provided by Irwin McSweeney.
74. British Library, *The American War of Independence 1775-1783* Exhibit by the Map and MS Division of the British Library 4 July-11 November 1975 (London: British Publications Ltd., 1975), p. 143.

11: The Losers

1. Sir James Wright's Address to Upper and Commons House of Assembly, Province of Georgia, Savannah, 16 June 1782, *CRG*, 15:662; Statement of James Moncrief, Chief Engineer, concerning the Governour's plantation, 2 February 1780, BHP, #2553 (1); Georgia Loyalists John Mullryne, Nathaniel Hall, and Josiah Tattnall "examined the Barn, Machine for boiling Rice, overseer's House, Negro houses, several store Buildings and Conveniences." They said the materials had been used to build bastions, embankments, and redoubts and determined that they could not be rebuilt for less than £450, BHP, 15 April 1780, #2553 (2). According to Sabine, the post James Wright had commanded during the siege had not been as fine as the one provided by his plantation. His redoubt was built of "green wood, strengthened by fillings of sand and mounted with heavy cannon," Sabine, *Biographical Sketches*, 2:459.
2. *CRG*, 15:662-665.
3. Siebert, 1:106; for Wylly family history see Parrish, pp. 477-478.
4. Memorial of William and Alexander C. Wylly to Lord George Germain, 4 February 1777, AO 13, Bundle 37; "Memorial of Susannah Wyly," 11 August 1784, Hugh Edward Egerton, *The Royal Commission on the Losses and Services of American Loyalists 1783-1785; Being the Notes of Mr. Daniel Parker Coke, M.P. One of the Commissioners During that Period* (Oxford, 1915), p. 171.

5. Leslie to Carleton, Secret, 11 June 1782, BHP, #4772.
6. Memorial of East Florida Inhabitants to Lt. General Leslie, Charles Town, 14 June 1782, BHP, #4793 (1)-(3). Some of the signers who later touched on Abaco were William Alexander. Farquhar Bethune, and Thomas Forbes.
7. Lt. Gen. Leslie to Guy Carleton, Secret, Charlestown, 27 June 1782, BHP, #4915 and #4916. General Leslie need not have marked his correspondence "Secret," his handwriting is nearly impossible to decipher.
8. *Royal Gazette* (Charleston: Robert Wells), 7 August 1782, p. 2.
9. Return of emigrating loyal inhabitants of Charleston as of 13 August 1782, signed by Charles Ogilvie and Gideon Dupont Jr., New York, 29 August 1782, BHP, #10316 (1).
10. Memorial of Loyal Inhabitants of Charlestown to Sir Guy Carleton submitted by Ogilvie and Dupont, New York, 10 September 1782, BHP, #5578 (1)-(6).
11. Return of Refugees from Georgia and South Carolina in New York, 13 November 1782, BHP, #6159; Return of Refugees from Georgia and South Carolina in East Florida, 25 December 1782, BHP, #6475. A report of the New York board to consider claims of refugees submitted 8 November 1782 showed only six refugee applications from North and South Carolina, Georgia and Florida, amounting to £20 immediate relief and £440 annual support, £200 of which went to one man, BHP #10330 (15A). A "List of Sundry distressed Loyalists who have taken Refuge within the British Lines at New York," and the sums recommended for their support from 1 January to 31 March 1783 shows only six more names, BHP, #7258 (8).
12. Rivington's *Gazette*, 8 January 1783, p. 2.
13. Thomas Jones, *History of New York During the Revolutionary War*, 2 vols. (New York; New York Historical Society, 1879; rpt. ed., New York: Arno Press, 1968), 2:235-236; same account in Crary, p. 358-359.
14. For Preliminaries to a General Peace see Rivington's *Gazette*, 26 March 1783, p. 3; for Laurens in Tower see British Library, p. 145; *Royal Gazette* (Charleston), 7 September 1782, p. 3.
15. Rivington's *Gazette*, 15 January 1783, p. 1.
16. Parrish, p. 24.
17. Johann David Schoepf, *Travels in the Confederation 1783-1784*, trans. and ed., Alfred J. Morrison (Philadelphia: William J. Campbell, 1911), pp. 226, 228, 229, 231, 240; The religious freedom clause was revoked by Spain in the Definitive Treaty, but His Catholic Majesty compensated by extending the withdrawal period, Lockey, intro., p. 5.
18. Food shortage, see Return of Provisions at St. Augustine 6 January 1783, BHP, #10355 (3) and Siebert, 1:132 and Schoepf, p. 244.
19. Article V, Sabine, *Historical Essay*, p. 99; Wylly property sold, "Sales of Confiscated Estates," *CRG*, 1 (1769-1782): 430, 420; Virginia Loyalist Alexander McKee had a grant on Abaco. For Kentucky land, see Isaac Samuel Harrell, *Loyalism in Virginia: Chapters in the Economic History of the Revolution* (New York: AMS Press Inc., 1926), p. 99; for New York property, see Van Tyne, p. 280.
20. Rivington's *Gazette*, 1 October 1783.
21. Egerton, intro., p. 36.
22. "Half Pay," *Royal Georgia Gazette*, 6 November 1783; West Florida, see Schoepf, p. 240; Mr. Pitt informed Loyalists that West Florida was the fortune of war whereas East Florida was the price of peace, *BG*, 2 September 1786, p. 3. In the Bahamas, John Wells printed "The Summary Case of the American Loyalists" in 1785, *BG*, 6 August 1785, p. 1. Loyalists who could not go to England or Nova Scotia to submit their claims in person could sign memorials to that effect left at the Printing Office on the Bay (Nassau), *BG*, 17 December 1785. Those memorials were sent by the sloop of war *Weazle* [sic] on 1 May 1786. Some of these claimants who may have been Abaco residents at the time were: John Cornish, Philip Dumaresq, John and Donald Ferguson, John Fox, William Gerard, Christopher Neeley, Richard Pearis, and Thomas Waters, "American Loyalists' Transcripts," transcribed from AO records in the PRO, 1783-1790 (New York Public Library, 1900), NYPL, v. 33 and Parrish, p. 31.
23. Egerton, intro., pp. 43, 44.
24. Final Report, Egerton, p. 40; *BG*, 17 October, 1789; New York claimants the largest, Van Tyne, p. 303; John Penn, American Claims, v. 109, p. 246, PRO; Loyalist betrayal, Egerton, intro., p. 31.
25. Sabine, *Historical Essay*, p. 99.
26. Carleton to Boudinot, New York, 17 August 1783, *State Records of North Carolina*, p. 868; St. Augustine invaded, Siebert, 1: 141; S.C. backcountry plundered, Rivington's *Gazette*, 5 November 1783.
27. Loyalist hint, *Royal Georgia Gazette*, 22 September 1783; panic, Egerton, intro., p. 30; American colours seized, *New York Post*, 7 November 1783, facsimile NYPL. Loyalists seized American colours from vessels in Nassau Harbour soon after their arrival in the Bahamas.
28. Rivington's *Gazette*, 8 December 1782; Maxwell murdered, McArthur to Carleton, 5 July 1783, BHP, #8332.
29. Parrish p. 13.
30. Thousands remain, Van Tyne, p. 298; exiles, *Case and Claims*, p. 10.
31. *Royal Georgia Gazette*, 22 September 1783.
32. Violence in N.Y., *State Rec. N.C.*, p. 868; Loyalists emigrate, Crary, p. 387; Flick, p. 171; Van Tyne, p. 294; Bode sketch, *RG*, 22 November 1823, p. 3. Tony Armbrister of Fernandez Bay Village, Cat Island, is the grandson of W. E. Armbrister.
33. Hawkins and Williamson to Gov. Martin, *State Rec. NC*, p. 865; Thelma Peters, "The American Loyalists and the Plantation Period in the Bahama Islands" (Ph.D. dissertation, University of Florida, 1960), p. 22.
34. *Royal Georgia Gazette*, 21 May 1783.
35. *Edinburgh Advertiser* (Scotland), 29 July 1783; Rivington's *Gazette*, 14 May 1783.
36. Roderick MacKenzie, *Tarleton's Strictures* (London: 1787) in Crary, p. 355.

37. Parrish, pp. 220, 221 and Crary, p. 354.
38. Sabine, *Biographical Sketches*, 1: 377; Deveaux's letter to a gentleman of St. Augustine, New Providence, 25 April 1783, *South Carolina Weekly Gazette* (Charlestown: Nathan Childs), 24 May 1783.
39. Siebert, 1: 147 and Crary, p. 354.
40. McArthur to Carleton, 20 May 1783, BHP, #7731.
41. Wheeler Deposition sworn 21 May 1783 at New Providence, CO 23/26, ff. 42-43.
42. The following account of Deveaux's seige of Nassau appears, with variations, in Siebert 1:146; MacKenzie and Deveaux's letter to Carleton 6 June 1783 in Crary, pp. 354-356; MacKenzie in Parrish, pp. 223-225; Deveaux in Sabine, *Biographical Sketches*, 1: 377-378; Wheeler Deposition CO 23/26, ff. 42-43; Deveaux's letter to St. Augustine in *SC Weekly Gazette*, 24 May 1783. Fanning missed Deveaux and returned to Halifax Inlet, Siebert, 1: 146.
43. The *Whitby Warrior* was probably named for Col. Thomas Brown, Parrish, p. 188; MacKenzie in Parrish, p. 223.
44. CO 23/15, f. 163A.
45. Moseley, p. 72.
46. Rumer Memorial, 21 February 1786, CO 23/26, f. 223; Rumer Memorial, Harbour Island Subscribers, 25 April 1786, CO 23/26, f. 224. Names: John (1) (2), Joseph (1) (2) and Jr., William *Albury*; Ephraim, John, Ruben, Thomas *Clear*; John (1) (2), Sr. and Jr., Joseph, Richard (1), (2), Thompson *Currey* [Curry]; Samuel *Higgs*; Nathaniel, Thomas *Johnson*; John *Kimblern*; Gideon *Lowe*; George *Parks*; Joseph, Thomas *Pierce*; John *Pinder*; Benjamin (1), (2), Jr., George, James (1), (2), John (1), (2), (3), (4), (5), Joseph (1), (2), Richard Sr., Jr., William *Roberts*; Benjamin Sr., Daniel, Joseph, Nathaniel, Thomas, William *Russell*; Benjamin *Sands*; Benjamin, & Jr., John (1), (2), Joseph Jr., Nathaniel Sr., Jr., Thomas, William Jr., *Sanders* [Saunders]; Admun Sr., Jr., Richard (1), (2), William *Sawyer*; Thomas, William *Sweeting*; John, Joseph Sr., Jr., *Tedder*; Nathaniel, Thomas *Thompson*.
47. Wheeler CO 23/26 f. 42; ORG, Book "M," p. 494; MacKenzie in Parrish. p. 224; *SC Weekly Gazette*, 24 May 1783. Major Archibald Taylor of the Royal Militia of North Carolina was allowed by the Commission £380 on his claim of £1,078, Am. Claims v. 109, p. 288 #721 NC. The *Bahamas Gazette* announced his marriage to Miss Eliza McNeil, daughter of William McNeil, on 24 October, 1789, in North Carolina, see Peters. His brother Duncan married Margaret O'Neil at Long Island in 1791, *BG*, 4 March 1791, p. 3. Major Taylor founded Clarence Town, Long Island, and his brother, Duncan Town, Ragged Island, Peters' interview with L. E. W. Forsythe, a direct descendant of Major Archibald Taylor, Nassau, 1958. Both brothers built and operated the successful Duncan's salt pond on Ragged Island, Peters, p. 160. Archibald died in New Providence in 1816, see Sabine. Duncan Taylor of Ragged Island died 7 April 1822, *RG*, 10 April 1822, p. 3.
48. *SC Weekly Gazette*, 24 May 1783.
49. MacKenzie in Parrish, p. 225.
50. Deveaux, 6 June 1783 in Crary, p. 356.
51. Hostages, see Parrish, p. 225; Deveaux's letter 6 June in Crary, p. 356.
52. "SC Council Journal," v. 33 (1767), pp. 144, 213, SCA.
53. Parrish, pp. 213-235.
54. *BG*, 15 January 1815, p. 3.
55. Rivington's *Gazette*, 8 November 1783, p. 1.
56. Claraco to Sterling, 12 August 1783 CO 23/26, f. 73; Letters between Maxwell and Claraco CO 23/25, f. 125.
57. Unzaga to Deveaux, Havana, 26 August 1783, enclosed in Hunt to Carleton, CO 23/25, f. 80.
58. Hunt to Carleton, New Providence, 27 October 1783, CO 23/25, ff. 86-87.

12: Homeward Bound

1. Claraco to Unzaga, New Providence, 19 May 1783 in Lockey, p. 112.
2. CO 23/26, f. 223.
3. McArthur to Carleton, St. Augustine, 20 May 1783, BHP, #7730.
4. McArthur to Carleton, St. Augustine, 16 June 1783, BHP, #8049; Tonyn to Townshend, St. Augustine, 15 May 1783 in Lockey, p. 97.
5. Carleton's orders to Wilson, New York, 14 July 1783, BHP, #8431.
6. Johnson to Lt. Gov. Graham, New Providence, July 1783, CO 23/26, ff. 26-28. Dr. Lewis Johnson, member of His Majesty's Council in Georgia, died at age sixty-nine in Edinburg, *BG* 26 January 1798, p. 3.
7. For Wilson see McArthur to Carleton, St. Augustine, 19 July 1783, BHP, #8478 and 12 September 1783, BHP #9105; committee, see Siebert, 1:183.
8. Carleton to the President of Congress, New York, 17 August 1783, *Royal Georgia Gazette*, 9 October 1783. Also from *Farmer's Journal* (Philadelphia), 10 September 1783 in Rivington's *Gazette*, 13 September 1783, p. 3 and Gaines's *Gazette*, 15 September 1783, p. 2.
9. Memorial to Carleton, New York, 25 June 1783, BHP, #8227 (1); sketch of Little Harbour, BHP, #8227 (3); Description of Abaco, BHP, #8227 (2).
10. Blake Memorial, 28 June 1783, BHP, #8237.
11. J. Barton Starr, *Tories, Dons, and Rebels: The American Revolution in British West Florida* (Gainesville: University Presses of Florida, 1976), pp. 229-230, 235.
12. Rivington's *Gazette*, 28 June 1783, p. 3. Tinian is one of the Mariana Islands in the western Pacific one hundred miles from Guam and noted for its sugar plantations. In August 1945 the runway of Tinian Island launched the plane that dropped the atomic bombs on the Japanese cities of Hiroshima and Nagasaki.

13. *Loyalist*, Rivington's *Gazette*, 2 July 1783, p. 3; Valleau's forty acres on Man-O-War Cay, Abaco was granted 23 December 1789, #478, CO 23/30, f. 223; *Nancy*, Rivington's *Gazette*, 24 July 1783; *Rover*, Rivington's *Gazette*, 13 August 1783 and Gaines's *Gazette*, 18 August 1783.

14. Rivington's *Gazette*, 5 July 1783, p. 3.

15. Watson to MacKenzie, Commissary General's Office, New York, 10 August 1783, BHP, #8686. On 16 August Watson directed the paymaster to pay "Mr. Richard Harris, a clerk of six years standing in this office, now in ill health and going to take refuge in Abaco, Six months' advance pay at 10s. per diem to 25th February next. Also to Philip Dumaresq six months advance pay as a commissary going to victual the loyal refugees there from 10 August to 9 February next at 7s. 6p. per diem." Brooks Watson to Major MacKenzie, 16 August 1783, BHP, #8739.

16. Article 7, "Orders," Headquarters New York, 15 April 1783 in Rivington's *Gazette*, 19 April 1783, p. 3 and "Book of Negroes," BHP, #10427 (1); "Boston King," Crow, p. 80.

17. Extract of a letter from an American at New York in Crary, p. 362; Appendix D, Part 2 of the "Book of Negroes" lists departures inspected from 31 July-30 November 1783, Ship *Nautilus* and the transport *William*, BHP, #10427 (98)-(101). Total number of Blacks embarking was 97. The only other vessel bound for the Bahamas was the brig *Elizabeth*, 341 tons bound for Cat Island on 3 November 1783 with 26 Blacks, their "present owners," Elias and Eve, Oswald Eve, Michael Clark, Cornel Gray of the British Legion and Joseph Shoemaker, (129)-(132).

18. Reverend George Gellard Huxtable, *Reminiscences of Missionary Life in the West Indies* (Kemptville, Ontario: Huxtable and Seily, 1902), p. 4. Huxtable arrived in Nassau in 1855.

19. Samuel Kelly, *An Eighteenth Century Seaman: Whose Days have been Few and Evil*, intro., Grosbie Garsten (New York: Frederick A. Stokes Co., 1925), p. 115. Since Joseph Paul's name does not appear on the 1788 Plan of Nassau, he may not have arrived there until 1790. Paul's church was constructed sometime between 1790-1793. Joseph Paul was succeeded at the Associates School first by his son Joseph Paul, Jr., then by his son William. See Colbert V. Williams, "The Methodist Contribution to Education in the Bahamas" (Ph.D. dissertation, University of Wales, 1977), pp. 184-185, NA. Williams writes that Joseph Paul, "who had gone over to the Anglicans died in 1802," p. 62. His will was dated 17 March 1802 and proved 19 April 1802 and he left to his wife and children land next to the meeting house and next to Anthony Wallace's lot, Wills, 1806, NA and C. Williams, p. 63. His younger son William took the leadership of the chapel in 1810 and Christ Church records show that "William Paul, free Black Man, Preacher of the sect of Episcopalian Blacks is buried in a vault of St. Paul's Church." He died 25 November 1813, "CC Book B," section marked "Blacks and Coloured" 1811-1828, p. 6.

20. Willis document of freedom and purchase of Hester from Cameron, ORG, Book "B," p. 338; also Peters, p. 58.

21. Rivington's *Gazette*, 13 September 1783, p. 2.

22. Blanchard to Powell, New Providence, 6 April 1785, ALM. Historian Steve Dodge pinpointed the location of Carleton Town by fixing the plots of John Jordan's forty and sixty acres on Pelican Bay and John Allender's eighty acre grant on Carleton Creek. He has placed Carleton Town at just northward of the present-day Treasure Cay Development. The point of land just south of Black Point, Dodge named Carleton Point. Steve Dodge, *The First Loyalist Settlements in Abaco: Carleton and Marsh's Harbour* (Hopetown, Abaco, Bahamas: Wyannie Malone Historical Museum, 1979).

23. This document written by the person, possibly a surveyor, who accompanied Lt. Wilson and General McArthur to Abaco in February, 1784, was discovered by William Holowesko in the British Library, #4/6405 or 4/6407?, ff 122-123A. The transcript was provided by E. Dawson Roberts and dated 4 November, 1976, p. 3. (hereinafter cited as Abaco 1784).

24. Blanchard 6 April 1785.

25. BHP, #9266.

26. There are *no names annexed* to this document, BHP, #10185.

27. BHP, #9407.

28. BHP, #9410. These supplies probably came from Barbados.

29. Hake Certificate, BHP, #9519. The actual memorial is not among these papers and as to be expected there is no list of the 509 names.

30. Stephens return, n.d. [1783], BHP, #9728 (5).

31. Moseley's source is the Report on the American MSS in the Royal Institute of Great Britain, v. 4. All page numbers listed in her note on page 59, except #490, correspond with the calendar of the British Headquarters Papers in New York. There is no document in or about 23 November 1783 there. Mary Moseley was a careful researcher and historian. It is possible that this document was not copied to be sent to New York and it is, as she said, in Great Britain. See also Siebert, 1: 150. Another historian made a detailed study of the British Headquarters Papers and did not locate this document either. Peter Culmer Kelly, "The Bahama Islands and the American Revolution" (Master's thesis, New York University, April 1959), pp. 54-55, copy in NA.

32. New York, 30 October, BHP, #9518 (1). Captain Ridley could have been living on Abaco at this time. This may be the same Ridley who was elected member of the House of Assembly for Abaco in 1785.

33. Brig *Hope* and John Davis, Rivington's *Gazette*, 25 October 1783, p. 3; Smith houses, Rivington's *Gazette*, 29 October, 1783, p. 2; *Felicity*, Rivington's *Gazette*, 1 November 1783, p. 2.

34. Rivington's *Gazette*, 5 November 1783, pp. 2, 4; *New York Post*, 7 November 1783, p. 3.

35. Rivington's *Gazette*, 12 November 1783, p. 2.

36. Shaw, Kennedy and Victor, New York, 30 October 1783, BHP, #9519 (1), see also Rivington's *Gazette*, 1 November 1783.

37. Rivington's *Gazette*, 15 November 1783.

38. Rivington's *Gazette*, 12 November 1783; Gaines's *Gazette*, 10 November 1783, p. 3.

39. Rivington's *Gazette*, 12 November 1783, p. 3.
40. Address, New York, 2 May 1782, BHP, #9982 (13), Memorial to Carleton, 8 June 1782, BHP, #9979 (1).
41. Egerton, pp. 159, 161; "American Loyalists Transcripts," Temporary Support, Old Claims, v. 2 (October-December 1782), p. 134.
42. Rivington's *Gazette*, 26 November 1783, p. 3.

13: "Double, Double, Toil and Trouble"

1. *East Florida Gazette* (St. Augustine: John Wells), 17 May 1783, p. 1. The *East Florida Gazette* was a weekly newspaper published from February, 1783, to April, 1784. The three extant issues are in the St. Augustine Historical Society Library.
2. Keep Florida, Address of Inhabitants of St. Augustine to Gov. Tonyn, 6 June 1783 in Lockey, p. 113; transients and troops, Extract of a letter to Captain Bisset in London, from a correspondent in St. Augustine, 20 May 1783 in Lockey, p. 173.
3. Extract from the *Gazette*, 26 July 1783 in Lockey, p. 140; Cowkeeper, 20 May 1783 in Lockey, p. 173; Claraco to Unzaga, New Providence, 19 May 1783 in Lockey, p. 112; Brown asked to stay, Tonyn to Carleton, St. Augustine, 11 September 1783, in Lockey p. 155; Indians betrayed and mode of life, Siebert, 1: 139.
4. Carleton to McArthur, 22 August 1783, BHP, #8780.
5. Treaty in Lockey, p. 142; ten thousand to emigrate, Petition of East Florida Inhabitants, 11 September 1783 in Lockey, p. 157. Siebert believed "perhaps as many as 17,000" left St. Augustine, 1: 183 and Lockey estimated "upwards of 16,000," intro., p. 9; Tonyn's return enclosed in Tonyn to Nepean, 2 May 1786, CO 5/561 in Lockey, intro., p. 11.
6. Florida banditti, Tonyn to Admiral Digby, St. Augustine, 10 September 1783 in Lockey, p. 152; McArthur to Carleton, St. Augustine, 15 September 1783, BHP, #9136 (1); Address of East Florida Inhabitants to McArthur, n.d. [1783], BHP, #9137 (1).
7. Lord North to Patrick Tonyn, Whitehall, 4 December 1783 in Lockey, p. 178; Tonyn's proclamation in *BG*, 28 March 1789, p. 3.
8. *BG*, 30 October 1784, p. 2.
9. Lockey, p. 174.
10. Petition of Loyalists to the Spanish King, St. Marys, 28 October 1784 in Lockey, p. 301; Memorial to Governour Maxwell, 28 October 1784, CO 23/26, f. 89; Maxwell's reply, Siebert, p. 190; Cruden to Zespedes, New Providence, 10 March 1785 in Lockey, p. 485-486; Zespedes to Galvez, St. Augustine, 23 March 1785 in Lockey, p. 484.
11. Tonyn to Sidney, St. Augustine, 6 December 1784 in Lockey, p. 321; *BG*, 20 November 1784, p. 3.
12. Address of Inhabitants to Tonyn, St. Augustine, 15 February 1785 in Lockey, p. 521 and Zespedes to Tonyn, St. Augustine, 20 February 1785 in Lockey, p. 323; Tonyn expecting appointment as governour of the Bahamas, Zespedes to Galvez, St. Augustine, 24 December 1785 in Lockey, p. 747. Zespedes alleged that Tonyn had used "indecorous" means to gain "his ambition." Lockey comments that there is "no confirmation of this assertion elsewhere in the correspondence," p. 947. Tonyn had forwarded to England the loyalist Resolution against Gov. Maxwell, Tonyn to Sidney, 21 October 1784 in Lockey, p. 287.
13. Confirmation McArthur to temporary government of Bahamas, North to McArthur, Whitehall, 15 December 1783, CO 23/25, f. 66; McArthur to Sidney, New Providence, 1 March 1784, CO 23/25, f. 68.
14. John Wilson, "Report on the Bahama Islands," 1784, MS in Boston Public Library Rare Book Room, f. 8.
15. These affidavits, had they been sent along to England, would have proved invaluable. Not only would they have provided more names of the New York refugees, but also some insight into the psychological and social factors which contributed to what was tantamount to civil war at Carleton, Abaco.
16. There is a document in the BHP, #9625, "List of Loyalist Commissions" Adjutant General's Office "to be dated" 15 November 1783. Samuel Isaacs, Cap^n, Abraham Wetmore, 1st Lt. and Jacob Boyce, 2nd Lt. Next to their names it reads: "dated the 10th [month and year blank] Island of Abbaco." Samuel Isaacs' commission is confirmed by another document which lists only his name on a "List of Loyalists for Commissions going to the Island of Abbaco," dated 10 November 1783, BHP, #9587. It is not certain whether the commissions Stephens withheld were these or some others.
17. The following is the location of Carleton and Marsh Harbour according to the writer of the British Library 1784 Abaco document. McArthur and company came to Abaco by way of the N.W. Providence Channel around "Hole in the Rock" and entered at Little Harbour, preceeded NNW, and stopped at Marsh Harbour. "From Marshes Harbour I went to Carleton which lies about W.N. West distant Six leagues and within Whale Key in lattitude 26°40' we proceeded within the Keys to Whale Key which is Separated from the Island of Abaco by a piece of water not more than Five feet [deep] at High Water. The Vessel was therefore obliged to go without side of this Key and Entered on the Westend carrying in Twenty one feet water. Carleton Harbour lies about Four miles within this Key and is Sheltered by the Keys without and a Sand Bank within, round which sand Bank the Vessel was anchored in Sixteen feet Water. At this place the Refugees from New York first settled. . . ."
18. McArthur's numbers fall short of the 1,458 reported to have left New York and the 1,500 anticipated from East Florida, CO 23/25, ff. 68-70.
19. Wilson, ff. 8-9.
20. Abaco 1784.
21. Pearis Memorial to McArthur, 18 July 1783, BHP, #10138 (1).

22. Abaco 1784. The small passage which separates Great from Little Abaco is called today Ben Curry Cut or The Crossing.

23. Walker to Lincoln, Nassau, 28 January and 10 February 1784, CO 23/26, ff. 46-47; *BG*, 5 March 1784, p. 3.

24. Moseley, p. 60.

25. Dumaresq, Memorial New York, 20 April 1783, BHP, #7466 and Moseley, p. 60; May 1782 Census, Wilson, f. 11.

26. Wilson, ff. 13-15; McArthur, CO 23/25, f. 69; Oswell Eve to Daniel Cox, Port Howe, Cat Island, 29 May 1784, CO 23/26, ff. 204-205; Hunt to Sidney, New Providence, 15 March 1784, CO 23/25, ff. 78-79.

27. Maxwell to Lord North, Leicester Field, 21 October 1783, CO 23/25, f. 64; Whitehall to the Lords of Treasury, 11 December 1783, CO 23/15, f. 154.

28. Extract of a letter from an American Loyalist now settled at New Providence, containing Remarks on the Bahama Islands, n.d. [after 17 May, probably autumn 1784], CO 23/26, f. 161.

29. Maxwell to Sidney, New Providence, 29 March 1784, CO 23/25, f. 76.

30. American Loyalist, CO 23/26, f. 161; CO 23/25, f. 69A and Commissary General's Office, Barbados, 4 March 1784, CO 23/25, f. 92.

31. Whitehall to Lords of Treasury, 24 October 1783, CO 23/15, f. 148.

32. Petition CO 23/24, f. 106 in Maxwell to Sidney, 17 May 1784, CO 23/25, f. 104; Maxwell to Sidney, 4 June 1784, CO 23/25, f. 108; Return of ironmongery from the ship *David*, 15 June 1784, CO 23/25, f. 139. That same month a list of fifty-two American Loyalist heads of families stated "from whence [they] came, number of Whites, number of Blacks, where settled and total." All who settled on Abaco, except John O'Halloran, came by way of East Florida. The first number after the name is the number of Whites including the head of the family, the second is the number of Blacks. John Cornish (1) (5), Martin Weatherford (7) (25), Farqhuar Bethune (3) (16), Robert Scott (1) (18), Lt. Col. Brown (3) (170), Alex. C. Wylly (3) (17), Joseph Smith (3) (10), David Scott (1) (20), William Armstrong (1) (10), Jonathan Belton (1) (10), Andrew McLean (2) (12), James C. Brown (3) (30), John O'Halloran from Georgia (1) (9), John Pritchard (2) (1), enclosure #10 in Maxwell to Sidney, 4 June 1784, CO 23/25, f. 131.

33. Maxwell to Sidney, 17 May 1784, CO 23/25, f. 103-104.

34. CO 23/25, f. 104A; proclamation, 4 June 1784, CO 23/25, f. 110; orders to masters of American vessels, CO 23/25, f. 114.

35. "Writing Libels," CO 23/25, f. 108; "To be Sold," CO 23/25, f. 112; Request for garrison, CO 23/25, f. 108; "stiff finger," Maxwell to Tonyn, 5 June 1784, CO 23/25, f. 128.

36. Handbill, CO 23/26, f. 96; Wells to Willet, Nassau, 29 July 1784, CO 23/25, f. 200; Willet to Maxwell, New Providence, 15 September 1784, CO 23/25, f. 220; Loyalists seize church, Maxwell to Sidney, 26 August 1784, CO 23/25, f. 158.

37. "Resolution," enclosure Tonyn to Sidney, St. Augustine, 21 October 1784 in Lockey, p. 287; Haven to Tonyn, Nassau, 6 December 1784 in Lockey, pp. 433-434; Hepburn recommendation, Tonyn to Maxwell, 15 July 1784, CO 23/26, f. 95.

38. Hepburn invades court, deposition of Atwood, Smith and Grant, 20 November 1784, CO 23/26, f. 91; Nassau, scene of riot, Maxwell to Sidney, 4 September 1784, CO 23/25, ff. 164-165; American Loyalist, CO 23/26, f. 161.

39. Return of Civil Officers "who all refused," enclosure Maxwell, 29 September 1784, CO 23/25, f. 198; Petition for Maxwell's removal, CO 23/26, f. 170-171; letter to Sidney, CO 23/26, f. 168-169.

40. Action of board illegal, supporters to Maxwell, 3 November 1784, CO 23/25, ff. 233-234; address of forty-five Loyalists to Maxwell, n.d. [1784], CO 23/26, f. 97; Maxwell dissolves Assembly, *BG*, 4 December 1784, p. 3; conchs and refugees, Kelly, p. 112; Abaco seats, *VHA*, (1779-1786), 1 February 1785, p. 1-2. Ridley is an old Eleutheran name. In order to be elected to a seat in the House of Assembly, the candidate must own property in the place he seeks to represent. Ridley must have been one of perhaps several Old Inhabitants from Eleuthera and Harbour Island who lived on Abaco and voted for him; Maxwell embarks for England, *BG*, 26 March 1785, p. 3; Maxwell Town *BG*, 9 April 1785; Arnold and Valentine, Tombstone makers, *BG*, 2 October 1784, p. 3.

41. The list of those who had reason to "deprecate Mr. Maxwell's return" was dated Nassau, 5 March 1784 and appeared in *BG*, 12 March 1785, p. 1; Maxwell to Sidney, n.d. [May 1785], CO 23/26, ff. 185-189. The 6 August 1790 issue of the *Bahamas Gazette* announced the death of John Maxwell in England.

42. Hepburn and Powell, Bates, p. 295; Powell thought there might be five hundred people on Abaco and Cat Island, but would "endeavour to ascertain their number," Memorandum from Powell regarding the State of the Bahama Islands, 7 March 1785, CO 23/26, ff. 190-191; also Powell to Sidney 19 March 1785, CO 23/25, ff. 303-304; address of British merchants to Powell, 14 April 1785, CO 23/26, ff. 157-160. Among the signers were: Hugh and Peter Dean, John Denniston, James and William Moss, Panton, Leslie and Co., John Petty, Alexander Taylor, John Wells and John Wood; smuggling, CO 23/26, f. 157A; request for cruiser, Powell to Admiral Tunis, 17 April 1785, CO 23/26, ff. 182-183; smuggled goods brought to Nassau, Powell to Sidney, 16 October 1785, CO 23/25, f. 351.

44. Wanted, *BG*, 18 September 1784; *Norman*, *BG*, 9 July 1785, p. 3.

45. VHA (1779-1786), 1785 session, pp. 8-14.

46. *BG*, 14 May 1785, p. 3.

47. Tonyn to Sidney, 4 April 1785 in Lockey, pp. 496-500; wreck of the *Cyrus*, Tonyn to Sidney, St. Marys, 15 September and 10 November 1785 in Lockey, pp. 738-739.

48. Powell to Tonyn, Nassau, 9 June 1785 in Lockey, pp. 695-696; Tonyn to Powell, St. Marys, 25 August 1785 in Lockey, pp. 696-697.

49. *BG*, 23 July 1785, p. 2.

50. Erratic weather, *BG*, 2 July 1785, p. 3; last transports, *BG*, 17 September 1785, p. 3; Hope, *BG*, 24 September 1785, p. 3 and 1 October 1785, p. 3.

51. Vessels lost in storm, *BG*, 1 October 1785, p. 3; "Council Journal," CO 23/25, ff. 376-378. Corn and flour were delivered to John Cameron and Capt. John W. Barclay to be carried by them to Carleton, Captain Cook to take to Maxwell Town and Spencers Bight, CO 23/25, f. 380. Cornelius Blanchard would distribute the supplies to the people at Carleton, Philip Dumaresq to Maxwell Town and Marsh Harbour and John Fergusson at Spencers Bight, CO 23/25, f. 377.

52. *BG*, 10 December 1785, p. 3.

14. "When the Hurly-Burly's Done"

1. McArthur to Sidney, 11 March 1786, CO 23/25, ff. 405-406; When the *Gazette* announced the funeral of the Honourable John Brown on 27 September 1796, it mentioned that Brown, age seventy-two, had been a resident of the Bahamas for fifty years and had "filled at different times, almost every office of respectability in the government." *BG*, 27 September 1796.

2. Lt. Gov. Powell died of dropsy, see G. Barry to Stokes, 15 January 1786, CO 23/26, f. 209; Brown to Grey Elliott, 21 April 1786, CO 23/26, ff. 211-212.

3. Memorial to Brown from fifty-two late arriving Loyalists who had received only four months' provisions, 21 February 1786, CO 23/25, ff. 395-396; Colonel Thomas Brown and other officers petitioned Brown regarding grants of land promised by Guy Carleton. They had been informed upon their arrival, "much to their mortification, that His Majesty's Bounty did not extend to these islands," CO 23/25, f. 4; Petition from the Old Inhabitants, who had been twice captured by Americans and once by Spain, Brown to Sidney, New Providence, 3 July 1786, CO 23/25, f. 439; Out Island smugglers, 9 March 1786, CO 23/26, f. 207; American Loyalist (1784), CO 23/26, f. 162A. One historian's statement may prove true for The Bahamas today; "Blackbeard might be dead, but his soul lives on." Michael Block, *The Duke of Windsor's War* (London: Weidenfield and Nicolson, 1982), p. 109.

4. Barry to Stokes, 15 January 1786, CO 23/26, f. 209; Exuma petition, #2 in Brown, 17 April 1786, CO 23/25, f. 432.

5. Cedar Harbour proprietors, *BG*, 16 September 1786, p. 3; "all things flourish," *BG*, 8 July 1786, p. 3; *Sally*, *BG*, 13 May 1786, p. 3.

6. *BG*, 28 January 1786, 19 August 1786, 7 October 1786, 30 December 1786, p. 3.

7. *Fair Abaconian* lost on Abaco, *BG*, 4 April 1789, p. 3; vessels built at Abaco, CO 23/29, ff. 68, 69, 70; see chart.

Type	# Tons	Name of Vessel	Master	Year Built	Owner
Sloop	21	*Huaebras* §	Edward Lane	1785	Barron & McKinnon
Snow	155	*Recovery*	Philip Lithybee	1786	P. Lithybee
Schooner	74	*Fair Abaconian*	Wm. Thurston	1786	Wm. & Thos. Armstrong
Schooner	47	*Carleton*	Ward Atwater	1786	Frederick Fine°
Schooner	12	*Resolution*	John Bromhall	1786	J. Bromhall
Schooner	119	*Ulyses*	James Hovey	1787	Smith & Hovey
Sloop	37	*Two Friends*	John McGillivray*	1787	Thos. Simson
Schooner	21	*Dolphin*	Henry Smith	1787	John Petty
Schooner	87	*Eliza*	Charles Brown	1788	Denniston & Co.

§ Could be *Hudibras*, a satirical mock-heroic epic poem written by Samuel Butler and published between 1663 and 1678.

° Frederick Fine, native of New York, arrived in the Bahamas in 1779 and resided in Nassau for forty-six years. *BG*, 26 February 1825, p. 3.

* John McGillivray, Indian trader and wealthy West Florida merchant raised a corps of one hundred men to fight in Willings Raid. Spain seized him on the high seas. J. Leitch Wright, *Florida in the American Revolution* (Gainesville, Florida: University Presses of Florida, 1975), pp. 50, 139, 102. McGillivray's name appears on the list of "loyalists lately settled in these Islands" dated 21 February 1786, in Brown CO 23/25, f. 395A.

Two other vessels were built at Abaco in these early years. John McKenzie offered for sale a "Brigantine on the Stocks (with Masts and Spars)" at Eight Mile Bay in 1789. *BG*, 10 January 1789, p. 2. In July, 1793, Thomas Forbes advertised for sale "the new sloop *Industry* built at Abaco of the best material, launched in March last." *BG*, 4 July 1793, p. 4.

8. Prices doubled, Bates, p. 297; price current for 18 April 1786, CO 23/25, ff. 433-434; For the years 1773-1774, exports to Great Britain = £5,216.8.10 (principally wrecked goods) and imports = £3,592.0.1, but for the years 1786-1787 exports = £58,707.10.1 "exclusive of a great deal of bullion, of which no account has been kept" and imports from Great Britain = £136,359.14.11. [William Wylly], *A Short Account of the Bahama Islands* by a Barrister at Law (London, 1789), NYPL and CO 23/29, ff. 191-213, NA, pp. 5-6, also in Siebert, p. 194; estimate of American refugees, Peters "near 4,000," p. 46 and Bates "at least 7,000," p. 297; As a means of helping loyalist refugees, Anguilla had sent some of their cotton seeds to the Bahamas. In the winter of 1786 Loyalists in the Bahamas sent some of their seeds to friends on the Georgia coast. Gray noted that the "Bahama strain" was superior to the "black-seeded cotton already in cultivation in English Colonies." Gray's *History of Agriculture in the Southern States* to 1860, v. 2, pp. 676-677 in Peters' research notes: Dunmore for Jamaica, *GG*, 7 May 1785; Dunmore for Bermuda, *BG*, 11 March 1786, p. 3; McArthur for Bahamas, *BG*, 22 July 1786, p. 3; Dunmore for Bahamas, *BG*, 26 August 1786, p. 3.

9. Small vessel, Dunmore to Sidney, Berkeley St. London, 10 November 1786, CO 23/25, f. 443; Dunmore refuge, Harrell, p. 32; description, Sabine, *Biographical Sketches*, 2:400, Harrell, p. 30 and Wylly to Stokes CO 23/29, f. 234; [John Matson] "An Account of the Present Situation of Affairs in the Bahama Islands," Most Secret and Confidential, CO 23/28, f. 149. Matson's letter to Philip Edwards, 10 November 1788, proves he is the writer of this Secret Account. Matson told Edwards that he left "a long account of all the situation of the colony" with Lord Sidney.

10. Loyalists hijacking Blacks, G. Baylis to Stokes, CO 23/26, f. 225; Dunmore proclamation dated 7 November extended pardon to Blacks to 12 November 1787, enclosed in Dunmore to Sidney, 28 November 1787, CO 23/27, f. 78; illegality of Negro Court, Wylly, p. 21.

11. Dunmore to Sidney, 20 December 1787, CO 23/27, f. 92.

12. Blanchard, 6 April 1785; John Ferguson reward, *BG*, 17 June 1786, p. 3; Abaco revolt, Dunmore to Sidney, 28 November 1787, CO 23/27, f. 75.

13. Transport *Mercury*, McArthur to Sidney, 27 November 1787, CO 23/27, f. 74; Dunmore detains troops, Wylly to Stokes, 6 July 1789, CO 23/29, f. 247; House prorogued, CO 23/27, f. 75; packed House, Wylly, pp. 11-13; Brown, *VHA* (1787), pp. 4, 6; Wylly to Abaco, *VHA*, 7 December 1787, p. 9.

14. Scott, *VHA*, 31 January 1788, p. 29. Robert Scott was Acting Surgeon's Mate of the Royal Artillery, Matson, f. 174; Brown and Forbes Exuma, *VHA*, 5 February 1788, p. 31; Brown/Murray, Forbes for Abaco, *VHA*, 9 March 1789, p. 50 and *BG*, 14, 21 February and 7, 14 March 1789; memorials to dissolve Assembly, Wylly, pp. 33-39; Abaco memorial in Dunmore, 12 March 1788, CO 23/27, ff. 119-121A. According to Wylly this Abaco memorial was dated 6 January 1788, p. 38.

15. Enclosed in Dunmore to Sidney, 29 February 1788, CO 23/27 ff. 102-105.

16. Dunmore to Sidney, 4 March 1788, CO 23/27, f. 112.

17. "Damned liar," Matson, f. 168; trial, Wylly CO 23/29, ff. 224-225; Wylly in England, Wylly to Nepean, Rye in Sussex, 7 August 1789, CO 23/29, ff. 217-218.

18. Wylly, CO 23/29, f. 219—and Matson, CO 23/28, f. 149.

19. See Benjamin Baynton, *Authentic Memoirs of William Augustus Bowles* (1791; rpt. ed., New York: Arno Press Inc., 1971) and J. Leitch Wright Jr., *William Augustus Bowles: Director General of the Creek Nation* (Athens: University of Georgia Press, 1967).

20. Panton memorial by attorney William Wylly to Grenville, 19 June 1789, CO 23/29, f. 163; Welbank, J. L. Wright, *Bowles*, pp. 31, 66 and BHP, #10427, f. 100.

21. Dunmore denial, Dunmore to Grenville, 1 March 1790, CO 23/30, ff. 192, 192A; *Lucayan Herald* (Nassau: Cameron), 19 August 1789, CO 23/30, ff. 194-195 and letter from Dr. William S. Coker, Editor of *The Papers of Panton, Leslie and Company*, 27 October 1982. Bowles received a five hundred acre grant on Eleuthera, Book "F," p. 150, LS. Dunmore wanted Bowles to get him a 20,000 acre grant from the Creeks, Dowdeswell to Chalmers, 6 September 1797 in *Aspinall Papers*, v. 10 (1871), p. 831 in Peters' research notes.

22. Bowles's sworn statement, 9 April 1788, enclosed in Dunmore to Sidney, 21 April 1788, CO 23/27, ff. 158-159. In 1803, John Forbes of the Panton, Leslie Company captured Bowles at the Hickory Ground conference and the United States turned him over to the Spanish. One of the half-breeds employed by John Forbes to seize Bowles was Charles Weatherford. Bowles languished in Morro castle in Havana until he died of starvation 23 December 1805. Some accounts allege that the Spanish were trying to poison him and for that reason Bowles refused to eat, but the true cause of his death may never be known. J. Leitch Wright poignantly stated that "Fate was not kind" to allow such a vital personality "to rot away in isolation at the prime of his life." J. L. Wright, *Bowles*, pp. 166, 171, 173-174.

23. Matson, f. 159; Mackay to Abaco, CO 23/27, f. 76; E. Williams, p. 56; Abaco smugglers, *RG*, 16 July 1825, p. 3.

24. Richard Pearis to William Coleman, 8 May 1788, CO 23/29 ff. 303-304 and Pearis' affidavit sworn before Joseph M. Moore J.P., 16 May 1788, CO 23/29, ff. 304A-305.

25. Spencers Bight memorial in Wylly pp. 40-41; Dunmore to Abaco, Wylly, p. 23; Dunmore's instructions to Mackay, footnote to copy of Spencers Bight memorial in Wylly, CO 23/29, ff. 283-284. Signatures which appear on this document are: Philip Dumaresq, J.P., John Ferguson J.P., Joseph Smith J.P., Richard Pearis, Martin Weatherford, John Cornish, J. M. Moore, J. P., Abraham Martinangle, William Armstrong, Senior and Junior, James O'Neil; "trifling rebellion," Wylly to Stokes, CO 23/29, f. 227; "impartial trial," Spencers Bight inhabitants to Dunmore, 2 June 1788, CO 23/27, ff. 168A-169.

26. Kennedy affidavit, 2 July 1788, CO 23/29, ff. 298-300.

27. Memorial to Lord Sidney from Kennedy by his attorney William Wylly, London, 15 November 1788, CO 23/28, f. 147; Richard Pearis to Dunmore, 13 May 1788, CO 23/27, f. 173.

28. Memorial from Abaco to William Pitt, n.d., no signatures, CO 23/27, f. 170-172.

29. CO 23/29, f. 247A.

30. Stokes to Nepean, Inner Temple, 3 June 1788, CO 23/28, f. 109; courts closed, Wylly, CO 23/29, f. 246A; Wylly to Sidney, London, 15 November 1788, CO 23/28, ff. 143-146.

31. Stokes to Committee of Correspondence, 23 October 1788, CO 23/28, ff. 124-128.

32. Bates, pp. 316-317; Wylly to Grenville, Queen's Row, Knightsbridge, 9 June 1789, CO 23/29, ff. 187-188.

33. Wylly to Nepean, Knightsbridge, 10 June 1789, CO 23/29, f. 214.

34. Wylly, CO 23/29, f. 247A-249 and ff. 228-230.

35. *BG*, 5 September 1789, p. 3.

36. Baker to Treasury, Account of expenses from October, 1789, to October, 1792, CO 23/32, f. 235A; Baker memorial to Dundas, CO 23/32, ff. 236-237.

37. Dunmore to Sidney, 29 June 1789, CO 23/29, ff. 117-122.

15: More Hurly-Burly

1. Wylly, p. 4; islands inhabited, CO 23/30, f. 334; population, "Report on the Bahama Islands," by Thomas Brown's committee, 28 April, JHA (1760-1784), p. 48, also in CO 23/29, ff. 172-177.
2. Wylly, p. 7; "State of the Bahama Islands," June 1788, CO 23/30, f. 334. For this report, the number and descriptions of New Inhabitants were ascertained from king's ration and donation lists: Old Inhabitants from poll tax, old muster rolls and parish registers. Information about dimensions of the islands came from old settlers and sea-faring people. Planters on Abaco, CO 23/30, f. 335; "Since Abaco climate was not favourable for cotton culture, the inhabitants have moved to Caicos." This notation appeared on "Bahamas" map #8, 1790, CO 700, map room, British Library.
3. Crop failure, Dunmore to Sidney, 31 August 1789, CO 23/29, f. 167A; Granada and Barbados, Council to Stokes, 1786, CO 23/26, f. 207; exodus predicted, BG, 26 September 1789; snow, BG, 28 February 1789, p. 3; worm, BG, 21 March, 20 June, 4 July, 18 July 1789.
4. "Out of Date," BG, 8 July 1786, p. 3; "Observations by Lord Dunmore on such of the Bahama Islands as he visited," New Providence, 1 September 1790, CO 23/30, ff. 238-239.
5. Dunmore's Spencers Bight purchase, 31 January 1789, ORG, Book "O," p. 341; Report 1789, JHA, p. 247; Abaco grapes, Dunmore to Dundas, 18 December 1793, CO 23/33, f. 43.
6. Powell's proclamation, BG, 1 October 1785, p. 1; purchase, Siebert, 1: 154, 193; "List of tracts of land granted . . . 8 April 1788-31 December 1789," enclosure #4 in Dunmore, 15 June 1790, CO 23/30, ff. 216-224A (hereinafter cited as G, year, grant and folio number); Gambier, G 1788 #215, f. 217A; Rolle complaint, Rolle to Lord Shelburne, 24 February 1783 in Lockey, pp. 58-59.
7. Allender, G 1788, #515, f. 233A; Stephens' Green Turtle Cay, plat certified by Josiah Tattnall, 6 December 1786. Grant Book "B," p. 61, LS and G 1789, #525, f. 223A; Stephens' Codicil, Book "I," pp. 312-314, NA.
8. Margaret Pearis G. 1788, #99, f. 220; goat warning, BG, 19 September 1789; Richard Jr., Marriage "CC Mar. Reg. (1753-1805)," p. 52.
    By April, 1807, Richard Jr. and his wife Margaret had established a residence in Georgia on the St. Johns River. RG, 23 April 1807. Colonel Richard Pearis died in Nassau 7 November 1794. BG, 11 November 1794. He left three tracts of land on Abaco to his wife Rhoda. To his son Richard and daughters Sarah and Margaret he bequeathed the land in Nassau and two hundred acres on the River Pensacola in West Florida. Richard Jr. received his father's Caicos land and all the property in the United States. Will Book "F," pp. 460-464, proved 15 December 1794. Not mentioned in the will is the colonel's son by his Cherokee wife. The headmen of the Cherokee nation granted to Richard Sr. and his son George Pearis a tract of land twelve miles square lying on the waters of the Saluda, Enoree and Ready Rivers in the South Carolina backcountry. SC "Journal of the House of Assembly" (1783-84), pp. 411-412, SCA, George Hite petition 3 February 1784. Richard Sr. became obnoxious early in the war, fought in the Seige of Ninety-Six in 1775 and was imprisoned in Charleston in 1776 with Robert and Patrick Cunningham. He took the oath of fidelity and was released. When he reached his home he was surprised to find that a Colonel Thomas had burnt his house, destroyed his mills, sold his cattle, and after stripping Mrs. Pearis and his children, had left them to shift for themselves. After a desperate search he found them a hundred miles away living among a "parcel of rebels." Wednesday, 18 September 1776, State Records, SC "General Assembly Journal" (1776-1783), p. 62, SCA and Parrish, p. 419.
9. "CC Mar. Reg. (1753-1805)," 12 April 1798; William Jones' death, BG, 14 May 1799.
10. Pearis's note lost, notice dated 13 April 1789, BG, 16 May 1789; runaway shot, VHA, 8 May 1789, p. 144; Caicos grant, 27 June 1792, Grant Book "M," LS.
11. Brown to Pitt, New Providence, 2 November 1790, CO 23/30, ff. 346-346A; Creek Indians visit Nassau, McArthur to Sidney, 13 April 1787, CO 23/27, f. 9; C. F. Taylor, CO 23/30, f. 249.
12. Caicos Petition, enclosure #15 in Dunmore 28 August 1792, CO 23/31, f. 148A.
13. BG, 26 November 1790. Sergeant John Armstrong appears on the muster roll of Captain Daniel Manson's Company of Royal North Carolina Regiment, Hillsborough, North Carolina, 24 February-24 April 1781 (Clark, 1: 397), Wilmington, North Carolina, 25 October-24 December 1781 (Clark, 1: 399), Quarter House, South Carolina, 25 April-24 June 1782 (Clark, 1: 400) and St. Augustine, 25 April-24 June 1783 (Clark, 1: 402). There was a lot for A. Blanchard near John Weatherford at Maxwell Town and a twenty-two acre plot for J. Armstrong at Spencers Bight. The sergeant John Armstrong who eloped from Abaco with his family is not the same John Armstrong, Solicitor General of the Bahamas in 1813, who had married Alicia Maria Yonge on 4 May 1800. "CC Reg. (1753-1805)."
14. "Perfect crop," and Eve's gin, BG, 5 February, 23 November, 24 December 1790. The Yankee inventor Eli Whitney did not manufacture a cotton gin until 1793; Sheep, BG, 16 February 1790; Dunmore to Grenville, 5 April 1790, CO 23/30, f. 200, drawings of Ft. Charlotte, CO 23/29, f. 49.
15. BG, 4 March, 12 August, 7 January, 23 August, 23 December 1791.
16. Abaco election, BG, 24 June 1791, VHA, 4 July 1791, p. 48, 8 July 1791, p. 51, 11 October, 1791, p. 14; Dumaresq, BG, 18 October 1791, Dunmore to Dundas, 12 April 1792, CO 23/31, f. 110.
17. Dunmore grants, 18 June 1790-31 May 1794, CO 23/30, ff. 114-118, fees, CO 23/31, ff. 10, 20, 24; Long Island survey map by Josiah Tattnall 1792, CO 700/14, PRO. This map shows a five thousand acre grant for Lord Dunmore.
18. Mississippi, Richards, 30 April 1791, USPG, Reel 2; Richards' population figures show 5,000 on Nassau, 1,500 on Eleuthera and Harbour Island, 2,200 on Long Island, 1,200 on Exuma, 16 December 1791, USPG, Reel 2; Siebert, 1: 197-198; Gordon, 17 June 1792, USPG, Reel 2.
19. Lark, BG, 17 January 1792, Cotton, BG, 17 January, 4 May, 5 June, 22 June, 27 November 1792.

20. Wilberforce, *BG*, 8 June 1792; Columbus, *BG*, 16 October 1792; 7 December 1792, M. K. Armbrister.
21. Proclamation, CO 23/32, f. 110; Dundas to Dunmore, Whitehall, 10 August 1793, CO 23/32, f. 118; French, Dunmore to Dundas, 17 July 1793, CO 23/32, f. 124.
22. French War—Arms had been sent to Long Island, Exuma, Cat, Crooked, and Caicos Islands but not to Harbour Island, Eleuthera, or Abaco. Council Minutes, CO 23/33, f. 36. When the threat of invasion ended, William Wylly resigned his commission in the artillery because he refused to serve under men of inferior rank. Muster Rolls Volunteer Troops, CO 23/33, ff. 18-24 and *BG*, 6 January 1794; storm Long Island, *BG*, 22 February 1793.
23. Wind insurance, *BG*, 28 November 1793; wind gin, *BG*, 21 March 1794; Eve, library, *BG*, 24 January 1800. The eulogy for John Wells appears in the *BG*, 1 November 1799 and Joseph Eve took over as editor, *BG*, 18 February 1800. Joseph Eve, youngest son of Oswell Eve and Anne Moore Eve of Philadelphia, died near Augusta, Georgia, 14 November 1825 or 1826. His son Joseph Adams Eve became a noted physician in Augusta. *Charleston News and Courier*, 14 November 1926? clippings provided by Mrs. Grace Eve Crawford of Augusta, descendant of Joseph Eve; loyalist contributions, *Nassau Guardian*, 18 October 1913, p. 20.
24. Abaco vote 1794, CO 23/36, ff. 132-134; dissolution of the Assembly, *BG*, 3 October 1794; 1795 election held 16 September, *BG*, 22 September 1795.
25. Dunmore expenditures, Bates, p. 320; *Parisienne*, *BG*, 18 December 1795.
26. Dunmore to Portland, 22 August 1795, CO 23/34, ff. 94-96. There is a copy of the wrecking licence issued by Dunmore enclosed in this correspondence.
27. Deposition of John Clear of Harbour Island sworn at Nassau, 28 June 1796 before Adam Chrystie. Incident occurred 4 June 1796 at Harbour Island. John Clear was over fifty-five years of age at the time. Chalmers Papers, Reel 1.
28. Dumaresq resigns, *BG*, 23 February 1796; Dumaresq jailed, CO 23/34, ff. 265-266, 275; Dumaresq fined, CO 23/35, f. 74. Philip's wife died in April 1791. *BG*, 8 April 1791. Philip married Miss Sarah Stirrup, daughter of the deceased Captain Daniel Stirrup. *BG*, 20 January 1792. The *Gazette* reported Philip's death in October 1800. *BG*, 3 October 1800. His will requested that he be buried in some convenient place, in a plain coffin and in the "most frugal manner." "Wills C2," pp 154-157, proved 13 Oct. 1800.
29. Bates, pp. 321-322.
30. Forbes's arrival, address of Inhabitants of New Providence with names, 13 November 1796, CO 23/35, ff. 47-49 and address of Harbour Island residents, 1 January 1797, CO 23/35, ff. 173-174; Wylly appointed Chief Justice, *BG*, 17 January 1797; anxiety over Dunmore's possible return, Bates, pp. 324-325; arrival of Dowdeswell, *BG*, 23 February 1798 and address of New Providence inhabitants, with names, *BG*, 30 March 1798.
31. Pascoe, pp. 221-222. Religion aside, inbreeding, particularly at Spanish Wells, Eleuthera has caused serious physical and mental defects.
32. Petition of inhabitants, St. Johns, Harbour Island, 7 June 1796, CO 23/34, ff. 280-281. This Joseph Curry may have been Harllee's Joseph Curry (3301), son of Joseph (33) and Rachel and husband to Patience, who died in 1806. According to Harllee, this Joseph would have been about forty-six years old in 1799. He also could have been the Joseph Curry who died on 4 July 1809 on his return from Charleston. This Joseph must have been the one who received lot #81 in Dunmore Town. But whether he was granted the land as a Loyalist or one of the "poor" but "industrious" Harbour Islanders is not certain.
33. "Prince belonging to Mr. Joe. Curry was baptized (being a negro man)" 19 August 1798, "Births and Baptisms," St. Johns, Harbour Island, p. 19, NA.
34. ". . . no owner, employer or Supervisor or gaol keeper shall on any account punish a slave with more than 39 lashes at one time and for 1 offense." "Act to consolidate several laws pertaining to the slaves" printed by John Wells, 1797, CO 23/54, f. 276. According to article 70, it was lawful for two justices giving notice to owners of the place of trial, to issue any punishment not exceeding 50 lashes, f. 283A.
35. Gordon to Franks and Stephen Haven, Harbour Island, 13 May 1799, USPG, Reel 2.
36. Gordon, third letter, n.d., USPG, Reel 2.
37. Gordon, 21 May 1799 and third letter, USPG, Reel 2.
38. *BG*, 2 November 1798.
39. Petition, CO 23/39, f. 258; "Cotton Questionnaire," CO 23/39, f. 264A.
40. CO 23/39, ff. 305-306A.
41. Instructions to grant office, JHA (1802), pp. 89-90 and 9 November 1802, p. 155; Yonge, JHA, 25 November 1803, p. 20; emigration to Georgia, CO 23/41, f. 110 and CO 23/44, f. 212; extract from James Moss's letter. CO 23/44, ff. 182-183; Brown to John Sullivan, September 1803, CO 23/44, ff. 212-215.
42. On 13 August 1805 James Moss and John McIntosh offered for sale 2,850 acres of land on Middle Caicos purchased from Lt. Col. Brown "some years ago," *RG*, 1 October 1805, p. 1; Brown, Piarra Coffee House, Covent Garden, n.d. [1803], CO 23/44, ff. 81-82.
43. Hall to Tattnall, New Providence, 20 January 1804, CO 23/46, f. 121.
44. French expected, Richards, 30 January 1804; St. Matthews, Richards, 23 July 1802, USPG, Reel 2. St. Matthew's church, built between 1800 and 1802 by Joseph Eve, is the oldest church building in The Bahamas. Gail Saunders and Donald Cartwright, *Historic Nassau* (London: Macmillan Caribbean, 1979), p. 20.
45. French soldiers, JHA, 1 April 1805, p. 282; Daniel McKinnon, *A Tour Through the British West Indies in the Years 1802 and 1803 Giving a Particular Account of the Bahama Islands* (London: printed for J. White, 1804), p. 117; Green Turtle Cay school, JHA, 31 December 1804, p. 208.
46. McKinnon, p. 261; Archer, July 1803, CO 23/47, f. 144A. Benjamin Archer of Marsh Harbour was appointed deputy surveyor for the Bahama Islands on 21 May 1805, *RG*, 7 June 1805, p. 3. Archer had a grant for one hundred acres in

the area of Carleton, dated 3 March 1807, recorded in grant Book "K," p. 143.
47. List of grants 18 May 1803-24 July 1804, CO 23/46, f. 10; Abaco election, 1804, 31 December 1804, CO 23/47; elected 1805; CO 23/47, f. 141.
48. CO 23/48, ff. 144. 146.

16: "Anything to Make a Living"

1. Peters, pp. 55, 62, 66.
2. Peters, pp. 63-64.
3. Catton, grant list 1801-1809, 28 June 1806, CO 23/56, f. 64A; interview with Mr. Harold Lowe, Green Turtle Cay, Abaco, 8 April 1981.
4. Benjamin, son of Richard and Mercy Curry of Green Turtle Cay, born 21 August 1803, CC; grants, Gideon Lowe, 27 March 1807, Book "K," p. 142, Jacob Adams, 31 March 1807, Book "K," p. 140, CO 23/56, ff. 64A-65A. Unless otherwise indicated all the foregoing tracts were located on the main of Abaco. The Benjamin Curry mentioned is probably Harllee's (3303).
5. Wylly, p. 4; Harbour Island names, CO 23/35, ff. 173-174 and Book "R," pp. 433-442; "A Record of Returns of Slaves" commonly called the "Slave Registers," 1821-1834, triennial, nine books, NA. James Armbrister was registrar.
6. Jenny, "Slave Registers:" 1822, p. 5; 1825, p. 525; 1828, p. 57; 1831, pp. 65-66 and 1834, p. 322; gifts of land Great Guana Cay, ORG, Book "Y3," pp. 10-11; boat, Book "S3," p. 189; Baker and Adams, oral history passed on by Alton Lowe from conversations he had with his great-uncle Oliver Saunders.
7. Adams's military history, Clark, 1:210, 52, 54, 272; RG, 13 June 1829.
8. Clement A. Penrose, "Sanitary Conditions of the Bahama Islands," in Shattuck (1905), p. 410.
9. Benjamin and Ephraim Malone (Melone), Clark, 1: 119, 122, 137, 140, 142, 236; Susannah Melone, Clark, 1: 145, 522; Ephraim Melone, Charleston, Clark, 1: 178. Clark's records show a James Malone taken at the surrender of Charleston 12 May 1780, Clark, 1: 477; Lewis Malone, "Oaths of Allegiance," Charleston, CO 5/527, British Library, Reel 21, p. 63, SCA. Dawson Roberts found a grant for a Cornelius Malone dated 1752 and located south of the river at Camden, South Carolina.
10. Penrose genealogical chart, p. 410; Ephraim Malone, Little Guana Cay acreage, Book "B," p. 82, dated 18 day of _____ 18_____, (record mutilated). The St. Matthew's Register shows the birth of Vienna Charlotte, daughter of Jacob and Winifred Adams of Abaco on 14 April 1804. The 1834 "Slave Register" records seven slaves belonging to the estate of Jacob Adams of "Elbow Cay, deceased." 1834 "Slave Register," 1:279.
11. Weatherford losses in Georgia, AO 13, Bundles 82 and 138; will dated 28 July 1800, witnessed by Joseph Curry, proved 23 March 1805, recorded in ORG, Book "C2," pp. 304-305 in "Wills 1790-1808," NA.
12. Archer's son, "St. Johns Register 1799," p. 24; RRG, v. 2 (1778-1785), p. 410. Loyalist, see Hazel Albury's Man-O-War My Island Home: A History of an Outer Abaco Island (Delaware: Holly Press, 1977).
13. Key grants, twenty-two acres 1807, Book "K," p. 145, 220 acres, Book "L1," p. 30; "Death Register," 1850; Philip Barton Key, "American Loyalist Claims," 35:381-389, 4:196-197, 6:288-289; return to Maryland, Sabine, Biographical Sketches, 1:601; Francis Scott Key, Wright, Bowles, p. 8.
14. Dunmore, CO 23/27, f. 103: return to Florida, VHA, 10 November 1812, p. 17. John Russell married Mary Hog 27 April 1796, "CC Mar. Reg. 1789-1803," Book 2, p.79. George Ely Russell, editor of the National Genealogical Society Quarterly, informed me that it is unlikely that shipwright John Russell was the father of John Russell (1770-1840) of Abaco. The shipwright's will, dated 18 January 1811 at New Providence, and the will of Mary (Hogg) Russell, dated 24 August 1830 in Liberty County, Georgia, mention no son John among their children. October 1983: personal communication.
15. "CC Baptisms," p. 5.
16. Huxtable, pp. 5-7; James Martin Wright, "The Wrecking System of the Bahama Islands," Political Science Quarterly 30 (1915): 632-633.
17. Kill lone survivor, Schoepf, p. 283; save lives and wrecking procedures, J. M. Wright, "Wrecking," pp. 630, 622.
18. Bahama Herald (Nassau), 4 June 1859.
19. Roman's chart, Charles Florence's response to "Observations on the Gulf Passage," in 11 December 1804 issue of the Royal Gazette, RG, 25 December 1804; Spanish chart, RG, 11 December 1804, p. 3.
20. Brig Samuel, RG, 13 November 1804; The men brought in by the John Bull could have been the Benjamin Saunders and Richard or William Sawyer who pillaged Benjamin Archer's property the year before. RG, 16 November, 1804.
21. Low, RG, 1 February 1805; Russel at Elbow Cay, RG 27 September, 1805.
22. Betsey, RG, 27 May 1806; Hurricane, RG, 19 September 1806; list of Harbour Island houses destroyed and people drowned at the Bogue, RG, 23 September 1806; Provisions sent by Council, Commissary receipt, 24 September 1806, CO 23/49, f. 109.
23. Burr, RG, 7 August, 1804, 26 September, 10 October 1807; at Abaco, RG, 17 February 1807.
24. Cut-off day for the cessation of slave trade set for 31 January 1808, RG, 16 April 1807; John D. Toy, printer, African Slave Trade in Jamaica and Comparative Treatment of Slaves (John D. Toy for Maryland Historical Society, 1854), p. 10.
25. RG, 21 May 1808, Flora Thompson granted lot #135, Book "R," f. 436.
26. Laurel, RG, 30 January 1810. In June of that year Benjamin Saunders and Richard Curry paid for and published an advertisement for Doctor W. F. McCarty who had rendered "dignified services" to the people of Green Turtle Cay and wished him prosperity in Nassau RG, 9 June 1810. This is possibly the Richard Curry who married the widow

Mercy Albury. Their daughter Jane was probably the Jane Curry who married James Lowe 30 September 1812. "St. Matthew's Register (1802-1903)," marriage certificate #92, p. 52; *Orion, RG* 7 November 1810, see also *The Republican and Savannah Evening Ledger*, 27 November 1810, Georgia Historical Society Library, Savannah.

27. Schools, JHA, 20 November 1812, p. 29 and CO 23/59, f. 9; 1812 census, CO 23/59, f. 57.

28. Munnings Address, CO 23/59, f. 84; in America, *BG*, 9 June, 5 July 1812.

29. *BG*, 21 March 1813.

30. Hurricane, CO 23/60, f. 68A; Love Curry, *BG*, 5 and 12 August 1813.

31. Prisoners of war, *BG*, 16 July 1814; American cruisers, *BG*, 15 September 1814; *Midas, RG*, 14 September, 5 October 1814 and 15 September 1814; peace, *BG*, 19 February 1815.

32. Reverend H. Bleeby, "The Story of a Mission: Abaco and its Cays," paper in ALM, p. 1 and Rutledge, 24 June 1815 in Deans Peggs, *A Mission to the West India Islands: Dawson's Journal for 1810-1817* (Nassau, Bahamas: The Deans Peggs Research Fund, 1960), p. 90; conversions, Ward, 11 August 1815 in Edwin L. Taylor, compiler, "The Letters of the First Four Missionaries to the Bahamas," in *Methodism in the West Indies 1760-1960 Bicentenary Souvenir* (Nassau: Methodist Church, 1960), p. 26; Ward, 28 July 1815 in Peggs, p. 91.

33. Turton, 30 January 1816 in Peggs, p. 95; early failure, Alan Betteridge, compiler, "The Spread of Methodism Through the Bahamas" in *Methodism in the West Indies 1760-1960*, p. 15.

34. Cartagena cruisers, *RG*, 22 February 1817.

35. J. M. Wright, *History*, pp. 430-432, 440; removal of slaves, Shaw to Goutburn, London, 31 July 1816, CO 23/63, f. 345.

36. Perpall, CO 23/63, ff. 187-188; U.S. accusations, CO 23/61, f. 110; Bathurst to Cameron, 2 February 1815, CO 23/62, ff. 152-153.

37. *BG*, 14 May 1812 and Petition of New Providence inhabitants to Gov. Munnings 1811, CO 23/58, f. 32.

38. CO 23/56, ff. 74-78.

39. *RG*, 27 April 1816. Isle de Los is probably Delos (Dhilos), a small island of S.E. Greece, and traditionally the birthplace of Apollo and Artemis. Collins *Gazetteer*, (1974), p. 137.

40. *RG*, 12 June 1816.

41. The *Bermuda* departed Nassau 24 June and returned from Abaco 28 June, *RG*, 26, 29 June 1816; *La Rosa* cargo seized, *RG*, 29 June 1816 and Pakenham to Cameron 28 June 1816 in Cameron to Bathurst 12 July 1816, CO 23/63, f. 201.

42. Nassau residents to Council, copy of minutes, 29 June 1816 in Cameron to Bathurst, 12 July 1816, CO 23/63, f. 206; Wylly to Cameron, 15 July and 29 October 1816, CO 23/63, ff. 269 and 274.

43. *La Rosa's* stranded goods, *RG*, 3, 13, 31 July 1816; petition, *RG*, 6, 13 July 1816; Curry report, Mancanger, 1828, #127, CO 23/79, f. 175.

44. Resolution, *RG*, 13 July 1816; Prouche acquitted, *RG*, 3 August 1816; *La Rosa* slaves "condemned," *RG*, 11 September 1816.

45. *RG*, 14 September 1816.

46. Murray to Lord Bathurst, 16 September 1816, CO 23/63, ff. 360-362; Abaco apprentices, Duplicate List of slave apprentices from Customs Office 1811, CO 23/66, ff. 203-211; A. Murray to Lord Bathurst, 27 September 1816, CO 23/63, f. 348. A notice appeared in the *Royal Gazette*, 9 September 1830 reminding proprietors that the *La Rosa* indentures would expire on the 24th. Planters were required to produce the Africans at the Customs House in Nassau where, upon application, the Africans would receive certificates of freedom signed by the governor.

17: The High Road to Freedom

1. Wright, *History*, p. 433; Bates, p.345 and mentioned in Committee of Correspondence to Chalmers, 4 February 1817, CO 23/64, f. 118A.

2. George Chalmers, *The Representation of the House of Assembly of the Bahamas to the Right Honourable Earl of Bathurst, the Colonial Secretary of State Respecting Their Proceedings during Their Last Session 1816/17 with an Appendix of Documents* (London: printed by Luke Hansard and Sons [but not sold], 1817), CO 23/66, pp. 37, 2, 4, NA, (hereinafter cited as Chalmers, *HA, 1816/17*).

3. "Evil genius," CO 23/64, f. 116; William Wylly, *Regulations for the Government of Slaves at Clifton and Tusculum in New Providence* (Nassau: *Royal Gazette*, 15 July 1815), CO 23/67, ff. 153-160.

4. Wylly's answers, *VHA* (1812-1814), p. 32; Wylly to African Institution, 26 December 1815, CO 23/64, f. 232.

5. Wylly, Blacks in court and "declared white," *Laws of the Bahamas*, v. 1 (1729-1802) and Chalmers, *HA 1816/17*, pp. 37-38; Wylly's revision, CO 23/64, f. 230.

6. Chalmers, *HA 1716/17*, p. 42. According to contemporary accounts, the eloquent lawyer "Lewis Kerr," Speaker of the House in 1817, was thought to be Harman Blennerhasset who was noted for his treasonous association with alleged conspirator Aaron Burr. Blennerhasset disappeared soon after Burr's trial. He came to Nassau, practiced law and married a Miss McPherson. In 1809, an American schooner arrived at Nassau from South America and a beautiful and accomplished lady of high society inquired after Mr. Blennerhasset. By accident she discovered Mr. Kerr, who was in fact her husband. He prevailed upon her not to reveal his true identity and she went back to America. A contemporary writer hinted that "Mr. K.," Speaker of the House, was the notorious Mr. Blennerhasset, but on the whole his friends guarded his secret. Adala Del Lorraine, *Miss Hart's Letters from the Bahama Islands written in 1833-34* (Nassau, Bahamas, n.p., 1827, rpt., 1948), letter XI, pp. 57-58; Stark, pp. 183-185.

7. Wylly affidavit, 27 January 1817, CO 23/64, ff. 87-91: also in Chalmers, *HA 1716/17*, pp. 44-46.

8. Chalmers, *HA 1716/17*, p. 47, 42.

9. **CO 23/64**, f. 63A and Chalmers *HA 1716/17*, p. 47.

10. Results of the close of session, Committee, of Correspondence to Chalmers, CO 23/64, f. 115A; Wylly horse-whipped, CO 23/64, f. 64; private quarrel, CO 23/64, f. 118; summary of documents relative to the Wylly affair: Wylly's answers to the slave bill questionnaire, 28 December 1815, CO 23/64, ff. 229-232; Office of Correspondence to George Chalmers, Nassau, 4 February 1817, CO 23/64, ff. 112-119; Chalmers *HA 1716/17*, CO 23/66, ff. 59-84.
11. "Drunk from Vanity," Chalmers *HA 1716/17*, p. 6; court battle, *RG*, 8 February, 19 April, 7 May 1817; Wylly refutation, *RG*, 18 July 1818.
12. *RG*, 25 July 1818; *RG*, 19 August 1818. The sixteen surnames are: Addams, Albury, Bartlum, Bethell, Curry, Johnson, Lowe, Melone, Pinder, Roberts, Sands, Saunders, Sawyer, Sweeting, Tedder, Weatherford.
13. *RG*, 5 April 1828, p. 3 and Wylly Family History, Parrish, pp. 477-481.
14. Interim, *RG*, 20 January 1819; "Act to establish a Triennial Registry of Slaves," *VHA*, 27 March 1821, p. 15; J. M. Wright, *History*, p. 445; *Carolina, RG*, 14 March 1818; 101 wrecked American slaves, *RG*, 25 March 1818; wreck Hole in the Wall, *RG*, 24 March 1919; census, *RG*, 24 July 1819.
15. Armbrister, *RG*, 13, 17, 24 June 1818; "A Bahamian Tragedy," in *Bahamas Handbook* (Nassau: Etienne Dupuch, Jr. Publications, 1974), pp. 15-25.
16. *RG*, 25 August 1821. Reverend John Turtle of the Wesleyan Methodist Society died at Turks Island 16 August 1825 "after a long and severe illness." *RG*, 1 October 1825.
17. *VHA*, 17 October 1822, pp. 13-15.
18. *Mary, RG*, 5 October 1822; *Iphigenia, RG*, 7 September 1822, p. 3.
19. *RG*, 5 June 1819.
20. *Cicero, RG*, 10 June 1818; *Horizon, RG*, 2 December 1818; *George Washington, RG*, 25 August 1819.
21. *Success, RG*, 19 June 1819. This advertisement also requested interested parties to apply to Richardson Saunders for terms. Richardson died at Abaco 11 November 1822 after a nine month illness. He was a forty-seven year old Nassau merchant who left a large family. *RG*, 16 November 1822; *Rebecca, RG*, 13 March 1822; Russell to the rescue, *RG*, 11 October 1823.
22. Martin Weatherford's will dated 28 July 1800 in "Wills 1790-1806," p. 304, NA.
23. *RG*, 17, 28 April, 5, 22 May, and 21 August 1824.
24. *RG*, 30 January 1828.
25. Governour Smyth's report on the state of the Bahama Islands, 17 September 1832, #178, "Governour's Dispatches 1832-1834," NA, (hereinafter cited as Gov. D.).
26. *RG*, 27 October 1827 and 2 February 1828.
27. *RG*, 1 September 1830.
28. Weather: a tornado, *RG*, 19 November 1825; severe gale at Abaco, *RG*, 8 October 1825; wrecks caused by storms, *RG*, 31 March 1827; wrecks at Hole in the Wall, *RG*, 27 May, 18 November 1826; a Dutch brig wrecked at Abaco, *RG* 28 July and 1 August 1827; De Mayne and *Clio, RG*, 3 January 1827; Blount's Nautical Book, *RG*, 15 June 1825, p. 3; *Plato, RG*, 8 December 1827, p. 3.
29. Gov. D. *1818-1825*, pp. 905, 906, 931, 1057, 1061 and *RG*, 23 September 1826.
30. *Abaco, RG*, 17 February 1830; wrecking regulations, Gov. D. 1829-1830, Smith, 12 December 1829, #4, pp. 20-25.
31. *Carpenter's Revenge, RG*, 11 February 1832. The *Carpenter's Revenge* was sold in 1833 for $406.50 after Gideon Lowe's death that same year. A document dated 28 October 183[3], Green Turtle Cay, concerning the division of money from the sale of the vessel appears in William Lowe's Ledger, Monroe County Public Library, Key West; *Hannah V, RG*, 25 August 1832; wreck of fifty-three emigrants, *RG*, 12, 22 December 1832 and Gov. D. 1832-1834, Carmichael-Smyth, 1 February 1833, #8, pp. 26-27.
32. "Slave Register," 1825, v. 1, n.p., return #22. Gideon Lowe died at Green Turtle Cay before 6 July 1833, the date his will was proved. The will was written [8?] January 1832 and was registered in Book "C4" (pages 31-33) in 1838. His wife Nancy Saunders is named, but the names of his children are obliterated in the old and torn document. William Lowe, John Roberts, and Martha Lowe were named executors. The estate notice in the *Gazette* was dated 16 September 1833 and signed by William Lowe, (*RG*, 5 October 1833). The oldest son, Benjamin, could not write and probably for that reason Gideon left his affairs in the hands of William. Benjamin had made his mark on the sworn statement in the 1825 "Slave Register." Gideon also made his mark on his will. According to William Lowe's ledger, two-thirds of the proceeds from the *Carpenter's Revenge* was shared equally among ten children listed: sons: William (executor), John, James, Benjamin and Mathew and daughters, no first names given, but married to John Roberts (Executor), William Sweeting, Benjamin Roberts, Randal Adams, B. John Roberts, and Benjamin Roberts. Martha Lowe, the third executor, could have been Gideon's sister. According to family tradition, two brothers, Gideon and probably Mathew, were shipwrecked on Bermuda and emigrated from there to the Bahamas, (Harllee, 2:1794-95). Joseph Loe emigrated to Bermuda in 1635, (Lefroy, 1:689). In 1664, John Loe and his wife of the Sandis tribe were fined for constantly absenting themselves from church "more out of slothfulness," than any acceptable reason, (Lefroy, 2:215; see also Julia E. Mercer, *Bermuda Settlers of the 17th Century: Genealogical Notes from Bermuda* (Baltimore: Genealogical Publishing Co. Inc., 1982).
Mathew Lowe, the would-be pirate of Harbour Island, was in the Bahamas in 1715. There was a Gideon, a Mathew, a Samuel and a John on the 1731 census for New Providence, together with a Mathew, a Gideon and a Martha at Eleuthera. The Gideon Lowe mentioned here was probably the same man who had aided Deveaux in the recovery of the Bahamas in 1783 and received the Dunmore grant for a town lot in Harbour Island in 1791. William Lowe emigrated to Key West in the 1840s. Artist Alton Lowe is descended from James Lowe. Harold and Floyd Lowe are descended from John Lowe.
33. African indentures, *RG*, 29 June 1825, Gov. D. 1818-1825, Grant to Bathurst, 5 May 1825 and *RG*, 8 September

1827; Africans on Out Islands, Munnings' Report on the State and Condition of the Liberated Africans, CO 23/79, f. 15A.

34. 160 American slaves rescued and brought to Nassau, *RG*, 12 January 1831, p. 3; petition, *VHA*, 14 and 18 January 1831, p. 40; *RG*, 15 January 1831.

35. At Hog Island, Gov. D. 1830-1831. Smyth to Bathurst, 31 January 1831, #78, pp. 46-47 and *RG*, 19 January 1831; investigation proceedings, JHA, 27 January 1831, pp. 38-39 and *RG*, 5 February 1831, p. 3.

36. Gov. D. 1829-1831, Smyth, 10 April 1830, pp. 498-499.

37. JHA, pp. 38-39 and *RG*, 5 February 1831, p. 3. Some of the land masses in the Bahamas designated islands are actually smaller than some cays.

38. Court ruling, *RG*, 13 February 1831; American agents, Gov. D. April-August 1831, Smyth to Goderich, 11 August 1831.

39. Thomas Brown Wylly finds paper, Gov. D. 1829-1831. Munnings to Foster, 19 February 1831, p. 989; judgement of Robinson and Gifford, Gov. D. 1830-1831, Smyth, 5 March 1831, #84, pp. 62-70 and CO 23/84, f. 67A.

40. *Comet* slaves freed and price of rescue, Gov. D. 1830-1831, pp. 65-66; "quiet and industrious," Gov. D. 1832-1834. Smyth to Goderich, 5 February 1832, pp. 62-63.

41. Smyth enforces slave code, J. M. Wright, *History*, p. 446. Another comprehensive work on slavery in the Bahamas is a dissertation by Gail Saunders, NA; villages, Gov. D. 1832-1834, p. 69; elevate Whites, J. M. Wright, *History*, pp. 479, 473 and Bates, pp. 361-362; reforms led to abolition, J. M. Wright, *History*, p. 441.

42. Gov. D. 1829-1831, 6 May 1830, pp. 519-525 and J. M. Wright, *History*, pp. 459, 458.

43. *Perseverance*, Gov. D., 31 January 1831, pp. 48-54; House disagrees, J. M. Wright, *History*, p. 458. There is a letter to the editor regarding the flogging of female slaves in *RG*, 18 April 1831.

44. Gov. D. 1829-1831, Smyth to Goderich, 23 June 1831, pp. 1105-1113; *VHA* (1828-1831), pp. 79, 95.

45. W. E. Armbrister, "A Short History of the Bahamas of Recent Date," Sandra Riley, transcriber, copy of original in NA and Historical Association of Southern Florida in Miami. The original document in the Nassau Archives was donated by Mrs. Frances Armbrister, mother of Tony Armbrister, who is the grandson of W. E. Armbrister and great grandson of John Armbrister, South Carolina Loyalist and brother of James Armbrister, Registrar of Slaves. The Honourable William Edward Armbrister served as a member of the House of Assembly in the Bahamas for over twenty years. Sandra Riley, "W. E. Armbrister's Loyalist Heritage," *Journal of the Bahamas Historical Society*, 2 (October 1980): 3-10.

46. J. M. Wright, *History*, pp. 468-469.

18: "Free at Last"

1. Ormond J. McDonald, *A Relic of Slavery: Farquharson's Journal for 1831-1832*, intro., Deans Peggs, preface, Ormond J. McDonald (Nassau, Bahamas: Deans Peggs Research Fund, 1957), pp. 44, 37, (hereinafter cited as *FJ*).

2. Plantation structures, *FJ*, Peggs intro., p. xi; jail, McDonald preface, p. xiii. Farquharson planted what he called one-one cotton, meaning he planted one bush here and one bush there, *FJ*, p. 2.

3. Ben Storr's funeral, *FJ*, p. 80; wreck of the *Enterprise*, *RG*, 24 March 1832; *FJ*, pp. 55-57.

4. When Charles Farquharson died at age seventy-five on 16 March 1835, the *Gazette* eulogized him as a "kind, hospitable, and honest man, *RG*, 4 April 1835; the author with the help of Elmore Nairn and Oliver Black rediscovered Farquharson's grave, Riley, "Journal III (1973-1979);" *Farquharson's Journal*, McDonald, preface, p. xiii and Peggs intro., p. viii.

5. Alexander Farquharson, "Colonial Plats," v. 6, p. 326, SCA; John Farquharson, "American Loyalist Transcripts." South Carolina Claimants, v. 53, p. 566; will James Farquharson, "Charleston County Wills 1780-1783," v. 19, pp. 52-54, SCA; Charles Farquharson's will, ORG, "C4," pp. 74-75; William Farquharson died in the wreck of the *Eleanor*, *RG*, 29 May, 9 June 1824. As a result of that same wreck John Armbrister, Jr., of Cat Island, half brother of W. E. Armbrister, was rescued by a Spanish brig after spending seventeen days on a small deserted cay.

6. *FJ*, 20-21 February 1832, pp. 50-52.

7. *FJ*, pp. 57, 62.

8. Gov. D. 1832-1834, Smyth, 4 May 1832, p. 127 and Memorandum, 1 May 1832, pp. 137-139.

9. *FJ*, p. 64. Another one of Alick's wives, Lisey, is mentioned on p. 51.

10. Gov. D. 1832-1834, Balfour to Stanley, 4 September 1833, #36 and *RG*, 8 August 1833.

11. Peters, p. 39.

12. Stout murdered, *RG*, 2 March 1808; Mary Stout's death, Peters, p. 72.

13. Estate appraisal Mary Stout, Book "Z," pp. 168-169; Tom Williams, Riley "Journal III" (1977), p. 77. James Thompson, Jr., wrote his master's thesis on the Burton Williams family for Hillsdale College, Michigan, 1982, copy in NA. His father James Maxwell Thompson, Sr., Nassau attorney, is the son of Maxwell James Thompson, O.B.E., retired judge of the Bahamas Circuit court who married Hazel Williams, direct descendant of loyalist Burton Williams.

14. Ianthe Bond Hebel, "Four Williams Families" (Daytona Beach, Florida, n.d.), p. 1; Robert O. DeMond, *The Loyalists in North Carolina During the Revolution* (Durham, N.C.: Duke University Press, 1940), p. 73; Caroline Garvin Chapelle, "Recollections," Georgia Historical Society Library, Savannah, genealogical chart.

15. Burton's forty acre grant, #351, CO 23/30, f. 221A. Burton's original forty acre grant underwent the process of escheat in 1834 for nonpayment of quit rent, *RG*, 25 January 1834, p. 3; Williams' grants located on Watling's Island, Samuel #331, Henry #330 (160 acres) and #332 (400 acres), CO 23/30, f. 221; Siebert, 2:367.

16. Samuel to New Smyrna, Victoria Margaret Williams Smith, "Oral History: Williams Family," 14 February 1917, p. 1; B. W. married Jane Hartley, "CC Mar. Reg. 1789-1803," Book 2, p. 91; indenture Muir/Williams, lease 1 September and release 2 September 1804, Book ?, pp. 174-175; Burton member for Eleuthera, *RG*, 1 October 1808.
17. *RG*, 16 March, 10 April, 3 September 1814.
18. Burton Williams elected for Abaco, *RG*, 27 December 1820. Later, John Irving was elected for Abaco in the place of Burton Williams "whose seat had been declared vacant" after an absence of twelve months. *VHA*, 15 October 1822, p. 46; departure of the *Midas*, "Slave Register" 1821-1822; to Trinidad, Peters, p. 163 and Eric Williams, compiler and ed., *Documents on British West Indian History 1807-1833* (Trinidad, B.W.I.: Trinidad Publishing Co. Ltd., 1952), p. 276.
19. Wife's death, *RG*, 14 December 1822; son's marriage, *RG*, 4 July 1827. Gloster is a name which has passed down in the Williams family for generations; snuff box, Chapelle, p. 1. There is a photograph of this snuff box in the Parrish Collection, but Mrs. Parrish did not identify the location of the heirloom. Maxfield Parrish, Jr., gave his mother's collection of photographs to Dr. Peters who has donated it to the ALM.
20. Williams return, a customs document dated 1836 showing 173 Blacks returning to the Bahamas is glued to the index in front of the "Slave Register" 1821-1822; Gov. D. 1832-1834, Smyth letter located between #63 and #64. On 17 December 1833 Stephen Dillet was elected to the House to represent the town of Nassau. Dillet, the first black man to sit in the Assembly, appears on a "Petition of Coloured Inhabitants" to Smyth, 1 July 1831, CO 23/84, f. 240. The first meeting of this General Assembly was held 15 February 1834. *Bahamas Election Book 1808-1868*.
21. In 1835, only eighty Blacks were listed as apprenticed to Burton Williams. *RG*, 6 May 1835, p. 4; will, "N4", pp. 113-115, 119, 131; Parrish, p. 49; Peters, p. 188.
22. Interview with Joseph Albury, now deceased, San Salvador Island, October 1973. Elmore Nairn said that they actually dug up Burton's grave and put Father Chrysostom in with him. Interview with Elmore Nairn, San Salvador, 1 April 1979 in Riley, "Journal III," p. 100. Both Mr. Albury and Mr. Nairn believed the smaller grave next to Father Chrysostom's tomb was that of Mrs. Burton Williams. Since Jane Hartley died in Trinidad, this can hardly be she. This fact also casts suspicion on the identity of the man lying in the ground with Father Chrysostom. He may be Burton Williams, the grandson of the elder loyalist Burton who bequeathed to his namesake his gold watch. The woman in the smaller grave could be *his* wife.
23. Hebel, p. 2.
24. House of Commons bills passed 7 August 1833, *RG*, 12 October 1833; proclamation by William IV, brother of George IV, *RG*, 30 October 1833; in Nassau, J. M. Wright, *History*, p. 492.
25. Apprentice classification, Emancipation Act, *RG*, 6 November 1833; see slave classification lists for Abaco, *RG*, 18, 21, 25 March 1835; work agreements, J. M. Wright, *History*, pp. 495-498; Abaco cottages, Magistrate's half year CO 23/113, f. 291.
26. Compensation, *RG*, 6 November 1833; petition, Gov. D. 1835-1836, pp. 546-560 with signatures; see also "Slave Compensation Lists" (eleven in all) which name the proprietors and number of slaves "for whom compensation is claimed," *RG*, 30 August, 6, 13, 20 September, 1, 8, 15, 22, 29 October, 26 November, 31 December 1834; special justices, Abaco, Benjamin Russel was reimbursed by the Assembly £1.4.0 for a pair of stocks for Abaco, *VHA*, 6 March 1835, p. 108. Population in Abaco for the year 1834 was 921. "Blue Book."
27. Special Justices' Report, Abaco May 1835 visitation by McLean and Munro, *RG*, 11 July 1835. According to Mr. Harold Lowe, the black settlement at New Plymouth ran from Mission Street to the steps of the school. Their turtle pond was Black Sound; jail at Green Turtle, *RG*, 11 July 1835; Archer, *Blue Book 1836*, pp. 114, 116; petition by apprentices at Green Turtle Cay, 4 April 1837, CO 23/102, f. 191. Asterisk by name indicates a manumitted apprentice; all others were apprentices: Nathaniel Adams, Thomas Brown, Richard Clear, Morris Cornish*, Charles Curry*, James Curry, Sr.* and Jr.*, Mathew Curry*, Thomas Holmes*, David Lowe, Jacob Lowe*, Thomas Lowe, Richard Russell*, Stephen Russell, Thomas Russell*, Richard Saunders, Richard Sawyer, Issac Sweeting*, John Webster.
28. Colebrook to Glenelg, 11 March 1836, CO 23/96, f. 225. One wonders what the governour meant by recent. The town was well established in 1815 when the Methodist missionary visited.
29. Gov. D. 1835-1836, Colebrook, 28 July 1836, pp. 1353-1354.
30. Lamotte, Gov. D. 1832-1834, Balfour to Stanley, 23 July 1833, #22 and Balfour, 15 March 1834, #82.
31. *RG*, 13 February 1834.
32. CO 23/92, ff. 246, 249, 255.
33. Return to America; *Hamlet*, III, i and Gov. D. 1832-1834. Balfour, 18 February 1834, #76; England must pay compensation, Gov. D. 1832-1834, Balfour to Stanley, 17 March 1834, #83. John Bull is an English political allegorical character created by John Arbuthnot, Tory satirist. One of his pamphlets, *John Bull in His Senses: Being the Second Part of Law Is a Bottomless Pit* was printed in London in 1712. See Alan W. Bower and Robert A. Erickson, eds., *John Arbuthnot's, The History of John Bull* (Oxford: Clarendon Press, 1976).
34. Reprint from the *Quarterly Review*, *RG*, 30 March 1836.
35. Gov. D. 1835-1836, Cockburn, 4 July 1838, p. 1272 and return of Africans wrecked on Cherokee Sound, signed 3 August 1838, f. 1278; Wright, *History*, pp. 518, 526.
36. Wright, *History*, p. 528.
37. Major McGregor, Gov. D. 1839-1842, Cockburn to Russell, 4 February 1841 and Cockburn 1 February 1842, p. 1429; J. M. Wright, *History*, pp. 563-564; petition, Gov. D. 1843-1846, Mathew to Stanley, 10 April 1845, pp. 1167-1170; CO 23/120, f. 100-102.
38. Limited emigration, J. M. Wright, *History*, p. 565; leaving Abaco, Colebrook to Glenelg, 9 July 1835, CO 23/93, f. 442; *Charlotte*, *RG*, 1 February 1834; "Blue Book," Abaco population 921 in 1834, p. 118 and 848 in 1836, pp. 166-167.

39. Gov. D. 1832-1834. Balfour, 19 February 1834, #78, p. 2; Abaco exported turtle and some shells. In 1849, the *Delight*, Lowe, arrived in Nassau with a cargo of sponge, *Nassau Guardian*, 22 December 1849. In 1847, Abaco supplied the city of Bridgetown, Barbados, with firewood. The wood was loaded at Abaco at £0.8.4 and sold at Barbados for between £2 and £3. Vessels returned from Barbados with cargoes of rum and molasses which found a good market in the Bahamas, Gov. D. 1847, C. R. Nesbitt to Grey, 7 August 1847, pp. 507, 571. See also public revenue schedule in *Nassau Guardian*, 3 November 1849 and revenue from Out Islands in *Bahama Herald*, 15 March 1850; oranges, *Nassau Guardian*, 17 October 1849, p. 2. In 1834, Abaco exported 23,625 dozen oranges and limes, "Blue Book 1834," p. 152. "China oranges lately shipped from Abaco to Charleston realized from £2.3.6 to £5.4.2 per thousand." A public meeting was held at Green Turtle Cay 19 November 1849 to formulate an address to the governor from the Abaco orange growers. *Nassau Guardian*, 24 November 1849, p. 2.
40. CO 23/128, f. 198. "Blue Book 1849" population pp. 132-133. House of Assembly for Abaco: C. R. Nesbitt, Colonial Secretary, J. G. Anderson, Receiver General and J. B. Farrington; Clyde, *Bahama Herald*, 29 May 1850, p. 3; on 27 April 1841 at Green Turtle Cay seventy-three leading inhabitants *signed* their names to a document recommending John Parvost Baldwin for an appointment as Her Majesty's Consul at Key West, CO 23/110, f. 351. The population of Green Turtle Cay in 1849 was 792. Chambers Report to SPG, 12 January 1849, p. 1, SPG, copy furnished by Father Irwin McSweeney; address of New Plymouth inhabitants, *Nassau Guardian*, 22 August 1849.
41. The base of the lighthouse at Hole in the Wall is eighty feet above high water and the tower another eighty feet high. The light revolves "once in every minute and may be seen in all directions except where the high parts of the Island intervene," *RG*, 21 December 1836, p. 4; two thousand ships, Gov. D. 1847, Nesbitt to Grey, 11 December 1847, enclosure, p. 968; American transport, Gov. D., Nesbitt to Grey, 4 November 1847, p. 820 and 7 August 1847. pp. 573-574.
42. Current wrecking regulations, Gov. D. 1847, pp. 573-574; too strong dependence, Magistrate's half year report 1842, CO 23/113, ff. 282, 291 and Gov. D., Cockburn, 22 October 1838, pp. 1506-1509; Gov. D., Mathew, speech to HA, 1 February 1848, #15, pp. 5-6; Gregory address to New Plymouth inhabitants, *Nassau Guardian*, 15 December 1849. Benjamin Curry, J.P., was one of the 139 persons who signed the New Plymouth address on the governour's arrival. He also signed a petition to Governor Gregory asking that small vessels be exempt from pilotage and harbour fees at Nassau. *Nassau Guardian*, 21 March 1849.
43. Demoralizing effect of wrecking and stone chapel at Green Turtle Cay, notes from "District meeting Abaco," book misplaced, Turton House, Nassau, and Betteridge, pp. 15-16; church held seven hundred people, Mr. Sweeney's visitation and state of the Bahama Islands, USPG, Reel 3; Baptists in Abaco, CO 23/113, f. 290; first Anglican church, Green Turtle Cay, *Nassau Quarterly*, 25 (December 1910), p. 88. Turton House, the residence of the Methodist chairman, Windsor Avanue, Nassau, is an important genealogical depository. The records of persons baptized, married or buried in Methodist churches throughout the Bahamas prior to 1850 are kept there.
44. *RG*, 19 April 1837; official report, Gov. D. 1835-1836 and number of voters, pp. 774-775.
45. J. M. Wright, *History*, p. 567; Gov. D. 1848, Mathew, 28 September 1848, letter just before #69.
46. Abaconian prejudice, Bayley to Duke of Newcastle, 25 April 1860, CO 23/162, ff. 264-265; Report of Governor Gregory accompanying the "Blue Book 1849," CO 23/135, f. 123.
47. Trew to SPG, 12 January 1848, pp. 3-4A, original in London at the SPG, copy furnished by Reverend Irwin McSweeney.
48. Trew on seating at Methodist chapel, 12 January 1848, p. 2A; Methodist ruling on seating and Annear, Turton House District Meeting Book, Abaco notes and Betteridge, p. 14; "angry disputation" Trew, 12 January 1848, p. 3; Bayley, CO 23/162, f. 266.
49. Lowe Ledger; sale of land to Thompson, ORG, Book "L4," pp. 338-341; Bartlum House moved to Key West, "Historic American Buildings Survey Report" prepared by Betty Bruce, Historic Research Committee Old Island Restoration Foundation Inc., Key West, Florida, 18 June 1965; insurrection at Green Turtle Cay, *Pensacola Gazette* 2 January 1847, p. 2.
50. Trew, 12 January 1848, pp. 5A-6; Chambers Report to SPG, February, 1848.

Appendix A: A list of surnames appearing on a "List of Baptisms, Marriages, and Burials in Ye Government of His Excellency Governour Phenney since his arrival November 13th, 1721 to this present year 1726."

Adams
Albury §
Alden
Allen
Artereal
Austen
Aynard

Babb
Baillis
Barbarx
Barker
Barnet (Barnett)
Beak
Behn
Bellon (Bellown)
Bennet
Bethel
Bill
Blake
Blay
Bloom
Bloucher
Bossard
Bourne
Bowen
Bradwell
Brooks
Brown
Buckley
Bullard
Bullock
Bunch

Capehort
Carey
Carr
Carter
Cash*
Caton
Charler
Clapp
Clapshaw
Cockrem
Collison
Comber
Comer
Connor
Constable
Cornish
Coverly*
Cox §
Crafton

Crawlin
Cray
Criswell
Croskin
Current
Curtis
Curry*

Darvil
Davis
Day
Dolrampl
Dorset*

Edwards
Evans

Fairfax
Fisher
Flemming
Force*
Fox
French
Frith
Fulford

Gale
Gething*
Gibbon(Gibbons)
Gorden
Green
Gridley
Griffin*

Hale §
Hall
Hain
Ham
Hardy
Harper
Harvey
Hawks
Herring
Hinkley
Hooper
Hotham
Howell
Hunnee
Hunter

Ingham
Inkley
Innes

Jeans
Jemizon
Johnson
Junes [Jones]

Kembling (Kimbling)
Kemp
King
Knight
Knowles

Lawford
Legget
Lintratt (Liptratt)
Lockinger
Londen (Louden)
Long
Low
Lyford

McKenzie
McKinney
McManus
Maylock
Miller
Mills
Mauley
Morton
Mourley
Moxey
Moyor

Norris
Nubal

Paddock
Palson
Peale
Pearce
Peltro
Penchand (Penzhand)
Pennell
Petty
Phileze
Pindar*
Prior
Pye*

Raddon
Raundell
Reston
Reynolds
Roberts*

Rogers
Rounsenel
Rowen

Sans [Sands]
Saunders*
Sawkins
Sawyer
Scadding
Scot
Spatches (Spatchers)
Spencer
Simonet
Sims
Shock
Shipton
Smith
Somershall
Spikeman
Steel
Stirrup
Stroud
Sweeting*

Tabor
Tate
Taylor
Tedder
Thomas*
Thompson*
Todd
Truefoot
Turner

Veasic
Vere

Wadworth
Walker
Walling
Waters
Watkins*
Welsh
White
Whitehead
Williams
Wishart (Wizhart)
Wood
Wright

§   Name appears on either the Harbour Island "Force" document or the "Fort Petition" *only*.

*   Name *also* appears on either or both of the aforementioned documents.

Appendix B: Woodes Rogers' Census [1731]
Book "C" Census [about 1740] (names in italics)

NASSAU, NEW PROVIDENCE

Albury
Albury
Anderson
Anderson

Baddon
Barnett
Barnett
Barone
Beane
Beasey
Belle
Belone
Beloon
Bennet
Berk
Besey
Bickman
Bill
Bill
Blay
Blay
Borouse
Bowen
Bradwell
Brazeel
Brooks
Brown
Bullard
Bullock
Bullock
Bunch
Burrum
Butler

Carey
Charles
Colebroke
Comber
Commer
Constable
Coverly
Cox
Cox
Cullimore
Cullimore
Cumber
Current
Current
Currie
Curtis
Curtis

Darvil
Darvill
Darville
Dowley
Demerrit
Dickens
Dickerson

Dormham
Dorsett
Downham
Driscoll
Driscoll
Duncombe

Edwards
Elding
Evans
Evans
Eyres

Fernando
Fife
Fisher
Fisher
Fitzgherald
Forester
Fowles
Fox
Fox
Frazer
Frith
Frith

Gardner
Gascoign
Gibbons
Gibson
Goudet
Graham
Graham
Griffin
Griffin

Hale
Hale
Hall
Hall
Harper
Harriott
Harris
Hatchett
Higgingbotham
Higgs
Hill
Howell
Hudson
Huggins
Hunter
Huntington

Innes
Irving

Jackson
Jackson
Jenners
Jennings

Johnson
Johnston
Jones

Kemp
Keown
Keown
King
Knight
Knowles

La Fountaine
Lauxy
Lawden
Lawford
Leafe
Leggett
Lemmon
Lemon
Lightwood
Limberlin
Lincoln
Lorey
Loverly
Lowden
Lowe
Lusher

March
Marshall
Mathews
Mawley

McKennie
McKenny
McKenzie
Meredith
Meyers
Miners
Minors
Mitchell
Morley
Morton
Morton
Mottes
Mounsey
Moxey

Neuman
Newton
Noules
Nusum

Oliver

Penshaw
Perkins
Petty
Phenney
Pichard

Pierce
Pindar
Pinder
Powell
Puissant
Purkiss
Purselle
Pye
Pyfrom

Reading
Redwood
Richardson
Rivers
Roberts
Roberts
Rogers
Ross
Rowland
Russell

Sands
Saunders
Saunders
Scott
Seares
Simonett
Simons
Simpson
Sims
Sims
Skinner
Skinner
Smith
Smith
Smithson
Spachers
Spencer
Spratches
Steward
Stowe
Stroud
Strowd
Supplee
Swearim
Sweeting
Sweeting
Symonds

Tedel
Thompson
Thompson
Todd
Turnley

Varner
Vaughan

Walker
Walker

Watkins
Watkins
Wells
Whitehead
Whitehead
Williams
Wright
Wright
Wrighton
Wyatt

Yates
Yerworth
Young
Young

ELEUTHERA   *indicates Harbour
Island 1731

Beak
Been
Bethel
Bethell
Bradwell
Bra'well
Bullard
Bullard

Cambell
Carey
Carey
Cash*
Champion
Carlow
Charlow
*Clare**
Colmer
Comber
Conner*
Coverly*
Crowley*
Curry*

Dickenson
Dorsett

Evans

Force*

Gladden
Griffin*

Havill*

Ingham
Ingraham

Johnson

Kemp
Kemp
Knowles

Le Comber
Loverly
Low
Lowe

Maycock*

Newbold
Newbold
Nouls

Oenshaw
Oliver

Pindar

Roberts*
Rowland
Russell*

Sands
Sands
Saunders*
Sawyer
Shower
Soyer
Smith
Spencer
*Sweeting**

*Tedder**
*Thompson**
Thone

Watkins
Weatherly
Weaverly

Appendix C: Curry Family Genealogy

Tradition maintains that Joseph Curry emigrated from Scotland to South Carolina. His father was probably a lowland farmer and because of the proximity of the English border, considered to be as much English as Scottish. Joseph may have first emigrated to the Ulster region of northern Ireland with his father, for he displays through the actions of his life in Carolina many of the best attributes of an Ulster-Scot: proud, persistent, ambitious, resourceful, aggressive, litigious, tough, and thrifty. These people had a passion for education, were not intellectual but intelligent, and could make anything grow in the ground.

Joseph Curry and his wife Jane Walker, an Irishwoman, settled in the Carolina backcountry about 1748.[1] Their union produced Joseph (father of Benjamin Curry of Green Turtle Cay, Abaco), William, John, Robert, Richard, Stephen and Hannah.[2] The Irish mix may account for the charming sense of humour and good looks found in the Currys of today.

He first settled on the Broad River, then moved to the Congarees where Joseph on land of his own chopped a homestead out of the savage wilderness. In 1756 he was appointed deputy surveyor of Craven County and in two years he ran over one hundred surveys.[3] By 1761, when Curry had acquired almost 1,200 acres and had earned his status as one of the backcountry's leading men, he was appointed magistrate.

During the Regulator trouble Curry was accused of consorting with criminals. The allegation struck deep, causing Curry to publish a statement rebutting the "scandalous reports" against himself. In the *Country Journal*, Curry recalled how in October, 1767, forty Regulators assembled at his house and "frightened my wife and family into terrors." He denied taking bribes from criminals and reminded his accusers that he had committed forty-two horse thieves to the jail.

Moses Kirkland published a sarcastic and lengthy reply in the *Gazette*. Kirkland pointed out that only five men had actually appeared at Mr. Curry's house, and of the forty-two horse thieves Curry claimed to have apprehended, only one had ever been convicted. Proceeding with his narrative, Kirkland related a wonderful story. Curry had gone to the home of Thomas Woodward and expressed a desire to join the Regulators. He even offered to try to persuade his regiment to join. Curry promised to swear to an oath, but told Woodward that it must appear as if he had been coerced into so doing. Woodward asked, "Swear? Swear to what?" Colonel Curry then presented Woodward with a paper he had prepared for the Regulators to administer to him. The document, reprinted in full in the *Country Journal*, contains eight oaths, written in colourful and somewhat legalistic fashion and prefaced by a letter extolling the many virtues of Colonel Joseph Curry, Esquire, who was addressed "Worshipfull Sir." After Curry signed the paper, Kirkland said Curry gave out the report that the Regulators had kept him prisoner for three days, refusing him food or drink until he signed the Regulator Oath.[4]

In September, 1768, illness and bad debts caused Joseph Curry to sign over a power of attorney to his wife. Jane Curry sold 250 acres in Craven County in February, 1775, and since the Release did not acknowledge her as "Sole Trader" Joseph Curry was presumed dead.[5]

The Revolutionary War loyalties of this Carolina branch of the Curry family and their connection with the Bahamas *may* be indicated through a discussion of the children of Colonel Joseph and subsequent Joseph Currys. This analysis is based on Colonel Harllee's extensive genealogical research on this and related families. Since no documented evidence of marriages, births, and baptisms exists, Harllee's theory can be supported only by the living memory of descendants of the Curry family on Green Turtle Cay and elsewhere who wrote to Harllee in the early 1930s; unfortunately, none of their letters have survived.

The 1721 List of Baptisms and the 1731 and Book "C" censuses show Currys in the Bahamas that early. Therefore, it can not be "safely concluded that all Currys whose records appear after 1786 [in the Bahamas] were the Curry refugees from South Carolina and their descendants," as Harllee maintained.[6]

Some time during or after the Revolutionary War, Joseph Curry (33) and his wife Rachel, who *may* have been a Weatherford,[7] moved to Harbour Island. By 1791 this Joseph *may* have been dead in that Rachel Curry received Lot #138 in Dunmore Town,[8] possibly as a result of her loyalty to the Crown during the late war. Other Carolina Curry brothers may have been divided in loyalties.

Stephen, the youngest son of Joseph (333), stayed in the backcountry with his mother Jane and sister Hannah. In May 1785, the United States paid him £3.17.8½ for one stack of corn and other provisions he supplied to the Continental Army in 1781.[9] There is no evidence of Joseph's (33) son Benjamin (3303) or Richard Curry (33305) in the Carolinas. They may have already been in the Bahamas before or during the war.

There are others of the family to consider. A William Currie (33302?), native of Scotland and merchant of Charleston, presented a Loyalist claim.[10] Harllee believed that the John Curry who died at Harbour Island in 1791 was a wealthy merchant in Charleston in 1786; however that Harbour Island planter who bequeathed his property "on this island and elsewhere" could not write his name. There was a Loyalist John Curry who made a similar mark on an oath of allegiance in Charleston in 1781.[11] He may have been the Harbour Island planter, but he was not a merchant.

Colonel Joseph Curry's son John was a magistrate of Craven County in 1764.[12] Later he may have been a merchant or even an inventor who stayed in Charleston after the war; for on 1 April, 1789, John Curry of the city of Charleston deposited in the Secretary's office "a model of a machine for picking or Ginning cotton." Several John Currys served in North and South Carolina loyal regiments: a few privates and one corporal, a tailor, and a refugee.[13]

There was a grant made to Robert, Jane, and William Currie of three hundred acres on the north fork of the Tyger River in South Carolina,[14] and a Robert Curry was granted eighty-five acres in New Providence.[15] The state of South Carolina also paid a Robert Curry £19.10.0 for Continental Army pay and a lost rifle.[16]

Rachel and Joseph's (33) son Joseph (3301), born before 1761, who died in 1809, may have been the Captain Curry who fought with David Fanning in North Carolina. Rebels had been destroying Loyalist property in the area of Coxe's Mill. Fanning, with Captains Joseph Currie, Stephen Walker, and one other man, set out to retaliate. The tiny band of Loyalists burnt the houses of Captains Coxe and Golson, killing several people, until the rebels were forced to make peace. Fanning and his two captains formulated the terms and stated that if any articles were violated, their swords would be "continually unsheathed." Later the proverbial shoe was to be on the other foot. In March, captains Walker and Currie fell in with a party of rebels and fired until their ammunition was spent. They sent a Major Griffith to inform the rebel officer that they desired peace. Colonel Balfour answered that "there was no resting place for a Tory foot upon the earth," whereupon Griffith killed Balfour and destroyed his plantation. In April a Captain Edward Gun of the Continental Army wrote to Colonel Fanning, "I would recommend that you order Joseph Currie and Blair to return the widow Dixon's property which they robbed her of and I will not write to the Governour concerning it, as *you* want peace." (Emphasis added.)[17] This Captain Currie was in East Florida at the Peace where he received six months' pay[18] and may have been the one who joined Andrew Deveaux's expedition to rescue Nassau from the Spanish in 1783.[19]

In the Bahamas there was a Joseph Curry, probably (3301), who was a member of the House of Assembly for Harbour Island in 1784 and received two grants, one for 220 acres in Eleuthera and a lot in Dunmore Town in 1791, and was captain of the militia of the Bahamas at Harbour Island in 1801.[20] If it is true that character traits skip a generation, this Joseph Curry's altercation with the Reverend Mr. Gordon at Harbour Island in 1799 proves he had his grandfather's determination and flair.

Joseph Curry (3301) had definitely kept his contacts in Charleston. In 1806, the *Charleston Times* announced the death at Harbour Island of Patience Curry, wife of Joseph Curry.[21] The *Royal Gazette* in Nassau announced the death on the 4th of July, 1809, of Joseph Curry, Esquire, aged fifty-six, "on passage from Charleston to Harbour Island. "On the same day at Nassau an infant son of Mr. Joseph Curry, Jr., of this place and grandson of the above Joseph Curry, Sr., Esquire, also died."[22] Thus far everything fits the history of Harllee's Joseph Curry (3301) except the identity of Joseph (33011). According to the *Kinfolks* Joseph, Jr., who died in 1833, had no male children and his wife Lavinia had died in 1817. However, the Joseph Curry who died in 1833 *may* have been the widower of Love Curry, who died in the hurricane of August, 1813, and who did have an infant son, Robert Joseph Wadham, born 15 November 1808.[23] There is no will for Joseph Curry who died in 1833 to prove which Joseph Curry he was. There remains only a totally illegible letter of administration.[24]

A Joseph Curry (33011) was perhaps alive after 1809 and possessed in Florida and South Carolina, certain lands which he could have acquired only through connection with colonial American Currys.

In 1823 the Private Lands Committee of Congress confirmed title to land in Florida of Joseph

Curry, heir of Joseph Curry. The resolution was adapted 17 January 1823 by an act of Congress which also gave Joseph Curry "leave to withdraw." In May, 1818, Joseph Curry purchased for $19 from Stephen Curry, possibly his great-uncle, one hundred acres in the Orangeburg District of South Carolina. Five months later he sold this property to Andrew Wolfe for $370.[26]

Anyone named Curry in Miami, Key West, or the Bahamas who recognizes the foregoing enterprising qualities of the aforementioned Joseph Curry may claim him as an ancestor.

Notes

1. *Country Journal*, 18 April 1768, p. 1.
2. Harllee, *Kinfolks*, p. 1501. Along with numerous collaborators, Admiral Harllee spent years compiling the *Kinfolk* genealogies.
3. "South Carolina Miscellaneous Records, Vol. 83A, 1754-1758," p. 428, SCA; all the survey information was compiled from the South Carolina Department of Archives Alphabetical Index. Entries under Joseph Curry for plats recorded during the years 1756 and 1757 appear on pages 7174-7178, SCA. This computer index was not available to Admiral Harllee when he was researching his *Kinfolk* books.
4. *Country Journal*, 18 April 1768, p. 1.
5. Jane Curry designated "Sole Trader" 30 September 1768 Misc. Records vol. NN, pp. 403-405, SCA; Jane Curry sold to James Chestnut 250 acres in Craven County on 23, 24 February 1775, Harllee, *Kinfolks*, p. 1527.
6. Harllee, *Kinfolks*, p. 1504. In his letters Harllee admitted his difficulty in obtaining records from Nassau. When he read A.T. Bethell's *Early Settlers* in 1932 he realized that "it throws a whole flock of flies in the ointment" and that Bethell's research "makes it difficult for us to separate our line of Currys from the descendants of those who propagated there over a hundred years before our Currys arrived." Harllee to Sweeting, 25 November 1932, "Harllee Papers" #1550, 5 Boxes, Wilson Library, University of North Carolina, Chapel Hill. Harllee corresponded with Mr. Bethell and commented later in another letter that "Mr. A.T. Bethell appears to be a fraud." Harllee to Sweeting, 17 March 1933, "Harllee Papers," Folder 47. Mr. Bethell was in error at times but it was unwise of Mr. Harllee to discount all of Bethell's work and conclude that all the Curry records in the Bahamas after 1786 are those of the "South Carolina refugee Curry family and their descendants." Betty Bruce is a Curry descendant who has spent many years tracing the family line and is close to connecting the living descendants with the Currys who first appear on the Bahamas Records in 1721. Her findings when completed would throw serious doubt on Harllee's theory. The numbers in parenthesis are Harllee's designations.
7. Harllee to Sweeting and Condrick, 25 November 1932, "Harllee Papers," folder #42.
8. Lord Dunmore issued these grants to lots in Dunmore Town, Harbour Island, to Bahamian as well as American Loyalists. Harllee page 1531 assumes that Joseph (33) was dead because his Dunmore Town grant was issued to "his heirs and assigns" but this is not necessarily true. All the grants were issued in the name of the person and his or her "heirs and assigns." Grant #81 could have been issued to either Joseph (33) or Joseph (3301) or even to a descendant of an Old Inhabitant. ORG Book "R," pp. 433-442.
9. "Revolutionary Claims," #1701, SCA.
10. AO claims in "American Loyalist Transcripts," 56: 105-115, NYPL.
11. John Curry, Harbour Island Planter, made his mark to sign his will which was recorded 18 October 1792, ORG, Book "I," pp. 410-412, NA. A similar mark can be seen on an oath of allegiance to Great Britain by a John Curry of Charleston in 1781, South Carolina Oaths of Allegiance (1779-1782), p. 38, SCA.
12. *South Carolina Council Journal*, 34:33.
13. *South Carolina Historical and Genealogical Magazine* 9 (1908): 57; Clark, see vol. 1.
14. "Royal Grants," 20: 459 and Harllee *Kinfolks*, p. 1552.
15. 85 acre grant dated 15 December 1789, CO 23/30, f. 224, #577.
16. "Revolutionary Claims," #1700, SCA.
17. 7 January 1782, CRNC, 22: 212-214; CRNC, 22: 220, 224.
18. CRNC, 22: 196; Clark, 1:361.
19. CO 23/26, f. 224.
20. 20 April 1784, VHA (1779-1786), p. 2; The 220 acres on Eleuthera granted 23 December 1789 was probably given to the Joseph Curry who assisted Deveaux in the recapture of Nassau. CO 23/30, f. 224, #545; Captain of Militia CO 23/40, f. 101. It may be coincidental but a Curry was master of the sloop *Regulator* which arrived in Nassau from Eleuthera on 20 July 1792, BG 31 July 1792.
21. *Charleston Times*, 9 December 1806.
22. RG, 12 July 1809.
23. "Joseph Wadham, son of Joseph and Love Curry born 15 November 1808, baptized 18 December 1808," St. Matthews Baptisms (1802-1835)" no pages, by year; Love Curry died in a hurricane, BG 12 August 1813, p. 2. Their infant daughter Lavinia who was born 4 May 1813 and baptized 19 August 1813 died 24 June 1814, "CC Births and Baptism (1802-1828)," p. 31; BG 26 June 1814. This Joseph Curry probably married Mrs. Jane Albury, widow, on 17 September 1814, RG 21 September 1814.
24. *Bahama Argus*, 25 January 1833; Letters of Administration ORG Book B, p. 43.
25. *Private Claims: Presented to the House of Representatives from 1st to 31st Congress*, vol. 1 (Baltimore: Genealogical Publishing Co., 1970), p. 442, North Carolina State Library, Raleigh.
26. Secretary of State, South Carolina *Memorial of Conveyances* Orangeburg Abstracts, January 1818 to January 1821, pp. 4-5, SCA.

Appendix D: "Book of Negroes"

"British Headquarters Papers" #10427 f. 83 No. 2 "Book of Negroes Registered and certified after having been inspected by the commissioners appointed by His Excellency Sir Guy Carleton K. B. and General and Commander in Chief, on board sundry Vessels in which they were embarked Previous to the time of Sailing from the Port of New York between 31 July - 30 November 1783 both days Included."

[f. 98:99] 21 August 1783 Ship *Nautilus* Mr. Kildare Williamson Commander bound Albaco [sic]

Names	Age	Description	Names of persons in whose possession they are now	Remarks
Joe Grant	19	Stout Fellow	John Shoemaker	Born free at Bristol in Barbadoes.
James Snow	25	S.F.* & marked	Capt. Patrick Kennedy	Formerly property of John Elwin from Jamaica who died at Charlestown 15 years agoe.
Anthony Townass	40	S.F.	William Lesner	Formerly property of Henry Touness Middletown New Jersey left him 4 years agoe.
Isaac Bush	28	S.F.	Isaiah Low	Formerly property of Lincy Opey of Cherry Point Potowmack River, Va.
Charles Harell	17	S.F. mulatto blind right eye	William Goldwast [?]	Says he was born free at New London.
Joseph Cox	40	S.F. cooper by trade	Patrick Kennedy	F.P. § John Bybant Tolloway, New Jersey left him 2 years agoe.
Flora Bush	26	Thin Wench	Isaiah Low	F.P. Patrick Simons Cherry Point, Va. left him 2 years agoe.
Sally Jones	25	S.W. Mulatto	Capt. Pat. Kennedy	F.P. James Jones of Charlestown, S.C. left him 3 years agoe.
Joseph Paul	30	Stout low Man	Capt. Pat. Kennedy	Free having purchased his freedom from Lawrence Cartwright of New York
Susannah Paul	30	S.W. mar. with 3 Children 13,5,2	Capt. Pat. Kennedy	Free having purchased her freedom from Mr. Brown of New York.
Ichabod Wilkins	25	Stout Man	Capt. Pat. Kennedy	F.P. of John Thomas of White Plains, New York left him 7 years agoe.
Phillis Wilkins	31	S.W. Mulatto	Capt. Pat. Kennedy	Born free on Long Island.
Ned Price	40	Stout little man	Capt. Pat. Kennedy	F.P. of Joshua Buntin of Crosswecks, New Jersey who he says gave him his freedom in 1776.
Kate	19	Stout little wench	Capt. Pat. Kennedy	Born free at Jerecko, Long Island served 10 years with John Duryee at [Jerecko].
Charles Johnson	49	Stout man of his age	Thomas Cartwright	F.P. of George Biscoe St. Mary's County Maryland left him 4½ years agoe.
Nancy Dixon	30	sick at present with dau. 6 yrs.	Thomas Cartwright	F.P. John Dixon of Williamsburgh, Va. left him 3 years agoe.
Jack Jordon	55	Stout little man	John Job	F.P. of Robert Jordon of Norfolk, Va. left him 7 years agoe.
Venus Jordon	64	Stout little wench	John Job	F.P. of Captain Wenyfield of Boston, New England left him 7 years agoe.
Timothy Snowball	37	S.F. Mulatto	Capt. Pat. Kennedy	F.P. of Cornelius Colbert of Norfolk, Va. left him 7 years agoe.
Peter Johnston	25	S.F. Scar forehead	William Smith	F.P. Daniel Seix of Savannah, Georgia.
Cuffy Lucas	38	S.F.	Humphry Massenburgh	F.P. Ann Luker of Eastern Shore, Va. left her 2 years agoe.

Name	Claimant	Description	Age	Notes
Isabella	Humphry Massenburgh	S.W.	40	F.P. of Charles Mifflin of Philadelphia left him 5 years agoe.
Thomas Miller	Isaac Punderson	S.F.	20	F.P. of John Whitten of Portsmouth, Va. left him 4 years agoe.
Jack	John Longley	S.F.	25	F.P. of John Longley purchased from Sarah Aymer as per Bill of Sale produced.
Robert Johnson	Thomas Cartwright	S.F.	49	F.P. George Biscoe of St. Mary's County, Maryland left him 4½ years agoe.
Hannah Johnson	Thomas Cartwright	S.W.	40	F.P. Simon Hallyar Hampton, Va. left him 4 years agoe.
Benjamin Harris	Thomas Cartwright	Stout Tall Fellow	39	F.P. Caleb Herman St. Mary's County Maryland left him 5 years agoe.
Hester Scott	Mathew Arnold	Stout Mulatto Wench	20	Free as per Governour Bull's certificate.
Tom	Charles Whitehead	S.F.	25	Free made his escape from Cape Francois.
Lucas	Joseph Pilgrim	S.F.	64	F.P. of Benedick Burgoyne of Savannah, Georgia left him 6 years agoe.
Hercules	Joseph Pilgrim	S.F. very flat nose	30	F.P. of Isaac Herleston who was killed at Eutaws of Irish Town, South Carolina left him 6 years agoe.
Nancy	Joseph Pilgrim	S.W.	16	F.P. Colonel Cole of Swynyard, James River left him 4 years agoe.
Tom	Robert Smith	Stout thin man	60	F.P. of Mr. Allen of Norfolk, Va. who was killed.
Adam	Richard Warner	Stout boy scar on forehead	10	F.P. of Richard Warner.
Rose	John Shoemaker	fine girl	11½	F.P. of John Shoemaker who purchased her from _____ Vanderwater Bedfor[d], Long Island.

22 August 1783 *William* Transport John Coom [sic] master bound Albaco

Name	Claimant	Description	Age	Notes
George	Patrick Kennedy	S.F.	20	Came from Jamaica where he says he was born free.
Sharp	Patrick Kennedy	S.F.	25	F.P. of John Cooke of Charlestown left him 4 years agoe.
Joe Elliott	John Reed	S.F.	36	F.P. of George Elliott of Charlestown, S.C. left him 3 years agoe.
James Nash	John Reed	S.F.	26	F.P. John Ash [sic?] near Stone [S.C.?] left him 3 years agoe.
Dianah	John Reed	S.W. 1 Child 10 mons.	28	F.P. Mr. Cross of Charlestown left him 4 years agoe.
Daphae Rivers	Elias Davis	S.W.	22	F.P. Samuel Fulton of Charlestown, left him 4 years agoe.
William Keney or Kenly	Cornelius Blanchard [sic]	S.F.	35	F.P. of William Pilery of St. John [East Florida] left him 5 years agoe..
John Jackson	Alexander Dean	S.F.	27	Says he is free, lived with Tom Hutchinson of Charlestown left him 5 years agoe.
James Cain	Joseph Moore	S.F.	26	F.P. of John Houston of Savannah, Georgia left him 4 years agoe.
Kate Johnson	Joseph Moore	S.W.	37	F.P. of Andrew Johnson of Charlestown left him 2 years agoe.
Jack Johnson	Joseph Moore	a fine boy	11	F.P. of Andrew Johnson of Charlestown, South Carolina left him 2 years agoe.
Esther Moore	Joseph Moore	a fine girl	16	F.P. of Joseph Moore.
Joseph Scott	Alexander Dean	S.F.	40	Says he is free lived in Charlestown, a carpenter.

* S.F. = Stout Fellow & S. W. = Stout Wench
§ F.P. = Formerly the property of

Names	Age	Description	Names of persons in whose possession they are now	Remarks
[f. 100-101] *William* John Cook bound Albaco cont.				
Primus Fortune	30	S.F.	Alexander Dean	F.P. of Isaac Warner of Philadelphia left him 4 years agoe.
Manuel Williams	25	S.F.	Alexander Dean	F.P. of Robert Miles near Savannah, left him 5 years agoe.
Sally Beauman	25	fine wench	Alexander Dean	F.P. of Thomas Beauman of Beaufor[d], S.C. left him 4 years agoe.
Juba	30	S.F.	Alexander Dean	F.P. of Alexander Dean by bill of sale produced.
Carolina	10	fine boy	Alexander Dean	Ditto.
Rebecca	22	S.W. w/1 yr old child	Alexander Dean	F.P. of Joseph Bradford of Charlestown left him 4 years agoe.
Paris	50	S.F.	John Wallis Barclay	F.P. of John Wallis Barclay by bill of sale.
Venus	33	S.W. w/4 children 11,8,4,1	John Wallis Barclay	F.P. of John Wallis Barclay by bill of sale.
George Taylor	28	S.F.	George Antill	Says he is free.
Hannah Taylor	22	S.W. w/6 mon. old child	George Antill	F.P. of Timothy Burges of Portsmouth Va. left him 4 years agoe.
Lettice London	29	S.W.	George Antill	F.P. of George Webb of Norfolk, Va. left him 6 years agoe.
Henry Jackson	25	S.F.	George Antill	F.P. of Thomas Gold of Richmond, Va. left him 4 years agoe.
Peggy	21	S.W. w/8 mon. old child	George Antill	F.P. of Jesse Barlow of Portsmouth, Va. left him 5 years agoe.
Jane Williams	60	ordinary wench	George Antill	F.P. of Nathaniel Burges of Portsmouth, Va. left him 5 years agoe.
Isaac Wickfall	45	S.F.	George Antill	F.P. of Joseph Wickfall of Waubaw, S.C. left him 4 years agoe.
Susannah Powell	35	S.W. w/boy 5 yrs. old	John Jordan	F.P. of Capt. Dixon who she says left her free.
Isaac Mannays	16	fine boy	Cornelius Blanchard	Certificate of freedom from Gabriel Manigault.
Luce	11	fine girl	John Hutchins	F.P. of said Hutchins by bill of sale.
Nancy	24	fine wench w/2 children 4 & 2	Blanchard	F.P. of said Blanchard.
Patty	21	fine wench w/6 month old child	William McDonald	F.P. of General Howe of the Continental Army left him 4 years agoe.
Bob Powell	32	S.F.	John Jordan	F.P. of John Powell of Charlestown left him 3 years agoe.
Tom Tanyard	31	S.F.	John Jordan	F.P. of John Tanyard of Stone, S.C. left him 4 years agoe.
Betsey	21	Idiot	Mrs. Barclay	Says she is free.
James Dickson	24	S.F.	William McDonald	Says he was left free by Capt Benjamin Dixon of Charlestown where he died 5 years agoe.
Fortune	23	S.F.	Cornelius Blanchard	F.P. of Thomas Haywood of Charlestown left him 6 years agoe.

	Age			
Thomas Grisswell	23	S.F.	John Jones	F.P. of Hector Grisswell of George Town, South Carolina left him 5 years agoe.
James Brown	23	S.F.	George Welbank	Born free at Salem Township, New Jersey served until 21 with Abraham Hewlins.
Peter Brown	35	S.F.	John Davis	F.P. of James Brice of Annapolis, Maryland left him 6 years agoe.
Ned Jackson	31	S.F. Carpenter	George Welbank	Says he was born free at Bermuda served his apprenticeship with John Morrell.
Bridget Wenton	22	Stout little woman w/ Small girl 5 yrs.	John Davis	F.P. of Col. Joseph Wanton of Rhode Island who at his death left him [sic] free.
William Willis	39	Stout lusty man	John Cameron	F.P. of Joseph Pente of New York who gave him his freedom 10 years agoe.
Hester Willis	26	Stout Wench	John Cameron	Ditto.

[f. 101] "In persuance of two orders from H. E. Sir Guy Carleton K. B. General and Commander in Chief of His Majesty's forces from Nova Scotia to West Florida inclusive both dated Headquarters New York 15 April 1783. We whose names are hereunto subscribed do certify that we did carefully inspect the foregoing Vessels on the 13th, 14th,* 21st ard 22nd days of August and that on board the said vessels we found the negroes mentioned in the aforegoing List Amounting to 80 men 39 women and 35 children, and to the best of our judgement believe them to be all the negroes on board the said Vessels, and we enquired of the Master of each vessel, whether he had any records, Deeds, or archives, or papers or other property of the Citizens of the United States, on Board, and to each enquiry we were answered in the Negative and we futher certify that we furnished each master of a vessel with a certified List of the Negroes on board the vessel and informed him that he would not be permitted to land—— any other negroes than those contained in the List, and that if any other Negroes were found on board the Vessel, he would be severely punished, and that we informed the Agent for the transports, of this matter and desired him to use means for returning back to this place all Negroes not mentioned in the Lists.

[signed] W. J. Smith Col., Samuel Jones Secretary, Nathaniel Philips M. B. and William Armstrong Deputy Quarter Master General

* vessels embarking on the 13th and 14th went to "Germany and Spithead" [England], numbers represent the total for all four vessels

Appendix E: Emigrants who touched Abaco's shores during the loyalist period, beginning in 1783 up to the first slave register in 1821.

Abbreviations used in chart

American Provinces: NY (New York), NC (North Carolina), SC (South Carolina), EF (East Florida), WF (West Florida), Ga (Georgia)
G (Dunmore grants 1788-1794, does not include early 1800's)
A (Acres)
X (Land escheated for non payment of quit rent by 1834)
MT (Maxwell Town, Marsh Harbour, Abaco)
SB (Spencers Bight, Abaco)
L (Indicates that the loyality of that person is documented)

Name	Proof of Loyalty	Native Country American Province	Occupation America/Bahamas	Earliest Date on Abaco Settlement	Removals/Date & Place of Death
Adams, Jacob	L	SC to Ga	Soldier/Planter	1789 G Little Guana Cay 1807	Died at Abaco 1829
Aiken, David				1789/90 G 140A Great Abaco X	
Allender, John	L	Maryland to NY	Soldier/Planter	1789 G 80A Allender's Cay X	
Anderson, Lt. John	L	Native NY to Ga to EF	Soldier/Planter	1790 G 100A Long Bay, Great Abaco X	1790 G Caicos, Cat Island Long Is, Died Nassau 1838
Antill, George	L	NY		1783 Carleton	
Archer, Benjamin		SC?	Surveyor & Planter	1805 Marsh Harbour	Died at Abaco?
Armstrong, John	L	NC to SC to EF	Soldier	SB	1790 Absconded to WF
Armstrong, John	L	NC to Ga to EF	Lawyer/Soliciter General 1813	1789 80AX SB	Died Bath, England
Thomas	L	NC to Ga to EF	Planter	1784 Great Abaco	Caicos, Died Ga 1816
William Sr.	L	NC to Ga to EF	Planter	1788 G 600A SB	Died Abaco 1790
William Jr.	L	NC to Ga to EF	Planter	1784 SB	Long Is. Died St. Simons Ga. 1849
Arnold, Matthew		NY	Tombstone-Maker	1783 Carleton 1785 MT	
Backhouse, George	L	Native England to EF	Tailor	G Abaco	
Ball, William	L	NY	Soldier	1785 MT	
Barclay, John Wallace	L	Maryland to NY	Soldier/Planter	1783 Carleton 1789 G 280 A Monjack Cay	1791 G Caicos
Bazely, James		NC		1785 MT	
Belton, Major Jonathan	L	NC to SC to EF		1785 MT 1789 G 140AX SB	Charleston, SC
Berry, Timothy	L			1789 G 140AX Great Abaco	
Bethune, Farquhar	L	WF to EF	Indian Agent	1784 Great Abaco	
Blanchard, Andrew				1789 G 60AX MT	
Blanchard, Cornelius	L	New Jersey? to NY	Soldier/Justice of Peace	1783 Carleton	1790 Left Islands to ?
Brown, Lt. James C.	L	SC to EF	Soldier	1788/89 G 700AX SB	Caicos
Brown, Theodora	L	EF	Widow	1789 SB	Caicos G 500A
Brown, Lt. Col. Thomas	L	Ga to SC to EF	Soldier/Planter	1788/89 G 1900AX SB 8 Mile Bay Little Har.	1789 Caicos, Nassau Died at St. Vincent 1825
Burnet, John				1789 G 100AX	
Cameron, Capt. Donald	L	NC? Ga? EF	Soldier	1789 G 260 A SB X	Died at Nassau 1785
Cameron, John	L	Native of Scotland SC to NY	Soldier	1783 Carleton	Died 1785, Lost at Sea

Name	Proof of Loyalty	Native Country American Province	Occupation America/Bahamas	Earliest Date of Abaco Settlement	Removals/Date & Place of Death
Campbell, Major Alex	L	NC to EF	Soldier	1789 G 40A	1791 G Rum Cay
Carrier, Thomas					
Carroll, Thomas				1789 G 40A Deep Sea Cay	
Cartwright, Thomas	L	VA to NY		1783 Carleton	
Clark, Col. John	L	WF		1789 G 40AX SB	
Clements, James				1789 G 40AX	Long Island
Cockran, John	L	New Hampshire to NY	Soldier	1789 G 40AX	Caicos
Cocks, Thomas			Soldier	1789 G 60AX Crossing Rocks Fig Tree Hill	
Cook, Capt. John	L	SC?		1789 G 140AX Near MT	Exuma?
Cornish, John	L	Ga to EF	Soldier/Clerk, Notary	1789 G 176A SB	Cat Is. Long Is. Died 1795
Crannel, Robert				1789 G 40AX Pensacola Cay	
Crispin, Silver	L		Soldier	1785 MT	
Curtis, William	L	Mass. to NY	Soldier	1789 G 80AX Carleton	
Dalby, Daniel				1789/90 G 140A Little Guana Cay Lubbers Quarter	
Davis, Capt. John	L	SC? to NY			
Dean, Hugh	L	Maryland? to NY	Merchant	1789 G 200AX Cedar Harbour	1786 New Providence Inagua, Long Is.
Dumaresq, Philip	L	Mass. to NY	Merchant/Planter, Receiver General	1783 Carleton 1789 G 220A MT	New Providence, died 1800
Dunmore, John	L	Native of Scotland NY to Virginia	Soldier/Governour	1789 480A Purchase SB	England
Ellorby, Thomas					
Ferguson, Donald	L		Surveyor	1789 G 100AX SB	Drowned near Tardum Bay Eleuthera 1808
Ferguson, John	L	EF	Sea Captain, Surveyor	1789 G 120AX SB	Died Long Is. 1807
Ferguson, Kenneth				1788/89 G 255½AX SB	
Fisher, Christopher				1789 G 40A Crab Key	1789 Nassau
Flynn, Dennis				1789 G 60AX Carleton	
Forbes, Gilbert Jr.	L	NY		1785 MT	
Forbes, Thomas	L	EF	Merchant, Council, Member Panion Leslie Co.	1789/90 G 400 A SB, Cedar Harbour	Exuma, Crooked Is. Caicos Died Nassau 1808
Fox, John	L	Ga to EF	Carpenter	1789-91 G 360A	Nassau?
Freeman, Seth				1789 G 80AX	1790 Long Is.
Fry, Philip				1789 G 40AX Little Guana Cay	1799 Caicos
Fryar, Anthony	L	NY	Soldier/Labourer	1789 G 80AX SB	
Gerrard, William		NY		1789 G 60AX MT	
Glenton, Henry	L		Planter & Provost Marshal	1783 Carleton	1784 Nassau, Long Is. Died Nassau 1809
Grant, Dr. Michael	L	WF to NY	Garrison Physician Council & Judge	1783 Carleton	1784 Nassau Died 1797
Hamilton, Capt. Wm.	L	EF	Soldier		
Harding, John	L	NY		1783 Carleton	Nassau
Harkness, George	L		Agent for Refugees	1789/90 G 280AX SB Long Bay	1792 Caicos

Name	Proof Of Loyalty	Native Country American Province	Occupation America/Bahamas	Earliest Date on Abaco Settlement	Removals/Date & Place of Death
Harris, John	L	NY	Commissary	1790 G 100AX Fig Tree Hill	
Harrold, Anne	L	NY	Midwife	1783 Carleton	1785 Nassau
Haskey, William			Schoolmaster	1789	
Haven, Stephen	L	EF	Lawyer	1789 G 320A	Nassau
Haynes, William				1789 G 20AX to MT	
Hield, William	L	NY		1783? Carleton	Nassau
Hodgens, William				1789 G 60AX SB	
Hunt, John	L	Mass?		1789 G 40AX SB	Cat & Long Is. Died 1807
Hutchins, John	L	NY		1783 Carleton	
Isaacs, Capt. Samuel	L	NY	Soldier; Doctor	1783 Carleton 1785 MT	Died 1785 at Sea
Jenkins, Griffin				1789 G 60A Matlos Cay	
Job, John	L	NY		1783 Carleton	
Jones, John	L	NY		1783 Carleton	
Jordan, John	L	Native of Ireland New Jersey to NY	Director of Ironworks/	1783 Carleton G 1789 100AX	Claim England Return Bah.?
Kennedy, Capt. Patrick	L	Maryland to NY to Nova Scotia	Soldier/Planter, Merchant	After 1786	1807 Nassau
Kennedy, Capt. William	L	NY	Sea Captain	1783 Carleton 1785 MT 1789 G 140AX	
Kerchner, Jacob				1789 G 40AX Cistern Point	
Kirk, Andrew				1787 Daughter born at Abaco	
Lane, James	L	SC		1789 G 40AX SB	1790 Grand Caicos
Lee, Ambrose	L	Maryland?		1789 G 40AX Rocky Harbour	1790 Grand Caicos
Linton, Robert				1789 G 80AX SB	
Lovell, John	L	Boston?	Merchant? Soldier/	1789 G 100AX	
Low, Isaiah	L	NY		1783 Carleton	
Marks, James				1789 G 40AX	
Marks, John				1789 G 80AX	
Marks, William				1789 G 40AX Carleton Creek	
Martin, John	L	NY?	Assistant Judge General Court?	1789 G 60AX MT	1790 Caicos G died Nassau 1796?
Martinangle, Abraham	L			Arrived 1786, 1789 G 180AX SB	
Massenburgh, Humphry	L	NY		1783 Carleton	
McDonald, Alexander	L	NY	Half Pay Agent	1783 Carleton? 1790 G 40A	
McDonald, Donald	L	NC?	Soldier	1789 G 100AX	
McDonald, William	L	NY		1783 Carleton	
McFarlane, John	L		Soldier		
McGillivray, John	L	WF	Indian Agent Merchant/Soldier		
McInness, Miles				1789 G 100A	
McIntosh, John	L	Native Scotland WF	Indian Commissary Soldier/Planter	1789 G 200AX Little Harbour	1790 Grand Caicos 930A
McKee, Alexander	L	VA? Maryland? NY		1789 G 60AX 1785 MT	

Name	Proof Of Loyalty	Native Country American Province	Occupation America/Bahamas	Earliest Date on Abaco Settlement	Removals/Date & Place of Death
McKee, John				1789 G 40AX 1785 MT	
McKee, Michael				1785 MT, 1789 G 40A Great Guana Cay	
Miller, B					
Moore, John Morris	L	NY		1789 G 40A	
Moore, Joseph Morris	L	EF		1789 G 100AX SB	1790 Caicos Died Caicos 1795
Moxey, William				1789 G 60AX	
Neeley, Christopher	L	Native American, SC	Soldier/Planter	1788 G 200AX SB	Died Nassau 1803
O'Halloran, John	L	Ga	Soldier / Postmaster, House of Assembly	1784	Died Nassau 1796
O'Neil, James	L	SC		1789 G 420A SB	Died Long Island 1793
Pearis, Margaret	L		Dau. of Richard Sr.	1788 G 40AX SB	
Pearis, Col. Richard Sr.	L	Native of Virginia SC to WF to Ga	Soldier/Planter	1788 G 140A SB	Rum Cay Died Nassau 1794
Pearis, Richard Jr.	L	EF			Caicos to Ga 1807
Peterson, Lt. William	L	EF	Soldier	1789 G 80AX SB Lit. Har. Gr. Guana Cay	
Pennybaker, Conrad	L	Ga to EF	Soldier/Planter	1789 G 60AX MT	Died Abaco 1828
Pennycooke, David				1789 G 100AX	
Philips, John	L	NY		1783 Carleton	
Pilgrim, Joseph	L	NY		1783 Carleton	
Pintard, John L.	L	NY		1783 Carleton?	
Plenis, Benedick			Merchant	1789 G 40AX Rocky Harbour	Died Nassau 1805
Pringle, James				1789 G 80AX Little Abaco	1789 G 100A Grand Caicos
Pritchard, William	L	EF		1788 G 80AX	1790 G Crooked Island 1794 Long Island
Punderson, Isaac	L	NY		1783 Carleton	
Ray, Phoebe			1789 G 40A	1789 G 80A SB	
Reinhart, William	L			1789 G 40AX Rocky Harbour	
Reister, Ernest	L			1783 Carleton? 1785 MT	
Ritter, Henry		Native American, NY		1789 G 40A SB	Died in Nassau 1823
Robinson, Hamilton			Shipwright	1789 G 600AX Pensacola Cay Gr. Abaco	
Russell, John	L	SC to EF		1789 G 200AX SB	
Scott, Robert	L	EF	Surgeon's Mate-Royal Artillery/Doctor	1783 Carleton?	1790 G Crooked Island
Shaw, Capt. George	L	NY	Soldier?	1783 Carleton	1805 G Caicos Died Caicos 1811
Shoemaker, John	L	NY		1789 G 80A SB Little Guana Cay	
Smith, George	L			1783 Carleton?	1790 G Caicos Nassau?
Smith, John		Phil. to NY		1783 Carleton?	
Smith, Henry	L	NY		1785 MT 1789 G 120A Man-O-War Cay	

Name	Proof Of Loyalty	Native Country American Province	Occupation America/Bahamas	Earliest Date on Abaco Settlement	Removals/Date & Place of Death
Smith, Robert	L	NY		1783 Carleton	
Smith, Thomas	L	Native of England Conn. to NY	Soldier	1789 G 40A	Died Nassau 1814
Smith, William	L	NY		1783 Carleton	
Stansbury, Isaac	L			Carleton	
Stephens, John				1783 G 80AX Cocoa Plum Creek	
Stephens, Capt. Thomas	L	PA to NY	Soldier/Planter	1783 Carleton 1789 G 140A G.T.C. 1786 Cedar Har. & 200A Lit. Ab.	Died in Abaco 1787
Tattnall, Josiah	L	Native of SC Ga to EF	Surveyor General	1785 Plat Cedar Harbour	Long Is. New Providence to Ga
Taylor, Alexander	L			1794 Free Holder	Cat Island
Taylor, Charles Fox	L	Native American WF to EF	Soldier	1788 G 160AX SB	1790 G Caicos Died About 1808
Taylor, Duncan	L			1785 MT, 1789 G 100A	1793 Long Is., Exuma Died Ragged Is. 1822
Underwood, Augustus	L	Native American Ga	Soldier/Master Mariner	1789 G 31AX SB	Long Is. Died Nassau 1809
Valentine, John	L	NY	Maker of tombstones	1789 G 100AX MT	1790 - Caicos
Valleau, Josiah	L	NY	Master of a Vessel	1789 G 40A Man-O-War Cay	
Victor, Thomas	L	NY	Master of a Vessel	1783 Carleton?	
Warner, Richard	L	NY		1783 Carleton	
Waters, Col. Thomas	L	Ga to EF	Soldier/Deputy Superintendent Cherokee Nation	1789 G 160A Cedar Harbour	
Weatherford, John	L	Ga to EF	Planter	Marsh Harbour	
Weatherford, Martin	L	Ga to EF	Planter	1789 G 130A SB Little Har. Bridges Cay	Died Harbour Is. 1805
Wegg, Edmund Rush	L	WF	Attorney General	1789 G 40AX Allens Cay,Cedar Har.	Died Nassau 1789
Welfling, Henry	L	Phil. to NY		1783 Carleton?	
Welbank, George	L	NY	Soldier	1783 Carleton to MT	
Wells, John	L	SC to EF	Printer	1794 Election-Free Holder	Lived in Nassau
Wells, Henry	L	NY		1783 Carleton 1789 G 100AX	
Whitehead, Charles	L	NY	Sea Captain?	1783 Carleton	
Wier, Robert	L	NY	Shopkeeper	1785 MT 1789 G 40AX	Died Nassau 1835
Willet, Thomas	L	NY	Planter/Magistrate	1783 Carleton? MT	
Wilson, William	L	SC?		1789 G 40AX SB Hurricane Hole	Long Is.? 1791 G Watling's
Wylly, Capt. Alexander C.	L	Ga to EF	Soldier/Planter Speaker House	1788 G 380A SB	1790 G Long Is. Lived Nassau, Died St. Simons Is. Ga 1833
Wylly, William	L	Native of Ga to EF to Nova Scotia	Soldier/Solictor General Chief Justice (St. Vincent)	1790 G 750AX Madeira Bay	Long Is. Nassau to St. Vincent Died in England 1828

Appendix F: "Slave Register" 1834

Name of Proprietor	# of Return in Slave Register	Residence	Occupation or Description	Total Number of Slaves	Field	Domestic/Field	Domestic	Mariner	Field/Mariner	Mariner/Field	Other	Children	Place of Employ other or in addition to residence of proprietor	Reason Not Counted
Addams (Adams), Jacob	279	Elbow Cay	Deceased Estate Of	5	3							2		
Addams (Adams), Randall	622	Green Turtle Cay	Planter	5	3							2		
Albury, John	315	Green Turtle Cay	Planter	6		1	1		1			3		
Albury, John	826	Little Guana Cay	Planter	14	5		2					7		
Albury, Joseph	303	Cotinary Cay	Planter	1				1						
Baker, Conrad P.	322	Great Guana Cay	(Formerly Pennybaker)	1	1									
Bethell, Elizabeth	136	New Providence	Widow	9			1				6 New Providence	2	Green Turtle Cay	
Bethell, John	282	Cherokee Sound	Planter	2	1						Runaway		Elbow Cay	
Bremen, John & Polly	317	Great Guana Cay		1	1									
Curry, Benjamin	271	Green Turtle Cay	Planter	7	3		1					3	Abaco	1 Died
Curry, Benjamin, Jr.	316	Green Turtle Cay	Planter	1					1					
Curry, Elizabeth (dec.)	623	Green Turtle Cay	Late wife of Richard Curry	3	2		1							
Curry, Jacob	624	Green Turtle Cay		4			2					2		
Curry, Mary	319	Green Turtle Cay		4		1		1				2	Crab Cay	
Curry, Richard Sr.	308	Green Turtle Cay	Planter	17 (15)			1		3	5	1 out on wages 1 Carpenter	4	Little Abaco	
Curry, Richard Sr. Jr.	420	Green Turtle Cay	Planters	5			1					4		
Greenleaf, Elizabeth	348	New Providence	Widow, formerly of Green Turtle Cay	7			4					3	Abaco	
Griffin, George Sr.	306	Green Turtle Cay	Late of Eleuthera	1	1								Abaco	
Holmes, Abraham, et al	437	New Providence		2			1					1	Abaco	
Johnson, Joseph	275	Cherokee Sound	Planter	2	1		1						Abaco	
Kemp, Samuel	304 & after 305	Abaco	Planter	25	3		5			1	1 Blacksmith	15	Green Turtle Cay & Little Abaco	1 Absconded in America

Name of Proprietor	# of Return in Slave Register	Residence	Occupation or Description	Total Number of Slaves	Field	Domestic/Field	Domestic	Mariner	Field/Mariner	Mariner/Field	Other	Children	Place of Employ other or in addition to residence of proprietor	Reason Not Counted
Kemp, William	1025	Harbour Island		2	1			1					Eleuthera and Abaco	
Lord, Margaret	15	New Providence	Free Woman of Colour	1									Abaco	
Lowe, Benjamin	604	Green Turtle Cay	Planter	9	4		1	1			A Carpenter and Sailor	3		
Lowe, Gideon (dec.)	296	Green Turtle Cay	Planter (Master of a Vessel)	23	8		2	4				8	Abaco and Spanish Cay	
Lowe, James	314	Green Turtle Cay	Planter	6	2	1				1		2		
Lowe, John	324	Green Turtle Cay	Planter	7					3			4		1 Manumitted in 1832
Lowe, Mathew Sr.	625	Green Turtle Cay	Planter	9	5	1				1		2		
Lowe, William Sr.	300	Green Turtle Cay	Planter	8	2		1			2		3	Abaco	
Lowe, William Jr.	302	Green Turtle Cay		3			1			2			Abaco	
Melone, Benjamin	277	Elbow Cay		1			1							
Pinder, Benjamin	278	Cherokee Sound	Planter	7	2		1					2	Abaco	
Roberts, Benjamin	323	Green Turtle Cay	Planter	11					11				Abaco	
Roberts, Caroline Elizabeth	621	Green Turtle Cay	Late Quince or Quance	5	1		1					3		
Roberts, John Sr.	305	Green Turtle Cay	Planter	1			1							
Roberts, John	281	Elbow Cay	Planter	7	3		1					3	Green Turtle Cay & Abaco	
Roberts, John	619	Little Guana Cay	Planter	7	3		1					3		
Roberts, Joseph	76	Cherokee Sound	Planter	9	3		3	1			Mariner also a Woodcutter	2		
Roberts, Richard	618	Green Turtle Cay	(Formerly Harbour Is.)	3			1		1	1				
Russell, Benjamin	69	Cherokee Sound		3			1					2		
Russell, John	81	Abaco (Green Turtle Cay)	Shipwright	45	26	4	4	2			1 Ship Carpenter	12		1 Sold 1 Died
Russell, Joseph	620	Green Turtle Cay	Planter	1	1								Crab Cay	
Russell, Thomas	307	Elbow Cay		3	1							2	Little Guana Cay	

Name	No.	Residence	Occupation						Notes		Location	Remarks
Russell, William	318	Green Turtle Cay	Planter	1	1							
Russell, Wm. et al*	312	Green Turtle Cay	Planter	16	1	8	3			4	Harbour Is. & Abaco	
Sands, Zachariah	617	Cherokee Sound	Planter	1				1				
Saunders, Albert	298	Green Turtle Cay	Planter	12	2	3	1	3		4	Cotinary Cay	
Saunders, Benjamin Esq.(dec)	609	Abaco	Planter	22	✓	✓			Woodcutter ✓			
Saunders, George	301	Green Turtle Cay	Planter	1		1	1				Abaco	
Saunders, Joseph	272	Green Turtle Cay	Planter	5		1		1		3	Abaco	1 Born & Died 1832
Saunders, Joseph	284	Green Turtle Cay	Mariner	1		1					Harbour Is.	
Saunders, Nathaniel	321	Green Turtle Cay	Planter	7 (6)		2	1			2		
Saunders, Uriah Esq.	309	Abaco (Green Turtle Cay)	Planter (Shipbuilder)	5	1	2	1		Ship Carpenter			1 Absconded 3 Died
Saunders, William (Jr.)	297	Green Turtle Cay	Planter	5	1	1	1	1	1 Jobbing Mason & Wrecker	1		
Sawyer, John Frederick	613	Green Turtle Cay	Planter	7		2		2		3		
Sawyer, Richard	283	Elbow Cay		2	2				Man-O-War Cay			
Sawyer, Samuel (Jr.)	608	Green Turtle Cay	Planter	3	2	1	1	1				
Sawyer, Sarah	610	Green Turtle Cay	Wife of Samuel Sawyer	1		1	1					
Sawyer, William	273	Green Turtle Cay		2		1		1		1		
Sawyer, William	611	Green Turtle Cay	Planter	1		1	1					
Skelton, John Esq.	612	Green Turtle Cay	Master of Vessel	5		3				2	Harbour Is.	
Sweeting, John	299	Green Turtle Cay	Planter	5	2			1		2	Little Abaco	
Sweeting, William	616	Green Turtle Cay		2		1		1		1		
Thompson, William	274	Elbow Cay	Planter	0								
Wallace, George	543	New Providence	Son of Anthony Wallace, free Black	5	4	5	1			1	Abaco	An African Died 1832

*Edward Russell
Matilda Russell
Mary Saunders
Maria Sweeting

BIBLIOGRAPHY

This bibliography is restricted to the works quoted in the text and does not include all references consulted.

Primary Sources - Unprinted

Boston. Boston Public Library Rare Book Room. "Report on the Bahama Islands" by John Wilson, 1784.
Chapel Hill. University of North Carolina, Wilson Library. 1550. Harllee Papers.
Columbia. South Carolina Department of Archives and History.
    Confiscted Estates: List of Returns made by Regimental Commanders, 1783 (File Drawer marked Loyalists).
    Oaths of Allegiance (to King George III) 1781 (Microfilm from British Library).
    Records of the Auditor General. Memorials. 1731-1775 (16 vols).
    Records of the Comptroller General. Accounts Audited of Claims Growing out of the Revolution 1778-1804 (328ff)
    Records of His Majesty's Council. Council Journals 1721-1774 (27 vols).
    Records of the Secretary of State. Miscellaneous Records. Main Series. 1671 to present (213 vols).
    ➡ Records of the South Carolina Court of Common Pleas. Judgment Rolls 1703-1790 (167ff).
    Records of the Surveyor General. Colonial Plats 1731-1775 (21 vols).
Key West, Florida. Monroe County Public Library. Lowe Family Register [by William Lowe]. [1833-?]
London. British Library. 4/6405 and/or 4/6407? Abaco. 1784.
London. Lambeth Palace Library. Fulham Papers. SPG.
London. Public Records Office.
    American Claims (Loyalist).
    Audit Office Series (Loyalist).
    Colonial Office Papers.
    Georgia Claims (Loyalist).
London. Society for the Propagation of the Gospel in Foreign Parts. Bahamas Box B or 3. Chambers Report, Governour's Harbour, 1848. Archdeacon Trew Report, Nassau, 12 January 1849.
Nassau, New Providence, The Bahamas. Nassau Library. Malcolm Collection (by permission).
Nassau, New Providence, The Bahamas. Public Archives.
    Bahamas Blue Books 1834-1850.
    Chalmers Papers, vol. 1 (1728-1796).
    Christ Church Registers. Births 1744-, Marriages 1792-, Burials 1806-. (by permission).
    C.O. 23 (Bahamas).
    Governour's Dispatches 1818-1850.
    Journal of the House of Assembly 1760-1836.
    Slave Registers 1821-1834.
    St. John's Harbour Island Marriage Register 1802-1819 (by permission).
    St. Matthew's Church Registers 1802- (by permission).
    USPG: Records Relating to the Bahama Islands. Reel 97132/1 (1726-1822), Reel 97132/2 (1790-1810), Reel 97132/3 (1834-1858).
New-York. Historical Society. "Declaration of Dependence," Y1776.
New York. Public Library, Rare Books and Manuscripts Division.
    American Loyalists: Transcripts. 1900.
    British Headquarters Papers. 1775-1783.
Tampa, Florida. University of South Florida. David O. True Collection.
Washington, D.C. Library of Congress. Forbes Collection. Vernon Wager Papers.

Primary Sources - Printed

Bartram, William. *Travels Through North and South Carolina, Georgia, East and West Florida.* 1791. Reprint. New York: Dover Publications, 1955.
Baynton, Benjamin. *Authentic Memoirs of William Augustus Bowles, Esquire, Ambassador from the United Nations of Creeks and Cherokees to the Court of London.* 1791. New York: Arno Press Inc., 1971.
Bellin, Jacques-Nicolas. *Déscription Géographique Des Isles Antilles Possedées Par Les Anglois.* Paris: n.p., 1758. Translation of the Bahamas section by James and Catherine Herlihy. Photocopy in the Albert Lowe Museum.
Black List: A List of Those Tories Who Took Part With Great Britain In the Revolutionary War and Were Attainted of High Treason, Commonly Called the Black List! Philadelphia: n.p., 1802.
British Library. *The American War of Independence 1775-1783: A Commemorative Exhibition Organized by the Department of Manuscripts of the British Library Reference Division 4 July-11 November, 1975.* London: British Museum Publications Ltd., 1975.

Bruce, Peter Henry. *Bahamian Interlude.* London, 1782. Reprint. London: John Culmer Ltd., [1949].

Bruzen de la Martiniere, Antoine Augustin. *Le Grand Dictionnaire Géographique Historique et Critique.* 6 Vols. Paris: n.p., 1768.

Calendar of State Papers: Colonial Series America and West Indies. 44 vols. (1570-1738). London: Her Majesty's Stationery Office, 1860-1939. Reprint. Vaduz, Germany: Kraus Reprint, 1964.

Case and Claims of the American Loyalists Impartially Stated and Considered. London: G. Wilkie, 1783.

Catesby, Mark. *The Natural History of Carolina, Florida, and the Bahama Islands.* 2 vols. London, 1754. Reprint. Savannah, Georgia: Beehive Press, 1974.

Chalmers, George. *The Representation of the House of Assembly of the Bahamas to the Right Honourable Earl of Bathurst The Colonial Secretary of State Respecting Their Proceedings during Their Last Session 1816/17 with an Appendix of Documents.* London: Luke Hansard and Sons, 1817, (CO 23/66, f. 59-84).

Clark, Murtie June. *Loyalists in the Southern Campaign of the Revolutionary War.* 3 vols. Baltimore: Genealogical Publishing Co. Inc., 1981.

Colonial Records of North Carolina. Collected and edited by William L. Saunders. 10 vols. Raleigh, N.C., 1886-1890.

Colonial Records of the State of Georgia. Compiled and Published under Authority of the Legislature by Allen D. Chandler. Atlanta: The Franklin Printing and Publishing Company, 1904.

Columbus, Christopher. *Journal of First Voyage to America.* Kettel Translation, 1827. Reprint. New York: Albert and Charles Boni, 1924.

Crary, Catherine S. *The Price of Loyalty: Tory Writings from the Revolutionary Era.* New York: McGraw-Hill, 1973.

Crowley, John. *A Description of the Windward Passage and the Gulf of Florida.* London: Corbett, 1739.

Defoe, Daniel. *A General History of the Pyrates.* Edited by Manuel Schonhorn. Columbia, South Carolina: University of South Carolina Press, 1972.

de Las Casas, Bartolomé. *The Devastation of the Indies: A Brief Account.* Translated by Herma Briffault. Introduction by Hans Magnus Enzensberger. New York: The Seabury Press, 1974.

------. *History of the Indies.* Translated and edited by Andrée Collard. New York: Harper and Row, 1971.

[Del Lorraine, Adela.] *Miss Hart's Letters from the Bahama Islands Written in 1823-24.* 1827. 2nd ed. edited by Jack Culmer. Nassau, Bahamas, 1948.

Documents Relative to the Colonial History of the State of New York. 15 vols. Edited by E. B. O'Callaghan, M.D. Albany: Weed, Parsons and Co., 1853-1861.

Edwards, Bryan. *The History Civil and Commercial of the British West Indies.* 2 vols. London: John Stockdale, 1794.

Egerton, Hugh Edward, ed. *The Royal Commission on the Losses and Services of American Loyalists 1783 to 1785: Being the Notes of Mr. Daniel Parker Coke, M.P. One of the Commissioners During That Period.* Oxford, 1915. Reprint. New York: Arno Press, 1969.

Esquemeling, John. *The Buccaneers of America.* 1684. London: Swan Sonnenschein and Co., 1893. Reprint. New York: Dover Publications Inc., 1967.

[Frost, John.] *The Heroes and Battles of the American Revolution or Thrilling Stories and Anecdotes of That Eventful Period.* Philadelphia: Willis P. Hazard, 1845.

Goldham, Peter Wilson, ed. *American Loyalist Claims, Vol. I, Abstracted from P.R.O. A.O. 13 Bundles 1-35 & 37.* Washington, D.C.: National Genealogical Society, 1980.

Graves, John. *A Memorial: or a Short Account of the Bahama Islands.* London: n.p., 1708.

Hooker, Richard J., ed. *The Carolina Backcountry on the Eve of the Revolution: The Journal and Other Writings of Charles Woodmason, Anglican Itinerant.* Chapel Hill, North Carolina: The University of North Carolina Press, 1953.

Huxtable, Reverend George Gellard. *Reminiscences of Missionary Life in the West Indies.* Kemptville, Ontario: Huxtable and Seily, 1902.

Jones, B. Alfred. *The Loyalists of Massachusetts: Their Memorials, Petitions and Claims.* London: The Saint Catherine Press, 1930.

Journal of the Board of Trade and Plantations. 14 vols. (1704-1782). London: Her Majesty's Stationery Office, 1920-1938. Reprint. Mendeln/Liechtenstein, Germany: Kraus Reprint, 1969-70.

Kelly, Samuel. *An Eighteenth Century Seaman Whose Days Have Been Few and Evil, to Which is Added Remarks etc., on Places He Visited during His Pilgrimage in This Wilderness.* Introduction by Grosbie Garsten. New York: Frederick A. Stokes Co., 1925.

Lefroy, Major-General J. H., compiler. *Memorials of the Discovery and Early Settlement of the Bermudas or Somers Islands 1515-1685.* 2 vols. London: Longmans, Green, and Co., 1877.

Lockey, Joseph Byrne. *East Florida 1783-1785: A File of Documents Assembled, and Many of Them Translated.* Berkeley: University of California Press, 1949.

McDonald, Ormond J., transcriber. *A Relic of Slavery: Farquharson's Journal for 1831-32.* Nassau, Bahamas: Deans Peggs Research Fund, 1957.

MacKenzie, Roderick, *Strictures on Lt. Colonel Tarleton's History to Which is Added the Recapture of the Island of New Providence.* London: n.p., 1787.

McKinnon, Daniel. *A Tour Through the British West Indies in the Years 1802 and 1803 Giving a Particular Account of the Bahama Islands.* London: Printed for J. White, 1804.

Manross, William Wilson, compiler. *Fulham Papers in the Lambeth Palace American Colonial Section Calendar and Indexes.* Oxford: Clarendon Press, 1965.

Minutes of a Conspiracy Against the Liberties of America. Philadelphia: John Campbell, 1865. Reprint. New York: Arno Press, 1969.

Minutes of the Trial and Examination of Certain Persons, in the Province of New York Charged with Being Engaged in a Conspiracy Against the Authority of the Congress, and The Liberties of America. London: n.p., [1776].

Moll, Herman. *A Man of West Indies on the Islands of America in the North Sea.* London: n.p., 1721.

Oldmixon, John. *The History of the Isle of Providence.* (Chapter on the Bahamas, taken from John Oldmixon, *The British Empire in America.* 2 vols. London: John Culmer, 1741.) Reprint. Nassau: The Providence Press, 1966.

Peggs, A. Deans, ed. *A Mission to the West India Islands: Dawson's Journal for 1810-1817.* Nassau, Bahamas: The Deans Peggs Research Fund, 1960.

Rawson, Sir R. W. *Report on the Bahamas for the Year 1864.* London: George E. Eyre and William Spottiswoode, 1866.

Revolutionary Records of the State of Georgia. 3 vols. Compiled and Published under Authority of the Legislature by Allen D. Chandler. Atlanta: Franklin-Turner Co., 1908.

Schoepf, Johann David. *Travels in the Confederation 1783-1784.* Translated and edited by Alfred J. Morrison. Philadelphia: William J. Campbell, 1911.

Siebert, Wilbur Henry. *Loyalists in East Florida 1774-1785: The Most Important Documents Pertaining Thereto, Vol. II: Records of Their Claims for Losses of Property in the Province.* Deland, Florida: The Florida State Historical society, 1929. Reprint. Boston: Gregg Press, 1972.

[Smith, John.] *The Historye of the Bermudaes or Summer Islands.* Edited by Sir J. Henry Lefroy. London: Printed for the Hakluyt Society, 1882.

------. *A Sea Grammar.* London, 1627. Reprint. New York: DaCapo Press, 1968.

State Records of North Carolina. 16 vols. Collected and edited by Walter Clark. Winston and Goldsboro, N.C.: n.p., 1895-1905.

Tarleton, Colonel Bannastre. *A History of the Campaigns of 1780 and 1781 in the Southern Province of North America.* London: Printed for T. Cadell, 1787.

Taylor, Edwin L., compiler. "The Letters of the First Four Missionaries to the Bahamas." In *Methodism in the West Indies 1760-1960 Bicentenary Souvenir*, pp. 21-27. Nassau: Methodist Church, 1960.

Thatcher, James. *A Military Journal During the American Revolutionary War from 1775-1783.* Boston: Cottons and Barnard, 1827.

The Tryals of Captain John Rackam, and Other Pirates. Jamaica: Robert Baldwin, 1721.

(U.S.) *Private Claims: House of Representatives from the 1st to the 31st Congress. Vol. I.* Baltimore: Genealogical Publishing Co., 1970.

Votes of the Bahamas House of Assembly (1729-1850). Nassau, Bahamas: Office of the *Royal Gazette* and *Nassau Guardian*, 1851-1910.

Werner, Raymond C., introduction and notes to *The Diary of Grace Crowden Galloway Kept at Philadelphia from June 17th, 1778, to July 1st, 1779.* Reprint. New York: Arno Press, 1971.

Williams, Eric, compiler and editor. *Documents on British West Indian History 1807-1833.* Trinidad, B.W.I.: Trinidad Publishing Co. Ltd., 1952.

Winthrop, John. *The History of New England From 1630-1649.* Edited by James Savage. Reprint (2 vols. in 1). New York: Arno Press, 1972.

[Wylly, William.] *A Short Account of the Bahama Islands: Their Climate, Productions, &c. to which are Added, some Strictures upon their relative and political Situation, the Defects of their present Government &c.* by a Barrister at Law, Late His Majesty's Solicitor General of Those Islands, and King's Counsel for the Provinces of Nova Scotia and New Brunswick. London: n.p., 1789.

Primary Sources - Newspapers

Bahama Argus. Nassau, Bahamas. 1831-1835. Nassau Library.

Bahamas Gazette. Nassau, Bahamas. 1784-1819 (some gaps). Nassau Library.

Bahama Herald. Nassau, Bahamas. 1849-1862. Nassau Library.

The Caledonian Mercury. Edinburgh, Scotland. 1779.

Charleston Times. Charleston, South Carolina. 1800-1824. Caroliniana Library, Columbia, South Carolina.

East Florida Gazette. St. Augustine, Florida. February 1783 to April 1784 (only three issues extant). St. Augustine Historical Society Library, St. Augustine, Florida.

Edinburgh Advertiser. Edinburgh, Scotland. 1783.

Lucayan Royal Herald and the Weekly Advertiser. Nassau, Bahamas. 19 August 1789 (the only issue extant). CO 23/30, ff194-195, Nassau Public Archives.

Nassau Guardian. Nassau, Bahamas. 1849 to present. Nassau Library.

New York Gazette and the Weekly Mercury (Hugh Gaine). New York. 1752-1783. New-York Historical Society, New York, New York.

New-York Post. New York. 7 November 1783. Facsimile, New York Public Library Rare Book Room. New York, New York.

The Royal Gazette (James Rivington). New York. Established 1733. 1776-19 November 1783. New-York Historical Society. New York, New York.

Royal Gazette (Robert Wells and son). Charleston, South Carolina. March 1781-1782. South Carolina Archives, Columbia, S. C.

Royal Gazette and Bahama Advertiser. Nassau, Bahamas. 1804-1810, 1813-1837. Nassau Library.

Royal Georgia Gazette. Savannah, Georgia. 1774-1783. Georgia Historical Society Library, Savannah, Georgia.

South Carolina Gazette (Peter Timothy). Charleston, South Carolina. 1732-1774. South Carolina Archives, Columbia, S. C.

South Carolina Gazette and Country Journal (Charles Crouch). Charleston, South Carolina. 1765-1773. South Carolina Archives, Columbia, S. C.

South Carolina Weekly Gazette (Nathan Childs). Charleston, South Carolina. 15 February 1783-? Charleston Library Society, Charleston, South Carolina.

Secondary Sources - Books, Periodicals and Manuscripts

Albury, Haziel L. *Man-O-War My Island Home: A History of an Outer Abaco Island.* Delaware: Holly Press, 1977.

Albury, Paul. *The Story of the Bahamas.* London: Macmillan Education Ltd., 1975.

Allen, Gardner W. *A Naval History of the American Revolution.* 2 vols. New York: Russell and Russell Inc., 1962.

Andrews, James E.; Shepard, Francis P.; and Hurley, Robert J. "Grand Bahama Canyon." Geological Society of America Bulletin 81 (1970):1061-1078.

Armbrister, Mary K. "Henrietta My Daughter." Typed Manuscript. Nassau Library, 1836.

Armbrister, W. E. "A Short History of the Bahamas." Transcribed by Sandra Riley. Original and photocopy. Nassau Public Archives, Nassau, The Bahamas, 1980.

Baer, Joel Herman. "Piracy Examined: A Study of Daniel Defoe's *General History of the Pirates* and Its Milieu." Ph.D. dissertation, Princeton University, 1970. University Microfilms, Ann Arbor, Michigan. Facsimile 71-24, 351, 1973.

"A Bahamian Tragedy." In *Bahamas Handbook,* pp. 15-25. Nassau: Etienne Dupuch, Jr., Publications, 1974.

Baird, Charles E. *History of the Huguenot Emigration to America.* vol. 2. New York: Dodd Mead, 1885.

Bates, H. E. and Saunders, Hilary St. George. "The Bahamas Story." Carbon copy of typed manuscript, 1954. Nassau Public Archives.

Benton, William A. "Peter Van Schaack: The Conscience of a Loyalist." In *The Loyalist Americans: A Focus on Greater New York,* edited by Robert A. East and Jacob Judd, pp. 44-55. Tarrytown, New York: Sleepy Hollow Restorations, 1975.

Besson, Maurice. *The Scourge of the Indies: Buccaneers, Corsairs and Filibusters.* New York: Random House, 1929.

Bethell, A. Talbot. *The Early Settlers of the Bahama Islands with a Brief Account of the American Revolution.* Norfolk, England: Rounce and Wortley, n.d.

Betteridge, Alan, compiler. "The Spread of Methodism Through the Bahamas." In *Methodism in the West Indies 1760-1960: Bicentenary Souvenir,* pp. 10-20. Nassau: The Methodist Church, 1960.

Bleeby, Reverend H. "Story of a Mission: Abaco and Its Cays." Mimeographed. The Albert Lowe Museum, Green Turtle Cay, Abaco, The Bahamas, n.d.

Block, Michael. *The Duke of Windsor's War.* London: Weidenfeld and Nicolson, 1982.

Bourne, Edward Gaylord. "Columbus, Ramon Pane and the Beginnings of American Anthropology." *Proceedings of the American Antiquarian Society* 17 (1906): 310-348.

Bradley, Arthur Granville. *Colonial Americans in Exile: Founders of British Canada.* New York: E. P. Dutton and Co. Inc., 1932.

Brinton, D. G. "The Arawak Language of Guiana in its Linguistic and Ethnological Relations." *Transactions of the American Philosophical Society* 14 (1871):427-444.

Britt, Kent. "The Loyalists." *National Geographic* 147 (1975):510-539.

Brown, Richard Maxwell. *The South Carolina Regulators.* Cambridge, Mass.: Belknap Press of Harvard University, 1963.

Brown, Wallace. *The King's Friends: The Composition and Motives of American Loyalist Claims.* Providence, Rhode Island: Brown University Press, 1965.

Browne, J. Ross. *Etchings of a Whaling Cruise.* Edited by John Seelye. Cambridge, Mass.: The Belknap Press of Harvard University, 1968.

Callahan, North. *Flight from the Republic: The Tories of the American Revolution.* Westport, Conn.: Greenwood Press Publishers, 1967.

Carr, Robert S. and Riley, Sandra. "An Effigy Ceramic Bottle from Green Turtle Cay, Abaco." *The Florida Anthropologist* 35 (1982):200-202.

Cashin, Edward J. *Story of Augusta.* Augusta: Richmond County Board of Education, 1980.

Christie, Henry Christopher. *Blackbeard: A Romance of the Bahamas.* Nassau, Bahamas: Bahamas Publishing Co. Ltd., n.d.

Coker, William C. "Vegetation of the Bahama Islands." In *The Bahama Islands,* edited by George Burbank Shattuck, pp. 185-268. New York: The Macmillan Co., 1905.

Craton, Michael. *A History of the Bahamas.* London: Collins, 1962.

Crow, Jeffrey J. *The Black Experience in Revolutionary North Carolina.* Raleigh, North Carolina: Department of Cultural Resources, Division of Archives and History, 1977.

Curry, Robert A. *Bahamian Lore.* Paris, France; By the Author, 1928.

De Booy, Theodoor. "Lucayan Artifacts from the Bahamas." *American Anthropologist* 15 (1913):1-7.

DeMond, Robert O. *The Loyalists in North Carolina During the Revolution.* Durham, North Carolina: Duke University Press, 1940.

DePauw, Linda Grant. *Founding Mothers: Women of America in the Revolutionary Era.* Boston: Houghton Mifflin Co., 1975.

Dexter, Elizabeth Anthony. *Colonial Women of Affairs: A Study of Women in Business and the Professions in America Before 1776.* Boston: Houghton Mifflin Co., 1924.

Dietz, Robert S.; Holden, John C.; and Sproll, Walter P. "Geotectonic Evolution and Subsidence of Bahama Platform." *Geological Society of America Bulletin* 81 (1970):1915-1928.

Dodge, Steve. *The First Loyalist Settlements in Abaco: Carleton and Marsh's Harbour.* Hope Town, Bahamas: Wyannie Malone Museum, 1979.

Dow, George Francis. "The Whale Fishery in Colonial New England." In *Whale Ships and Whaling: A Pictorial History of Whaling During Three Centuries.* Salem, Mass.: Marine Research Society, 1925.

Durlacher-Wolper, Ruth. 1982. Who was Christopher Columbus? Paper read at the 3rd Bahamas Conference on Archaeology, 18-21 March 1982, at San Salvador, The Bahamas.

Flick, Alexander Clarence. *Loyalism in New York During the American Revolution.* New York: The Columbia University Press, 1901.

Ford, Cecil G. Untitled manuscript written between July 1948-July 1953. Photocopied. Albert Lowe Museum, Green Turtle Cay, Abaco, The Bahamas.

Frye, John. *The Search for the Santa Maria.* New York: Dodd Mead and Co., 1973.

Giddings, Joshua R. *The Exiles of Florida.* Columbus, Ohio: Follett, Foster and Co., 1858.

Goggin, John M. "An Anthropological Reconnaissance of Andros Island, Bahamas." *American Antiquity* 5 (1939):21-26.

Granberry, Julian. "A Brief History of Bahamian Archaeology." *Florida Anthropologist* 33 (1980):83-93.

Hanke, Lewis. *Spanish Struggle for Justice in Conquest of America.* Boston: Little, Brown & Co., 1965.

Harllee, William Curry. *Kinfolks: A Genealogical and Biographical Record, vol. 2, Fulmore Curry, and Kemp Sections.* New Orleans; Searcy and Pfaff Ltd., 1935.

Harrell, Isaac Samuel. *Loyalism in Virginia: Chapters in the Economic History of the Revolution.* New York: AMS Press Inc., 1926.

Harrison, G. D., editor. *Shakespeare: The Complete Works.* New York: Harcourt, Brace and Co., 1948.

Hassam, John T. "The Bahama Islands: Notes on an Early Attempt at Colonization." *Massachusetts Historical Society Proceedings* 13 (1899):4-58.

Helps, Sir Arthur. *The Spanish Conquest in America.* Vol. 4. London: n.p., 1904.

Hoffman, Charles A., Jr. "The Palmetto Grove Site on San Salvador, Bahamas." *Contributions of the Florida State Museum Social Sciences, No. 16.* Gainesville, Florida: University of Florida, 1970.

Hughson, Shirley Carter. "The Carolina Pirates and Colonial Commerce, 1670-1740." In *Johns Hopkins University Studies in Historical and Political Science,* vol. 12, edited by Herbert Adams, pp. 5-134. Baltimore: Johns Hopkins Press, 1894.

Jones, Thomas. *History of New York During the Revolutionary War.* New York: New York Historical Society, 1879. Reprint. New York: Arno Press, 1968.

Josephy, Alvin M., Jr. "Was America Discovered Before Columbus?" *American Heritage* 6 (1955):16-19 & 103.

Keegan, William F. "Lucayan Fishing Practices: An Experimental Approach." *Florida Anthropologist* 35 (1982):146-161.

------. 1982. Settlement Pattern in the Bahamas Region. Paper read at the 3rd Bahamas Conference on Archaeology, 18-21 March 1982, at San Salvador, The Bahamas.

Kelly, Peter Culmer. "The Bahama Islands and the American Revolution." Master's thesis, New York University, April 1959. Photocopied. Nassau Public Archives.

Kenyon, J. P. *The Stuarts: A Study in English Kingship.* London: Fontana/Collins., 1970.

Kinnaird, Clark. *George Washington: The Pictorial Biography.* New York: Hastings House, 1967.

Labaree, Benjamin W. *America's Nation-Time 1607-1789.* Boston: Allyn and Bacon, Inc., 1972.

Labaree, Leonard. "The Nature of American Loyalism." *Proceedings of the American Antiquarian Society* 54 (1945):15-58.

Lambert, Robert S. 1975. Loyalism in Back-Country South Carolina. Paper read at the Conference on American Loyalists, 6-8 February 1975, at St. Augustine, Florida.

Lawson, Edward W. *The Discovery of Florida and Its Discoverer Juan Ponce De Leon.* St. Augustine, Florida: Edward W. Lawson, 1946.

Lee, Robert E. *Blackbeard the Pirate: A Reappraisal of His Life and Times.* Winston-Salem, North Carolina: John F. Blair, 1974.

Little, Bryan. *Crusoe's Captain: Being the Life of Woodes Rogers, Seaman, Trader, Colonial Governor.* London: Odhams Press Ltd., 1960.

MacLeisch, Fleming and Krieger, Martin L. *The Privateers: A Raiding Voyage to the Great South Sea.* New York: Random House, 1962.

McNair, Raymond F. "The Spirit of America." *Plain Truth* 41 (1976):6-13.

Macy, Obed. *The History of Nantucket.* Boston: Hilliard, Gray and Co., 1835.

Melville, Herman. *Moby Dick; or, the Whale.* Edited by Robert Maynard Hutchins. Great Books of the Western World Edition. Chicago: Encyclopedia Britannica Inc., 1952.

Miller, W. Hubert. "The Colonization of the Bahamas, 1647-1670." *William and Mary Quarterly* Third Series 2 (1945):33-46.

Mitchell, Steven W. "Analysis of Tidal Growth Sequences in Populations of *Codakia Orbicularis* (Linnaeus) from the Lucayan Arawak Pigeon Creek Site, San Salvador." In *Bahamas Archaeological Project Reports and Papers,* pp. 1-20. San Salvador, Bahamas: CCFL Bahamian Field Station, 1980.

Molander, Arne. "The Search for San Salvador." *Journal of the Bahamas Historical Society* 4 (1982):3-8.

Morison, Samuel Eliot. *Admiral of the Ocean Sea.* Vol I. Boston: Brown and Co., 1942. Reprint. New York: Time Inc. 1962.

Morley, F. V. and Hodgson, J. S. *Whaling North and South.* London: The Century Co., 1926.

Moseley, Mary. *The Bahamas Handbook.* Nassau, Bahamas: The Nassau Guardian, 1926.

Nassau Quarterly: Mission Papers. Vol. 16 (1901) and vol. 25 (1910). Nassau, Bahamas: Anglican Church.

Newton, A. P. *The European Nation in the West Indies 1493-1688.* London: A. & C. Black Ltd., 1933.

Norton, Mary Beth. *The British-Americans: The Loyalist Exiles in England 1774-1789.* Boston: Little, Brown and Co., 1972.

------. 1975. Loyalist Women: A Case Study in the Social Impact of the Revolution. Paper read at the Conference on American Loyalists, 6-8 February 1975, at St. Augustine, Florida.

Ober. Frederick. "Aborigines of the West Indies." *American Antiquarian Society* 9 (1894):270-313.

------. *A Guide to the West Indies, Bermuda and Panama.* New York: Dodd, Mead and Co., 1920.

Olson, Storrs L. "Biological Archaeology in the West Indies." *The Florida Anthropologist* 35 (1982):162-168.

Parrish, Lydia Austin. "Records of Some Southern Loyalists: Being a collection of manuscripts about some eighty families, most of whom immigrated to the Bahamas during and after the American Revolution." Collected from 1940 to 1953. Typed manuscript. Widener Library, Harvard University. Microfilm copy. Nassau Public Archives.

Pascoe, C. F. *Two Hundred Years of the S. P. G.: An Historical Account of the Society for the Propagation of the Gospel in Foreign Parts 1701-1900.* London: The S. P. G., 1901.

Penrose, Clement A. "Sanitary Conditions of the Bahama Islands." In *The Bahama Islands,* edited by George Burbank Shattuck, pp. 387-415. New York: The Macmillan Co., 1905.

Peters, Thelma Peterson. "The American Loyalists and the Plantation Period in the Bahama Islands." Ph.D. dissertation, The University of Florida, 1960. University Microfilms, Ann Arbor, Michigan. Mic 60-5143, 1973.

Peterson, Mendel. *The Funnel of Gold.* Boston: Little Brown and Co., 1975.

------. "Reach for the New World." *National Geographic* 152 (1977):724-767.

Powell, William S. *The War of the Regulation and the Battle of Alamance, May 16, 1771.* Raleigh: State Department of Archives and History, 1965.

Randall, Willard S. "William Franklin: The Making of a Conservative." In *The Loyalist Americans: A Focus on Greater New York,* edited by Robert A. East and Jacob Judd, pp. 56-73. Tarrytown, New York: Sleepy Hollow Restorations, 1975.

Riley, Sandra. "W. E. Armbrister's Loyalist Heritage." *Journal of the Bahamas Historical Society* 2 (1980):3-10.

Robertson, William. *The History of America.* 4 vols. London: Printed for Cadell and Davies, 1808.

Robotti, Frances Diane. *Whaling and Old Salem: A Chronicle of the Sea.* Salem, Mass.: Newcomb and Gauss Co., 1950.

Rose, Richard. "The Pigeon Creek Site, San Salvador, Bahamas." *The Florida Anthropologist* 35 (1982):129-145.

Rouse, Irving. "The Circum-Caribbean Theory, an Archaeological Test." *American Anthropologist* 55 (1953):188-200.

Ryerson, Egerton. *The Loyalists of America and Their Times from 1620-1816.* 2 vols. First published 1888. Reprint. New York: Haskell House Publishers Ltd., 1970.

Sabine, Lorenzo. *The American Loyalists or Biographical Sketches of Adherents to the British Crown in the War of the Revolution.* 2 vols. Boston: Charles C. Little and James Brown, 1847.

------. *A Historical Essay on the Loyalists of the American Revolution.* Foreword by Benjamin Keen. Springfield, Mass.: The Walden Press, 1957.

Salley, A. S. *The Lords Proprietors of Carolina.* N.p: General Assembly of South Carolina, 1944.

Saunders, D. Gail. "The Slave Population of the Bahamas 1783-1834." M.A. dissertation, University of the West Indies, 1978. Photocopied. Nassau Public Archives.

Saunders, Gail and Cartwright, Donald. *Historic Nassau.* London: Macmillan Caribbean, 1979.

Sears, William H. and Sullivan, Shaun O. "Bahamas Prehistory." *American Antiquity* 43 (1978):3-25.

Shy, John. "The Loyalist Problem in the Lower Hudson Valley: The British Perspective." In *The Loyalist Americans: A Focus on Greater New York,* edited by Robert A. East and Jacob Judd, pp. 3-13. Tarrytown, New York: Sleepy Hollow Restorations, 1975.

Siebert, Wilbur H. *Loyalists in East Florida 1774-1785.* Vol. I. Deland, Florida: The Florida State Historical Society, 1929. Reprint. Boston: Gregg Press, 1972.

Simms, W[illiam] Gilmore, Esquire. *Mellichampe: A Legend of the Santee.* New York: W. J. Widdleton, 1864.

Smiley, Nixon. "The Lost Tribe of Andros." *Tropic, Miami Herald.* 20 February 1972.

Southey, Captain Thomas. *Chronological History of the West Indies.* 3 vols. London: A. & R. Spottiswoode for Longman, Rees, Orme, Brown and Green, 1827.

Stark, James H. *Stark's History and Guide to the Bahama Islands.* Norwood, Mass.: Plimpton Press, 1891.

Starr, J. Barton. *Tories, Dons, and Rebels: The American Revolution in British West Florida.* Gainesville: University Presses of Florida, 1976.

Sullivan, Shaun. 1982. Astronomical Alignments of Stone Line Formations at Two Arawakan Sites on Middle Gaicos Island. Paper read at the 3rd Bahamas Conference on Archaeology, 18-21 March 1982, at San Salvador, The Bahamas.

------. 1982. Modeling of Economic Strategies Based Upon Analysis of Resources Within Site Catchment Areas. Paper read at the 3rd Bahamas Conference on Archaeology, 18-21 March 1982, at San Salvador, The Bahamas.

------. "An Overview of the 1976 to 1978 Archaeological Investigations in the Caicos Islands." *The Florida Anthropologist* 33 (1980):120-142.

Toy, John D., printer. *African Slave Trade in Jamaica and Comparative Treatment of Slaves.* N.p.: printed for the Maryland Historical Society, 1854.

Trevelyan, G. M. *English Social History: A Survey of Six Centuries Chaucer to Queen Victoria.* London: The Reprint Society, 1944.

Tripp, William Henry. *There Goes Flukes.* New Bedford, Mass.: Reynolds Printing, 1938.

Troxler, Carole Watterson. *The Loyalist Experience in North Carolina.* Zeblon, North Carolina: Theo. Davis Sons Inc., 1976.

Van Tyne, Claude Halstead. *The Loyalists in the American Revolution.* New York: Peter Smith, 1929.

Whittleton, Eric. "Family History in the Bahamas." *Genealogists Magazine* 18 (1975:187-191.

Williams, Colbert V. "The Methodist Contribution to Education in the Bahamas." Ph.D. dissertation, University of Wales, 1977. Photocopied. Nassau Public Archives.

Williams, Eric. *From Columbus to Castro: The History of the Caribbean 1492-1969.* New York: Harper and Row, 1970.

Wilson, Richard, ed. *Stories from Hakluyt.* New York: E. P. Dutton and Co., 1921.

Winter, John. 1982. Preliminary Results for a Cuban migration. Paper read at the 3rd Bahamas Conference on Archaeology, 18-21 March 1982, at San Salvador, The Bahamas.

Wright, Esmond. "The New York Loyalists: A Cross-section of Colonial Society." In *The Loyalist Americans: A Focus on Greater New York,* edited by Robert A. East and Jacob Judd, pp. 74-94. Tarrytown, New York: Sleepy Hollow Restorations, 1975.

Wright, J. Leitch, Jr. *Florida in the American Revolution.* Gainesville, Florida: University Presses of Florida, 1975.

------. 1975. Southern Black Loyalists. Paper read at the Conference on American Loyalists, 6-8 February 1975, at St. Augustine, Florida.

------. *William Augustus Bowles: Director General of the Creek Nation.* Athens: University of Georgia Press, 1967.

Wright, James Martin. "History of the Bahama Islands, With a Special Study of the Abolition of Slavery in the Colony." In *The Bahama Islands,* edited by George Burbank Shattuck, pp. 419-582. New York: Macmillan Co., 1905.

------. "The Wrecking System of the Bahama Islands." *Political Science Quarterly* 30 (1915):618-644.

Yachtsmans Guide to the Bahamas. 1974 Edition. Edited and illustrated by Harry Kline. Coral Gables, Florida: Tropic Isle Publishers Inc., 1973.

Oral Sources

Albury, Joseph. San Salvador, The Bahamas. Interview, October, 1973. (Now deceased.)

Chapelle, Caroline Garvin. "My Aunt Chapelle's Recollections of Her Ancestors." Dictated to her granddaughter Carrie Williams probably between 1870 and 1880, Mimeographed. Georgia Historical Society, Savannah, Georgia, n.d.

Forsythe, L. E. W. Former inspector of schools, Nassau, New Providence, The Bahamas. Interviewed by Thelma Peters, July, 1958. (Now deceased.)

Hebel, Ianthe Bond. "Four Williams Families." Daytona Beach, Florida, n.d. Photocopied. Bahamas Title Research Co. Ltd., Nassau, The Bahamas.

Lowe, Harold. Green Turtle Cay, Abaco, The Bahamas. Interview, 8, 11 April 1981.

McSweeney, Reverend Irwin. Bahamian historian. Hipoint, Nassau, New Providence, The Bahamas. Interview, 6 July 1981.

Moseley, Mary. Bahamian editor and historian. Nassau, New Providence, The Bahamas. Interviewed by Thelma Peters, 28 July 1958. (Now deceased.)

Nairn, Elmore. San Salvador, The Bahamas. Interview, 1 April 1979 and 24 March 1982.

Sawyer, Mizpah. Native of Green Turtle Cay, Abaco, The Bahamas. Interview at Boca Raton, Florida, 10 August 1982.

Smith, Victoria Margaret Williams. Untitled declaration. 14 February 1917. Mimeographed. Bahamas Title Research Co. Inc., Nassau, The Bahamas.

Thompson, Hazel Henrietta Rosanna nee Williams and Albury, Maude Louisa, nee Williams. Direct descendants of loyalist Burton Williams. Nassau, New Providence, The Bahamas. Interview, 9 April 1982.

Index

Commonwealth of The Bahamas

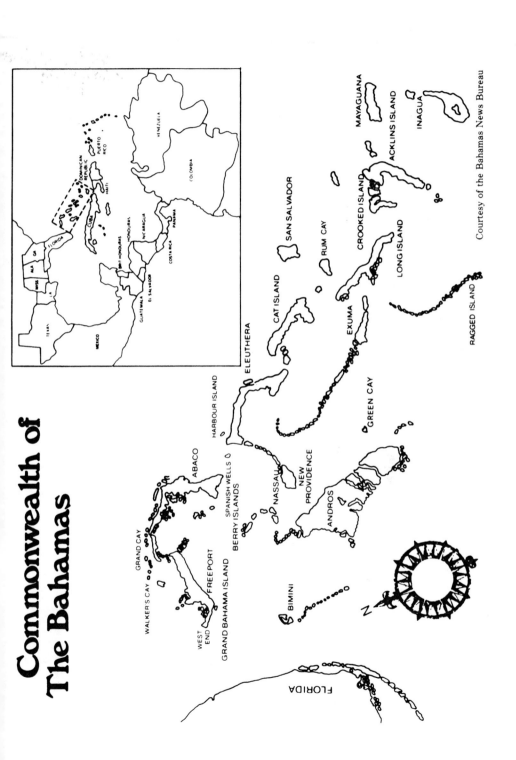

Courtesy of the Bahamas News Bureau

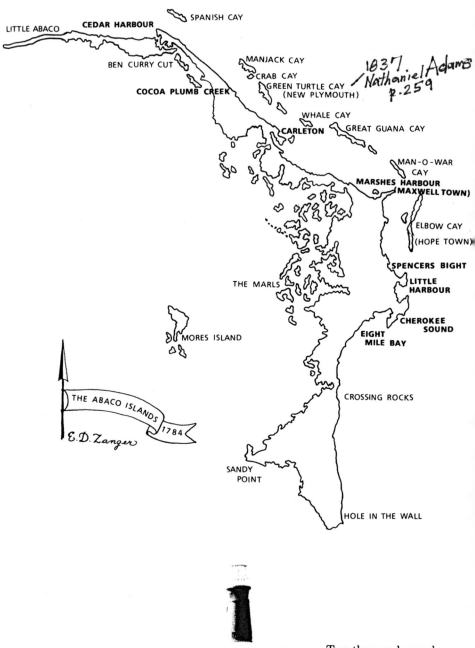

LITTLE ABACO **CEDAR HARBOUR**

SPANISH CAY

BEN CURRY CUT

MANJACK CAY

CRAB CAY

COCOA PLUMB CREEK

GREEN TURTLE CAY
(NEW PLYMOUTH)

1837.
Nathaniel Adams
p. 259

WHALE CAY

CARLETON

GREAT GUANA CAY

MAN-O-WAR
CAY

**MARSHES HARBOUR
(MAXWELL TOWN)**

ELBOW CAY

(HOPE TOWN)

THE MARLS

SPENCERS BIGHT

**LITTLE
HARBOUR**

**CHEROKEE
SOUND**

MORES ISLAND

**EIGHT
MILE BAY**

THE ABACO ISLANDS

1784

E. D. Zanger

CROSSING ROCKS

SANDY
POINT

HOLE IN THE WALL

Two thousand vessels
passed the Abaco Light
at Hole in the Wall
in 1846. (Photograph
by Diane Armbrister
Sauleda.)

CPSIA information can be obtained at www.ICGtesting.com
Printed in the USA
BVOW05s1539110614

356060BV00002B/487/P

9 780966 531022